Democracy and Political Theory

CLAUDE LEFORT

Democracy and Political Theory

Translated by
David Macey

UNIVERSITY OF MINNESOTA PRESS,
MINNEAPOLIS

Library of Congress Cataloging Number: 88–22034

Published by the University of Minnesota Press
2037 University Avenue Southeast, Minneapolis MN 55414.

The University of Minnesota is an equal-opportunity educator and employer.

Printed in Great Britain.

Contents

Translator's Note

The essays in this volume were first collected in Claude Lefort, *Essais sur le politique (XIX^c–XX^c siècles)* (Paris: Seuil, 1986). Details of previous publication are given below.

'The Question of Democracy' originally published as 'La Question de la démocratie' in Denis Kambouchner et al., *Le Retrait du politique* (Paris: Galilée, 1983).

'Human Rights and the Welfare State', originally published as 'Les Droits de l'homme et l'Etat-providence', *Revue interdisciplinaire d'études juridiques*, 13 (1984).

'Hannah Arendt and the Question of the Political', originally published as 'Hannah Arendt et la question du politique', *Cahiers du Forum pour l'indépendence et la paix*, 5 (March 1985). The essay is the text of a lecture given at the Centre Rachi.

'The Revolutionary Terror', originally published as 'La Terreur révolutionnaire', *Passé-Présent*, 2 (1983).

'Interpreting Revolution within the French Revolution', originally published as 'Penser la révolution dans la Révolution Française', *Annales*, 2 (1980).

'Edgar Quinet: The Revolution That Failed', originally published as 'Edgar Quinet: La Révolution manquée', *Passé-Présent* 2 (1983).

'The Revolution as Principle and as Individual', originally published as 'La Révolution comme principe et comme individu', in *Différences, valeurs, hiérarchie: Mélanges offerts à Louis Dumont* (Paris: Ecole des Hautes Etudes en Sciences Sociales, 1984).

'Rereading *The Communist Manifesto*', originally published as

'Relecture du *Manifeste communiste*', in *Dictionnaire des œuvres politiques* (Paris: Presses Universitaires de France, 1986).

'Reversibility: Political Freedom and the Freedom of the Individual', originally published as 'Reversibilité: Liberté politique et liberté de l'individu', *Passé-Présent*, 1 (1982).

'From Equality to Freedom: Fragments of an Interpretation of *Democracy in America*', originally published as 'De l'Egalité à la liberté: Fragments d'interprétation de *De la démocratie en Amérique*', *Libre*, 3 (1978).

'The Permanence of the Theologico-Political?', originally published as 'Permanence du théologico-politique?', *Le Temps de la Réflexion*, 2 (1981).

'The Death of Immortality?', originally published as 'Mort de l'immortalité?', *Le Temps de la réflexion*, 3 (1982).

Whilst every effort has been made to avoid sexist formulations in the translations, the political and historical context often necessitates the use of 'man' and its derivatives in a universalist sense.

Introduction

The project of interpreting or reinterpreting the political with a view
to addressing the questions that arise from the experience of our time
is certainly not one that can be undertaken unless we ask ourselves:
what is the political? Does this mean that a definitional answer is
necessary from the outset, or even that we have to look for such an
answer? Or does it not, rather, mean that we must accept that any
definition, any attempt to establish the essence of the political will
hinder the free movement of thought, that its free movement requires
us, on the contrary, not to prejudge the limits of the political, to agree
to go on a journey of exploration without knowing our path in advance?
The essays included in this collection are exploratory. They do not
represent so many stages in a systematic research project. It need
scarcely be pointed out that they were not written as chapters of a
book. They are in fact so obviously disparate that, even though they
are grouped together around a small number of themes, no such
illusion should arise. I would add that some, like 'Rereading *The
Communist Manifesto*' are occasional pieces – a commission provided
an unexpected opportunity to re-evaluate Marx's project – whilst
others, such as the essays on the French Revolution, on Tocqueville
and on religion and politics originated in seminars. Yet others, like
'The Death of Immortality', are the result of a deliberate enquiry,
even though they are based on very inadequate data.

Whatever their origins and their subject matter, the one thing that
they have in common is an intention to look for signs of the political
in areas where its existence usually goes unnoticed or is denied, and
a willingness to recognize and identify those signs. I deliberately use
this double formula to make it clear that, whilst our search for the
political is obviously a deliberate project, it is also determined by our
experience, in the here and now, and in a previously unknown form,
of our mode of our political existence or, to use Aristotle's terminology,
of our political animality.

The motivation behind an interpretation of the political differs, then, from the motivation behind political science and political sociology, and we must therefore examine our links with the tradition of political philosophy. Let me briefly say what distances these essays from the former and what links them to the latter. Political science and political sociology relate to a domain which has been delineated in response to the imperatives of positive knowledge – the imperatives of objectivity and neutrality – and which is, as such, circumscribed and distanced from other domains which are defined as, for example, economic, social, juridical, religious, aesthetic and so on. The reader will see, especially in the essay entitled 'The Permanence of the Theologico-Political?', why I consider such a division to be artificial, but by no means accidental. In this brief introduction, let me simply say that it loses all pertinence when we consider most of the societies revealed to us by anthropologists and historians, that it testifies to the existence of a *form of society* which appeared in the West and, given the long history of humanity, at a relatively recent date; that this form of society has to be distinguished from earlier forms and that, if science cannot do that, it will be powerless to elucidate and justify its foundations. There can, then, be no doubt that a critique of this kind brings us within the orbit of political philosophy. An investigation into differences between forms of society and into the categories which allow us to account for them and to found a political judgement was originally central to its undertaking, and it remained a central concern throughout its existence as a living discipline. Such an investigation means that it is impossible to designate a particular sector of social life as 'politics'; on the contrary, it implies the notion that relations between human beings and the world are generated by a principle or body of principles. The most eloquent expression of this notion is probably also the oldest. Plato (or Socrates) was probably the first to forge the idea of what I have termed a 'form of society' by examining the *politeia*. We have become accustomed to translating the word as 'regime', a term which is now used in a restrictive and perhaps misleading acceptation. As Leo Strauss rightly observes, the word is worth retaining only if we give it all the resonance it has when used in the expression 'the Ancien Regime'. Used in that sense, it combines the idea of a type of constitution with that of a style of existence or mode of life. But, as Strauss notes, we still have to specify the meaning of those words. 'Constitution' is not to be understood in its juridical acceptation, but in the sense of 'form of government' – in the Anglo-American sense of the term; I would even venture so far as to say that it refers to a structure of power which, in its executive, judicial and legislative functions (regardless of whether or not they are explicitly differentiated), is considered legitimate and which, in its turn, provides the basis for a legitimate distinction between social ranks. The expressions 'style of existence' or 'mode of life' should, for their part, evoke everything that is implied by an expression such as 'the American way of life', namely, those mores and beliefs that testify to the existence of a set of implicit norms determining notions of just and unjust, good and evil, desirable and undesirable, noble and ignoble. Far from placing limits upon politics, the investigations undertaken by Plato in *The Republic* – and it will be recalled that they were undertaken in order to arrive at a theoretical definition of the good regime – introduced a set of questions which touched simultaneously upon the origins of power, the conditions of its legitimacy, upon the authority–obedience relationship throughout society, upon relations between the City and the outside world, upon social needs and the division of professional activities, upon religion, and upon the respective ends of the individual and the social body. They even led him to posit an analogy between the constitution of the *psyche* and that of the *polis* and, finally, to make the equally remarkable suggestion that discourse on the *politeia* and, in more general terms, dialogue as such involved political relations. As we know, Plato did not think that everything was political: he did not confuse relations between father and son, between master and disciple, between head of household (*oikos*) and slaves or dependents with the relationship between those who hold power in the City and citizens; nor did he assert that education or religion are reducible to their political functions. And, far from taking the view that the same principles determine the good of the City and the good of the individual, he suggested that the two are ultimately discordant, and showed no hesitation about asserting the excellence of the philosophical life as opposed to the political life.

Whatever difficulties the interpretation of *The Republic* may pose, the one reading that we can unreservedly regard as radically mistaken is that made by certain of our contemporaries, who find in it the earliest expression of a totalitarian theory. The misunderstanding is worthy of note in that it stems from an inability to accept the idea of a social order that is of necessity instituted politically, the idea of a space that can, despite its internal heterogeneity, perceive itself in its entirety – or from an inability to conceive of unity without assuming that a coercive force has to be applied in order to compress various modes of activity, behaviour or belief into a single mould and, simultaneously, to subject individuals to the will of a master. This view implies, quite apart from a failure to understand Plato's philosophy, a misunderstanding of the point of political philosophy in general, and we must therefore investigate its origins. We have already spoken of a break between political science and political philosophy; we now have to examine a different kind of break, although the two are not unrelated. I refer to the break which inaugurates the Marxist conception of history. This conception does not simply privilege the analysis of relations of production and class relations. That analysis is assumed to account for the origins of politics, morality, law and religion – or even, and despite the obvious contradiction, science – and for their particular characteristics at any given stage in the history of humanity. The fact is that any such theory – and I am not the first to make this observation

– shares, to some extent, the ambitions of both philosophy and science. Like science, it demands objective knowledge but, at the same time, it transgresses its principles by claiming to have a vision of a totality. From political philosophy, it retains the ambition to distinguish between 'social formations' but, at the same time, it makes a radical departure from philosophy by forging the notion of a reality which contains its own meaning, and it therefore views human relations as having been originally established in the absence of any representation of a common identity, in the absence of any power to guarantee it and in the absence of any law which assigns the origin and scope of that power, as it assigns groups and individuals their names and their places in the world. As these problems are touched upon in the essays that follow, and as I have dealt with them at length elsewhere, it seems unnecessary to dwell upon a critique of Marxism here. I will therefore simply draw attention to a curious and disappointing phenomenon which is to be observed, I believe, at the present time. Although Marxism has, as a result of the collapse of the myth of Soviet or Chinese socialism, been declining in popularity in recent years – in France in particular, this has been the case since the early seventies – it is only in restricted circles that this has led to a rehabilitation of the notion of the political. It is as though the condemnation of totalitarianism implied the condemnation of the political as such, as though the belated discovery of a regime in which an all-powerful authority destroys its citizens' freedoms, intervenes in the most personal aspects of the lives of individuals, tends to subject behaviour and beliefs to common norms and, when people resist, locks them up in concentration camps, revealed, as under a magnifying glass, the evils of all power, the real function of law as an instrument for 'normalizing' behaviour and, finally, the totalitarian character of the modern state. This climate has resulted in a vocal return to the timeless truths of religion or ethics, in a garrulous critique of history itself, of the dialectic, of totality, of revolution, and of everything which now seems to have been no more than a phantasy on the part of the post-war generation. Yet ultimately, it is simply the outcome of an inversion of what was once the dominant ideology.

No doubt the lessons critics wish to learn from totalitarianism and from the blindness it induced are sometimes less naive than this. But one wonders about the benefits of sophistication when it results in a restoration of rationalism combined with liberal humanism, in the wilful ignorance of the latter's inability between the wars to undertsand the drama that was unfolding in the world, and in particular its inability to understand the depths from which the collective identifications and death wishes sprang, its inability to grasp the link between the unbridled pursuit of individualism and economic competition, on the one hand, and the attractions of communist or fascist collectivism, on the other. One also wonders what good can come of a return to a Kantian or post-Kantian ethics – divorced, one might add, from the theory of knowledge with which it was articulated – when it becomes a means of avoiding any reflection on the insertion of the subject into the world and into the history he is investigating and on how knowledge of both self and other is rooted in an unconscious matrix.

It need scarcely be stressed that, brief as they may be, these exploratory essays presuppose that we do not surrender to the charms of the little havens that others construct in haste from text-book instructions. In our day, reinterpreting the political requires a sensitivity to the *historical*; and far from destroying it, rejection of the Hegelian or Marxist fiction of history makes that sensitivity more important than ever. It is only by looking for signs of the new, by asking what came into being with the formation and development of modern democracy – and, to mention some of the themes touched upon here, by asking what issues were raised by the progressive separation of state and civil society, by the increase in demands that resulted from the proclamation of the rights of man, by the notion of the individual, by the withdrawal of religion from the sphere of the social and the various modes in which belief survives – it is only by trying to see how theatres of conflict are displaced, how the ambiguities of democracy are transferred from era to era, and how the debate that accompanies change and which to some extent constitutes it evolves, that we can possibly hope to take cognizance of the political, as others did in the past, and sometimes with incomparable acuity and boldness, albeit on the basis of a different experience.

It will, no doubt, be objected that it is something of a paradox to declare one's allegiance to the earliest traditions of political philosophy and at the same time to assume that our experience can reveal something that escaped the philosophers of Antiquity. It could of course be argued that the paradox is not new, and that the works of Machiavelli, Montesquieu and Tocqueville testify to that fact. But it seems preferable to face up to the issue, without calling upon witnesses who are themselves at times targets for the criticisms of historicism; it seems preferable to assume the paradox openly, and to state that the very exercise of thought requires us to do so. Attempts to force us to choose between historicism and a philosophy of human nature on the one hand, and a traditional philosophy of transcendence on the other appear to signal the presence of a mode of thought which knows nothing of its own workings. None of the criticisms that are addressed to historicism – and they are quite justified when it is erected into a thesis and is used to dismiss any claims to be able to go beyond the temporal limits of knowledge – can prevail in the face of the experience of the advent of thought unto itself; and that experience occurs as thought encounters something that comes to it from *outside*, because it is inscribed in a social–historical world. Similarly, none of the valid criticisms that can be made of the idea of human nature, or of that of an unconditional subject, of pure consciousness, of pure will, can prevail against thought's experience of a primal ability to discriminate

between true and false, just and unjust, good and evil – or, to cite
Plato again, between noble and base – or its experience of the need
to judge and to be judged, an experience that attests to a universal
intention. And so, when I speak of *interpreting* and *reinterpreting* the
political, I am deliberately putting forward the idea of a task which
has been the same ever since it was first formulated and which,
nevertheless, must always be started anew in every age, because the
knowledge it procures cannot be divorced from that which is given to
each to investigate from his own position.

This is why we must situate these essays in relation to Hannah
Arendt, who is one of the few writers to have attempted to give the
notion of the political its true meaning. I share her conviction that the
events of this century, and above all the rise of totalitarian regimes,
are unprecedented, and that they mean that thought must begin anew.
But I do not share her conviction that they have destroyed the
categories of Western thought, and that we must therefore begin our
reflections by breaking with all the teachings of political philosophy –
an assumption, it should be said, which she fortunately contradicts by
constantly entering into debate with the great authors of the past.
Arendt does, it is true, reject the terms of the above-mentioned
alternative, as I do. She rejects both historicism and the representation
of a human nature, but she does so in such a way as to escape the
tension which mobilizes thought. I am not confusing her project with
that of other contemporary thinkers whom I have described as retreating
in the face of the need to interpret. But, although she opens up new
avenues, she places arbitrary restrictions on the scope of interpretation.
Her resolve to remain free of all traditions – or, and this is a more
subtle version of the same thing, to return to their sources only so as
to perceive the absolute novelty of the present – is bound up with her
confidence in her own ability to define the political. All her
investigations are therefore subordinated to a clear and distinct idea
of what is political and what is not political. Hence the familiar, clear-
cut distinctions she makes between the political and the social realms,
between the realm of nature, life, necessity and labour, and the realm
of culture, freedom and action; between the public and the private
realm; between the existence of the individual and that of the citizen.
And hence, finally, the confidence she places in a critique of the
increasing corruption of modern democracy, in her own ability to
detect events which could give rise to totalitarianism.

The approach adopted in the following essays is very different. They
explore certain avenues in an attempt to find the mark of the political
in various facts, acts, representations and relations without automatically
assigning them to one or another register of our 'condition'. By paying
attention to signs of repetition and to signs of the new, they attempt
to reveal the symbolic dimension of the social.

Part I

On Modern Democracy

1

The Question of Democracy

My purpose here is to encourage and to contribute to a revival of
political philosophy. I am not alone in working to that end. Our
numbers are, no doubt, small, but they have been increasing for some
time, although it must be admitted that there is as yet little enthusiasm
for the task. What surprises me is that most of those who ought to be
best-equipped to undertake it because of their intellectual temperament,
which inclines them to break with dogmatic beliefs, because of their
philosophical culture, because of their desire to find *some* meaning
behind the events, confused as they may be, that take place in our
world, who might be expected to have become sufficiently disenchanted
with the rival dominant ideologies to want to discern the preconditions
for the development of freedom, or at last to shed some light on the
obstacles that stand in its way, are and remain stubbornly blind to the
political. 'Freedom', the simple word I have just used, is usually
banished from scientific language or relegated to the vernacular, when,
that is, it does not become a slogan for small groups of intellectuals
who declare that they have taken sides and who are content with anti-
communism. They can be ignored, no matter how much noise they
make, as we have seen their kind before. I am more concerned with
those intellectuals and philosophers who claim to belong to the left or
the far left. Although they live in an era in which a new form of
society has emerged under the banner of fascism on the one hand and
under that of socialism on the other, they refuse to contemplate or
even perceive that momentous event. In order to do so, they would
of course have to give new meaning to the idea of freedom. And yet
they abandon it to the vagaries of public opinion, apparently on the
grounds that everyone defines it in accordance with their own wishes
or interests. By doing so, they cut themselves off, not from public
opinion, but from political philosophy, even though they claim to be
in search of rigorous knowledge. For the sole motivation behind
political philosophy has always been a desire to escape the servitude
of collective beliefs and to win the freedom to think about freedom in

society; it has always borne in mind the essential difference between the regime of freedom and despotism, or indeed tyranny. Yet now that we are faced with the rise of a new type of despotism (which differs, let it be noted, from ancient despotism as much as modern democracy differs from classical democracy), of a despotism which has, moreover, world-wide ambitions, despotism itself is becoming invisible. Whenever they hear the word 'totalitarianism', philosophers ask, 'What are you talking about? Is it a concept? How do you define it? Does not democracy mask the domination and exploitation of one class by another, the standardization of collective life and mass conformism? Even if we do agree that history has given birth to a monster, what caused the mutation? Was it an economic cause, a technological cause, or does it relate to the rise of state bureaucracy?' I am, as I said, surprised: how can they handle ontological differences with such subtlety, vie with one another in exploiting the combined resources of Heidegger, Lacan, Jakobson and Lévi-Strauss, and then fall back upon such crass realism when the question of politics arises? Marxism, of course, has been through this stage too; it destroyed the old relationship that once existed between philosophy and naivety by teaching us that the establishment of a concentration-camp system, the extermination of millions of men and women, the suppression of freedom of association and freedom of expression, and the abolition of universal suffrage or its conversion into a farce which gives one party ninety-nine per cent of the vote, tells us nothing about the nature of Soviet society. But the most remarkable thing of all is that the withering away of that ideology has done little to set thought free or to help it return to political philosophy. It may well be admitted that it is not socialism, or 'true' socialism as they quaintly say, that is being constructed in the USSR, in Eastern Europe, in China, Vietnam, Cambodia, or Cuba, but how many intellectuals are still haunted by the spectre of the correct theory, by the belief that it will reveal the laws that govern the development of societies and that it will enable them to deduce a formula for a rational practice? At best, we find expressions of sympathy for the dissidents persecuted by communist regimes or for popular uprisings. But such feelings have no lasting intellectual effect. They are unable to discern freedom in democracy, because democracy is defined as bourgeois. They are unable to discern servitude in totalitarianism.

It would, however, be a mistake to restrict ourselves to a critique of Marxism. If we are to reinterpret the political, we must break with scientific points of view in general and with the point of view that has come to dominate what are known as the political sciences and political sociology in particular.

Political sociologists and scientists, for their part, do not attempt to define politics as a superstructure whose base is to be found at the supposedly real level of relations of production. They obtain their object of knowledge by constructing or delineating political facts, which they regard as particular facts and as distinct from other particular social facts, such as the economic, the juridical, the aesthetic, the scientific or the purely social, 'social' being defined as designating modes of relations between groups or classes. This approach implies a surreptitious reference to the space that is designated as society. It claims to be able to provide a detailed survey or reconstruction of that space by positing and articulating terms, by forging specific systems of relations, or even by combining them into an overall system, as though the observations and constructs did not themselves derive from the experience of social life, an experience which is at once primordial and uniquely shaped by our insertion into a historically and politically determined framework. One effect of this fiction is immediately obvious: modern democratic societies are characterized by, among other things, the delimitation of a sphere of institutions, relations and activities which appears to be political, as distinct from other spheres which appear to be economic, juridical, and so on. Political sociologists and scientists find the preconditions that define their object and their approach to knowledge in this mode of appearance of the political, without ever examining the form of society within which the division of reality into various sectors appears and is legitimated. The fact that something like *politics* should have been circumscribed within social life at a given time has in itself a political meaning, and a meaning which is not particular, but general. This even raises the question of the constitution of the social space, of the *form* of society, of the essence of what was once termed the 'city'. The political is thus revealed, not in what we call political activity, but in the double movement whereby the mode of institution of society appears and is obscured. It appears in the sense that the process whereby society is ordered and unified across its divisions becomes visible. It is obscured in the sense that the locus of politics (the locus in which parties compete and in which a general agency of power takes shape and is reproduced) becomes defined as particular, while the principle which generates the overall configuration is concealed.

This observation is in itself an invitation to return to the question that once inspired political philosophy: what is the nature of the difference between forms of society? Interpreting the political means breaking with the viewpoint of political science, because political science emerges from the suppression of this question. It emerges from a desire to objectify, and it forgets that no elements, no elementary structures, no entities (classes or segments of classes), no economic or technical determinations, and no dimensions of social space exist until they have been given a form. Giving them a form implies both giving them meaning (*mise en sens*) and staging them (*mise en scène*). They are given meaning in that the social space unfolds as a space of intelligibility articulated in accordance with a specific mode of distinguishing between the real and the imaginary, the true and the false, the just and the unjust, the permissible and the forbidden, the normal and the pathological. They are staged in that this space contains within it a quasi-representation of itself as being aristocratic, monarchic, despotic, democratic or totalitarian. As we know, the corollary of the desire to objectify is the positioning of a subject capable of performing intellectual operations which owe nothing to its involvement in social life. Such a neutral subject is concerned only with detecting causal relations between phenomena and with discovering the laws that govern the organization and the workings of social systems or sub-systems. The fiction of this subject is vulnerable to more than the arguments of critical sociologists and Marxists who object to the distinction between factual judgements and value judgements, and who show that the analyst is working within a perspective forced upon him by the need to defend his economic or cultural interests. Well-founded as it may be, this argument itself comes up against limitations which will not be examined here. It fails to recognize that any system of thought that is bound up with any form of social life is grappling with a subject-matter which contains within it its own interpretation, and whose meaning is a constituent element of its nature. By ascribing neutrality to the subject, it deprives the subject of the means to grasp an experience generated and ordered by an implicit conception of the relations between human beings and of their relations with the world. It prevents the subject from grasping the one thing that has been grasped in every human society, the one thing that gives it its status as human society: namely the difference between legitimacy and illegitimacy, between truth and lies, between authenticity and imposture, between the pursuit of power or of private interests and the pursuit of the common good. Leo Strauss's attacks on what might be termed the castration of political thought as a result of the rise of the social sciences and of Marxism are sufficiently eloquent for us not to dwell on the issue here; we have only to turn to the critique that opens *Natural Right and History*.[1] Let me say simply that if we ignore distinctions that are basic to the exercise of the intellect on the grounds that we cannot supply their criteria, and if we claim to be able to reduce knowledge to the limits of objective science, we break with the philosophical tradition. If we refuse to risk making judgements, we lose all sense of the difference between forms of society. We then fall back on value judgements, either hypocritically, beneath the cloak of a hierarchy in the determinants of what we take to be the real, or arbitrarily, in the crude statement of preferences.

I would like now to draw attention to what reinterpreting the political means in our times.

The rise of totalitarianism, both in its fascist variant (which has for the moment been destroyed, though we have no grounds to think that it might not reappear in the future) and in its communist variant (which is going from strength to strength) obliges us to re-examine democracy. The widespread view to the contrary notwithstanding, totalitarianism does not result from a transformation of the mode of production. In the case of German or Italian fascisms, the point does not have to be stressed, as they adapted themselves to the maintenance of capitalist structures, whatever changes they may have undergone as a result of increased state intervention into the economy. But it is important at least to recall that the Soviet regime acquired its distinctive features before the era of the socialization of the means of production and of collectivization. Modern totalitarianism arises from a political mutation, from a mutation of a symbolic order, and the change in the status of power is its clearest expression. What in fact happens is that a party arises, claiming to be by its very nature different from traditional parties, to represent the aspirations of the whole people, and to possess a legitimacy which places it above the law. It takes power by destroying all opposition; the new power is accountable to no one and is beyond all legal control. But for our purposes, the course of events is of little import; we are concerned with the most characteristic features of the new form of society. A condensation takes place between the sphere of power, the sphere of law and the sphere of knowledge. Knowledge of the ultimate goals of society and of the norms which regulate social practices becomes the property of power, and at the same time power itself claims to be the organ of a discourse which articulates the real as such. Power is embodied in a group and, at its highest level, in a single individual, and it merges with a knowledge which is also embodied, in such a way that nothing can split it apart. The theory – or if not the theory, the spirit of the movement, as in Nazism – may well turn everything to account as circumstances demand, but it can never be challenged by experience. State and civil society are assumed to have merged; this is brought about through the agency of the ubiquitous party which permeates everything with the dominant ideology and hands down power's orders, as circumstances demand, and through the formation of a multiplicity of microbodies (organizations of all kinds in which an artificial socialization and relations of power conforming to the general model are reproduced). A logic of identification is set in motion, and is governed by the representation of power as embodiment. The proletariat and the people are one; the party and the proletariat are one; the politbureau and, ultimately, the *egocrat*, and the party are one. Whilst there develops a representation of a homogeneous and self-transparent society, of a People-as-One, social division, in all its modes, is denied, and at the same time all signs of differences of opinion, belief or mores are condemned. We can use the term despotism to characterize this regime, but only if we specify that it is modern and differs from all the forms that precede it. Power makes no reference to anything beyond the social; it rules as though nothing existed outside the social, as though it had no limits (these are the limits established by the idea of a law or a truth that is valid in itself); it relates to a society beyond which there is nothing, which is assumed to be a society fulfilling its destiny as a society produced by the people who live in it. The distinctively modern feature of totalitarianism is that it combines a radically artificialist ideal with a radically organicist ideal. The image of the body comes to be combined with the image of the machine. Society appears to be a community all of whose members are strictly interdependent; at the same time it is assumed to be constructing itself day by day, to be striving towards a goal – the creation of the new man – and to be living in a state of permanent mobilization.

We can ignore other features, which I have described at length elsewhere, such as the phenomenon of the production–elimination of the enemy (the enemy within being defined as an agent of the enemy without, as a parasite on the body, or as an interference with the workings of the machine). Nor am I trying here to reveal the contradictions totalitarianism comes up against. Even this brief outline allows us to re-examine democracy. When seen against the background of totalitarianism, it acquires a new depth and cannot be reduced to a system of institutions. In its turn, democracy too is seen to be a form of society; and our task is to understand what constitutes its uniqueness, and what it is about it that leads to its overthrow and to the advent of totalitarianism.

Anyone who undertakes such a project can learn a great deal from Tocqueville. The thing that marks him out from his contemporaries is in fact his realization that democracy is a form of society, and he arrives at that conclusion because, in his view, democracy stands out against a background: the society from which it emerges and which he calls aristocratic society – a term which it would not be appropriate to discuss here. Tocqueville helps us to decipher the experience of modern democracy by encouraging us to look back at what came before it and, at the same time, to look ahead to what is emerging, or may emerge, in its wake. His investigations are important to us in several respects. He posits the idea that a great historical mutation is taking place, even though its premises had long been established, and he puts forward the idea of an irreversible dynamic. Although he attempts to locate the fundamental principle of democracy in a social state – equality of condition – he explores change in every direction, takes an interest in social bonds and political institutions, in the individual, in the mechanisms of public opinion, in forms of sensibility and forms of knowledge, in religion, law, language, literature, history, etc. His explorations lead him to detect the ambiguities of the *democratic revolution* in every domain, to make, as it were, an exploratory incision into the *flesh* of the social. At every moment of his analysis, he looks at things from both sides, moves from one side of the phenomenon to the other, and reveals the underside of both the positive – new signs of freedom – and the negative – new signs of servitude.

It is only recently that Tocqueville has become a fashionable thinker, that he has been defined as the pioneering theorist of modern political liberalism. But his intuitive vision of a society faced with the general contradiction that arises when the social order no longer has a basis seems to me to be much more important than his reputation. He traces this contradiction by examining the individual, who has been released from the old networks of personal dependency and granted the freedom to think and act in accordance with his own norms, but who is, on the other hand, isolated, impoverished and at the same time trapped by the image of his fellows, now that agglutination with them provides a means of escaping the threat of the dissolution of his identity. He then examines public opinion as it conquers the right to expression and communication and at the same time becomes a force in its own right, as it becomes detached from subjects, thinks and speaks for itself, and becomes an anonymous power standing over them. He examines law which, because it is drawn to the pole of the collective will, accepts the new demands that are born of changes in mentalities and practices, and which, as a result of equality of condition, is increasingly dedicated to the task of standardizing norms of behaviour and, finally, he examines power, which has been set free from the arbitrariness of personal rule, but which, precisely because it destroys all the individual instances of authority, appears to belong to no one, except to the people in the abstract, and which threatens to become unlimited, omnipotent, to acquire an ambition to take charge of every aspect of social life.

I am not saying that Tocqueville's analysis of this contradiction, which is inherent in democracy, is irrefutable, but it does open up a very fruitful line of research which has not been pursued. Without wishing to discuss the difficulties into which he stumbles – I have given some indication of these elsewhere[2] – let me simply observe that his explorations are usually restricted to what I have termed the underside of the phenomena he believes to be characteristic of the new society, and that he does not pursue his explorations by examining the underside of the underside. True, a century and a half have gone by since the publication of *Democracy in America*. We therefore enjoy the benefits of experience and have the capacity to decipher things that its author could only glimpse. But it is not simply his lack of experience which restricts his interpretation; there is also, I believe, an intellectual reluctance (which is bound up with a political prejudice) to confront the unknown element in democracy. As I cannot develop my criticisms here, I will merely state that in his attempt to bring out the ambiguous effects of equality of condition, Tocqueville usually tries to uncover an inversion of meaning: the new assertion of singularity fades in the face of the rule of anonymity; the assertion of difference (of belief, opinion or morals) fades in the face of the rule of uniformity; the spirit of innovation is sterilized by the immediate enjoyment of material goods and by the pulverization of historical time; the recognition that human beings are made in one another's likeness is destroyed by the rise of society as abstract entity, and so on. What he fails to see, and what we are in a position to observe, is that another influence or counter-influence is always at work and that it counteracts the petrification of social life. Its effects are revealed by the appearance of ways of thinking and modes of expression that are won in the face of anonymity, of the stereotyped language of opinion; by the rise of demands and struggles for rights that place the formal viewpoint of the law in check; by the irruption of a new meaning of history; by the unfolding of multiple perspectives on historical knowledge as a result of the dissolution of an almost organic sense of duration that was once apprehended through customs and traditions; by the increasing heterogeneity of social life that accompanies the dominance of society and state over individuals. We would of course also be mistaken if, in our turn, we claimed to be able to limit our explorations to the underside of the underside. On the contrary, we must recognize that, so long as the democratic adventure continues, so long as the terms of the contradiction continue to be displaced, the meaning of what is coming into being remains in suspense. Democracy thus proves to be the historical society *par excellence*, a society which, in its very form, welcomes and preserves indeterminacy and which provides a remarkable contrast with totalitarianism which, because it is constructed under the slogan of creating a new man, claims to understand the law of its organization and development, and which, in the modern world, secretly designates itself as *a society without history*.

We will, however, remain within the limits of a description if we simply extend Tocqueville's analyses, as they themselves urge us to identify those features which point to the formation of a new despotism. The indeterminacy we were discussing does not pertain to the order of empirical facts, to the order of economic or social facts which, like the gradual extension of equality of condition, can be seen to be born of other facts. Just as the birth of totalitarianism defies all explanations which attempt to reduce that event to the level of empirical history, so the birth of democracy signals a mutation of the symbolic order, as is most clearly attested to by the new position of power.

I have tried on several occasions to draw attention to this mutation. Here, it will be enough to stress certain of its aspects. The singularity of democracy only becomes fully apparent if we recall the nature of the monarchical system of the Ancien Regime. This is not in fact a matter of recovering from a loss of memory but, rather, of recentering our investigations on something that we failed to recognize because we lost all sense of the political. It is in effect within the framework of the monarchy, or that of a particular type of monarchy which, originally developed in a theologico-political matrix, gave the prince sovereign power within the boundaries of a territory and made him both a secular agency and a representative of God, that the features of state and society were first outlined, and that the first separation of state and civil society occurred. Far from being reducible to a superstructural institution whose function can be derived from the nature of a mode of production, the monarchy was the agency which, by levelling and unifying the social field and, simultaneously, by inscribing itself in that field, made possible the development of commodity relations and rationalized activities in a manner that paved the way for the rise of capitalism.

Under the monarchy, power was embodied in the person of the prince. This does not mean that he held unlimited power. The regime was not despotic. The prince was a mediator between mortals and gods or, as political activity became secularized and laicized, between mortals and the transcendental agencies represented by a sovereign Justice and a sovereign Reason. Being at once subject to the law and placed above laws, he condensed within his body, which was at once mortal and immortal, the principle that generated the order of the kingdom. His power pointed towards an unconditional, other-worldly pole, while at the same time he was, in his own person, the guarantor and representative of the unity of the kingdom. The kingdom itself was represented as a body, as a substantial unity, in such a way that the hierarchy of its members, the distinction between ranks and orders appeared to rest upon an unconditional basis.

Power was embodied in the prince, and it therefore gave society a body. And because of this, a latent but effective knowledge of what *one* meant to the *other* existed throughout the social. This model reveals the revolutionary and unprecedented feature of democracy. The locus of power becomes *an empty place*. There is no need to dwell on the details of the institutional apparatus. The important point is that this apparatus prevents governments from appropriating power for their own ends, from incorporating it into themselves. The exercise of power is subject to the procedures of periodical redistributions. It represents the outcome of a controlled contest with permanent rules. This phenomenon implies an institutionalization of conflict. The locus of power is an empty place, it cannot be occupied – it is such that no individual and no group can be consubstantial with it – and it cannot be represented. Only the mechanisms of the exercise of power are visible, or only the men, the mere mortals, who hold political authority. We would be wrong to conclude that power now resides *in* society on the grounds that it emanates from popular suffrage; it remains the agency by virtue of which society apprehends itself in its unity and relates to itself in time and space. But this agency is no longer referred to an unconditional pole; and in that sense, it marks a division between the *inside* and the *outside* of the social, institutes relations beween those dimensions, and is tacitly recognized as being purely symbolic.

Such a transformation implies a series of other transformations, and they cannot be regarded merely as effects, as cause and effect relations have no pertinence in the order of the symbolic. On the one hand, the phenomenon of disincorporation, which we mentioned earlier, is accompanied by the disentangling of the sphere of power, the sphere of law and the sphere of knowledge. Once power ceases to manifest the principle which generates and organizes a social body, once it ceases to condense within it virtues deriving from transcendent reason and justice, law and knowledge assert themselves as separate from and irreducible to power. And just as the figure of power in its materiality and its substantiality disappears, just as the exercise of power proves to be bound up with the temporality of its reproduction and to be subordinated to the conflict of collective wills, so the autonomy of law is bound up with the impossibility of establishing its essence. The dimension of the development of right unfolds in its entirety, and it is always dependent upon a debate as to its foundations, and as to the legitimacy of what has been established and of what ought to be established. Similarly, recognition of the autonomy of knowledge goes hand in hand with a continual reshaping of the processes of acquiring knowledge and with an investigation into the foundations of truth. As power, law and knowledge become disentangled, a new relation to the real is established; to be more accurate, this relation is guaranteed within the limits of networks of socialization and of specific domains of activity. Economic, technical, scientific, pedagogic and medical facts, for example, tend to be asserted, to be defined under the aegis of knowledge and in accordance with norms that are specific to them. A dialectic which externalizes every sphere of activity is at work throughout the social. The young Marx saw this only too well, but he mistakenly reduced it to a dialectic of alienation. The fact that it operates within the density of class relations, which are relations of domination and exploitation, should not make us forget that it stems from a new symbolic constitution of the social. The relation established between the competition mobilized by the exercise of power and conflict in society is no less remarkable. The erection of a political stage on which competition can take place shows that division is, in a general way, constitutive of the very unity of society. Or to put it another way, the legitimation of purely political conflict contains within it the principle of a legitimation of social conflict in all its forms. If we bear in mind the monarchical model of the Ancien Regime, the meaning of the transformation can be summarized as follows: democratic society is instituted as a society without a body, as a society which undermines the representation of an organic totality. I am not suggesting that it therefore has no unity or no definite identity; on the contrary, the disappearance of natural determination, which was once linked to the person of the prince or to the existence of a nobility, leads to the emergence of a purely social society in which the people, the nation and the state take on the status of universal entities, and in which any individual or group can be accorded the same status. But neither the state, the people nor the nation represent substantial entities. Their representation is itself, in its dependence upon a political discourse and upon a sociological and historical elaboration, always bound up with ideological debate.

Nothing, moreover, makes the paradox of democracy more palpable than the institution of universal suffrage. It is at the very moment when popular sovereignty is assumed to manifest itself, when the people is assumed to actualize itself by expressing its will, that social interdependence breaks down and that the citizen is abstracted from all the networks in which his social life develops and becomes a mere statistic. Number replaces substance. It is also significant that in the nineteenth century this institution was for a long time resisted not only by conservatives and bourgeois liberals, but also by socialists – and this resistance cannot simply be imputed to the defence of class interests. It was provoked by the idea of a society which had now to accept that which cannot be represented.

In this brief sketch of democracy, I have been forced to ignore a major aspect of the empirical development of those societies which are organized in accordance with its principles – a development which justified socialist-inspired criticisms. I am certainly not forgetting that democratic institutions have constantly been used to restrict means of access to power, knowledge and the enjoyment of rights to a minority. Nor am I forgetting – and this would merit a lengthy analysis – that, as Tocqueville foresaw, the emergence of an anonymous power facilitated the expansion of state power (and, more generally, the power of bureaucracies). I have, on the other hand, chosen to concentrate upon a range of phenomena which are, it seems to me, usually misunderstood. In my view, the important point is that democracy is instituted and sustained by the *dissolution of the markers of certainty*. It inaugurates a history in which people experience a fundamental indeterminacy as to the basis of power, law and knowledge, and as to the basis of relations betweel *self* and *other*, at every level of social life (at every level where division, and especially the division between those who held power and those who were subject to them, could once be articulated as a result of a belief in the nature of things or in a supernatural principle). It is this which leads me to take the view that, without the actors being aware of it, a process of questioning is implicit in social practice, that no one has the answer to the questions that arise, and that the work of ideology, which is always dedicated to the task of restoring certainty, cannot put an end to this practice. And that in turn leads me to at least identify, if not to explain, the conditions for the formation of totalitarianism. There is always a possibility that the logic of democracy will be disrupted in a society in which the foundations of the political order and the social order vanish, in which that which has been established never bears the seal of full legitimacy, in which differences of rank no longer go unchallenged, in which right proves to depend upon the discourse which articulates it, and in which the exercise of power depends upon conflict. When individuals are increasingly insecure as a result of an economic crisis or of the ravages of war, when conflict between classes and groups is exacerbated and can no longer be symbolically resolved within the political sphere, when power appears to have sunk to the level of reality and to be no more than an instrument for the promotion of the interests and appetites of vulgar ambition and when, in a word, it appears *in* society, and when at the same time society appears to be fragmented, then we see the development of the fantasy of the People-as-One, the beginnings of a quest for a substantial identity, for a social body which is welded to its head, for an embodying power, for a state free from division.

It is sometimes said that democracy itself already makes room for totalitarian institutions, modes of organization and modes of representation. Whilst this is certainly true, it is also still true to say that a change in the economy of power is required if the totalitarian form of society is to arise.

In conclusion, I return to my initial considerations. It seems strange to me that most of our contemporaries have no sense of how much philosophy owes to the democratic experience, that they do not explore its matrix or take it as a theme for their reflections, that they fail to recognize it as the matrix of their investigations. When one recalls how certain great philosophers were drawn to Nazism, at least in its early stages, and, to a much greater and lasting extent, to Stalinism, one begins to wonder whether, in modern philosophy, the ability to break with the illusions of both theology and eighteenth- and nineteenth-century rationalism does not carry with it, in turn, quasi-religious faith, a nostalgia for the image of a society which is at one with itself and which has mastered its history, for the image of an organic community. But can we restrict discussion to the idea of a separation between philosophical thought and political belief? Can either remain unaffected, once they have come into contact? It appears to me that the question is worth asking, and that we might be able to shed some light on it by following the evolution of the thought of Merleau-Ponty. A similar necessity led him to move from the idea of the body to the idea of the flesh and dispelled the attractions of the Communist model by allowing him to rediscover the indeterminacy of history and of the being of the social.

2

Human Rights and The Welfare State

As soon as we begin to ask ourselves about human rights, we find ourselves drawn into a labyrinth of questions.[1] We must first ask ourselves if we can in fact accept the formula without making reference to a human nature. Or, if we reject the notion of human nature, without surrendering to a teleological vision of history. For can we in fact say that human beings have embarked upon a voyage of self-discovery, that they create themselves by discovering and instituting rights in the absence of any principle that might allow us to decide as to their true nature and as to whether their evolution does or does not conform to their essence? Even at this early stage, we cannot ignore the question. Even if we attempt to avoid it and simply examine the import of an event such as the proclamation at the end of the eighteenth century of the rights known as the rights of man, other difficulties lie in store. If we adopt the latter course, our investigations appear to be guided, if not by observation, at least by a reading and interpretation of the facts. We begin by asking ourselves about the meaning of the mutation that occurred in the representation of the individual and of society. That question leads to another: can the effects of that mutation elucidate the course of history up to the present time? To be more specific: is it the case that human rights merely served to disguise relations established in bourgeois society, or did they make possible, or even give rise to, demands and struggles which contributed to the rise of democracy? Even this is too crude a statement of the terms of the alternative. Even if – and I believe that the organizers of this debate would accept the hypothesis – we agree that the institution of human rights has come to support a dynamic of rights, do we not have to investigate the effects of that development? It is one thing to say that social, economic and cultural rights (notably those mentioned in the United Nations Charter) arise as an extension of those original rights. It is quite another to say that they derive from the same inspiration, and it is yet another to take the view that they promote freedom. The question takes us further still if we ask whether the rise of new rights might not signal a perversion of the principle of human rights, or might not even undermine the whole democratic edifice. We cannot leave matters there. All these questions concern only the formation and the transformations of Western societies. No one can be unaware of the fact that over the great part of our planet, the idea of human rights is either unknown – because it is incompatible with communal traditions which in some cases date from time immemorial – or is furiously denied. How can anyone be unaware of that? It is in my view impossible to investigate the meaning of human rights if, at the same time, we ignore the spectacle provided by certain dictatorial regimes that have been established in some of the great countries of the modern world, notably in Latin America, and by those totalitarian regimes that are described as socialist.

A labyrinth of questions, then. I am quite prepared to admit that we might get lost if we tried to give each question all the time it needs, but let us at least not confine ourselves to a single question, for, whilst it may well be a distinct question, it is inseparable from all the rest.

In their preparatory document, M. François Ost and his associates invite us to examine 'the limitations of the explanatory and mobilizing power of this category [human rights] in the context of current transformations' and 'the extent to which this notion can be extended without being distorted or even negated'. The question seems to me to be fully pertinent and timely. It is one of the questions to which I have just alluded. But it cannot, of course, be completely divorced from a more general investigation which is at once philosophical and political. Indeed, the document will not let us forget that. At one point, it raises the possibility that a self-management model might involve the risk of totalitarian oppression. And the final section warns us that 'The mutations affecting the notion of human rights definitely mean that the philosophical question of their anthropological basis must be raised once more.' It even goes so far as to ask 'To what extent can the new historicist basis replace the original naturalist basis without dissolving the very category of human rights?' I take this as an invitation to place the principal theme of the debate within a broader context.

'The topicality of human rights in the welfare state' is the theme on which we have been invited to reflect. Assessing its topicality presupposes, however, that we agree as to the meaning that has been given to the establishment of human rights in the past, and as to the nature of the transformations that have taken place in the state. And it is by no means self-evident that we are in agreement here. 'It seems proven', we are told, 'that our Western societies developed out of the model of the liberal *état de droit*, and that they now correspond to the model of the welfare state.' Without wishing to reject this hypothesis, I wonder to what extent we can rely on an opposition between two model states, and if we might not be restricting the scope of our investigations by deciding to apprehend human rights from a viewpoint which circumscribes within the present only the economic and social functions of the state. 'Henceforth, its primary task is to ensure the well-being of its citizens'; it is assumed to have become 'an enabling state' which is responsible for 'ensuring free access to the various markets for material and symbolic goods'. If we accept this definition unreservedly, the answer is implicit in the question. For it goes without saying that human rights would no longer count for anything, or would represent no more than the survival of an outdated model, if the authority of the state were measured solely in terms of its ability to enable (the very term 'authority' would no longer be appropriate), and if citizens' demands were reducible to a demand for well-being. But we can question the validity of the hypothesis because it leaves aside the nature of the political system, which is not reducible to the management of the needs, or supposed needs, of the population. And we can also question the validity of the representation associated with the old model of the state, which has been defined as a liberal *état de droit*.

Let us begin by developing my last remark. The liberal state became, in theory, the guardian of civil liberties; but, in practice, it ensured the protection of dominant ruling interests with a consistency that was shaken only when the masses were mobilized and began their long struggle for their rights. Neither resistance to oppression, nor property, nor freedom of opinion and expression, nor the freedom of movement mentioned in the great Declarations were judged sacred by most of those who called themselves liberals, so long as they applied to the poor, or so long as they damaged the interests of the rich or threatened the stability of a political order based upon the power of elites, of, that is, those who possessed 'honours, riches and intelligence', as they said in France until the middle of the nineteenth century.

Although Marx failed to recognize the meaning of the mutation signalled by the advent of the liberal-democratic system, and although, as I myself have tried to show, he fell into the trap of the dominant ideology by describing the rights of man as a disguised form of bourgeois egotism, he was perfectly correct to denounce the relations of oppression and exploitation that were concealed behind the principles of freedom, equality and justice. And if, while discussing the liberal state, we think, finally, of the era when the right of everyone to participate in public affairs was effectively instituted by universal suffrage, and when freedom of opinion combined with freedom of association to give workers the right to strike – and it appears to us that these phenomena have become inseparable from the democratic system – we have to admit that it was only thanks to a combination of force of numbers and the principle of right that this model prevailed. In other words, the liberal state cannot be viewed simply as a state whose function is to guarantee the rights of individuals and citizens and to grant civil society full autonomy. It is at once distinct from civil society, is shaped by it, and is a force which shapes it.

The name of Benjamin Constant is often mentioned in discussions about the birth of political liberalism. And it is of course true that no other thinker so clearly delineated, in theory, the prerogatives of central government, so firmly asserted the sovereignty of right as opposed to the sovereignty of one man, one group or even the people, or so extolled the freedom of the individual. But, if we look at France, Guizot did more than Constant to formulate the practice of liberalism. Guizot proclaims the sovereignty of right just as loudly, but at the same time he attempts to forge a strong government which will both emanate from the bourgeois elite and become the agency which transforms it from being a potential aristocracy to being a real aristocracy – although it will of course be a new kind of aristocracy, as men will no longer be ranked according to birth, but in accordance with their functions and their merits. And I do not think I am mistaken in taking the view that Guizot's liberalism already implies the notion of a state based upon the power of norms and controls. That his state is very different from ours need scarcely be stressed. But the tendency whose effects we are assessing is already visible, and it is important to note that it takes shape on a truly political register as a result of the acceleration of what Tocqueville will term the *democratic revolution*. It seems to me that what Constant fails to see is that the increase in power is not the result of a historical accident, of an act of usurpation that gives rise to an arbitrary government, but that it goes hand in hand with the irreversible movement which brings into being a unified society or, more accurately, *society as such* from the ruins of the old hierarchies – and that this movement itself goes hand in hand with the emergence of individuals who are defined both as being independent and as being shaped in one another's likeness. And what appears to have escaped Guizot is that the conspicuous ramparts he wanted to erect around the ruling stratum, primarily by restricting the exercise of political rights, and the distinction he made between citizens, between the men who were worthy of that name and those who could be ranked on a scale ranging from mediocrity to penury, formed an edifice which would not be able to withstand the gradual onslaughts of the excluded – assaults which would be led by those members of the bourgeoisie he excludes. The man who did so much to bring bourgeois society into the world did not understand that it required divisions that were much less conspicuous and much less rigid, for, although it was a class society, it had the features of democracy.

Guizot and Constant are liberals who see democracy simply as a form of government. For them democracy is what it was for Aristotle and what it was for Montesquieu: a regime in which the sovereignty of the people is asserted and in which the government acts in the name of the people. Neither of them has any idea that it implies an unprecedented historical adventure whose causes and effects cannot be localized within the sphere that is conventionally defined as that of government.

Let us not, then, succumb to the illusions of liberalism, or to the illusion that a model of the state is sufficient to indicate the difference between the Old and the New that was introduced by the establishment of the rights of man. The liberal state may well become an abstraction if we try to extract it from the configuration of the new democratic society by isolating certain of its pertinent features. Let us turn, instead, to Tocqueville, whose works teach us that the questions we are asking had already arisen in the first half of the nineteenth century. If we cling to the conventional image of the liberal state, we will fail to understand that he was already expressing the fears that we are formulating, that he foresaw the possibility that the regime of freedom might turn into despotism or, rather – and since he ultimately rejects that term – into a system of oppression of a new kind which he cannot name.

He writes:

I think, then, that the species of oppression by which democratic nations are menaced is unlike anything that ever before existed in the world; our contemporaries will find no prototype of it in their memories. I seek in vain for an expression that will accurately convey the whole of the idea I have formed of it: the old words *despotism* and *tyranny* are inappropriate: the thing itself is new, and since I cannot name, I must attempt to define it.[2]

Tocqueville's work certainly alerts us to these questions, as it means that we must try to understand how, knowing nothing of the economic and social upheavals we associate with the formation of the welfare state, he was able to conceive of individuals being subjugated by an all-powerful state and of freedoms being lost behind a facade of freedom.

I am thinking in particular of the picture he paints in the final section of *Democracy in America*, where he invites us to imagine 'the novel features under which despotism may appear in the world'. Having mentioned the isolation of citizens ('Each of them, living apart, is as a stranger to the fate of all the rest'), he goes on:

Above this race of men stands an immense and tutelary power, which takes upon itself alone to secure their gratifications and to watch over their fate. That power is absolute, minute, regular, provident and mild. It would be like the authority of a parent if, like that authority, its object were to prepare men for manhood; but it seeks, on the contrary, to keep them in perpetual childhood: it is well content that the people should rejoice, provided they think of nothing but rejoicing. For their happiness such a government willingly labours, but it chooses to be the sole agent and the only arbiter of that happiness; it provides for their security, foresees and supplies their necessities, manages their principal concerns, directs their industry, regulates the descent of property, and subdivides their inheritances: what remains, but to spare them all the care of thinking and all the trouble of living?[3]

He then describes this power as covering the entire surface of society with a network of small, complicated rules, and specifically states that: 'It does not tyrannize, but it compresses, enervates, extinguishes and stupifies.' Finally, Tocqueville sums up his views: 'I have always thought that servitude of the regular, quiet and gentle kind which I have just described might be combined more easily than is commonly believed with some of the outward forms of freedom, and that it might even establish itself under the wing of the sovereignty of the people.'[4]

These lines are well known, but I cite them in my turn because they are singularly pertinent to our present investigations into the topicality of human rights in the welfare state. Do they not teach us that the liberal stage contains within it the seeds of what we are calling the welfare state and of what Tocqueville calls tutelary power? And does not his ability to see into the future stem from his exemplary sensitivity to the enigma of democracy? And are we not still faced with the same enigma?

As we all know, Tocqueville devoted himself to exploring the ambiguities of democracy and, more specifically, the ambiguities of what he regarded as the mainspring of the democratic revolution: equality of condition. I would merely add that this phenomenon (or the inscription on the reverse side: the destruction of the ranks, orders and principles which had previously been used to classify human beings) seems to him to have a double effect. On the one hand, there is the full affirmation of the individual, which is bound up with 'the wish to remain free', and, on the other, the subjugation of the individual to an anonymous or sovereign power, which he terms 'social power' and which he associates with the 'need to be led'.

Contrary to the views advanced by certain critics, Tocqueville certainly does not regard the independence of the individual as a delusion. He never derides it. On the contrary, in a passage in *L'Etat social et politique de la France*, he unequivocally states his belief in the democratic conception of freedom: 'According to the modern, democratic and, I would venture to say, correct notion of freedom, every man, being presumed to have received from nature sufficient intelligence to conduct his own affairs, is born with an equal and imprescriptible right to live independently of his fellows in all matters that regard him alone and to govern his destiny as he sees fit.' Our author does, however, note that the same process leads both to independence and to a new subjugation of the individual – and his subjugation is, and we must not be afraid of saying so, now more fearful than ever. It seems to Tocqueville that when man is freed from the old networks of personal dependency (which meant that he always recognized authority in the shape of someone placed above him, or that he embodied authority for someone placed beneath him) he is threatened with insignificance in a uniform society which condenses what were once multiple and disparate forces. This society is invested with a formidable authority – an authority which is simultaneously actualized in public opinion by the fantastic assertion of unanimity, in law by the fantastic assertion of uniformity, and in state power by the fantastic assertion of reglementation. There is no need to go into the details of Tocqueville's interpretation, and it is not my intention to do so. Suffice it to say that he is acutely aware of the social nature of man; as an individual, man may well wish to be the master of his own thoughts, to shape his own life and even to determine what is meant by good laws and good government, but he is still necessarily dependent upon received ideas and principles of behaviour which are beyond the control of his will and knowledge. As a result, the passion with which man strives to break the bonds making him subject to persons invested with social authority – the passion for equality leading him to challenge the figure of the master – cannot make him his own master. Paradoxically, the passions he directs against the visible master force him to submit to a faceless domination. As Tocqueville once put it: 'Every man allows himself to be put in leading-strings, because he sees that it is not a person or a class of persons, but the people at large who hold the end of his chain.'[5]

This sentence has long seemed to me to be one of the clearest expressions of Tocqueville's thought; it is a sentence which sheds the greatest possible light on the paradoxes of democracy. Let us note in passing that it is now more pertinent than ever. For, when this sentence was written, and for a long time afterwards – basically, until very recently – class divisions were sufficiently acute to make the features of class domination at least partly visible. As class divisions become blurred, however, domination tends increasingly to detach itself from any visible representative. It is even more important to note the distinction Tocqueville makes between personal power and impersonal power, and his representation of the latter as an omnipresent power which is destined by its very invisibility constantly to increase its hold over men. I would add, however, that democratic power is not reducible to impersonal power or, to be more accurate, that it masks two phenomena which, whilst they are inseparable, are also quite distinct. We must not, therefore, lose sight of the fact that the destruction of personal monarchical power has the effect of creating a vacuum at the very spot where the substance of the community was apparently represented by the king, by his body. In view of this phenomenon, the operation of negativity and the institution of political freedom are one and the same. And the fact is that political freedom survives so long as it is recognized that the guardians of public authority are forbidden to appropriate power, so long as it is deemed impossible to occupy the locus of power. Power becomes and remains democratic when it proves to belong to no one. It is, I believe, this which led

Tocqueville to reject the old words 'despotism' and 'tyranny' in his description of the new kind of oppression which menaced democratic societies. And it is this which leads me to criticize one of the judgements we have mentioned; it is inappropriate to speak of a form of servitude being combined with the outward forms of freedom. So long as institutions are so regulated to make it impossible for the ruler or rulers to appropriate power, we cannot say that they are a matter of pure form. What I have termed the operation of negativity is no less constitutive of the democratic space than the erection of the state into a tutelary power. The system thrives on this contradiction and, so long as the system is perpetuated, neither of its terms can lose its efficacy. It is in fact quite clear that Tocqueville himself saw that it was impossible to resolve or abolish this contradiction, despite the impulse that led him to imagine a sort of democratic despotism of a previously unknown kind. Commentators who dwell on that image tend to forget its conclusion:

> A constitution republican in its head and ultra-monarchical in all its other parts has always appeared to me to be a shortlived monster. The vices of rulers and the ineptitude of the people would speedily bring about its ruin; and the nation, weary of its representatives and of itself, would create freer institutions or soon return to stretch itself at the feet of a single monster.[6]

This idea is obviously of great importance to Tocqueville, as he reformulates it years later in a fragment written when he was preparing the final section of *L'Ancien Régime et la Révolution*. Having fully re-established the distance that separates democracy from an absolutist government which rules 'by law, and in the midst of institutions which favour the condition of the people', he states: 'Its meaning [that of democracy] is intimately bound up with the idea of political freedom. To apply the epithet "democratic government" to a government in which there is no political freedom is a palpable absurdity'. The point need scarcely be stressed: the freedom he is talking about is not reducible to the outward forms of freedom.

Why do I attach such importance to this last point? My audience will, I suspect, have already realized why. In our day we often heard it said that the only difference between democracy and the totalitarian system is the degree of oppression. Certain critics even go so far as to talk about 'totalitarian democracy'. To cite Tocqueville again, *this is a palpable absurdity*. We do of course have good reason to believe that the evolution of democracy has made possible the appearance of a new system of domination – be it fascism, Nazism or what is known as socialism – whose features were previously inconceivable. But we must at least recognize that the formation of that system implies the ruin of democracy. It does not represent the culmination of the historic adventure inaugurated by democracy; it inverts its meaning. The ambiguities of democracy cannot be resolved by furthering one of the tendencies that coexist within it, namely the tendency to reinforce the power of the state apparatus. For the state apparatus itself is dismantled for the benefit of the party apparatus, and the aim of the party is certainly not to ensure the well-being of citizens. We must never tire of considering this fact: totalitarianism does not simply mark the destruction of political freedom; it destroys the basis of the tutelary power or of the welfare state. Whatever the features of the new regime, be it fascist, Nazi or Stalinist, and no matter whether it was established in the wake of Soviet socialism or under the influence of that model in Europe, China, Korea, Vietnam or Cuba, it is not the principle of well-being that governs the development of the state.

'Isn't the welfare state like Janus?' someone will ask. 'Doesn't it have a hidden face: that of the police state?' This is a legitimate question. There is good reason to suspect not only that the repression directed against strata eroded by the economic crisis may increase, but that it is in the very nature of the welfare state to 'neutralize the expression of social conflicts'. But let us not forget that it does have two faces, and that as one becomes harsher, the other becomes more benign. And nor should we forget to look at the obstacles which block the expansion of the coercive state; I refer to the democratic apparatus, which prevents the agencies of power, law and knowledge from fusing into a single leading organ. If we fail to remember that, we will fail to recognize the specific dimension of the political in our societies. If we concentrate our attention upon the increasing prerogatives of the administration and, more generally, on the strengthening of public authorities, we will no longer be able to discern the specific nature of a power whose exercise always depends upon competition between parties – with all that competition implies – and upon a debate which is sustained by public liberties and which preserves them. It is primarily because there is no master that the welfare state does not become a police-state. If a master did appear, the state would lose the disturbing ambiguity which characterizes it in a democracy. And the fact that there is no master means that there is a gap, which is deemed to be intangible, between administrative power and political authority. The existence of that gap means that the representational imperative is still efficacious. Ultimately, that imperative is incompatible with the full implementation of the norm for two reasons. First, it both necessitates and legitimates the expression of a multiplicity of positions on the part of both individual and collective social agents. Secondly, it proves to be indissociable from freedom of opinion, of association and of movement, and from the freedom to express conflict throughout society. We may certainly wonder as to the current ability of political parties to ensure that representation is correctly exercised. We may even look for signs of new apparatuses capable of regenerating their ability to do so. But we cannot escape the need to compare the totalitarian regime and the democratic regime, and we cannot conceive of the state being transformed unless we take the political into account.

Let it not be thought that I have strayed away from the object of our discussion. These last observations are designed to recall our attention to what, in an essay published a few years ago, I termed the political significance of human rights.[7] It is true that my essay provoked objections to which I am not insensitive, notably from Pierre Manent, who criticized me on two counts. First, he believes. I failed to measure the extent of the gulf opened up between state and civil society by the modern conception of right – an argument which leads him to rehabilitate the analysis made by Marx in *On The Jewish Question*. Secondly, he believes that I failed to recognize the constant benefits that accrue to the state from the extension of social and economic rights which reinforce its statutory powers – an argument which leads him, unlike Marx, to detect the effect of the change that has taken place within the framework of the state rather than that of civil society.[8] Perhaps I was wrong not to give sufficient weight to the latter phenomenon. I was concerned primarily with combating the widespread interpretation which reduces human rights to individual rights, and which simultaneously reduces democracy to a relationship between only two terms: the state and the individual. But I remain convinced that it is only by recognizing in the institution of human rights signs of the emergence of a new type of legitimacy and of a public space, only by recognizing that individuals are both the products and the instigators of that space, and only by recognizing that it cannot be swallowed up by the state without a violent mutation giving birth to a new form of society, that we can possibly hope to evaluate the development of democracy and the likely fate of freedom.

Allow me, then, to return briefly to the interpretation of the 1791 Declaration, as it seems to me to invalidate the conception I have just mentioned.

Having proclaimed the end of social distinctions (art. 1), the Declaration pronounces resistance to oppression to be an imprescriptible right (art. 2); it then states that the principle of all sovereignty resides within the nation. 'No body and no individual can exercise any authority that does not emanate from it' (art. 3). It then makes law the expression of the general will and further states that 'All citizens have the right to contribute to its formation, either personally or through their representatives'. The Declaration is of course governed by the idea of natural rights, of rights which reside within every individual. As we know, it refers to political society as a 'political association' and defines its goal as the preservation of those rights. But how can we fail to see that, behind the mask of its language, it makes use of notions which are meaningful only if they are contrasted with those that governed the principle of the old political order, the order of the monarchy. Sovereignty, the nation, authority, the general will and the law which is assumed to be its expression are all described in such a way as to escape all appropriation. Sovereignty is said to reside within the nation, but the nation can no longer be embodied by anyone; similarly, authority can only be exercised in accordance with rules which guarantee that it is legitimately delegated; the general will makes itself known in law, and the elaboration of law implies the participation of citizens.

This body of propositions does not, let us note, depend for its coherence on a reference to human nature, or on the idea that every individual is born with inalienable rights. Its coherence is ensured by the principle of political freedom. What we refer to in positive terms as 'political freedom' can of course be called 'resistance to oppression'. And it is true that the latter concept is included, along with freedom, property and security, within the category of universal natural and imprescriptible rights, and that all political associations are designed to protect those rights. But, once again, we must bear in mind what might become of the principle of resistance in the real. The Constituant Assembly believed, of course, that this principle had its roots in human nature. But it formulated it in opposition to a regime in which power denies its subjects the ability to oppose anything they deem illegitimate, and claims to have the right to force them to obey. In short, the formulation of the rights of man at the end of the eighteenth century was inspired by a demand for freedom which destroys the representation of power as standing above society and as possessing an absolute legitimacy, either because it derives from God or because it represents a supreme wisdom or justice which can be embodied by the monarch or the monarchical institution. These rights of man mark a disentangling of right and power. Right and power are no longer condensed around the same pole. If it is to be legitimate, power must henceforth conform to right, but it does not control the principle of right.

We are told that freedom, property and security are rights of individuals, that the state acquires the function of preserving them, and that this function already indicates its potential strength – which will soon be greatly increased by the rise of new rights – because its apparent neutrality, its position as a guarantor or arbiter, mean that it can develop without, apparently, doing anything more than respond to its citizens' expectations. As I have already noted, this argument ignores one other phenomenon: an assertion of right which has the effect of challenging the omnipotence of power.

Whilst the Declaration stipulates the right to resist oppression, it is inconceivable that it should give the state responsibility for ensuring that that right is respected. It is certainly the task of the state to guarantee the property, security and freedom of its citizens, but the threat of oppression poses a different problem. Although the threat may emanate from one individual and may be directed against another individual, it culminates, of course, in the hypothesis of an assault on the sovereignty of the nation. And therefore no appeal is made to the state to guarantee the right to resist; that is the responsibility of the citizens themselves. Let us note in passing that when jurists argue that right exists only if its holder can be defined and only if it is demurrable, they are being very formalistic. In the present instance, the holder's identity is uncertain, and the tribunal before which his right is asserted is not visible.

If we now examined those rights which appear to refer solely to individuals, we would find that they too have a political import.

It is, however, true, that we will not discern that import if we stick to the letter of the great Declarations; we must also investigate the effects of the exercise of these new rights in social life. Critics of the rights of man always concentrate upon the form in which they are stated. This is especially true of their most virulent critic, namely Marx, who pursues every sign of individualism and naturalism in order to assign to it an ideological function. Marx sees in the freedom of action and the freedom of opinion granted to everyone, and in the guarantees of individual security, no more than the establishment of a new model which enshrines 'the separation of man from man' or, at a more basic level still, 'bourgeois egotism'.

Marx does of course display here a characteristic feature of the thinking of his time, but when he dismisses the upheaval in social and political relations implicit in the bourgeois representation of these rights, he still occupies the ideological terrain he claims to be undermining. The author of *On the Jewish Question* is trapped by this representation, and he is convinced that it reveals the effective reality of civil society – a society shattered into a diversity of private interests and individuals – a reality whose formation coincides with that of its counterpart: a state destined to embody a fictitious sovereignty. If Marx is to be belived, we have only to tear away the veil to reveal the 'trivial face' of that society. But the rights of man are not a veil. Far from having the function of masking a dissolution of social bonds which makes everyone a monad, they both testify to the existence of a new network of human relations and bring it into existence.

Without going into the details of the argument in the essay I mentioned earlier, I will put forward three points to support this proposition.

1 The declaration that freedom consists in being able to do everything which does not harm others does not imply that the individual withdraws into the sphere of his own activities. The negative formula 'which does not harm', upon which Marx concentrates, is indissociable from the positive 'being able to do everything'. This article gives full recognition to the right of freedom of movement; it enshrines the lifting of the prohibitions which restricted that right under the Ancien Régime, and it therefore facilitates the multiplication of human relations. Everyone now has the right to settle where they wish, to travel as they wish across the territory of the nation, to enter places which were previously the preserve of privileged categories, to embark upon any career for which they believe they are qualified.

2   Freedom of opinion does not transform opinion into private property, and it is not modelled on the ownership of material goods; it is a relational freedom. According to the text of the 1791 Declaration, 'The free communication of thoughts and opinions is one of the most precious rights of man, every citizen may therefore speak, write and freely print, unless what he does constitutes an abuse of that liberty in the particular cases laid down by law.' As everyone acquires the right to address others and to listen to them, a symbolic space is established; it has no definite frontiers, and no authority can claim to control it or to decide what can and what cannot be thought, what can and cannot be said. Speech as such and thought as such prove to exist independently of any given individual, and belong to no one.

3   The guarantees of security – in which Marx sees only the most sordid expression of civil society, a 'concept of *police*' designed to protect the bourgeois – teach us that justice has been separated from power, that it has its own principle and that, by protecting the individual from arbitrariness, it makes him a symbol of the freedom which founds the existence of the nation. From Constant to Péguy, it will therefore be asserted again and again that an injustice done to an individual not only harms the individual, but degrades the nation itself, not because everyone fears that they will fall victim to arbitrariness if their neighbour's rights are violated, but because the very fabric of social relations in a political community depends upon the citizen's trust in a justice which is independent of all masters.

Pierre Manent criticizes me for failing to recognize the paradox which Marx sees so clearly: 'At the very moment when the men of the Revolution gave the political instance all powers and rights, and gave themselves those powers and rights as rulers,' he observes, 'they justified politics as such as a means to be used by egotistic men in civil society.' And, having cited *On the Jewish Question*, he states that Marx sees quite clearly that 'When circumstances make it aware of its importance and of its eminent value, this civil life, which has no content of its own and no opinions of its own, cannot but take the form of pure negation, and cannot but turn against the conditions of its possibility, namely the bourgeois society of which it is still, in its own view, no more than an instrument.' But is the contradiction facing the men of the Revolution the contradiction of the rights of man?
Marx excels, as we know, at dialectical arguments which turn opposites into complementaries. The illusion of politics is, he notes in the early *On the Jewish Question*, twinned with the illusion of the rights of man. His argument relies for its coherence upon the thesis, which is certainly not shared by Manent, that communism will mark the abolition of class divisions, and that the distinction between the economic, the juridical and the political will therefore be abolished within the purity of the social. If that thesis proves to be inaccurate, and it seems to me that history in fact demonstrates that the thesis culminates in the

totalitarian fantasy, Marx's critique collapses. The lines cited by Manent reveal terror to be the hidden face of the rights of man. But does terror stem from a realization of the vanity of a society which, as a result of the separation of man from man, materializes only by breaking up? Or is this Marxist image of civil society no more than a fiction? And, far from complementing civil society, does not terror signal the destruction of political freedom as such? Does it not signal, as Michelet and Quinet will show, a surreptitious return to the tradition of absolutism, the emergence of a society whose faith in the monarch and in religion has collapsed, and of an insane power which claims to be the earthly embodiment of law and knowledge? It seems to me that it is all the more difficult to accept the argument put forward by Manent, who follows Marx here, in that it prevents us from understanding why democracy succeeded in freeing itself from terror and in basing itself upon the rights of man.

I quite realize that the principal thesis is that democracy could not have triumphed without instituting a separation between civil society – a locus for opinions with no power – and the secular liberal state – a locus for power with no opinions. It is claimed that, as a result of this system, the state grows stronger behind its mask of neutrality, whilst civil society grows weaker, but remains a theatre for the noisy expression of opinions which, because they are merely the opinions of individuals, neutralize one another. And yet this thesis seems unilateral, to say the least, in that it leads us to ignore the great event which determined both the formation of a neutral power and that of free opinions; I refer to the disappearance of an authority which subjugated each and every individual, to the disappearance of the natural or supernatural basis which, it was claimed, gave that authority an unassailable legitimacy and an understanding both of the ultimate ends of society and of the behaviour of the people it assigned to specific stations and functions.

The political originality of democracy – and it appears to me to have gone unrecognized – is signalled by a double phenomenon: a power which is henceforth involved in a constant search for a basis because law and knowledge are no longer embodied in the person or persons who exercise it, and a society which accepts conflicting opinions and debates over rights because the markers which once allowed people to situate themselves in relation to one another in a determinate manner have disappeared. This double phenomenon is itself a sign of a single mutation: power must now win its legitimacy without becoming divorced from competition between parties, if not by finding a basis in opinion. Now competition stems from, sustains or even stimulates the exercise of civil liberties. The state does, it is true, appear to be neutral, to have no opinions or to be above opinion, but the fact remains that the transformations it has undergone in the last 150 years (including the transformation which, by separating it from the Church, constituted it as a secular state), occurred as a result of changes in public opinion, or in response to them.

The early liberals and the Saint-Simonians were wrong to see public opinion as a completely new force – 'the sovereign of the world', as they liked to call it – which would gradually disarm the old prejudices and arbitrary power. Tocqueville came closer to the truth in that he realized that the process of the condensation of opinion might subject people to new norms of thought and conduct, and might encourage them to take a passive attitude towards the state. And yet, I repeat, the democratic process has more than one meaning. We should be able to identify a new 'tyranny of opinion', to use Tocqueville's expression; a new freedom to express opinions which are, as Manent puts it, destined to neutralize one another; and a new freedom which has the effect of undermining prejudice and of modifying the general feeling as to what is or is not socially acceptable and legitimate and as to what can or cannot be demanded.

I am not confusing rights and opinions. On the contrary, and as I am about to explain, the confusion of the two appears to me to me to stem from a perversion of the notion of right. My primary concern is to promote recognition of a public space, which is always in gestation and whose existence blurs the conventional boundaries between the political and the non-political. From this point of view, the distinction between civil society and state, to which I myself have referred, cannot fully account for what comes into being with the formation of democracy. Let us say that it is pertinent only if we refuse to see it as a pure division. Marx, it will be recalled, did define it in that way. He contrasted the model of feudal society, in which political relations appeared to him to be interwoven in socio-economic relations, with the model of bourgeois society, in which the sphere of the political tends to coincide with that of the state and in which it is divorced from a specifically civil sphere characterized by the fragmentation of interests and by conflicts beween their agents. He forgot only one thing, namely that the Ancien Regime had to a large extent already destroyed the feudal system, and that the state appropriated the principle of authority before it was in a position to make effective use of all its mechanisms. What he calls bourgeois society is certainly characterized by the strengthening of the power of the state, but it is also characterized by the representative system and by the fact that the government must emanate from society as a whole. These two features are of course indissociable; although we may choose to emphasize one rather than the other, they cannot be analysed separately.

It must be admitted that, all too often, we fail to recognize the import of the constitution according to whose terms a public authority is established, exercised and periodically renewed as a result of political competition and the import of the conflicts which, thanks to that competition, find their expression in social life. It is true that the efficacy of this representation is marred by the permanence of a state apparatus of increasing complexity, and that we are therefore tempted to ignore it. But we must resist that temptation.

It must also be pointed out that the formation of a totalitarian type of power which is not subject to competition signifies not only the end of political freedoms, but also the end of civil liberties themselves.

It is therefore impossible to restrict the terms of our argument to state and civil society. Civil society (if we are to retain the term) is itself inscribed within a political constitution, and it is bound up with the system of democratic power. Moreover, and regardless of its size and complexity, the state apparatus cannot be unified so long as every sector within it remains subject to pressure from specific categories of citizens or from social actors defending the autonomy of their spheres of competence, and so long as the managerial logic which officials try to impose comes into conflict with the logic of representation which imposes itself upon the elected authorities. In short, the same factors which make it impossible for the state to become a closed system, to become a great organ controlling the social body's every movement, also mean that those who hold political authority are obliged to submit the principle of the conduct of public affairs to periodic contests.

It is at this point in my argument that I return to the question around which our debate centres. My argument is not designed to invalidate the question, but to reformulate it in such a way as to make it impossible to answer it whilst avoiding its political implications. In fact I accept that the new rights that emerge as a result of the exercise of political freedoms help to increase the state's statutory powers.

Indeed, it seems to me that the political system lends itself to that development. Parties and governments in fact welcome demands which seem to them to be popular so as to sanction their own legitimacy; they modify legislation accordingly, and legislation gives the administration new responsibilities, new means of control and new opportunities for coercion. Naturally! But we cannot leave matters there. It is not enough for this or that demand to find a sympathetic hearing in the upper echelons of the state for new rights to receive juridical recognition. Even if a demand concerns only a single category of citizens, it must first meet with at least tacit approval from a broad section of public opinion; in other words, it must be inscribed within what we have called the public space. We must obviously not underestimate the articulation of force and right – no matter whether the force in question emanates from interests capable of mobilizing effective means of pressure or whether it is to be assessed in purely numerical terms. But one of the preconditions for the success of any demand is the widespread conviction that the new right conforms to the demand for freedom enshrined in existing rights. Thus, in the nineteenth century, the right of workers to associate and the right to strike resulted from a change in the balance of power, but at the same time even those who did not instigate those rights recognized them as a legitimate extension of the right to freedom of expression or the right to resist oppression. Similarly, in the twentieth century, the right of women to vote and a number of social or economic rights seem in their turn to be an extension of earlier rights, and so-called cultural rights seem to be an extension of the right to education. It is as though new rights seemed in retrospect to be linked organically with what are considered to be constituent elements of public freedoms.

It is, however, to be noted that this feeling initially inspires those who take the initiative in formulating the demand. In formulating it, they are of course defending their own interests but, so long as their voices are not heard, they are also aware of being the victims of a wrong rather than an injury.

This observation merits serious consideration. The democratic apprehension of right implies the affirmation of speech – be it individual or collective – which, whilst it is not guaranteed by existing laws or by a monarch's promise, can assert its authority in the expectation of public confirmation because it appeals to the conscience of the public. We cannot ignore the novelty of this phenomenon. Whilst speech of this type is intimately bound up with a demand addressed to the state, it is also distinct from that demand. In that respect, a comparison with the totalitarian regime is once more instructive. There is, let us note, no room in a totalitarian regime for the welfare state model; but that does not prevent it from taking countless measures concerning employment, public health, education, housing and leisure in order to meet certain of the population's needs. But it is not a guarantor of rights in any strict sense. The discourse of power is self-sufficient; it ignores any speech which leaves its orbit. Power decides and bestows, but it is always arbitrary; it is always selective, choosing between those to whom it gives the benefit of its laws and those it excludes. Individuals receive no more than requisites disguised as rights because they are treated as dependents and not as citizens.

If we consider the mainsprings of right in a democracy, it is tempting to conclude that no distinction can be made between rights which are regarded as fundamental – those which came into being as the rights of man – and other rights which have been acquired with the passage of time. And, in a sense which I am about to define, I believe that this is indeed the case.

Does this mean that we have to abandon a naturalist thesis only to adopt a historicist thesis? On the contrary, it means that we have to reject both these terms. The idea of human nature, which was so vigorously proclaimed at the end of the eighteenth century, could never capture the meaning of the undertaking inaugurated by the great American and French declarations. By reducing the source of right to the human utterance of right, they made an enigma of both humanity and right. Specific statements aside, they granted recognition of *the right to have rights* (the expression is borrowed from Hannah Arendt, although she uses it in a rather different sense), and thus gave rise to an adventure whose outcome is unpredictable. In other words, the naturalist conception of right masked an extraordinary event: a declaration which was in fact a self-declaration, that is, a declaration by which human beings, speaking through their representatives, revealed themselves to be both the subject and the object of the utterance in which they named the human elements in one another, 'spoke to' one another, appeared before one another, and therefore erected themselves into their own judges, their own witnesses.

The representation of *human nature* is not an isolated aspect of this event. Whatever its distinguishing mark may be, it cannot be divorced from the ascription of a 'nature' to the self; the self being, if I can put it this way, at once individual, plural and communal; its existence being indicated at once in every individual, in the individual's relations with others, and in the people. For the same reason, we can neither define the notion of human nature, see it as a nature-in-itself – unless we lapse into the imaginary – nor subscribe to any critique of the rights of man which claims to deny their universal import on the grounds that we must turn from fiction to reality. Paradoxically, the criticisms of naturalism put forward by thinkers as different as Marx and Burke invoke historical reality, yet they fail to see that the philosophical illusion which ignores 'concrete' human beings in favour of an abstract being becomes something that is absolutely new as a result of the affirmation of humanity. Neither of them actually perceives that the idea of the rights of man is a challenge to the definition of power has having rights, to the notion of a legitimacy whose basis is beyond the grasp of human beings, and, at the same time, to the representation of an ordered world in which human beings are 'naturally' ranked. They both attack the abstraction of an indeterminate humanity, denounce the fictional universals of the French Declaration, but fail to see what it bequeathes us: the universality of the principle which reduces right to the questioning of right. This last formula cannot be annexed by historicism; it implies that the institution of the rights of man is much more than an event, as we described it earlier; it is more than something which appears within time and which is destined to disappear into time. A principle arises, and henceforth we cannot understand the individual, society or history unless we go back to it.

And yet, the view that naturalism and historicism are equally inappropriate tools for conceptualizing the rights of man does not simplify the basic problem; it complicates it. It would seem that we can neither say that these original rights make up a bedrock because we have rejected all belief in human nature, nor that they and the rights that were subsequently won form a chain each link of which is similarly marked by circumstances, because we have discovered in the institution of those first rights a foundation, the emergence of a principle of universality. And nor can we trace a dividing line between first rights and new rights, because we have recognized that the latter are based upon the former.

It seems, however, necessary to complicate the argument in this manner. The advantage of doing so is that we do not lose sight of the distinction we must constantly investigate: that between a democratic and a totalitarian regime. It would be a mistake to translate this distinction into one between a regime governed by laws and a regime without laws (to use the terminology of classical philosophy), or into one between a regime in which power is legitimate, and a regime in which it is arbitrary.

As Hannah Arendt quite rightly observes, totalitarianism is indeed characterized by its scorn for positive rights, but it is still organized beneath the aegis of the Law, which, like power, is fantastically asserted to be above human beings, at the very moment when it is posited as being the law of the human world, as having been brought down from heaven to earth.

The distinguishing feature of democracy is that, whilst it inaugurates a history which abolishes the place of the referent from which the law once derived its transcendance, it does not thereby make law immanent within the order of the world, nor, by the same criterion, does it confuse the rule of law with the rule of power. It makes the law something which, whilst it is always irreducible to human artifice, gives meaning to human actions only on condition that human beings desire it, that they apprehend it as the reason for their coexistence and as the condition of possibility of their judging and being judged. The division between legitimate and illegitimate is not materialized within the social space; it is simply removed from the realm of certainty, now that no one can take the place of the supreme judge, now that this empty place sustains the demand to know. In other words, modern democracy invites us to replace the notion of a regime governed by laws, of a legitimate power, by the notion of a regime founded upon *the legitimacy of a debate as to what is legitimate and what is illegitimate* – a debate which is necessarily without any guarantor and without any end. The inspiration behind both the rights of man and the spread of rights in our day bears witness to that debate.

But, if we accept that this debate pertains to the essence of democracy, we may be in a better position to circumscribe the symbolic import of the rights stipulated in the first Declarations without making any concessions to the opposition between historicism and naturalism, and without misrecognizing the continuity between everything that has been affirmed from the original Declarations to our own times.

The singular thing about the freedoms proclaimed at the end of the eighteenth century is that they are in effect indissociable from the birth of the democratic debate. Indeed, they generate it. We therefore have to accept that whenever these freedoms are undermined, the entire democratic edifice is threatened with collapse, and that, where they do not exist, we look in vain for the slightest trace of it. Whilst economic, social and cultural rights, on the other hand, are not contingent, they may cease to be guaranteed or even to be recognized (I can in fact think of no country – not even Mrs Thatcher's Britain or Mr Reagan's America – where they have been abolished in principle), without that causing a fatal lesion; the process is still reversible and the fabric of democracy can still be repaired, not simply because conditions may make it possible to improve the lot of the majority, but precisely because the conditions that allow protests to be made are still intact.

I can anticipate the objections that will be raised. It will be said that freedoms remain formal when they coexist alongside poverty, insecurity of employment, and destitution in the face of illness. I find the argument untenable. When applied to Western societies, it ignores the fact that these formal freedoms made it possible to raise demands which succeeded in improving the human condition. It passes over in silence the status of the first freedoms which resulted from workers' rights to associate and to strike, the fact that they are so bound up with the original rights of man that their suppression would now imply the destruction of democracy, and the fact that they are bound up with economic and social rights.

If, moreover, this argument is applied to societies in which a wretched proportion of the population is the victim of savage exploitation, it can all too easily be turned against those who invoke it. What, they ask, is the point of talking about human rights in this context? Human rights are seen as a luxury that cannot be coveted by people who have to face the drama of penury, famine, epidemics or infant mortality. Those who use this argument forget only one thing: in such countries the oppressed are denied freedom of speech, freedom of association and often freedom of movement itself. In other words, they are denied everything that might give them legitimate and effective ways to protest and to resist oppression. And experience teaches us only too clearly that scorn for human rights encourages would-be revolutionaries to construct totalitarian-style regimes, or to dream of doing so. It masks an underlying refusal to grant individuals, peasant communities, workers, and peoples in general *the right to have rights*.

It is true that when we argue that democracy establishes a debate as to the legitimate and the illegitimate, we are getting to the heart of the problem. This principle in fact suggests that whatever is judged legitimate in the here and now is henceforth legitimate. But upon what criterion is that judgement based? We could of course say that it resides in the conformity between the new right and the spirit of the old rights. I myself would suggest that this is so: the feeling that there is such a connection motivates those who are or will become the defenders of unprecedented demands. It also motivates public opinion, which accepts those demands, and the agencies which provide them with a juridical outlet. But this answer does not remove all doubt. Fundamental rights may well be constitutive of a public debate, but they cannot be constrained by a definition; and we therefore cannot agree on any universal basis as to what conforms or does not conform to the letter or the spirit of those rights. We therefore lay ourselves open to the argument that what is judged legitimate in the here and now may be legitimate only in terms of the criteria of the majority. But, in order to support that thesis, we would have to forget what we have already said, namely that right cannot be immanent within the social order without the very idea of right being debased. At the beginning of the nineteenth century a paradox had already been perceived, not only by liberals resolutely hostile to the establishment of democracy, but also by thinkers such as Michelet and Quiret, who were equally attached to the sovereignty of the people – which was in their view implicit in social and economic progress – and to the sovereignty of right. The paradox was that rights are named by human beings – and that this in itself indicates their ability to name themselves, to designate themselves in their humanity, in their existence as individuals, and to designate their humanity in their mode of coexistence, in the manner of their living together in the 'city' – and that right is not reducible to human artifice.

The legitimacy of the debate as to what is legitimate and what is illegitimate presupposes, I repeat, that no one can take the place of the supreme judge: 'no one' means no individual, not even an individual invested with a supreme authority, and no group, not even the majority. The negative is effectiv: it does away with the judge, but it also relates justice to the existence of a public space – a space which is so constituted that everyone is encouraged to speak and to listen withuot being subject to the authority of another, that everyone is urged to *will* the power hc has been given. This space, which is always indeterminate, has the virtue of belonging to no one, of being large enough to accommodate only those who recognize one another within it and who give it a meaning, and of allowing the questioning of right to spread. As a result, no artifice can prevent a majority from emerging *in the here and now* or from giving an answer which can stand in for the truth. And the fact that every single individual has the right to denounce that answer as hollow or wrong is the one thing which confirms the validity of the articulation of right and opinion, of the irreducibility of conscience to the right to have an opinion; in the event, the majority may prove to be wrong, but not the public space. If, in the absence of the debate it implies, it proved to be the case that a compact, constant body of mass opinion took decisions under cover of darkness instead of majorities being made and unmade, instead of the turmoil of exchange and conflict stimulating uncertainty and a happy diversity of convictions, the debasement of right would stem, not from the errors of the majority, but from the debasement of the public space itself.

We therefore have to ask whether this space is shrinking or even withering away. Is it, as some claim, no longer anything more than a simulacrum which the state uses to further its claims to being democratic? Can we now see anything more than a gathering groundswell of opinion which is becoming more compact and which is being shaped to accommodate itself to the emergence of an omnipotent power? Let us pose the question, by all means, but let us also agree that this is a question of politics and that it would be rash to resolve it in one way or another.

The paradox which I have described and which pertains, I believe, to the essence of democracy, has in our day been considerably accentuated by the entry into what was once constituted as the public space of a mass of people who were formerly excluded from it. How are we to assess the effects of this change with any accuracy? The state's increasingly strong position as the guarantor of social, economic and cultural rights certainly tends to reduce the legitimacy of right to the sanctioning of opinion by an agency which appears to be a condensation of social power. At the same time, opinions tend increasingly to find a common denominator, regardless of the fact that they emanate from different categories, because they expect to be sanctioned and because they are in effect virtually legitimized if they have force of numbers of their side.

There is, in my view, no doubt as to the validity of this observation. But it must not be allowed to obscure the fact that, far from abolishing it, the intervention of the masses into the public space has extended its boundaries considerably and has led to an increase in its networks. Contemporary neo-liberalism (which is at the moment regaining an astonishing prestige) refuses to see the meaning of this adventure because it still clings to the theory that an elite can maintain itself in power by denying the more populous – and especially the poorest – strata of society the right to speak. It thus blinds itself to the problems that now confront us, as no return to the past is conceivable within the framework of democracy. And it makes it impossible to speak out in defence of the cause of right, as the generalization of the right to speak is inseparable from the diffusion of the *meaning* of right throughout society. It is all the more important to investigate the effects of new rights, to reveal their ambiguities and to attempt to make the correct distinction bewteen right and opinion – a distinction which many no longer see – in that it seems pointless to deny that, for millions of people, blind obedience to norms which served only to meet the needs of a minority or to maintain its dominance over numerous registers, has given way to a willingness to challenge the notion of the legitimate and the illegitimate.

Think, for example, of the demands which led to new conditions for women. Who could claim in good faith that those demands simply reflected a change in public opinion, or that they were governed by a mere demand for well-being? The debate over contraception, in particular, or that over abortion, brought into play an idea of freedom which some may certainly challenge, but which touches upon the essence of the individual, of interpersonal relationships and of social life. That is of course the most eloquent example. But if we think of rights as diverse as those of wage-earners who have lost their jobs, of entrepreneurs faced with management problems, of social security claimants, of immigrants, prisoners, conscientious objectors, soldiers (who are currently denied freedom of expression), or those of homosexuals – and all these rights have for years been the subject of constant debate, especially in France – we have to admit that they express a sense of right which is incomparably more acute than it once was. It is often said that the power of the state is increasing as a result of these new demands, but the extent to which it is being challenged tends to be forgotten.

Recent debates over employment, social security, reforms in public health and medical care, and over the status of private schools – and they have all provoked strikes and massive conflicts – prove that indifference and passivity are not the rule. It will be objected that these debates represent conflicts between coalitions of interests, corporate resistance to threats, or the reawakening of prejudice. But was the defence of rights ever free from the influence of interests and opinions in the past? When there are, for example, quarrels over the organization of medicine or education, do we not hear something more than the clash of interests? Some critics still believe that the economic crisis is the driving force behind the new expansion of technocratic bureaucracy. But is it not the case that, on the contrary, it reveals, in an unexpected way, a conflict of rights, that it exposes the underside of certain evils which are still evils, and of certain gains which are still gains?

I have said that the survival and extension of the public space is a political question. I mean by that that it is the question that lies at the heart of democracy. I do not pretend to have an answer. To look for even the outline of an answer would require a separate debate. I will restrict myself to this conclusion: there is no institution which can, by its very nature, guarantee the existence of a public space in which it is possible to question right on an increasingly broad basis. But, conversely, that space presupposes that the image of its legitimacy is reflected on a stage erected by distinct institutions, on a stage upon which actors entrusted with political responsibilities can be seen to move. And when parties and Parliament no longer assume their responsibilities, it is to be feared that, in the absence of a new form of representation capable of responding to society's expectations, the democratic regime may lose its credibility. It must also be feared that what I have termed the distinction between power, law and knowledge, which lies at the origins of the modern consciousness of right, may lose its symbolic efficacy when the exercise of justice on the one hand and the dissemination of information through the press, radio and television on the other are no longer seen to be essentially independent of one another. In other words, when political, juridical and intellectual actors so often appear to be acting in accordance with orders dictated by interests, by the need for group discipline or by the need to court public opinion, we have good cause to worry about the corruption they are spreading.

In order to demonstrate the role of those who appear on the public stage, let me end with a simple observation borrowed from an article by Pierre Pachet.[9] When Alain Peyrefitte was Minister of Justice he said in substance that, speaking as an individual, he was not opposed to the abolition of the death penalty, but public opinion was not ready for it. In saying so, he both elevated bad temper, fears and a lust for vengeance to the consistency of opinion, and legitimized them. There can have been few more striking examples of the degradation of right at the hands of the authority which is supposed to guarantee it. His successor, Robert Badinter, had only to speak the language of justice once more to make the spectre of the omnipotence of opinion disappear.

3

Hannah Arendt and The Question
of the Political

In the United States Hannah Arendt was recognized to be a major political thinker at a very early stage in her career, even though her writings did at times provoke violent polemics. In France, however, one is struck by the fact that she was ignored for so long, especially by the left-wing intelligentsia, even though many of her works had been translated. Raymond Aron was the man who played the decisive role in introducing her to the French public. In one sense, this is not surprising. Raymond Aron was an authentic liberal; although his liberalism differed from that of Arendt, they shared a common understanding of fascist and Stalinist regimes, and they both eluded conventional definitions of left and right. The fact that there are still great differences between Aron's liberalism and that of Arendt is indicated by the way Arendt was drawn to the revolutionary phenomenon and, more specifically, by the interest she took in the formation of the workers' councils during the Hungarian revolution. For Arendt, a revolution was not an object of curiosity. For her, it was the moment of *beginning*, or of *beginning again*.

It seems in fact that the ignorance, neglect and even hostility to which Hannah Arendt was subjected in France relate to the influence of Marxism, which was an obvious obstacle to the reception of her ideas. But we now live in an age in which a certain disenchantment is apparent, in which a certain number of new questions are being asked more and more frequently. For some years, it has, for example, been possible to note the presence of a critique of rationalism which is directed not only against modern science and its destructive effects, but also against the ideal of reason itself. And it is not only the philosophy of the Enlightenment which has come under attack; it is also the philosophy of history as such. The philosophy of history is now seen as an extension of the philosophy of the Enlightenment, whereas it was once seen as its critique, if not as its negation. Marx is no longer regarded as the thinker who overthrew rationalism, but as the thinker who did most to further the project of subjectivity by

embodying it in history and most to further the project of man's
domination over nature; and as the thinker who fostered the illusion
of the One, the illusion that humanity can become closed in upon
itself.

This critique, and this appears to be worthy of note, even goes so
far as to call into question the very notion of history itself; not simply
the notion of history as the 'tribunal of reason', but also the notion of
history as the advent of meaning, as a milieu within which we are
situated, by which we are shaped, and upon which we depend for
access to our past. This critique is also often directed against the very
notion of social reality, of the reality which was, it was once assumed,
to be found at the level of relations of production.

These criticisms find their clearest expression in the critique of the
state, which is regarded as an organ for the homogenization of the
social and for domination, as an organ which acquires increasing
powers as a result of the demand and the satisfaction of collective
needs.

The mood of a section of the contemporary intelligentsia, as
compared with that of the immediate post-war period, leads them to
discredit everything to do with the realm of violence, and to reject
politics as though politics and violence were one and the same. Anyone
who now reads Hannah Arendt for the first time cannot fail to see
the vigor with which she paves the way for the questions that are now
being asked, or the rigour with which she articulates them and attempts
to answer them. This does not necessarily mean that the answers she
gives will meet our expectations. But the spirit of investigation which
inspires her in her task merits our full attention.

I would like here to bring out the demand for thought which is
apparent throughout her work.

This demand was born of an encounter with an *event*, of her lived
experience of an event which overwhelmed her and which seemed, at
the same time, to be 'the central event of our times': the victory of
Nazism in 1933.

She says that her interest in politics and history dates from 1933.
Much more specifically, she evokes 27 February, the day of the
Reichstag fire: 'For me, it was an immediate shock, and from that
moment onwards I felt that I was responsible.'[1] This is neither an
anecdotal fact nor a biographical detail. The feeling that she was
responsible, that she had to respond to the fearful challenge of
totalitarianism made her aware of the motor force behind all thought.

In her preface to *Between Past and Future*, she writes: 'My assumption
is that thought itself arises out of incidents of living experience and
must remain bound to them as the only guideposts by which to take
its bearings.'[2] Arendt was certainly a woman of great erudition. She
was a brilliant Greek scholar, studied under Husserl, and was a disciple
of Jaspers and Heidegger. When she writes that 'thought arises'

'thinking' does not simply mean moving through the realm of *what has already been thought*; it means making a new beginning and, more specifically still, *beginning again on the basis of events*. These lines from Merleau-Ponty's preface to *Adventures of the Dialectic* are perfectly in keeping with the thought of Hannah Arendt:

> In the crucible of events we become aware of what is not acceptable to us, and it is this experience as interpreted that becomes both thesis and philosophy. We are thus allowed to report our experience frankly with all its false starts, its omissions, its disparities, and with the possibility of revisions at a later date. By doing so we manage to avoid the pretence of systematic works, which, just like all others, are born of our experience but claim to spring from nothing and therefore appear, at the very moment when they catch up with current problems, to display a superhuman understanding when, in reality, they are only returning to their origins in a learned manner.[3]

No other writer identified the link between thought and events more rigorously than Arendt. No writer saw more clearly that the unknown, the unexpected element that irrupts into our beliefs, and the universe that we share with our fellows, are the very birthplace of thought, the forces that generate thought. Facing up to the unknown, which was Arendt's attitude, takes on its full meaning if we recall the weakness displayed by German intellectuals in 1933 – by the intellectuals who dedicated the most deceitful and fallacious constructions to a 'refusal to think' and who, as she says, made her resolve to turn her back on intellectuals for ever because she knew that she had nothing to learn from them.

We cannot fully appreciate Arendt's work unless we grasp both this demand for thought and the need to remain faithful to it. Arendt was indeed a theorist, even a philosopher, but it is no accident that she always rejected that label, for we find in her work a constant tension between a desire to elaborate a theory and a wish to remain free to react to events. Similarly, her critique of the history of the historians becomes clearer in the light of her concern not to dissolve the new into a temporal continuum which makes it seem, a posteriori, to be no more than an effect of a development implicit in its premisses.

Arendt constantly draws a distinction between the task of *understanding* and the high theory which, in one way or another, always attempts to subordinate the particular to the rule of a principle, and between understanding and the explanations of the historian, which consist of chains of causal relations.

For Arendt, understanding means, primarily, relying upon a precritical understanding, upon common sense.[4] And does not common sense in fact spontaneously distinguish between truth and lies, good and evil, tyranny and freedom? And does not a reliance upon this non-critical understanding in itself help us to glimpse something that poses a challenge to thought? It is, however, true that this precomprehension gives us only a partial insight into the unknown. As Arendt notes, common sense regards totalitarianism as tyranny, whereas it is of course something very different; it is neither a new art of lying nor a new mode of an evil that has already been identified.

But, for Arendt, *understanding* also means being receptive to the times in which we live. It does not mean resigning ourselves to whatever happens, but attempting *to reconcile ourselves to time* and, ultimately, *understanding ourselves*, that is attempting to understand how something like totalitarianism could come into being in the world in which we live, given that it was not, after all, born of nothing and did, after all, spring from within a culture with which we were familiar.

The words 'thought arises out of incidents of living experience and must remain bound to them' convince me that the greater part of Arendt's work is bound up with her experience and interpretation of the totalitarian phenomenon. Although she does not make explicit the articulation between her conception of politics and of history and her analysis of the totalitarian phenomenon (one might call it the articulation between her conception of metaphysics and, more generally, of the human condition, and that analysis), it is in my view a rigorous articulation, and I would like to begin by bringing it to light.

Firstly, totalitarianism is a regime, it seems, in which everything appears to be political: the juridical, the economic, the scientific and the pedagogic. We observe how the party penetrates every domain and distributes its orders. Secondly, totalitarianism appears to be a regime in which everything becomes public. Thirdly, and this is why we cannot confuse totalitarianism with a vulgar tyranny, it cannot be regarded as an arbitrary type of government insofar as it does refer to a law, or at least to the idea of an absolute law which owes nothing to human interpretation in the here and now: the law of history in communist-style totalitarianism, and the law of life in Nazi-style totalitarianism. In this regime, action appears to be the dominant value, in that the people must be mobilized and must always be involved in tasks serving the general interest. It is also a regime in which discourse rules. Finally, it is a regime which appears to be revolutionary, which sweeps away the past and devotes itself to the creation of a 'new man'.

The other side of this full affirmation of politics is, however, a negation. It is not simply that we may discover that the ideal of mastering society in fact finds its expression in total domination, that it involves the exercise of powers which owe nothing to any ethical or religious reference, powers which recognize no limits to the realm of the possible, and which mean that the creation of the famous 'new man' becomes an attack on the very things that have always represented the dignity of the human condition. It is not simply that the fantastic elevation of the law to superhuman status has in reality the effect of suppressing entirely the validity of positive laws and of all juridical guarantees. It is not simply that the mystique of the One, of a sort of collective body, leads in fact to the extermination of the enemy within. If we leave matters there, we are merely stating the obvious. But if we go beyond appearances, we discover that totalitarianism is in no sense a matter of politics, public life, law, action or speech, or of revolution as beginning. We must recognize, rather, that these references were destroyed to allow the project of total domination to be realized.

How, in fact, can we cling to the idea that politics invades everything? If there is no boundary between politics and that which is not political, politics itself disappears, because politics has always implied a definite relationship between human beings, a relationship governed by the need to answer the questions on which their common fate depends.

Politics can exist only in the presence of a space in which human beings recognize themselves as citizens, in which they situate one another within the limits of a *common world*; and social life cannot exist in any true sense unless human beings experience their mutual interdependence solely as a result of the division of labour and of the necessity of satisfying their needs. This is tantamount to saying that the apparent expansion of the public sphere or (and this amounts to the same thing) the tendency for the public to swallow up the private – and we often hear it said that this is happening – are equally illusory. The truth of the matter is that, when the distinction between public and private disappears, both the public realm and the private realm disappear. What appears in their place is something that might be termed 'the social', a vast organization, a network of multiple relations of dependence whose workings are governed by a dominant apparatus.

It is said that in totalitarianism the law proclaims itself to be superior to human beings. In a sense, this phenomenon testifies to the impossibility of confusing totalitarianism with any other kind of tyranny, but it is equally clear that the very idea of law is destroyed, and not merely violated, as is the case within the bounds of an arbitrary power. When the law is believed to have materialized in the supposed movement of history, or in the movement of life, the notion of the transcendance of law is indeed lost; the criteria for distinguishing between the permissible and the prohibited vanish; there is no opposition to techniques of organization and domination. For the very same reason, the ideal of action, of which we hear so much and which is, moreover, supported by constant appeals to the activism of militants, is a lure, as is the ideal of an efficacious word which can transmit to the whole of society knowledge of its ultimate ends and immediate aims.

What we call 'action' is not 'action' when there are no actors, when, that is, no initiative is taken in response to novel situations, when a mere decision on the part of a leader is presented as an effect of the movement of history or of life, when the role of contingency is denied, and when the leader's only requirement of others is that their *conduct* shall conform to norms and orders. Similarly, what we call 'speech' is not speech when speech no longer circulates, when all trace of dialogue disappears, when only one master has the right to speak, and when everyone else is reduced to the function of hearing and transmitting.

This is also why the very idea of revolution disappears behind the mask of the national-socialist or communist revolution, for a revolution implies the appearance of the majority on the public stage or, rather, the building of that stage as a result of the agitation which brought human beings into contact with one another by bringing them out of their private universe, by mobilizing their initiative and by instituting a common debate. Moreover, revolution's characteristic ability to *begin* is not one of the distinguishing features of totalitarianism. On the contrary, the distinguishing mark of totalitarianism is the triumph of an ideology, which has an answer to every question, to any question that might arise from events; it is the triumph of an intellectual machine which uses principles to manufacture effects, as though thought had been disconnected from the experience of the real.

Arendt's reading of totalitarianism, in both its Nazi and Stalinist variants, governs the subsequent elaboration of her theory of politics. She conceptualizes politics by inverting the image of totalitarianism, and this leads her to look, not for a model of politics – the use of the term 'model' would be a betrayal of her intentions – but for a reference to politics in certain privileged moments when its features are most clearly discernable: the moment of the Greek City in Antiquity and, in modern times, the moments of the American and French Revolutions. The moment of the workers' councils in Russia in 1917, and that of the Hungarian workers' councils of 1956, might also be added to the list.

In the purest case, that of Greece, we see, according to Arendt, the organization or emergence of a 'space' within which men recognize one another as equals, and discuss and debate together, a space wherein they are removed from the private matters characteristic of the bounds of the *oikos* – a domestic unit of production governed by the constraints of the division of labour and of master–servant relations. Within this space men can, as Arendt puts it, vie with one another in attempting to attract public attention or to imprint their image on the public memory with their 'fine words' and their 'exploits'.

Here, power is exercised within an inter-personal relationship, and words are exchanged in an attempt to reach decisions that concern everyone. The very existence of this space is a precondition for the appearance of a 'common world', of a world which is not *one*, but which is the same because it is open to multiple perspectives. This is a truly human world, which neither perception alone nor labour alone could establish because, again according to Arendt, it is quite obvious that the mere use of life cannot transcend needs that have to be satisfied and the constraints they impose, and cannot give birth to this very different need – but the word is inappropriate – to *the desire for a human world which transcends the contingency of institutions.*

It is impossible to emphasize too strongly the idea that it is by participating in this space, by acceding to the *visibility* of a public stage than men define and apprehend one another as equals. Alternatively, we might say that it is by apprehending one another as equals that they gain access to the stage. According to Arendt, there is a very close connection between equality and visibility. The possibility, or even the reality, of equality implies that each person can appear before others in this space, and that others can appear before them. When power is circumscribed within an organ or an individual, it escapes everyone's gaze. Inequality and invisibility go hand in hand.

This in itself is enough to suggest that, for Arendt, equality is not an end in itself. It is not, for example, that at a given moment in history men make the discovery that they are born equal. Equality is an invention; it is an effect or simply a sign of the moment which raises men above life and opens them up to a *common world.*

This brief evocation of Greek politics allows us to bring out the oppositions which govern all Hannah Arendt's analyses. The primary object of her book *The Human Condition* is the opposition between action and work or labour.[5] She makes further oppositions between the public and the private realm, between the realm of politics and the realm of social life, between power and violence, between unity and plurality, and between the active life and the contemplative life.

With regard to the latter opposition, Hannah Arendt takes the view – and ultimately this is why she refuses to call herself a philosopher – that philosophy originates in Plato's misrecognition or disavowal of politics. The freedom that had once been found in action, in the democratic City, in debate and in *manifestation* was rejected by philosophy and was transferred to thought, which became divorced from the human world, a world which was disparaged as a realm of confusion. According to Arendt, the birth of philosophy gave a new meaning to the distinction between the sacred and the profane, between the enchanted world of politics and prosaic life, to the distinction which located the sacred or enchantment in the realm of the visible, in the appearance of the public space; because for philosophy it was the invisible (the invisibility that had once characterized private occupations) that was invested with the nobility characteristic of interiority, whilst political activity fell into disrepute.

The strength of the tradition inaugurated by Plato is, according to Arendt, such that its effects can still be seen in Marx, who attempts to revive political activity simply by *realizing* philosophy, in other words by projecting on to an empirical history and an empirical society the idea of a logic and a truth which arise precisely because the original nature of action has been forgotten.

We now have to ask how Arendt articulates this idea of politics with her reading of modern history. Modern times – the expression is vague, but the lack of precision can be imputed to Arendt herself – are, she suggests, the theatre of a considerable change. In Antiquity, in the time of the *polis*, society did not exist; the world was divided between the affairs of the city and the affairs of the *oikos*, whereas the distinctive feature of modernity pertains to the advent of the social.

In other words, growth, technology and the division of labour, together with the rise of modern science – which aims to control nature – had the effect of establishing a general network of dependence. This network binds together individuals, activities and needs, and implies increasingly complex organizational tasks; it leads to the emergence of relations of domination on a new scale: that of the nation.

The process of the expansion of the social and of the debasement of politics was briefly interrupted – at a point when, it is true, it was still in its early stages – by the American Revolution and the French Revolution, but neither had any lasting effect. Indeed, Arendt notes that the latter was almost immediately perverted by the rise of the 'social question'.

The problem was, she says in substance, that political equality inevitably became confused with social equality. This is a tragic confusion, as equality can only be political, and it found a philosophical expression in the insensate idea that individuals are equal by birth, in the chimera of the rights of man. It must be noted that for Hannah Arendt, as for Burke, only the rights of citizens are real; the rights of man are a fiction.

A glance at the way societies developed in the nineteenth and twentieth centuries reveals the increasing role of the state, of the organ responsible for the administration of the social. At the same time, politics tends increasingly to lose its status, whilst the public space withers away and whilst private space becomes atrophied. In their place, we see the emergence of, on the one hand, social organization and, on the other, the little world of the individual, which Arendt calls the world of intimacy. As a result of the standardization of mores and behaviour, the latter become a *trompe l'œil* painting.

It is at this point that we have to return to the origins of totalitarianism, a phenomenon which Arendt describes as being without any historical precedent and as having destroyed the categories of the Western trdition. Whilst she stubbornly refuses to assign a cause to it, she describes how it emerges from within modern societies, and does so in terms which leaves us in no doubt as to its *raison d'être*.

According to Arendt, totalitarianism is born of a depoliticized society in which there are no longer any limits to indifference to public affairs, to atomization, to individualism or to unbridled competition. Although she also recognizes that bourgeois individualism is an obstacle to the strong man's seizure of power, she is not afraid to say that 'in this sense, the bourgoisie's political philosophy was always "totalitarian"';[6] the bourgoisie had always assumed the identity of politics, economics and a society in which political institutions served only as a façade for private interests.

Nor is she afraid to write:

> The philistine's retirement into private life, his single-minded devotion to matters of family and career was the last, and already degenerated, product of the bourgeoisie's belief in the primacy of private interest. The philistine is the bourgeois isolated from his own class, the atomized individual who is produced by the collapse of the bourgeois class itself. The mass man whom Himmler organized for the greatest mass crimes ever committed in history bore the features of the philistine rather than of the mob man, and was the bourgeois who in the midst of the ruins of his world worried about nothing so much as his private security, and was ready to sacrifice everything – belief, honor, dignity – on the slightest provocation.[7]

Arendt does in fact refuse to establish a continuity between bourgeois democracy and totalitarianism, but that is because she finds in the crises that followed the war (the First World War) a decisive accident, namely the collapse of a class system and the liberation of the masses from what had by then become traditional bonds: the emergence of people who were quite literally *disinterested* because they no longer had any interests to defend, and who were in that sense ready for anything, including death.

Hannah Arendt's interpretation calls for numerous comments. The first concerns the clear-cut distinction she establishes between the political realm and the private realm, and the related distinction between political equality and social inequality.

Even presupposing that we can speak of politics having been invented in Greece, as Moses Finlay suggests,[8] it is worth asking which circumstances, which conflicts – and they can only have been social – and which aims – and they can only have been military – led highly differentiated and hierarchical societies to accept that peasants, shopkeepers and artisans should be admitted to assemblies in which decisions concerning public affairs were taken.

We must also ask how decisions were actually taken behind the mask of political equality, and we must ask ourselves about the nature of the means by which certain men succeeded in exercising a lasting authority over one or other section of the people. The latter question is never raised by Arendt, who is convinced, on the one hand, that speech is the sole medium of persuasion and, on the other – which is equally naive – that the exchange of words is in itself egalitarian, that it cannot transmit any inequality of powers. To turn to her interpretation of the French Revolution, it is difficult to see how she can make a distinction between political equality and the struggle that was waged against the hierarchy of the Ancien Regime. This struggle, as Tocqueville explains, was inscribed within the process of 'equality of condition', which certainly cannot be confused with economic equality but which, as Tocqueville again demonstrates, could not fail to have both social and political effects. It was a struggle both for freedom and for the recognition that human beings are made in one another's likeness.

In terms of Arendt's critique of the concept of the rights of man and her claim that it derives from the fiction of human nature, it is difficult to see the philosophical basis for the argument that the mutual recognition of individuals as being made in one another's likeness must stop at the gates of the City. If that were indeed the case, it is particularly difficult to see how we can possibly justify our condemnation of totalitarianism, except on the crude and almost accidental grounds that its conquests are a threat to our society.

Hannah Arendt sees the project of total domination as an expression of a wish to explore the limits of the possible, and as revealing the ultimate possibility of changing human nature itself. I do not wish to dwell upon the purely formal contradiction between the rejection of the idea of human nature and the assumption that human nature can be changed, but I think it important to stress that if we do not regard the distinction between truth and lies, good and evil, just and unjust, and real and imaginary as constitutive of political thought, or even of thought in general, we ultimately lend credence to the hypothesis that the only obstacle to totalitarianism is the power of its adversaries, and to the view that, in itself, it is free from all internal contradictions.

Arendt's formula 'The power of man is so great that he can be whatever he wants to be' is derived from historicism or from what Leo Strauss calls nihilism, a theory which Arendt herself attacks elsewhere.

Let us note, finally, that the way in which she defines politics presents us with a radical alternative. Politics, so to speak, either exists or does not exist. We cannot explain which politics emerges in any given context; it is the sign of a radical beginning and, moreover, it appears and then disappears without trace. When, for example, Arendt speaks in the preface to *Between Past and Future* of the Resistance as a 'lost treasure' – an expression she borrows from René Char – she adds:

> The men of the European Resistance were neither the first nor the last to lose their treasure. The history of Revolutions – from the summer of 1776 in Philadelphia and the summer of 1789 in Paris to the autumn of 1956 in Budapest – which politically spells out the innermost story of the modern age, could be told in parable form as the tale of an age-old treasure which, under the

most varied circumstances, appears abruptly, unexpectedly, and disappears again, under different mysterious conditions, as though it were a fata morgana.[9]

Arendt's intellectual style appears to reveal something of the inspiration behind the work of certain great contemporary thinkers. For Leo Strauss, the possibility that a regime conforming to nature – the regime conceived by Plato – might never exist in no way discredits it. For Heidegger, whose concerns are rather different, the greater the occultation of Being, the greater the danger; but as the danger increases, we are in a better position to understand the question of Being with greater acuity. Arendt, for her part, suggests that even if politics, as she understands politics, can no longer be embodied in the real, it is still politics, and she also leads us to suppose that, as the shadow of totalitarianism spreads, we are better placed to discern its features.

Despite the differences between them, all three thinkers concur in calling modernity into question. *From a political point of view, the questioning of modernity means the questioning of democracy.*

The disturbing thing about Hannah Arendt – and it is a sign of a shortcoming – is that, whilst she rightly criticizes capitalism and bourgeois individualism, she never shows any interest in democracy as such, in modern democracy. Could it be that this is because modern democracy is representative and because the notion of representation is alien or even repugnant to her? Yet if there is one thing that Nazi totalitarianism and Stalinist-style totalitarianism have in common, it is a hatred of democracy. Arendt refuses to see that. Although she wishes to restore plurality, as opposed to the One, she fails to see that the fantastic attempt to turn society into a unified body welded to its head – the Führer, the supreme guide – stems from the overthrow of the regime which established itself thus; by making a distinction between the pole of power, the pole of law and the pole of knowledge, and by accepting social division and conflict; by accepting a heterogeneity of mores and opinions, and by distancing itself, as no previous regime had done, from the fantasy of an organic society.[10]

PART II

ON REVOLUTION

4

The Revolutionary Terror

A SPEECH BY ROBESPIERRE

Let us examine a speech by Robespierre. Let us examine, for example, the speech he made on 11 Germinal Year II (31 March 1794). To tell the truth, it is no accident that I should have chosen this speech. The circumstances were exceptional. On that day, it seems, the Convention almost frustrated a bid for power by the Committee of Public Safety. Had it done so, revolutionary politics might have changed abruptly. '*Almost* frustrated . . .'? The decisive factor was of course Robespierre's intervention. Let us briefly recall the facts: Danton had been arrested the previous night, together with Camille Desmoulins, Lacroix and Philippeau. For less than a year, there had been an increase in the rate of major purges. The fall of the leaders of the Gironde had been followed in turn by the fall of the Enragés, the Hébertistes and then the old leaders of the Paris Commune. The victims were all distinguished, but none of them had enjoyed Danton's prestige. Not one of them had embodied the spirit of the Revolution to the same extent, and, unlike Camille, none of them could have claimed to be the father of the Republic. This time, Robespierre and the Committees were striking very close to home. The launching of an offensive against what was termed the Indulgent faction had of course been announced, notably to the Jacobins, but the news of the arrests, which had been ordered without the knowledge of the Convention, still came as a surprise. The bid for power was also a *coup de théâtre*; it provided a sign that the Terror had reached a paroxysm.

The fact is – let us note in passing – that the elimination of Danton and his friends appears, with hindsight, to have marked a turning point in the course of the Revolution. Perhaps, as has sometimes been said, it announced the fall of Robespierre. It certainly allowed him to impose unprecedented terroristic measures in the coming months; by destroying his opponents, the Germinal events paved the way for the creation of the Bureau de police générale and for the adoption, some two months

later, of the decree of 22 Prairal and the reorganization of revolutionary
justice.

And yet it is not really because of its circumstances, its timing or
its import that I have singled out Robespierre's speech for attention.
It stands out because of its style, its tone and its composition, because
of the strategy we can detect beneath the rhetorical effects. Robespierre
does not attempt to prove that Danton and his friends are guilty; he
says not a word to that effect. Nor does he try to convince the
Assembly of the need to maintain the Terror; he only uses the word
once, and then it is to evoke the fear his adversaries wish to inspire
in him. His art is the art of displacing the object of the debate; he
draws his interlocutors into the snares of an argument which they have
to recognize as their own. He simultaneously imposes himself as master
and obliterates the place of the master. Finally, he uses all the artifices
of speech to do away with speech itself; the revolutionary truth of
which he is the organ silences all debate. In short, Robespierre's speech
does not take the Terror as its object; it exercises the Terror; it
represents an important moment of the Terror in action. It speaks
Terror.

On 11 Germinal, then, the sitting of the Convention opens in accordance
with the usual procedures, but the Assembly is alive with rumours
about the night's arrests. The members of the Committees have yet to
arrive. Representative Legendre immediately asks leave to speak. He
declares that he is astounded, asserts that Danton is as pure as he is,
and makes an appeal: 'The man who, in September 1792, saved France
thanks to his energy deserves to be heard, and must have the right to
put his case if he is to be accused of betraying the Fatherland.' His
words no doubt express the feelings of the greater part of the Assembly:
how can it refuse one of its most illustrious members the right to
defend himself before it? The debate is already under way when
Robespierre appears, ahead of his colleagues on the Committees, and
eager, we can assume, to know the Assembly's reactions. He rises to
speak, and with his very first words he uncovers the hidden motives
behind Legendre's initial arguments: 'It is easy to tell from the turmoil
that prevails in this Assembly, a turmoil that has long been unknown,
and from the agitation provoked by the opening remarks of the last
speaker but one, that a major issue is at stake here: the issue is
whether or not a few men are to prevail against the Fatherland today.'[1]
The object of the debate is immediately displaced. Indeed, the orator
ignores its manifest object, and invites his listeners to look at the real
issue. Not content with denouncing the plans of Danton's supporters,
he then gives voice to a suspicion which weighs upon the whole
Assembly: 'What, then, is the change that appears to have manifested
itself in the principles of the members of this Assembly, and especially
in the principles of those who sit on the side which prides itself on
having given refuge to the most intrepid defenders of liberty?'

What was the object of the debate? – The right of members of the Convention who have been arrested without its consent to justify their conduct before their peers. Implicitly, it touched upon the guarantees accorded to the representatives of the people. Robespierre is careful not to condemn those guarantees in principle, and does not even evoke the restrictions that may have to be placed upon liberty in revolutionary times; he exploits an allusion to the Mountain to praise the 'refuge of liberty' but, basing his argument upon the fact that Bazire, Chabot and Fabre d'Eglantine were recently denied a right which the accused Danton demanded on their behalf – and his interlocutors cannot have forgotten the fact – he expresses his surprise that a principle should have been abandoned. This would be a weak argument if it merely revealed the instability of the Assembly, particularly in that a sovereign assembly is not bound by its previous decisions, and in that the immunity of *députés* cannot, as a matter of principle, be challenged. Robespierre's question does not, then, centre upon the fact that the Convention has reversed its position; he asks for the reasons for the change; he asks why some should be granted a right refused to others. His *why* is the instrument of suspicion. And the answer is obvious from the question itself: 'The issue is whether or not the interests of a few ambitious hypocrites are to prevail against the interests of the French people.' Robespierre, who is in no hurry to name Danton and his friends, is, then, pointing out to the Assembly that it is according privileged treatment to certain individuals.

The individuals in question are, it is true, described as ambitious hypocrites; and the orator now asks, 'Whether we have made so many heroic sacrifices, amongst which we must number certain acts of painful severity, ... only to come under the yoke of a few plotters who wanted power.' A forceful, and perhaps surprising, phrase. And so, guessing what everyone is thinking as he speaks, he dismisses the idea that the accused have rendered the Republic services, the very services which Danton and Camille would not fail to enumerate with such eloquence before the Assembly, had they the opportunity to do so. 'What do fine speeches matter to me?' cries Robespierre, as though he had heard them. What do tributes to oneself or to one's friends matter? We have learned from long and painful experience what we must think of such oratorical phrases. We no longer ask what a man and his friends boast of having done at a particular time, in particular circumstances of the Revolution; we ask what they have done throughout their political careers.' Without even giving his adversaries any real credit for their past services – he mentions only the services they claim to have rendered – he is obviously attacking the very principle that there can be objective proofs of revolutionary conduct (and thus anticipates the spirit of the Prairal law). But he does not mention his adversaries directly. It is not his intention to discuss the case of the accused in any depth; to do so would expose him to objections, denials or simply questions. What is his intention? He wishes to make the Assembly aware of its image of Danton and, more generally, of its image of the exceptional individual; of the spell cast by the name of Danton, by a *name*.

Hence the return to Legendre's intervention, to the man who opened the debate. 'Legendre seems to be unaware of the names of those who have been arrested. His friend Lacroix is one of their number. Why does he feign not to know that? Because he well knows that no one can defend Lacroix shamelessly.' The allusion to Legendre's immorality reveals the orator's remarkable cunning, for at the very same moment when he criticizes Legendre for not mentioning Lacroix's name, he himself fails to mention other names, notably the name of Camille. He exploits Legendre's silence in order to denounce the privileges granted to Danton. Legendre, he goes on, 'has spoken of Danton, no doubt because he believes that a certain privilege attaches to that name; no, we want no privileges; no, we want no idols.' He has now scored a direct hit on the target he set up at the beginning of his speech. And the hit appears to have been appreciated, as the transcript of the sitting speaks of applause from the Assembly. He will return to the same target a moment later by asking, 'Who are ... these men who sacrifice the interests of the Fatherland to personal loyalties, or perhaps to fear?, who, *at the very moment when equality has triumphed, dare to try to destroy it inside this Assembly?*' (emphasis added). The initial question – 'Whether or not a few men are to prevail against the Fatherland today', 'Whether or not the interests of a few ambitious hypocrites are to prevail against the interests of the French people' – was too closely bound up with the character of the detainees. It now proves to have been superseded. The second question concerns only a universal principle: equality. The accusation is no longer directed solely against the Dantonistes as such, but also against those who are trying to set individuals above the common law by focusing the Convention's attention on them. We should also note how Robespierre controls the thoughts of his audience – thoughts which cannot, of course, be expressed but which could thwart his plans. 'No, we want no idols', he cries; a happy expression and, apparently, one designed to please, but it has the disadvantage of suggesting that Danton is indeed an idol of the people, and therefore of reawakening fears as to what will happen if he is attacked; it has the disadvantage of giving him a new prestige which no principle will be able to expunge from the public imagination. And so he adds, 'We will see today whether the Convention will dare to break *a so-called idol which has long been rotten*, or whether that idol will crush the Convention and the French people when it falls' (emphasis added). He condenses a whole argument into three words. The substance of the argument is as follows: do not tolerate an idol, as you must venerate equality alone; and do not be deceived by rumours: Danton is not an object of worship; and besides, his image is bankrupt and rotten. He cannot of course actually deploy such an argument; the three statements are incompatible, but that is of little importance, and the strength of the discourse of terror lies precisely in its ability to abolish any articulation that might lend itself to contradiction, and to simulate a conclusion which leaves the audience with no choice. In the present context, it is not a matter of resolving whether the Assembly should or should not destroy Danton; he is a rotten idol and will fall of his own accord. The only issue at stake is whether his fall will damage the Convention, or whether the Convention will abandon him in order to save itself. There is, then, no alternative, particularly as the Convention is not confronted with a new situation: the fall of Danton, we are now told, is simply the latest episode in the series of events which destroyed Brissot, Pétion, Chabot and Hébert. Everything that is being said of Danton could have been said of them too: they all 'made France ring with the ostentatious sound of their deceitful patriotism'.

Robespierre, it will be noted, still refrains from producing even the slightest proof of Danton's guilt; he uses the fashionable argument of guilt by association by comparing him with traitors who have already been struck down: 'In what sense is Danton better than his colleagues? And what privileges does he have?' And he combines this argument with a defence of equality: 'In what sense is he better than his fellow citizens?' That is enough. The name of Danton will not be mentioned again.

The question is now displaced for a third time. Here, we must presumably imagine a pause, a sharp intake of breath or a change of tone. Suspicion now falls on the Assembly. Robespierre now addresses its members directly, something he has not done before: 'Citizens, the moment has come to speak the truth.' The challenge is calculated to make his audience shudder. He begins by saying that he has recognized 'a sinister omen of the destruction and decadence of principles' (a moment later, he will ask, 'Who are the men who wish to destroy equality?'), but that relates to his earlier argument. His next declaration introduces something new:

They want to make you fear (*on veut vous faire craindre*) abuses of power, of the national power you have exercised and which does not reside with only a few men. What have you done that you have not done freely, that has not saved the Republic, that has not been approved by the whole of France? They want to make us fear (*on veut nous faire craindre*) that the people will fall victim to the Committees, to the Committees which have won the people's trust, which emanate from the national Convention, and which they (*on*) want to divorce from it, for all those who defend its dignity are doomed to be calumniated. They fear (*on craint*) that the prisoners are being oppressed, and therefore they distrust our national justice, and the me who have won the trust of the nation; they therefore distrust the Convention which gave them that trust, and the public opinion which sanctioned it.

The basic argument seems clear: the Convention and the nation are one; the Convention's decisions are sovereign, and are made in accordance with the will of the people; the Committees and the Convention are one, because they are merely its emanation. Similarly, the organs of national justice derive their authority from the Convention, and it follows that any suspicions directed against the Committees and their justice are also directed against the Convention itself, that suspicion of any kind is intended to destroy the Convention by divorcing it from its own organs. In short, everything is deduced from the principle that the people, the Convention, the Committees and justice are one and the same; the legitimacy and pertinence of the decisions that have been taken therefore cannot be questioned. The exploitation of language is, it should be noted, as remarkable as the argument itself. Something is being implied without being stated explicitly; the explicit condemnation of the abominable suspicions that have been directed against the Committees and which are attributable to an enemy gives rise to a much more serious suspicion: the orator suspects the Convention. It is by slipping from *on* to *vous*, from *vous* to *nous*, and then back to *on* that Robespierre causes an ill-defined threat to hang over his audience. He began by evoking 'men who sacrifice the interests of the Fatherland to personal loyalties, or perhaps to fear'. They have not, of course, been named, but they could be. The *on* is then used to indicate the existence of an anonymous will; it refers to a power which wants to inspire far, and not to individuals who are *perhaps* motivated by fear. But at least the *on* still seems to be unrelated to those Robespierre is addressing; he is suggesting that 'they are manipulating you' [*on vous manipule*]. And, as though to win over his interlocutors, he then converts the *vous* into *nous*. He himself is one of the enemy's targets: *on veut vous faire craindre* becomes *on veut nous faire craindre*. The *nous* condenses the Committees and the Assembly, which they [*on*] want to divorce. But at the same time, an imperceptible shift in the position of the *on* insinuates it into the Convention itself; *on veut nous faire craindre* now becomes *on craint* (that the prisoners are being oppressed), *on se défie donc* . . . The enemy is no longer stirring up fears outside the Assembly; the enemy is inside the Assembly, on its benches; the enemy is among us [*entre nous*], among those Robespierre is addressing.

There can be no mistake as to what is happening when Robespierre suddenly abandons *nous* to hurl the thunderbolt of *je*: 'I say [*je dis*] that anyone who trembles at this moment is guilty; for innocence never fears public scrutiny.' Here, the master appears. His gaze takes in all the *députés*. Of course, no one is named. The point is that 'anyone' has no definite place, that he is here, there and everywhere. The word seeks out the trembling it causes; and the word is at one with the gaze that detects the trembling of fear. Fear and guilt are one and the same; fear is not simply a betrayal of guilt: *he who is afraid is guilty*.

The master appears, I said, but it is also true that the sudden distance between self and other that is imprinted on the 'I say' is immediately transferred from each listener to the next. For they can all see each other, and can be seen by one another. Robespierre's words therefore institute an ordeal by mutual gaze, an ordeal in which everyone must see and be seen. Everyone must open his eyes and look at his neighbour without dropping his eyes before his penetrating gaze. The master's 'anyone' thus diffuses throughout the whole Assembly the distinction between those who are afraid and those who are not afraid, and that distinction produces the distinction between the guilty and the innocent. And so, when Robespierre adds in the same breath that 'innocence never fears public scrutiny', he is not simply evoking the scrutiny of the Committees, but the mutual scrutiny of each by all. It is that which gives the Assembly and all its members a physical presence, and which indicates the all-seeing gaze of the Assembly; indeed, it is that which indicates the gaze of the public, which coincides, ultimately, with Robespierre's gaze. That is his great achievement; whilst the Assembly shrinks beneath his gaze, he escapes its gaze. Another of the orator's remarkable artifices is to be noted. At the very moment when he assumes the position of the master, and when his gaze becomes the organ of the public's vision, he in his turn exposes himself to the gaze of his colleagues as one individual among others. He has, he admits, been entrusted with 'a particular duty' to defend principles. In short, he, like everyone else, has been subject to intimidatory manœuvres or to friendly pressures:

> They have tried to inspire terror in me too, to make me feel that
> if I associated with Danton, I might be in danger too. They (*on*)
> described him to me as a man by whom I must stand, as a shield
> that could defend me, as a rampart whose destruction would
> leave me exposed to the shafts of my enemies. They wrote to
> me; the friends of Danton sent me letters and importuned me
> with their speeches.

Better still, he recalls that he was Danton's friend, that he was once Pétion's friend, even that he had links with Roland. Once again, we have here a sign of the perspicacity we saw earlier: he can read the thoughts of his audience. And they of course are thinking of his relationship with Danton, and of the vulnerability of a powerful man who has lost his closest supporters. Everyone is tormented by doubts and questions: after Danton, why not me? Why not him, the man who is now demanding Danton's death?

Robespierre draws attention to himself solely in order to demonstrate that he is not afraid to come under scrutiny. It is certainly not that he claims to be invulnerable. No, he accepts that *the danger that threatens Danton could in future threaten him too*; it is simply that he does not see that possibility as a 'public calamity'. The implication is that it would be a personal accident, that it would not count for anything. 'What does danger matter to me? My life belongs to the Fatherland; my heart is free from fear; and if I were to die, I would do so without reproach and without ignominy.' In other words, the reason why Robespierre is not afraid, why he can both let his gaze rest on others and expose himself to their gaze is not that he feels himself to be removed from danger, or that he refuses to admit that he can be attacked ('They will not dare to' said Danton, when his friends warned that he was about to be arrested); on the contrary, he delights in exposing himself to the enemy. It is because he is not afraid of death that he is so serene. Others do not frighten him because death does not frighten him, because his life is not his: it belongs to the Fatherland. The transcript of the session tells us that this declaration was punctuated with applause. Indeed, but applause is probably not enough for Robespierre. He is probably alert to the danger of exposing himself to the accusations of presumption, for he ends this confession by slipping back into the bosom of *nous*.

The speech now takes on a precious inflection:

> It is at this point that we no doubt require a certain courage and a certain fortitude (two virtues which, be it noted, he is careful not to claim explicitly for his own). Vulgar souls or guilty men are always afraid of seeing their fellows fall, for when they are no longer protected by a rampart of guilty men, they are exposed to the light of the truth; but whilst such vulgar souls do exist, there are also heroic souls in this Assembly, for it governs the destinies of the world and annuls all factions.

A subtle appeal to the sublime, then. But in order to appreciate it fully, we have to recall the original object of the debate; the refusal to hear Danton and his friends involves a vehement denial of the right of individuals – who are, as it happens, representatives of the people – to be recognized as *subjects*. They are described as being guilty in the absence of any proof of their guilt; they are symbolically destroyed before being physically destroyed. Regardless of his talents, Robespierre cannot conceal the fact that the revolutionary hero depends for his existence on the words that name him as such. Or, to put it more accurately, that the power of speech is bound up with the spell it casts; and its spell is such that, when it is uttered by the orator, it appears to be more than the speech of a single man: it is the speech of the collective hero, of the Assembly or of the people which speaks through it. Yet the source of this power's strength is also the source of its fragility. If the audience is not completely won over, or if a majority remains unconvinced, it becomes apparent that nothing in what

Robespierre is saying can ward off the possibility of a new torrent of accusations, the possibility that today's heroes may be tomorrow's guilty men. If the Assembly is to be convinced, the present must represent a plenitude. Precedents have of course been invoked, but they have only served to make the present more intense; the will to destroy enemies is supported by the re-presentation of the will that destroyed yesterday's enemies, and those of the day before yesterday: the Hébertistes, the Brissotins. But how can men fail to be haunted by the unknown future? As we have already noted, each of them can say to himself: 'after Danton, why not me?'

Once again, Robespierre has of course guessed what his listeners are thinking. Abandoning the register of the sublime, he therefore moves without transition to the register of the trivial. I say 'without transition', but we are reading his words, and we cannot see or hear him. Again, we must imagine a pause, a change of tone or of facial expression. He then goes on: 'The number of guilty men is not so great; patriotism and the National Convention can distinguish between errors and crimes, between weakness and conspiracy. We well know that public opinion and the National Convention attack faction leaders directly, and that they do not strike indiscriminately.' And in order to heighten the effect of his words, he repeats: 'The number of guilty men is not so great; I call as my witness the unanimity or the near-unanimity with which you have voted for these principles in recent months.' In short, he reassures his audience. Having cried, 'Anyone who trembles at this moment is guilty', he now removes the knife. 'Do not tremble so,' he murmurs, 'we tolerate your failings.' Having condemned the vulgar souls and the men who fear the death of their neighbours because they fear their own death, he now states in quite vulgar terms: 'You will not die.' But even this promise contains a veiled threat for, by invoking the unanimity or near-unanimity of recent months, he lets it be understood that the consensus of the day will determine how many are to die.

After this, Robespierre can allow himself the time to recall the scandal of the accusations that have been made against the Committees, to extol their actions in representing the nation, and to show that they are at this very moment watching over its safety. The precondition for safety is silence. And such is that silence, we are finally told, that it should never have been broken. 'Moreover, the discussion which has just begun represents a threat to the Fatherland; it is in itself a guilty blow against liberty, for it is an outrage to liberty to have raised the issue of whether one citizen should be granted more favours than another . . .' What better conclusion could one hope for? Discussion is superfluous. Even Robespierre's words are superfluous. Speech itself is guilty. Liberty implies silence.

It is as though Robespierre had replace his 'Anyone who trembles at this moment is guilty' with the words 'Anyone who speaks at this moment is guilty.'

In concentrating upon a speech by Robespierre, I am not claiming that
a theory of the Terror can be found within its confines. Other speeches
or texts by Robespierre himself, or by Marat, Saint-Just, Billaud-
Varenne or Barrère would also provide essential elements of that
theory. Nor am I being influenced by some vague theory of language
that might allow us to ignore economic, social and ideological conflicts.
Finally, I do not wish to explain every feature of the Terror in terms
of Robespierre's personality. The art with which he bends the members
of the Assembly to his will is, let us remember, efficacious only because
the Assembly lends itself to his art. Imagine these men; some of them
may fear the popularity which the orator, the Committees and the
Sections still enjoy at this point, whilst others may dread a trial of
strength whose outcome would decide not only the fate of the
Dantonistes, but also that of the Convention, or even the fate of the
Revolution itself. Many of them are certainly reluctant to reverse a
policy which was once theirs and to find themselves trapped by a logic
which, regardless of the enormity of its consequences, they have always
supported until now. Robespierre is in fact quick to remind them of
their past decisions; he makes much of his surprise at seeing them
reverse what had been a joint policy. Whilst it might have been
dangerous to evoke the role Danton or Camille Desmoulins played in
the elimination of the Girondins, the Enragés and the Hébertistes, or
the role of the Girondins in the elimination of the *Parti modéré*, he
could rightly have pointed out that neither party had been unduly
concerned with the formalities of justice. I am not, then, giving
Robespierre sole responsibility for the Terror. Many others used the
same means before falling victim to it. And when, for example, he
boasts of having denounced his friends, he is in effect quoting Camille,
and the words he uses are all the more striking in that the latter wrote
them at the time when he was campaigning in *Le Vieux Cordelier* for
an end to the Terror, or at least for a temporary halt. But it is still
true to say that, unlike many facts which are the subject of interminable
controversies, Robespierre's intervention of 11 Germinal does allow
us to grasp certain of the mechanisms of the workings of the Terror,
which converts the universalist principles of liberty and equality into
principles of death, which forges a collective will out of the diffusion
of fear, and which conceals the position of power behind a façade of
democratic heroism. It is also true to say that its workings reveal
Robespierre to be a virtuoso organizer of terror. In that sense, the
never-ending debate as to his intentions, in which the image of the
apprentice tyrant is contrasted with indications of prudence and
clemency, suddenly appears to be pointless. Even if the indications
are irrefutable, they provide no proof, and do not allow the debate to
be concluded in any definite way. They can be interpreted both as
evidence that he had scruples and as evidence that he was merely
calculating. When, for example, the deposition of the king and the
transfer of executive power to the Legislative Assembly were being

discussed in July 1792, Robespierre told the Jacobins: 'I see in this confusion of powers only the most unbearable despotism. No matter whether the despot has one head or seven hundred heads, despotism is still despotism. I know of nothing more fearful than unlimited power being given to a large assembly which is above the law, even if it is an assembly of sages.' But this declaration tells us nothing about his convictions, or about the manner in which his views have changed. It could quite rightly be pointed out that his adversaries held a majority in the Assembly whose despotism he is denouncing, and that he fears an extension of its powers. I myself take that view. But such comments, whilst they may be convincing, are not decisive, for no single statement can provide certainty, even if it is taken in context. Our best source of information lies in an argument whose workings reveal the position from which Robespierre is speaking, the means he uses to conceal that position, and the art with which he reduces others to silence.

THE TERROR SPEAKS

Why did the revolutionary Terror give rise to such a lengthy historiographical and political debate? There always have been, and there always will be, lofty-minded individuals who have expressed their surprise at the spell it casts, and who have found it *suspect*. After all, the Terror did not last long, no matter what starting point we ascribe to it. If, like Taine, we suggest that its beginnings coincide with the beginnings of the Revolution itself (Taine invokes the opinion of *constituant* Malouet, who claims that it began on 14 July 1789, but Burke's views could also usefully be taken into account), we may as well say that criticizing the Terror means criticizing the Revolution.[2] If, like Mortimer-Ternaux, we see the *journée* of 20 June 1793, when the Legislative Assembly resigned in the face of mass action, as the first episode in the Terror, we may as well admit to dreaming of a policed revolution from which the people and their furies are excluded. And, once again, we attack the Revolution itself, for the work of the Constituant Assembly had been in gestation since before 1789, and it did not take such a great political upheaval to obtain full recognition of equality and civil liberties.[3] If, on the other hand, we reserve the term 'the Terror' for the measures dictated by the Committee of Public Safety, and the term 'excesses' for the policy inaugurated by the Prairal law, make a distinction between the dynamic of the Revolution and what Thiers calls 'the Extreme Terror', and regard the Terror simply as a sign that a repressive machine whose mechanisms were originally designed as a response to necessity had skidded out of control, then we have to admit that a fever which lasted for less than six months and which resulted from a national crisis does not deserve to be discussed at such length. According to such views, the spell exercised by the Terror is suspect in that it is an index of the artificial or even hypocritical *construction* of an object which does not designate anything specific or consistent in the real; it is an index of a desire to claim that the Revolution invented some evil system or that it was carried away by some mysterious passion for murder, and an index of a desire to distract attention from the violence unleashed by the other regimes history has called upon us to witness.

It is in fact true that if we restrict the argument to the number of atrocities and murders committed during the French Revolution, the balance sheet is modest, compared with the cumulative crimes of the despots of the Orient and the tyrants of Greece and Rome, or, to turn to modern Europe, of the Inquisition and the divine-right monarchy. This is still the case even if we are careful not to underestimate the number of victims who fell to the revolutionary Terror: over forty thousand, if we are to believe Georges Lefebvre, who uses, with some corrections, the data collected by an American historian.[4] Whatever the statistical truth may be, no one can claim that the use of terror as a system of government or as a temporary means of enslavement was an invention of the French Revolution; in previous centuries, the same system had been used against groups who were deemed to be heretical, or who simply refused to pay taxes. It might also be added that in 1793 or 1794 we do not find the refined tortures which were so often the pride and joy of the great masters of punishment.

We would, however, attempt in vain to reduce the Revolutionary Terror to the level of historical banality. The primary reason why it poses a particular problem, and why it has exercised – and still does – such fascination over those who have studied the event is that it was combined with a quest for liberty. And there is, I believe, a second and related reason: its actions cannot be dissociated from the workings of speech.

The Revolutionary Terror *speaks*. It implies self-justification, a debate as to its function, its ends and even its limits. It also implies that it can be challenged. It can, that is, be challenged by the men who took part in it.

Listen to Saint-Just; speaking in the name of the Committee of Public Safety, he is addressing the Convention on 'the necessity of imprisoning persons who have been found guilty'. The speech was made on 8 Ventôse Year II (26 February 1794), just over two months before Robespierre made the intervention analysed above. Like Robespierre, the orator takes as his target the *indulgent party*, those who are calling for an investigation into the arrests and for the release of those who have been arrested without proof. Although he never mentions him by name, his main target is in fact Camille Desmoulins. He declares:

> You wanted a Republic. If you want nothing of the means needed
> to constitute it, the people will be buried beneath its rubble;
> what constitutes a republic is the total destruction of everything

opposed to it. We hear complaints about revolutionary measures!
Yet we are moderates compared with all other governments. In
1788, Louis XVI massacred 8,000 people of all ages and both
sexes in the rue Meslay and on the Pont-Neuf. The court repeated
these scenes on the Champ-de-Mars. The court hanged people
in the prisons; the drowned bodies found in the Seine were its
victims. Every year, 15,000 smugglers were hanged, and 3,000
men were broken on the wheel. There were more prisoners in
Paris then than there are today. In times of famine, regiments
marched against the people. Cast your eyes across Europe: there
are more than four million prisoners in Europe; you do not hear
their cries, yet your parricidal moderation allows all the enemies
of your government to triumph. Fools that we are! We take a
metaphysical delight in flaunting our principles; the kings are a
thousand times more cruel than we are, but their crimes do not
prevent them from sleeping.[5]

There is no need to cite more. But we should at least note that in the
same passage Saint-Just evokes the Spanish Inquisition, and that he
twice draws a parallel between the Terror exercised by revolutionaries
and that exercised by oppressors: 'Do you not have the right to treat
the supporters of tyranny in the same way that the supporters of liberty
are treated elsewhere?' He later adds: 'Being jealous of its authority,
the monarchy waded through the blood of thirty generations, and you
hesitate to treat a handful of guilty men harshly.'
    What is particularly striking about these vehement statements
is the link that is established between the requirements of
foundation–destruction, the argument used to justify it, and the idea
of the folly of speech: 'Fools that we are!' In a flash, Saint-Just
perceives the contradiction inherent in revolutionary terror, in the
alliance between terror and liberty. But he is powerless to overcome
it. He can only dream of 'kings whose crimes do not prevent them
from sleeping'. This is in fact an astonishing association, and one which
suggests more than he dares to say or think; it is as though he were
nostalgic for a world in which it was possible to kill without feeling
guilty. And yet his speech displays signs of the very folly he is
denouncing. For no one took more 'metaphysical delight in flaunting
principles' than Saint-Just. No one else forces himself to explain that
'what constitutes a republic is the complete destruction of everything
opposed to it'. No one else feels obliged to justify himself in this
manner: 'Do you not have the right to treat the supporters of tyranny
in the same way that the supporters of liberty are treated elsewhere?'
    We have mentioned the views of those who have doubts about seeing
the Revolutionary Terror as a special case, and who argue that seeing
it in that light is a device to mask the terror exercised by oppressive
regimes. If we accept that argument, the Revolutionary Terror is
merely a counter-terror which is temporary and, ultimately, quite

moderate, and it is a mistake to exhibit it as though it were a historical
monstrosity. But this argument was not born *post festum*; it is part of
the discourse of the Terror. It is impossible to overlook the articulation
between the theory and the practice of terror which appears during
the Revolution; it is the actors and not the historians who discover the
singularity of the Revolutionary Terror.

Saint-Just would like to be able to act in silence; he would like
everything opposed to the Republic to be destroyed in the name of a
certainty that can do without words, but that is not possible. The
Convention has doubts, and is raising questions as to the reasons for
the Terror, and as to its limitations. Saint-Just wants to convince it
that it is acting within its rights, but all rights must be shown to be
well founded. The Terror poses a question because it has to be
founded. Saint-Just does not, we must note, say: 'Do you not have
the right to treat the supporters of tyranny as others acting elsewhere
have the right to treat the supporters of liberty?' He merely says: 'are
treated elsewhere'. Paradoxically, the statement of right is paralleled
by an absence of right. And the paradox reveals that, despite the
apparent symmetry which makes the terror of liberation seem to be a
response to the terror used by tyrants, there is a hiatus between them,
and that Saint-Just is aware of it. The former has no consistency of its
own; it is consubstantial with a system of government; it raises no
questions that have not already been formulated by an analysis of that
system. What is referred to as 'terror' designates, in this case, no more
than the intensification of a mode of repression, a concentration of
the means of coercion, or the exacerbation of an authority in which it
was already potentially present. Indeed, the word 'terror' could without
difficulty be replaced by some other expression such as 'extreme fear',
'widespread fear', or 'the unleashing of arbitary violence', depending
on whether we take into consideration its victims or the actions of the
government. But when the Convention *places Terror on the agenda*
(and it is impossible to imagine a tyrant or his advisers pronouncing
that formula), it creates a new *political space*, and gives substance to
what was no more than an attribute of arbitrary power. When it is
named and, so to speak, exposed to the gaze of all or sanctioned, the
Terror is set free. It is now impossible to assign it a master. The
individual now has no alternative but to serve it, to will it, just as one
wills virtue or wills freedom.

In the speech we are discussing, Saint-Just, who is alarmed to observe
that 'the rise of the revolutionary government which established the
dictatorship of justice' has slowed down, exclaims; 'One might think
that each person was afraid of his own conscience and of the inflexibility
of the laws, and had said to himself: "We are not sufficiently virtuous
to be so terrible".' And shortly afterwards, when he addresses the
Convention again on 23 Ventôse, he asks: 'What do you want, you
who do not want virtue in order to be happy? What do you want, you

who do not want the Terror to be used against the wicked?' He does of course add: 'What do you want, you who are without virtue, you who turn the Terror against liberty?' Nor should we forget his other statement: 'The Terror is a doubled-edged weapon.' Virtue and terror therefore do not have the same status. But the fact that they can be bracketed together suggests that the latter is much more than an instrument. When it becomes an instrument of liberty rather than of tyranny, it does not simply change hands; it does not simply have a good and a bad side to it. When it is revolutionary, it conforms to its essence; in other circumstances, it becomes perverted. When it is revolutionary, it is – to use expressions which are contradictory but which also point to the impossibility of localizing it – both the 'dictatorship of liberty' and the 'sword of the law'. Alternatively, we might say that it is the law in action, the law which makes the sharp distinction between good and evil, between being and nothingness. The terror of the tyrant, in contrast, does not have this great ability to discriminate; the tyrant suppresses that which resists, disturbs or displeases him. Having no knowledge of good and evil, he can have no knowledge of the nature of society; he strikes cruelly, but at random, without even knowing who the enemy is. In that sense, the revolutionary Terror seems to have converted the terror of old into a truth or, more accurately, to have elevated it to the status of truth. It has mastered the principle of eliminating the evil that remained concealed beneath the arbitary rule of the criminal prince. What other meaning can we ascribe to the formula Robespierre uses on more than one occasion: 'the despotism of liberty'? He even uses a similar formula in his final speech of 8 Thermidor when, transposing its terms, he declares himself to be the 'slave of liberty'. The Terror, then, is not a means; it is imprinted upon liberty just as, for Saint-Just, it is imprinted upon virtue.

And yet, once it has been enunciated, the idea outstrips the certainties of the revolutionaries, of the very men who are calling for the nation to be purged, for the guilty, or the suspects, to be hunted down, who approve and even provoke 'the vengeance of the people'. For, once the despotism of liberty is exercised by men against men, the dividing line between crime and virtue, between oppression and liberty, must be visible in the here and now, at the level of the facts. No doubt the Girondins, the Dantonistes and the Enragés did, like the Robespierristes, at some point succumb to a representation of absolute terror as liberty and as virtue, to the representation of an excess which raises man to superhuman status, and to the status of a principle that can generate a social order. But, at some point they also notice that they have lapsed into barbarism, into vulgar despotism, and realize that a void has opened up at their feet. That they should be assailed by doubts when they feel themselves to be threatened is not irrelevant, but it is ultimately of secondary importance. The Girondins, for example, adopt the *loi de police générale* of 10 August, which invites citizens to denounce conspirators and suspects and which gives the municipal authorities power to take prisoners into custody, but, as soon as they have taken that step, they attempt to give legally recognized agents responsibility for administering the Terror, and Brissot condemns 'the *chambres ardentes* which certain men seem to want to borrow from despotism'.[6] At the same time, Danton's friend Thuriot vehemently rejects the link between liberty and crime: 'I love liberty and I love the Revolution, but if it took a crime to secure it, I would rather stab myself.'[7]

The rifts that appeared in the Convention after the September massacres were much more serious. At the time, the massacres did not result in any interventions or protests from the *députés*, or even from the Girondins themselves, but they subsequently gave rise to a bitter debate that lasted for months, and were denounced as murders disguised as measures of public safety. In general, those who shared responsibility for the terrorist laws were trapped in a contradiction. Over a period of only a few days the same Thuriot who, in the autumn of 1793, was calling for the arraignment of the Girondins[8] – in other words for their execution – declared that 'Throughout the Republic, the idea is being put about that it can survive only if all positions are given to the men of blood, to the men who, since the beginning of the Revolution, have distinguished themselves only by their love of carnage to the party of rogues and villains', and stated that 'We must halt this impetuous torrent which is sweeping us towards barbarism; we must halt the triumph of tyranny.'[9] The Convention greeted this appeal with applause, as though Thuriot were voicing its fears. At the time, those who had been denounced as extremists, as *enragés*, were in prison. But, because they themselves had used terror, they could foresee the danger of a return to the barbarism of old. Jacques Roux wrote in his newspaper: 'We cannot make men love and cherish a government if we rule them through terror', and 'It is not by casting men into prison, by overturning everything and setting it ablaze, by staining everything with blood or by turning France into one huge Bastille that our Revolution will conquer the world. To accuse a man of crimes because of the circumstances of his birth is to revive fanaticism; there are more prisoners than there are guilty men.'[10]

It will of course be said that everyone naturally wants to direct the Terror against their adversaries or rivals, and that, in order to understand why the actors changed their views, we must therefore make a detailed reconstruction of the social and ideological conflict. But, whilst such an analysis may be necessary, it may lead us to overlook the doubts which subtend the Terror. These doubts imply questions, and *they make the actors talk*. The image of 'a terrible virtue', of 'the despotism of liberty' casts its spell over everyone, but it also reveals a void in which the markers of social reality and of history are destroyed, in which, in other words, the distinction between revolution and oppression disappears.

No one saw this void more clearly than Camille Desmoulins, and no one did more to try to restore a sense of reality. Witness the campaign he launched in *Le Vieux Cordelier*.[11] 'Do you want to exterminate all your enemies with the guillotine?' he asks in the fourth issue. 'Has there ever been a greater folly than this? Can you put one person to death on the scaffold without making ten enemies among his family and friends? Do you believe that it is the women, the old men, the dodderers, the egotists and the sluggards of the Revolution whom you are imprisoning that are dangerous?' Camille began his previous article by praising democratic virtue, but he did so in very different terms to Saint-Just: 'One difference between the monarchy and the republic ... is that, whilst the people may be mistaken, they do at least love virtue, and believe that they are giving positions to men who merit them, and not to the rogues who are the essence of the monarchy.' He thus refutes in advance the idea that what constitutes the republic is the destruction of everything opposed to it (this is not a reply to Saint-Just; but in his Ventôse report, Saint-Just does attack Camille). If Camille is to be believed, the principle of virtue cannot be embodied in society; it merely gives it form, and the evil therefore cannot be extirpated. Attempts to exterminate the wicked merely create more enemies for the republic. But the greatest folly of all is to try to drive a wedge between the camp of virtue and the camp of crime, as though all cowards and all those who are irresolute or indifferent were to be found in the latter. And it is precisely that folly which inspires Saint-Just to go so far as to denounce the judges for colluding with the guilty, with the men who say, 'We are not virtuous enough to be so terrible'. But the folly is not his alone. The same folly lies at the heart of the *loi des suspects* of 17 September 1793, and the Paris Commune's *comité de surveillance* takes it still further with the directive which defines as suspects 'those who, having done nothing against liberty, have done nothing for liberty either'.[12] The directive predates the Prairal decree by seven months.

How can one distinguish revolutionary power from despotic power when the notion of 'suspect' becomes allied with that of 'guilty', when it takes on a fantastic extension and applies not only to those who are suspected of being implicated in a conspiracy but also to those who may, it is imagined, join it, not only to those whose opinions or intentions seem dangerous but also to those who show no sign of being real or potential enemies? In the third issue of *Le Vieux Cordelier*, Camille Desmoulins does more than formulate this question; he invites his reader to formulate it for himself by describing Tacitus' picture of the perverse reign of the Roman Emperors, and showing how it was based upon the hunt for suspects. He begins cleverly by stating that the picture is designed to make the Republic's adversaries see things in their true proportions. But he in fact paints it in such a way as to confuse revolutionary terror with despotic terror rather than to justify it. When he enumerates the crimes of *lèse-majesté* that were committed under the Roman Empire, he deliberately calls them 'counter-revolutionary crimes', and when he describes one tyrant's victim, he paints him as a new Brutus; he is worrying 'because of his pallor and his Jacobin wig'. He thus blurs the markers of history before finally declaring: 'And let no one tell me that an ill-disposed reader will find in this third issue and in my translations of Tacitus similarities between those deplorable times and the times in which we live. I know that only too well, and it is in order to put an end to such comparisons and to ensure that liberty does not resemble despotism that I have armed myself with my pen.'

The suspect is a product of the delusions of despotism. With the help of numerous quotations from Tacitus, Camille displays his portraits of the suspect: the man who is made conspicuous by his popularity or by his aversion to popularity, by his wealth or his poverty, by his melancholy humour or by his love of pleasure, by the austerity of his morals, by his literary renown, by his military successes. And he punctuates each portrait with the same word: 'suspect'. Robespierre spoke of the despotism of liberty. The author of *Le Vieux Cordelier* brings imaginations that have been inflamed by the idea of sacrificing the individual to the service of the new sovereign back to the realistic discovery that liberty disappears when despotism is resurrected. And in his next article he destroys the illusion that liberty can use the methods of despotism on a provisional basis. He asks if his adversaries think they can refute him or justify themselves 'simply by saying: we know that our present state is not a state of liberty; but, be patient, one day you will be free.' Without mentioning him by name, he uses La Boétie's language to dismiss their arguments: 'They believe that liberty, like a child, must go through a stage of tears and weeping in order to reach maturity. *On the contrary, the nature of liberty is such that we need only desire it in order to enjoy it.*' (emphasis added). In the face of the stupidity of men who say that they are willing to die for the Republic, like the 'Vendéean fanatics .... for the delights of paradise, which they will never enjoy', he argues that liberty is not *an unknown God*: 'We are fighting to defend our gains, and liberty will ensure that those who invoke her name will enjoy them now.'

Yet if these texts are worthy of our attention, it is not simply because they represent the most radical challenge to the Terror, but because they are the work of a major actor in the Revolutionary Terror. It is not enough to recall his role in all the bids for power that punctuated the elimination of the enemies of the people, as that might simply lead us to conclude that he has changed his opinion. The remarkable thing is that he is determined to remain true to his past behaviour. He does of course exploit his reputation for being an inflexible revolutionary who has denounced very plot and even his own friends to further the appeal for clemency he is making to the Committee, it is because he showed enemies no pity that he has the right to speak out against the

Terror. And yet, we can detect something else in this plea. He is torn between the idea that 'it was less dangerous and better to carry the Revolution to extremes than to hold back' (an idea which is, he says, shared by Danton), and the idea that liberty knows no restrictions. He maintains that the statue of liberty must be veiled, but tries to make a distinction between a 'veil of transparent gauze' and 'the shroud beneath which it was impossible to recognize the principles that lay in the coffin'. Even when he displays the most acute awareness of the immoderation of the Terror, he is still trying to find a formula for a gap, for an excess which will not go beyond acceptable limits. This is an astonishing contradiction, for he is familiar with every register of terror. At one point, he evokes the time of Nero and remarks that 'Men were afraid that their very fear would make them guilty'. On another occasion, he recalls one of Robespierre's sayings ('What difference is there between me and Le Pelletier, except death?'), and denounces the rhetoric of the sublime: 'I am not Robespierre; but although it disfigures a man's features, death does not in my view embellish his shade, and it does not heighten the lustre of his patriotism sufficiently to make me believe that I have served the Republic better than Le Pelletier, even though he lies in the Panthéon, and even though I have been expelled from the Club des Cordeliers.'

What can be said and what cannot be said

The Terror speaks: this does not simply mean that it requires more than police directives, that it implies laws which are the products of public debates, or that the actors must discuss, explain and justify it. What can be said in the discourse of the Terror reveals a trace of what cannot be said. The unspeakable usually remains concealed, but it sometimes becomes imminent, and it reveals to us the mouth of the Terror, which both generates and swallows up speech. This may escape us if we look only at the circumstances in which arguments are formulated, if we attempt to find a theory in statements of principle – the foundation of the body politic, the absolute sovereignty of the people, the reign of virtue, of liberty or of equality – or if we see effects – the endless elimination of enemies – as explanations. And yet the obsessive fear of revolutionary silence which accompanies the flowering of eloquence, and which is so obvious in Robespierre and more obvious still in Saint-Just, should alert us to this fact, for it does more than express the dream of a coincidence between feelings and action: it testifies to a vague realization that the causes of speech cannot enter into language.

Robespierre's formula 'the despotism of liberty', which we noted earlier, and his final declaration, 'I am the slave of liberty' imply something that cannot be said. We glossed over these words too quickly when we said that they revealed the depths of the oppression of old and the danger of lapsing back into the darkness of the past. They open up a new abyss for thought: the absolute assertion of liberty merges with its negation; meaning empties into meaninglessness. What can be said in this case is that the establishment of a free regime implies recourse to terrible means, to the methods of despotism, if the roots of despotism are to be extirpated. But Robespierre's words reveal a trace of something that cannot be said; they burn his lips as he speaks; articulation breaks down, and the Terror speaks amidst the ruins of human speech. A moment later, the same speech provides an answer to another of Saint-Just's formulations ('What constitutes the Republic is the total destruction of everything that is opposed to it'): 'The liberty of a people can scarcely be established by the sword alone.' This time, he does not go beyond the limits of what can be said. That the establishment of liberty requires extraordinary violence, and that the principle of the republic and the principle of other regimes are incompatible is certainly debatable; it could be argued that the distinguishing feature of a republic is precisely its ability to accommodate opposition without allowing it to destroy it. That, however, is unimportant, as it can, apparently, be articulated; at most we have to ask what remains unsaid. Even if it were in fact true that the constitution of the Republic requires the destruction of everything that is opposed to it, why remain silent about the problem posed by the gestation of the body politic *in reality*? Why conceal the identity of its founder? What does 'what constitutes' mean when it has to be related to the figure of an actor? And if that actor is the people, or the Convention which represents the people, how can one define or circumscribe *everything* that is opposed to it, how can we relate that to the specific figure of an adversary? Could it be, one begins to wonder, that what has been left unsaid cannot be said? When an attempt is made to conceptualize the foundation of the republic, what can be said sometimes obviously gives way beneath the weight of what cannot be said. Listen, for example, to Billaud-Varenne as he expounds 'the theory of democratic government' to the Convention during a sitting on 1 Floréal year II (20 April 1794) in a report on behalf of the Committee of Public Safety. Not content with criticizing the old monarchy, he demonstrates that it had plunged its roots into the people: 'The habit of wallowing in slavery for centuries, the passions it generates, the prejudices it allows to take root, the vices it propagates and the misery it exacerbates became, in the hands of despotism, so many mechanisms *to make the people crush the people*'[13] (emphasis added). The picture he paints clearly reveals the difficulty inherent in constituting a new body politic. The difficulties are in fact at this point obvious to all from the real society's stubborn resistance to attempts to inculcate new principles. When Billaud-Varenne tries to provide a solution, his words contradict one another as they come under the influence of fantasy:

The French people have set you a task which is as vast as it is difficult to carry out. The establishment of a democracy in a nation that has languished in chains for so long might be compared to the efforts made by nature during the astonishing transition from nothingness to existence, and those efforts were no doubt greater than those involved in the transition from life to annihilation. We must, so to speak, recreate the people we wish to restore to freedom.

His words are an attempt to justify the Terror, but Terror as object of discourse – the extermination of enemies – cannot be divorced from the Terror that is imprinted on speech. Birth and death cannot be represented or conceptualized; and nor can the foundation of the body politic, the establishment of democracy or the annihilation of what once existed; the workings of politics are comparable with the workings of nature. In other words, they are inhuman. That is what Billaud means. But that too can be said, provided that no attempt is made to penetrate the mystery or to draw conclusions. What destroys the consistency of what can be said is, however, the thought of the people entrusting the Convention with the task of their re-creation. This idea is doubly absurd: the people ask their delegation to give birth to them, but the delegation is part of the people. In fact it is triply absurd, for if it is true that *the people crushed itself*, how could they wish to be restored to liberty ... to a liberty they have never known?

We can only grasp the function of what we have termed a fantasy – and we are, I believe, using the word in its true sense, as we are dealing with something which contains contradictory representations and which cannot itself be represented – if we take into consideration all that it allows us to disavow. Billaud-Varenne ignores the freedoms that existed in the past: under the monarchy, servitude must have been total if the Revolution is to usher in a new era, if its foundations are to be absolute, and if the people are to be re-created. And although he speaks of restoring the people to liberty, he refuses to accept that there might be a distinction between liberty and the will of the people, as that would oblige him to examine its will and its possible weaknesses, and to look for guarantees of liberty. Similarly, the very idea that power might be disassociated from the people is dismissed; the Convention derives its ability to re-create the people from the people. And it is because of these disavowals that a policy of terror can be outlined. As the people must be extracted from within the people, the only means to extract them from themselves is to make a distinction between being and nothingness. The term 'means' is, however, ambiguous, and it would be more accurate to say that the gestation of the people implies that those who respond to their call from, so to speak, within must undertake a labour of creation–destruction.

Let us look more closely at what Billaud-Varenne is saying in his

historic speech. Whatever one may think of it, his argument appears
to be logical insofar as he evokes the battle between the revolutionaries
and the enemies of the people, whose sole aim is 'to reduce the people
to servitude through terror and devastation.' Skilfully, but like so many
others before him, the orator points to the terror the enemy wants to
unleash in order to justify a democratic terror. On the one hand, we
have an attempt to destroy the social body; on the other an attempt
to destroy those who would destroy it at birth. 'Only the death of the
conspirators can prevent the premeditated murder of the body politic.
We are killing a murderer so as not to fall victim to his blows. The
Revolution has won a major victory in this battle because it has been
able to strike at the leaders of two equally powerful coalitions' – by
which he means the *Exagérés* and the *Indulgents*, the Hébertistes and
the Dantonistes. But at the very moment when he mentions the
Revolution's latest victory and names its adversaries, he denies that
there is any criterion we can use to measure the progress it has made
in eliminating its adversaries, and gives the enemy a power that can
be neither localized nor defined. 'It is not', he says, 'that malevolence
falls silent when it has less room than ever to manœuvre. It watches
over every political nuance in order to turn it to its advantage, dreams
only of the chaos and disorder which will ensure it victory, and
constantly *spies on both good and bad actions* in order to poison good
and exacerbate evil' (emphasis added). In other words, we must
abandon the idea of being able to identify the conspirators, of being
able to identify the murderer whose death we are demanding. They
are the straw men of an invisible force, of a force which has no
empirical existence: *malevolence*. Malevolence is everywhere or, and
this amounts to the same thing, nowhere. And, whilst it is invisible,
it has eyes and is *constantly spying* on us. This enriches the fantasy
considerably. The murder of the social body is now associated with
the evil powers of eyes which can see through everything. Implicitly,
the gestation of the social body now means the gestation of the eye
of the people, of the eye of innocence which can unmask the evil eye.
I noted earlier that the Revolutionary Terror differs from the terror
exercised by tyrants in that it is assumed to understand the principle
behind the distinction between good and evil, whereas the latter is
delivered over to the arbitrary will of the prince. But we must now
add that the Revolutionary Terror constructs a symmetrical enemy
terror.

The symmetry can be seen most clearly in Saint-Just's speech of
23 Ventôse Year II. Saint-Just denounces all plots and traces them
back to a primary plot that has been fomented abroad by the English
government. Its agents are everywhere, disguised as the exiled victims
of persecution in their own countries (in Paris, its agents are 'Italians,
bankers, Neapolitans and Englishmen'), or as patriots ('Mimicry is the
hallmark of crime'). And what are they doing? 'They spy on everything.'
Having dwelt at length on the art of dissimulation, Saint-Just appeals

to revolutionaries to be vigilant: 'Let us draw aside the veil which conceals their plots; let us spy upon the words, the gestures and the mind of everyone.' The image is important to him. He returns to it; keeping one's eyes open is not enough for, while he is spying, the enemy can make himself invisible, and hides behind seemingly rival factions: 'The aim of this policy is to let them tear themselves apart and to deceive the *vigilant eye* of popular justice' (emphasis added). The task, then, is to penetrate something invisible.

What is the meaning of this appeal? In theory, it means that one power is behind the entire mechanism of conspiracy: perfidious Albion and its execrable genius, Pitt. In fact, something else is at stake: from now on, each person must watch the *other*, as his revolutionary garb may conceal a possible scoundrel. The closer the *other*, the more similar the *other*, the greater the need for suspicion. No obvious sign and no established proof is enough to identify the enemy. He can be recognized only at the moment when he is unmasked, at the moment when someone has the power to unmask him. The power to do so certainly presupposes that the man who has it is not motivated by private interests; when he uses it, he is a vehicle for the suspicions of the people, for the vision of the people. But the fact remains that it is his desire to be suspicious and to see, a desire which others do not have, that gives him the ability to know; it is his ability 'to watch everyone's consistency', to use Saint-Just's striking formula, his ability to find signs of an adverse will in modes of behaviour, gestures and words. In other words, it is only his knowledge of the enemy that designates him a revolutionary, both to himself and to others, but that is something that cannot be said. To put it another way, it is the enemy who gives the revolutionary his identity.

The Terror thus leads to the construction of a social space organized around the twin poles of a desire for good and a desire for evil, but the nature of that space is such that it consists of a network of dual relations. The revolutionary's correct position is established only in relation to the position of the other, and he can keep it only if he does not flinch before the gaze of the other. As we know, the decree of 22 Prarial brings to a paroxysm the image of a struggle to the death. The struggle is assumed to involve all citizens on an individual basis, but at the some time it in practice dissolves the criteria of guilt and the criteria of judgement. A struggle to the death: Article 8 stipulates that 'The penalty for any offence within the cognizance of the revolutionary tribunal is death.' Involving all citizens: Article 9 stipulates that 'Any citizen has the right to seize conspirators and counter-revolutionaries, and to bring them before the magistrates. *The citizen is expected to denounce them as soon as he discovers them*' (emphasis added). Dissolution of the criteria of guilt: the extent of punishable offences is such that no one can be certain to escape revolutionary justice. Article 6, which lists the enemies of the people, mentions 'those who have tried to sow despondency, and even those who have spread false rumours or have tried to lead public opinion astray with counter-revolutionary or insidious writings, *or by any other machinations*' (emphasis added). Dissolution of the criteria of judgement: according to Article 8, material proof is not required; moral proof is sufficient. 'Sentences will be decided by the conscience of the jurors, as guided by their love of the Fatherland; their goal is the triumph of the Republic and the ruin of its enemies.' The preliminary interrogation of prisoners is abolished, as is the role of the defence. We thus have an extraordinary face-to-face encounter, and the revolutionary and the other come into intimate contact with one another. At the same time, we see the quasi-abolition of the time which was previously allowed for suspicion and for the spectacle of punishment. As Couthon, who reported on the bill, put it so brutally, 'The time prescribed for punishing the enemies of the Fatherland must be reduced to the time it takes to recognize them; it is a matter of annihilating them rather than of punishing them.'

With the Prairal decree, the Terror declares that it knows no limits; the very dimension of law disappears. The reference to the reality which is supposed to justify the Terror also tends to vanish. Even at this early stage, the threat posed by foreign armies can no longer be invoked. In the coming months, the country's military position is to become consolidated. But, far from rejoicing at this, Robespierre is worried. In his view, the removal of the external threat merely exacerbates another threat: the threat born of insecurity. To the very end he goes on denouncing the illusion of trusting in the future. On the eve of his fall, he asks in his speech of 8 Thermidor, 'Why do those who once said, "We are walking on volcanoes" now believe they are walking on a bed of roses? Yesterday, they believed in conspiracies; I state that I believe in them at this very moment.'[14] His objective is to maintain the climate of fear: 'They talk to you at length and with academic frivolity of your victories. What have they done to turn our military victories to the advantage of our principles, *to ward off the dangers of victory* or to secure its fruits?' (emphasis added). He goes on: 'Our enemies are withdrawing and leaving us to our internal divisions. Think of the end of the campaign. Fear internal factions; fear the intrigues that exile in a foreign land promotes.' Behind the usual rhetoric, it is possible to perceive this 'truth': the Terror is interminable. It must not end; without it, the Revolution will be nothing. Obviously, that conclusion cannot be formulated. That leaves Robespierre at a loss for words and so, when he emphatically recalls the testament he once read to the Convention, he can only say: 'I bequeath you *the terrible truth and death*' (emphasis added).

Whilst it is true that arrests and executions became more frequent between Prairal and Thermidor, it would be a mistake to imagine that there was a major break in the course of the Terror. Certain historians try to convince us that there was such a break. Thiers, who is one of the first to take this line, tries to identify a period of 'extreme terror' in order to distinguish between that an 'ordinary terror' – in other words functional terror. That is the meaning of his comments on the events of June 1794: 'Now that the danger was over and that the Revolution was victorious, they no longer killed out of indignation, but because they had contracted the fateful habit of killing. The fearful machine which they had been obliged to construct to resist enemies of all kinds was beginning to be unnecessary; but once it had been set in motion, no one could stop it. Any government must have its moment of excess, and no government perishes until it has reached its moment of excess.'[15]

In other words, passion and a sense of necessity combine until the practice of extermination becomes a habit or an automatic reaction. This is a convenient way of clearing up anything that cannot be explained in terms of positive causes. The September massacres were perpetrated nineteen months before the Prairial law; they were not the result of popular indignation, and still less did they correspond to any necessity. Can anyone seriously claim – as did a circular issued by the Commune calling for similar carnage in other communes across France – that the prisoners were preparing to attack the Parisians in the rear at a moment when they were being threatened by the enemy without? We know that the massacres were planned by a small group of men, that the killers were to have been paid – and in some cases were paid – and that there were very few witnesses.[16] From this point onwards, it is ludicrous to rationalize the Terror. The purges in the prisons were, like the great purges Saint-Just was later to call for, motivated by a desire to furnish proof of the reality of the Revolution in the shape of the death of its enemies, to conjure up an actor and to give him a face by exploiting an event which indicated the existence of an *absolute gap*.

There are also broader rationalizations, and it is tempting to succumb to them, even though they conceal rather than reveal the basis of the Terror. One of the most important is the rationalization of *Public Safety*. In August 1792, Danton likens the Revolution to a ship which is in danger of sinking; he calls upon the nation to 'cast out from its bosom anything that might hurt it', just as 'a ship's crew casts into the sea anything that might expose them to death.'[17] The idea that a major amputation will restore the social body to health is a further rationalization. Baudot expresses this best: 'The egotists, the insouciants, the enemies of the city and the enemies of nature herself cannot be numbered among its children. Even if they number a million, would you not sacrifice eight tenths of yourself in order to destroy a gangrene which might infect the rest of your body?'[18] And yet this language, and even the language of Marat, who is regarded as the most resolute of the terrorists – the language of vengeance and punishment, the language of a dictatorship which is ready to sacrifice '26,000 persons' – always falls short of the requirements of the Terror, of what we have termed the *absolute gap*. The reference to the real, which allegedly makes the Terror inevitable – foreign invasion – and the reference to knowledge – of the nature of the social body – are always there to ward off the question which haunts the thought of the Terror: without the operation of the Terror, what would become of the real, of the level at which they see the need for a struggle to the death, and what would become of the knowledge in whose name that struggle takes on its full meaning? It is simply because this question becomes more and more pressing that the Terror intensifies. The image of a society which is at one with itself and which has been delivered from its divisions can only be grasped during the administration of the purge, or, better still, during the work of extermination. Severing virtue from crime, the people from their enemies, is not a means of instituting the Republic; it is a way of making the social visible and conceivable. More accurately, it is the act which generates vision and knowledge. In that sense, the Terror threatened from the outset to be interminable. It is as though the terrorists constantly had to create the ground in which they want the Republic to take root. Their fascination with being is at the same time a fascination with the abyss. This is why they all call down death upon their own heads in an attempt to find a sign of their inscription in the people, in nature and in history.

The end of the interminable

The interminable ordeal of the Terror did in fact come to an end. Is it enough to say that the vague consciousness of the threat it posed to the terrorists themselves became sufficiently acute for their instincts for self-preservation to bring them back to a sense of reality? In general terms, the argument is convincing. The fact is that, although the Dantonistes and especially Camille Desmoulins failed in their attempt to moderate the course of revolutionary politics, they did have a considerable impact, and the Thermidoreans, who were united (despite the factions that existed in their ranks) by a fear of being annihilated one after another, did succeed in changing it. And it is possible that the memory of Danton's execution was still alive. When the Assembly turned against him on 8 Thermidor, Robespierre is said to have murmured in stupefaction: 'Ah, you want to avenge Danton.' The reasons why what had appeared impossible now proved to be possible seem in themselves to be clear. Between Germinal and Thermidor, the Prairal decree had, at least implicitly, given the Committees a new and exorbitant power: the power to arrest members of the Assembly and to bring them before the revolutionary tribunal without its consent. The Assembly did, of course, adopt the decree. But the next day, having been alerted to a threat it had not previously noticed, it again debated the article which worried it. It was only the pressure brought to bear by Robespierre during its next sitting that put an end to this unaccustomed resistance. Although it submitted to terrible measures, the Convention was now on the alert. There is also one other, and more important, factor: as we have noted, the intensification of the Terror after Prairial coincided with the restoration of security throughout the country; the rebellions appeared to have been defeated, and the French armies were victorious on every front. One of the great justifications for the Terror – fictional as it may have been – had now been removed. Other factors support this hypothesis and make it still more pertinent, but they take us on to a different register.

Without going into a detailed account of the events themselves, it must be recalled that, since the end of Germinal, a profound change had taken place in the organization of the government.[19] The Committee of Public Safety was trying to take all power into its own hands. The number of administrative commissions acting under its orders increased. The provisional Executive Council, which had been made up of ministers appointed by the Convention, was abolished; it was replaced by twelve commissions whose agents were appointed by the Committee of Public Safety. Whilst the administrative organs were being purged of elements suspected of having Hébertiste sympathies, an offensive was launched against the popular Sections, and they were finally forced to disband. Representatives like Fouché in Lyons and Tallien in Bordeaux, who had previously distinguished themselves in the service of the Terror but who now seemed to be displaying moderate leanings, were suspended from their missions. Repression became increasingly centralized; most provincial revolutionary tribunals were abolished, and revolutionary justice was concentrated in Paris. All these measures reveal the hand of Robespierre and that of close associates like Saint-Just and Couthon. It was of course the Committee of Public Safety which created the new organ known as the Bureau de police générale at the beginning of Floréal, but it was administered by the triumvirate. That the Prairial decree was drafted by Robespierre and Couthon without the knowledge of the other members of the Committee is an indication of the divisions that were beginning to tear the Committee apart. The activities of the Bureau, which tended to overlap with those of the Comité de sûreté générale, and its attempts to take responsibility for matters that appeared to be in the latter's remit, further reveal the existence of a power struggle which had previously been carefully contained. The most telling signs of the new tension are provided by Robespierre's refusal to appear before the Committee of Public Safety and by the incidents that occurred during the Feast of the Supreme Being, which was organized at his instigation. Having become separated from the head of the procession, he was insulted by certain *représentants* who showed no qualms about describing him as a tyrant.

  These facts shed a new light on the crisis which put an end to the policy of Terror, if not to violent repression which, as we know, began again under the Directory. We must, then, re-examine the way in which the use of Terror was combined with the search for a position of power. It was in order to reveal the link between the two that we began by analysing a speech by Robespierre. We noted his remarkable ability to bend the Assembly to his will – his will to exterminate the Dantonistes – by using devices which allowed him both to appear to be in possession of knowledge, speech and vision, and to conceal the position from within which he was using them. He did not call for a decision, but revealed that there was nothing to decide that had not already been decided by virtue of the logic of principles and by virtue of the essence of the Convention as representation of the people. He did not take part in the debate, but revealed that the debate should never have taken place, and even condemned himself to silence. Whilst his words caused a terrible threat to hang over the Assembly, he offered its members the means to escape it by turning on one another. By transferring suspicion, he effected a transfer of power.

The events we thought we observed taking place within the space of the Convention are a reflection of what had been happening on a larger scale throughout society since August 1792. The Terror gave rise to a multiplicity of positions of power by giving those who had won them an opportunity to conceal from others and, if need by, from themselves the fact that they were exercising their omnipotence. That, however, would have been a banal phenomenon, had it been solely a matter of using principles for purposes of dissimulation. It becomes extraordinary if we note that the dissimulation is a result of the obligation, which is incumbent upon everyone, to leave the place of power apparently empty. Robespierre's ploys are no more psychological than those of the other terrorists, great or small. The Terror is revolutionary in that it forbids anyone to occupy the place of power; and in that sense, it has a democratic character. Only Marat called openly for a dictatorship (and even he thought of it as a temporary measure). The accusation hurled against factions one wishes to destroy and against men one wishes to discredit is always that of wanting to establish a dictatorship – Louvet, Guadet, Barbaroux and even Camille himself use it against Robespierre in the autumn of 1792, and his adversaries will use it again in the spring of 1794. In other words, the Terror implies that the terrorists must recognize one another as individuals who are equal before the law – the law of which the Terror is said to be the sword, but which it embodies in fantasy. These individuals are therefore confronted with a terrible imperative: they are all required to take responsibility for the Terror, but the strength they derive from it always lacks the cement that might have been provided by an institution guaranteed by a definite, reliable and general power. It is, perhaps, Saint-Just himself who best perceives the role played by individuals, even though he expresses it badly, when he imagines the magistrates secretly admitting that *We are not sufficiently virtuous to be so terrible*'. It would be more accurate to imagine them saying 'Fearful as it may be, our power is too hollow to be so terrible', but that would have been inconceivable to him.

The fact is that the organization of the Terror was never such that its agents could free themselves from their own will or imprint themselves in a body whose cohesion was ensured by the existence of its head. In short, they could not act as bureaucrats. This observation means that we cannot be content with the arguments mentioned above. It is not simply an instinct for self-preservation which restores a sense of reality; paradoxically, it is Robespierre's very attempt to consolidate the system of the Terror which makes it unviable. Far from giving the terrorists the security they lack – the real security of a life free from danger and the symbolic security of a mind free from doubts – his attempts to do so in fact result in the destruction of what remains of the unity of terrorism, the unity it had acquired with the collusion of the furies of repression and as a result of the egalitarian fiction.

Robespierre, we must note, is the first to promote that fiction, and he cannot both escape it and attempt to acquire a total mastery of power. Historians have discussed the possibility that he could have mobilized the forces of the streets against his adversaries in Thermidor. It has rightly been noted that the measures he took against the Hébertistes and then against the Paris Sections deprived him of mass support when the time came for the final conflict with the Convention. But it cannot be denied that he did have considerable forces in Paris, and that he did not use them. His objective was to take control of the police and revolutionary justice into his own hands, and to use them to ensure that the convention would agree to his wishes. In other words, Robespierre was constantly obliged to cover up the paths that had brought him to power, but this was not because of some character trait; as we said above, it was because everyone who sought power was under an obligation to disappear as an individual. The means Robespierre used to institutionalize the Terror were – apart from the administrative measures described above – essentially of a symbolic nature; he had to provide a criterion which could finally reveal the doctrinal unity of terrorism. The project never went beyond the outline stage, but there can be no doubt about its meaning. In Robespierre's view, belief in the Supreme Being is, in this final period, the vital and ultimate guarantee of public safety – of, that is, a terrorist dictatorship. It is therefore no accident that the Feast of the Supreme Being, which he organized and which was so staged as to designate him the most important figure in the state, took place on 10 Prairial and almost coincided with the new legislation on the Terror (22 Prairial). His praises of the Supreme Being ring so hollow that historians have been tempted to see the invention of the new cult as no more than a whim or as a sign of a naivety which is in stark contrast with its author's implacable severity, and which might even excuse it. They fail to see the function of Robespierre's invention: to articulate the Terror with an orthodoxy. From the end of Prairial onwards, Robespierre continues to speak of the virtue and happiness of the people, and of the unity of the body politic, but he also constantly denounces atheism, naturalism, materialism and philosophism.

A programme is being outlined for a split between those who know why they are killing and those who do not. Chaumette and the Hébertistes are numbered amongst the former, but so are the Dantonistes who, because they do not know why they kill, have gone over to the party of indulgence, and who are now the most dangerous of all the adversaries plotting against Robespierre. To take an example of his strategy: in his final speech on 8 Thermidor, he exclaims in indignation: 'People of France, do not allow your enemies to degrade your souls and sap your virtues with their doctrine of despair! No, Chaumette, no, death is not an eternal sleep.' Now no one could be unaware of the fact that it was Fouché, the enemy of the moment, who had suggested marking graves with a statue of sleep rather than with a cross. Turning to the real terrorists, he calls upon them to free themselves from their own will (to employ a phrase we have already used) and to rely upon a tribunal that is higher than the tribunals of mere mortals; they must love only the Terror, and can perform their duties in all innocence. Robespierre hides behind the mask of the Supreme Being in order to promote a dictatorship. But the mask betrays the new face of the inquisitor rather than concealing it. Nothing could be more menacing than an orthodoxy which will in future make it possible to introduce divisions into the body of terrorism, which, in order to resolve the unknown elements in the Terror, places it under divine authority and thereby turns revolutionaries into the executive agents of the man or the Bureau who represents it.

When the enemy of the people becomes the enemy of God, everything changes. Robespierre may well go on denouncing the conspiracies that are being hatched in secret, but the whole economy of evil has been overturned. The interminable has come to an end. Revolutionary Terror or modern terror cannot accommodate itself to a theocratic institution (not to mention the fact that the Supreme Being lacks the support of any religion).

As the future will reveal, Robespierre's dream is false. It is in philosophism, naturalism, materialism and in perverted visions of science – a science which succeeds in merging with the representation of a people which wins its identity by ridding its body of enemies – that the Terror will find new formulae for its institution, and that it will anchor the desire for *an absolute gap* and the fantasy of *the interminable* in an organization.

5

Interpreting Revolution within the French Revolution

In the introduciton to his *L'Ancien Régime et la Révolution*, Tocqueville declares: 'The book I am publishing at this time is not a history of the Revolution; its history has been written with such distinction that I would not dream of rewriting it. This is a study of that Revolution.' And he adds in a fragment: 'I am talking about history; I am not recounting it.' François Furet has been able to make these words his own. In his latest work he does not attempt to make a further contribution to our knowledge of the facts, to exhume previously unknown documents, to redistribute the roles of individual and collective actors or to modify their accents, or even (and this is where he differs from Tocqueville) to reassess the balance sheet of the Revolution.[1] None of these projects is, of course, alien to his concerns, as is evident from the book he wrote in collaboration with Denis Richet, where he does touch upon these questions in passing.[2] His purpose here is of a different order: he is 'talking about history' or, to be more accurate, trying to reorient revolutionary historiography by making it meet a demand that is usually neglected; he demands that it must be an interpretation of the French Revolution.

How are we to define this demand? What does interpretation mean in this context? The reader may think that he will find the answer in a passage in which the author complains that the history of the Revolution has been the last to adopt a method that 'history in general' adopted long ago. The latter, we are reminded, 'has ceased to be a body of knowledge where the "facts" are supposed to speak for themselves, once they have been established according to the rules. It must state the problems it seeks to analyse, the data it uses, its working hypotheses and the conclusions at which it arrives.[3] Such formulations are certainly worthy of attention. It is not that they are strikingly original: they are simply a condensed statement of principles which have long been recognized by the best historians, but they also represent a welcome invitation to subject events to the common law of science. He displays here a boldness which is borne out by his entire book.

'Event-bound' history [*histoire événementielle*] cannot, Furet suggests, be deduced from the specificity of its object. Being concerned with reconstructing sequences of events on the basis of accurate observation, it is a naive and dogmatic history, which believes that the meaning is inscribed within the picture, and which conceals the effects of perspective. It is because of these prejudices, and not because it deals with *events*, that a distinction must be made between event-bound history and the history of modes of production, technologies, mentalities and morals, or the history of structures and long time-spans, always assuming that event-bound history does not in its turn fall into the trap of objectivism. The widespread view to the contrary notwithstanding (and, curiously enough, this view is shared by the supporters of different schools), it is not because of the nature of their objects that there is a difference between the two modes of historical knowledge; the difference is one between two ways of conceiving knowledge's relationship with its object. In one case, knowledge knows nothing of its own operations; in the other, it understands how much it owes to its operations, and tests its own resistances. Events do of course appear to resist conceptualization, but that is merely because the historian apprehends them as something which has already been named, which has already been invested with meaning by actors or witnesses. That is because the historian, perhaps more than anyone else, is a prisoner of the illusion that appearance coincides with being, and because, in order to construct his object, he must begin by 'deconstructing' it on the basis of the position he has adopted.

Important as this revalorization of the history of the event may be, it does not allow us to understand fully the injunction to interpret the French Revolution. Indeed, to restrict it to a demand for a new 'conceptual' history would, I believe, perpetuate an ambiguity. Furet's formula is of course designed to win the support of a new school of historians, but it tends to obscure a project which breaks with most contemporary work. Furet is in fact trying to redirect history towards a path from which it has, on the whole, strayed: the path which links it to a reflection on politics.

He himself signals his intentions in his first essay when he concludes a lengthy argument which contains the essentials of his problematic with the words: 'The first task of the historiography of the French Revolution must be to rediscover the analysis of its political dimension (p. 27). It must immediately be pointed out that, when the author refers to 'the analysis of the political dimension', he does not mean the analysis of a category of particular facts, of those facts which are normally described as political or which are assumed to be more pertinent than others, such as the economic and social facts that have long been privileged by historians. On the contrary, he wishes to break with the idea of politics as a regional science. This is now a conventional idea, but it first appeared in the modern era – and indeed it was a late development – as a result of the rise of the social sciences (which went hand in hand with a fracturing of the objects of knowledge): and as a result of the rise of Marxism, which has always primarily been concerned with circumscribing relations of production in order to accord them the status of the real, and with relegating politics to a superstructural level. His statement of intent testifies to a return to the sources of classical political thought: he wishes to uncover a schema or a body of schemata of actions and representations which govern both the shaping [*mise en forme*] and staging [*mise en scène*] of a society, and, at the same time, its dynamic. And, if power seems to him to be the central object of any reflection on politics, it is not because he regards as decisive the relations established between actors whose aim it is to win or keep power, to appropriate or modify its exercise, or because he regards property relations and class relations as being less important. It is because the position and representation of power, and the figuration of its locus are, in his view, constitutive of the social space, of its form and of its stage. In other words, he recognizes that, quite apart from its real functions and the effective modalities of its exercise, power has a symbolic status, and claims that the Revolution becomes intelligible only if we examine the way that status changes or, as he puts it, how 'the site of power is displaced'. If we fail to grasp his intentions, we will fail to recognize the meaning of his interpretation of the Revolution, raise irrelevant objections, or fail to answer the questions it raises. One would, for instance, reproach him in vain for underestimating the conflicts which, on the eve of the Revolution, resulted from a mode of exploitation and class domination, from the expansion of the bourgeoisie and from the obstacles it encountered, from the increasing burden of taxation imposed upon the peasantry, from the redistribution of property and from economic crises; or for ignoring conflicts of interest during the revolutionary period. Our historian certainly does not neglect the analysis of social divisions; he merely challenges the view that they in themselves can explain the outbreak of the Revolution or the specific course it took.

Although they are not always explicit, the principles behind his reasoning can easily be reconstructed. Firstly, he believes that class oppositions or, more broadly, socio-economic oppositions, are not fully significant at their own level. Social actors do not see their behaviour as being strictly determined either by their material condition or by the mutual relationships which define them in relation to one another. They decipher their condition and relationships in the context of the common situation imposed upon them by the fact of belonging to the same society, and that situation itself cannot be disassociated from a general system of representation. In other words classes do not represent small societies within a *wider* society – what could be the meaning of such a global term? – and they are not bound up with one another simply because they are inserted into a network of economic operations. They are, by their very division, constitutive of a single social space, and are generated within that space. The relationships they establish with one another are caught up in a more general relationship – society's relationship with itself – and it is that which decides their nature. This in itself implies that the outbreak of a revolution cannot be deduced from a degree of class domination or exploitation, or from a degree of conflict between interests. If a revolution is to occur, either there has been a shift in the markers of the common situation, which once allowed it to be represented and apprehended as natural (painful and conflictual as it may well have been), or new markers have become at least partially visible.

Secondly, this general relationship implies a division between power and society as a whole. Paradoxically, power is established and represented as being distanced from every part of the social whole, as though it existed outside society; and yet it is consubstantial with it, and therefore assumes the function of guaranteeing its integrity, no matter who is invested with it or who exercises it. It provides society with a reference point which allows it to become potentially visible to itself, which allows social articulations within a common space to be deciphered, and which allows actual conditions to appear within the register of the real and the legitimate. When, therefore, it becomes generalized, opposition to power is not directed solely against those who control the decision-making and coercive apparatus, who are an obstacle to the destruction of certain hierarchies and who defend the interests of dominant groups. It is directed against the reality principle and the legitimacy principle which support the established order. It is not only political authority which is shaken; it is the validity of conditions of existence, and the modes of behaviour, beliefs and norms which affect every detail of social life. It follows that revolutions are not born of an internal conflict between the oppressed and their oppressors; they occur at the moment when the transcendance of power vanishes, and when its symbolic efficacy is destroyed.

Thirdly, it therefore proves impossible to establish a boundary between that which pertains to the realm of action and that which pertains to the realm of representation. At a certain level, such a distinction is of course well founded, but no political analysis worthy of the name can be restricted to the manifest, specific aspects of actions and representations. It cannot be confused with an analysis of what are commonly termed political facts, and must be combined with the study of behaviour and institutions; with the study of the discourses and ideas they vehicle; and with a search for the system within which they are ordered, for the logic which animates them. And that logic cannot be said to be either a logic of action or a logic of representation, as it operates on both registers.

Furet does, it is true, speak of the system of action and the system of representation which appear with the Revolution, but he does not disassociate the two. And when he describes the dynamic of the

Revolution as being at once 'political, ideological or cultural' (p. 27), he is attempting to use the latter terms to reinforce the meaning of the former, and not to disassociate them. The political character of the Revolution becomes perceptible only if we grasp, on the one hand, the signs of the *imaginary* elaboration by virtue of which social relations are assumed to be organized, to escape indeterminacy, and to be subject to the will and understanding of human beings, and, on the other hand, the signs of a new intellectual, moral, religious or metaphysical experience of the world.

The revolutionary phenomenon is in fact the most convincing proof that an analysis of the political implies not only an analysis of ideology, but also an analysis of the experience of the world, and of modes of thought and belief which are conventionally assigned to the realm of culture. Until such time as a fracture appears in society, it is tempting to study the structure of power, class structure, the workings of institutions, and social actors' modes of behaviour as though they were meaningful in themselves, and to overlook the imaginary and symbolic foundations of their 'reality'. It is because representations are, so to speak, so enkysted in social practice that they are so easily overlooked; that we identify them only when they appear at a certain remove from that practice in discourses which are explicitly religious, philosophical, literary or aesthetic and that we fail to grasp their political significance. The French Revolution is, however, the moment when all discourse acquires an import within the generality of the social, when its political dimension becomes explicit, and it therefore enables the historian to recognize the political dimension in areas where it was invisible under the Ancien Regime. This does not, of course, mean that representations, as defined by their manifest content, now render reality transparent. Furet even claims that their opacity is at its height in revolutionary ideology. But this opacity is, he should point out, an effect of the dissimulation of something that has entered the register of the thinkable for the first time. Misrecognition and recognition go hand in hand, as do the occultation of practice and an opening on to the question of the real. We therefore cannot decipher ideology unless we simultaneously relate to the new requirements of thought the new representations of history and society, of the power of the people, of its enemies' plots, of citizens and suspects, and of equality and privilege. And nor can we detect mutations in knowledge or the requirement to redefine the condition of everything that affects the establishment of the social unless we examine the advent of a new idea of time, of the division between past and present, true and false, visible and invisible, real and imaginary, just and unjust, between that which conforms to nature and that which goes against nature, between possible and impossible. This is precisely why our author says that the historian must rediscover the analysis of the political dimension. By this, he means an analysis which does not circumscribe the political within the boundaries of power relations, or within the boundaries of the social;

he means, that is, a metasociological analysis. But he might add that the Revolution is the very phenomenon which promotes such an analysis, that it forces us to interpret the political.

No doubt such a history could be described as 'conceptual' insofar as it is inscribed under the sign of the political. But, as we have already said, the term is still ambiguous; its extension is so wide that it cannot be distinguished from other modes of historical knowledge. This history implies a reflection upon society and culture; it is a philosophical history or (to use a term which certain of our contemporaries may find less disturbing), an interpretative history, in the sense that it cannot claim simply to be inspired by the ideal of objectivity; in that it cannot be verified by quantitative means; and in that it asks the reader to mobilize his or her experience of social life in order to shrug off the weight of his or her opinions, and to combine knowledge of the past with knowledge of the present.

Let us look at how Furet proceeds with his analysis. He begins by demonstrating how the history of the Revolution was pressed into the service of the national ideology, whose features were established during the nineteenth century and, more specifically, during the formation of the Third Republic. Not content with showing that most historians identified with the actors of the Revolution and appropriated their discourses instead of investigating them, he reveals the mechanisms behind that identification: their desire to have roots in the nation and to have links with a real point of origin reproduces the revolutionaries' desire to found the nation, to situate themselves at a point of origin, and to wipe out every trace of an earlier usurping people which perpetuated its domination by disguising itself as a nobility. The denunciation of the illusions of legacy and foundation is inseparable from this initial argument, and the reader cannot subscribe to it unless he or she can escape myths of identity and origins. Furet then looks at the displacement the history of the Revolution underwent when it was pressed into the service of socialist ideology. Once again, posterity's illusions are shown to be bound up with an image promoted by the revolutionaries themselves. 'The French Revolution,' he notes 'is not only the Republic. It is also an unlimited promise of equality, and a special form of change. One only has to see in it not a national institution, but a matrix of universal history, in order to recapture its dynamic force and its fascinating appeal. The nineteenth century believed in the Republic. The twentieth century believes in *the* Revolution. The same founding event is present in both images' (p. 5). Personally, I am particularly impressed by the wisdom of an interpretation which, having described the effects of the Russian Revolution on the history of the French Revolution, notes in passing that: 'The idea of a new beginning and of a nation in the vanguard of history' was grafted on to the Soviet phenomenon (pp. 11–12). This remark both illuminates the hidden connection between national ideology and socialist ideology, and shows how the efficacy of a logic of representation can outlive the displacement of its contents. But it is still true to say that this type of analysis is not and cannot be supported by the mechanisms of proof; it implies that the reader enjoys the freedom to reject both the image of the Revolution as the absolute beginning of history and the image of the USSR as a model for the good society.

The principles behind Furet's approach become fully apparent when he describes the conditions which now make it possible to view the French Revolution from a critical distance. The new factor is, he observes, that the hopes that were once invested in the regime which emerged from the Revolution have faded. So long as the right has a monopoly on the indictment of the regime, there can be no new reflection of politics, for in order to indict it, the right 'has no need to adjust any part of its heritage and can simply stay within the bounds of counter-revolutionary thought' (p. 11). On the other hand, 'What does matter is that a left-wing culture, once it has made up its mind to think about the facts – namely, the disastrous experience of twentieth-century communism – in terms of its own values, has come to take a critical view of its own ideology, interpretations, hopes and rationalisations' (p. 11). One could not hope for a more eloquent description of how the relationships we establish with the past are implicated in those we establish with the present, of how our knowledge of history is governed by the experience of history. This certainly does not mean that we have to invert our identifications, rediscover totalitarianism in the ideal of Jacobinism or confuse the system of the Terror with that of the Gulag, and I do not think that this is what Furet is saying. But, and this is a considerable step in the right direction, he does encourage us to question revolutionary discourse rather than taking it literally, to detect the contradiction that arose between ideology and practice, and, finally, to look for a meaning in the historical process which led to the emergence of a regime of oppression rather than simply explaining the corruption of the principles of the Revolution in terms of 'circumstances'. The author does of course also point out that the 'disinvestment' of the French Revolution or, to use Lévi-Strauss's terminology, 'the "cooling off" of the object "French Revolution"' (p. 10) is implicit in the mutations in historical knowledge' (p. 11). He believes that the time has come to make due allowance for 'another *primum movens* of the historian, namely intellectual curiosity and the free search for knowledge about the past' (p. 10). He is, then, rightly concerned not to fall into the trap of relativism, and wishes to avoid dissolving the thought of history into the history of thought – which would simply conceal its presuppositions still further. He also wishes to avoid divorcing the critique of the illusions that accompany our political convictions from the quest for truth which is an intrinsic part of scientific endeavour. It would, however, be a mistake to believe, as certain of Furet's formulations suggest, that historical science will sooner or later lead to an 'interpretation' of the French Revolution as a result of some internal necessity, for, if we are to interpret it, we must do more than divorce it from its heritage. One might even venture so far as to say that developments in historical science have led to a 'cooling off' of both the subject and the object, that it is becoming increasingly reluctant to reflect upon politics, and that it is attempting to adopt a position which spares it the experience of the mutual imbrication of subject and object. Indeed, the very fact that Furet calls for a rediscovery of the political dimension indicates that he is aware that, despite the progress knowledge has made, something has been lost or forgotten, and that this has nothing to do with the immaturity of the science. But he is, perhaps, reluctant to make a more radical critique of the idea of progress.

We see an indication of this reluctance in what appears at times to be a simplification of revolutionary historiography. Furet's failure to examine more closely the break in the conception of history that occurred in the latter part of the nineteenth century is all the more regrettable in that his critique of the myths of identity and origins does seem convincing. It is not only Tocqueville who perceives a discrepancy between the actors' discourse and their actions; Benjamin Constant had already arrived at that perception, as had Chateaubriand and as did, from very different perspectives, Thierry and Guizot, Michelet and Quinet, and Leroux and Proudhon. They all pursue their investigations beyond the manifest evidence of an upheaval in society and culture, and regard its meaning as being at once political, philosophical and religious. To restrict the discussion to Michelet, Furet contrasts him with Tocqueville in rather dubious terms which, moreover, have little to do with his inspiration. 'Michelet', he tells us, 'communes and commemorates, while Tocqueville constantly examines the discrepancy he discerns between the intentions of the actors and the historical role they played. Michelet installed himself in the visible or transparent Revolution: he celebrated the memorable coincidence between values, the people and men's actions' (p. 16). If we wish to do Michelet justice, we should, rather, be looking at the conflicting views expressed in his work. It is quite true that he does commune, but it is also true to say that he identifies with something invisible. It is true that he does take a global view of the Revolution; but it is also true to say that he breaks down the received image of the sequence of events, of its unity and of its positivity. It is true that he does commemorate, but it is also true to say that he believes that the Revolution cannot be commemorated, that its monument should be a void, as he puts it in the 1847 Preface (its symbol is the Champ-de-Mars; with 'its sand, as white as Arabia'). It is also true that he claims to be able to put himself in the actors' shoes, but it is not true that he appropriates their discourse; he wants to reconstruct the work of time, which fragments their actions and beliefs, which gradually takes them apart as though they were puppets. The idea that he celebrates a coincidence between values, the people and men's actions seems to me to be equally groundless. He sees the people as an omnipresent but latent force, whose name is taken in vain, and who are elevated to the status of a subject and a judge. Again and again, he observes that the people are absent from the theatre of events; one thinks, for example, of his comments on the people's absence from Paris from the end of 1792 onwards.[4] His critique of the distance separating the people from the men who speak in their name and who make them speak, of the 'heroes of conventional history', as he calls them, is so acute that it is astonishing that Furet does not use it to cut the ground from under the feet of his detractors, who accuse him of using 'right-wing' sources. For it is not Tocqueville, but Michelet who says of the Girondins and the Montagnards that 'These doctors, just like those of the Middle Ages, believed that they alone possessed the gift of reason, that it was their patrimony; they also believed that reason had to come from on high, in other words from them. . . . Both parties . . . took their inspiration from men of letters, from an intellectual aristocracy.'

He also uses an even more striking formula: 'There is a terrible aristocracy among these democrats.'[5] And it is not Cochin but Michelet who writes: 'The Jacobins frequently appealed to the violence of the people and to their physical strength; they bribed the people, and urged them on, but they did not consult the people . . . All the measures that were voted by the clubs of 93 and by all the *départements* were voted on orders from the holy of holies in the rue Saint-Honoré. They boldly pronounced on national issues with only an imperceptible minority, displayed such horrifying scorn for the majority, and believed with such unshakeable faith in their own infallibility that they sacrificed a world of living men to it without any remorse' (pp. 300–1). Finally, it was Michelet who, long before Furet, said of the Terror: 'It had to overcome incredible obstacles, but the most terrible of those obstacles were of its own making' (p. 297). But it is, perhaps, more important to recall that the basis of his interpretation is as political as that of Tocqueville's, even though they are very different. He wanted to bring out the one thing that escaped the latter's notice, namely the monarchical principle of the Ancien Regime, the principle of a general constitution of society, which cannot be adequately defined in terms of social and economic relations. It is the principle of an architecture which imbricates the representation of the king in that of the nobility, the orders, and the corporate bodies and ranks; the principle of an architecture whose scaffolding was, despite the changes that had occurred, still theologico-political. It is to Michelet that we we the idea that royal authority was transferred to the revolutionary government. When one looks at the work of Michelet and that of certain of his contemporaries, one begins to wonder whether, paradoxically, it may not have been the rise of a positivist-inspired history (and I include Marxist works in this category, as they represent a major variant on the same theme) which set the seal on the myth of origins and of national or revolutionary identity by partially masking it. If that is indeed the case, it is tempting to see Furet's project both as a critique of a certain historiographical tradition and as a sign of a return to the source of the modern idea of history.

Let us try to reconstruct the principal articulations of Furet's argument, for they are not all obvious, in order to arrive at a better appreciation of the subtlety of his interpretation and to raise certain questions in passing.

His starting point is, as has already been noted, a critique of the historiography which became dominant by the end of the nineteenth century and which finds its rationalization and its canonization in Marxist writing. This historiography is, he demonstrates, a combination of explanation and narrative. The former is based upon an analysis of the Revolution and of its balance sheet. The latter deals with the events that took place between 1789 or 1787 and Thermidor or 18 Brumaire. The explanation is determined by the narrative in the sense that the historian adopts the actors' image of an absolute break between past and future, between the Ancien Regime – defined in terms of the rule of absolutism and the nobility – and the new France – defined in terms of the rule of liberty and the people (or of the bourgeoisie, with popular support). At the same time, the narrative is determined by the explanation, for it is organized 'as if, once the causes are set out, the play went on by itself, propelled by the initial upheaval'. This 'mingling of genres' stems from the confusion of two irreducible objects: 'It fails to distinguish between the Revolution as a historical process, a set of causes and effects, and the Revolution as a mode of change, a specific dynamic of collective action' (p. 18). The confusion arises as a result of the adoption of a postulate whose validity is never questioned: the postulate of a historical necessity which dissolves the singularity of the events:

> If it were true that objective reasons necessarily – and even inevitably – compelled men to take action to shatter the "Ancien" Regime and to install a new one, then there would be no need to distinguish between the problem of the origins of the Revolution and the nature of the event itself. For not only would historical necessity coincide with revolutionary action, but there would also be a perfect "fit" [*transparence*] between that action and the general meaning attributed to it by the protagonists, who felt that they were breaking with the past and founding a new history (p. 19)

I accept Furet's comments, and would merely add, for my part, that anything that seems to depart from what is assumed to be the predictable or, so to speak, natural course of the Revolution is explained in terms of circumstances and that it can never alter its meaning: the excesses of the Terror are explained in terms of the war, and the war is explained in terms of the plots of the enemies of the people, and so on. This postulate, notes Furet, 'is a classic retrospective illusion of historical consciousness' (p. 19). What happens seems, after the event, to have been the only possible future for the past. But, in the case of the French Revolution, this assumption overlaps with a second postulate, namely the postulate that the Revolution marks an absolute break in the history of France. As a result, the new is not simply seen as arising out of the old; it contains within it the seeds of the future. Because it is linked with the postulate of the Revolution as destruction-advent, the postulate of necessity has, in other words, the power to unify the historical and social process. Marxism simply takes over this schema when it introduces the concept of a *bourgeois revolution* which 'reconciles all levels of historical reality and every aspect of the French Revolution' (p. 19). The Revolution is assumed to have been the midwife of capitalism, which was still embryonic in the eighteenth century, of the bourgeoisie, whose ambitions had been thwarted by the nobility, and of a set of values which are believed to be consubstantial with the bourgeoisie. It is assumed to have unveiled the nature of the Ancien Regime as a whole by 'defining it *a contrario* by the new' (p. 20). Finally, it is assumed to have established premises from which the future will draw the necessary conclusions. From this point of view, the dynamic of the Revolution becomes transparent; it accomplishes the destruction of the feudal mode of production; it has an agent which is perfectly suited to its task; and it speaks the language required of it by the tasks of the day. It is by denouncing the artifices of this construct that Furet advances towards his goal. There is little point in dwelling on the details of his critique, which he formulates most clearly in an essay entitled 'The Revolutionary Catechism' (pp. 81–131), but we can at least bring out the essential points by summarizing the argument. The analysis of history in terms of modes of production is, he implies, pertinent only if it takes the long-term view. If it is applied in the short term, it is incapable of proving that any structural changes occurred in France between the time of Louis XVI and that of Napoleon. If we cling to this view and insist upon seeing the Revolution as a mutation in the economy which coincides with the bourgeoisie's victory over the nobility, we inevitably have to overlook the economic expansion which characterizes the eighteenth century, the establishment of capitalism within the pores of seigneurial society, and the role played by a fraction of the nobility in the expansion of the economy, and especially in the expansion of industry. If we remain trapped by the image of feudalism, we confuse the features of a feudal regime with those of a seigneurial regime, and take no notice of how much the exploitation of the peasantry owes to a new form of economy. We take it for granted, without proving the point, that the existence of a nobility was in itself incompatible with the development of trade and with a profit economy; so long as we remain blind to signs of continuity between the pre- and post-revolutionary periods, we fail to ask how the break-up of property, which was accelerated by the Revolution, encouraged the development of capitalism in France, or whether it might not have hindered it. Secondly, an analysis conducted in terms of class struggle not only fails to recognize the vitality of one section of the nobility, both in economic life and in terms of participation in the rise of a new culture centred upon the Enlightenment; it also obscures the multiple oppositions which divided the nobility, which testify to its increasing heterogeneity and which, insofar as they relate to the conflict between the new nobility and the old, reveal a division which, although it takes different forms, is no less significant than a class division. In more general terms, such an analysis prevents us from seeing the increasingly complex interplay between two systems of social classification and identification, between a long-standing system based upon distinctions between ranks, orders, ancestry, and *corps*, and a system resulting from the fusion within the elite of strata sharing the values of wealth, knowledge and power.

In order to perceive the ambiguity of the Ancien Regime, we have to take into account the role the absolute monarchy played in transforming society through the practice of selling offices and through ennoblement, and through the modernization of the administration and the encouragement of trade. As Furet notes:

> The monarchy gradually undermined, chipped away at and destroyed the vertical solidarity of the various orders, especially the nobility, both socially and culturally. Socially, it created, notably through its offices, another nobility, which was different from that of the feudal period and by the eighteenth century constituted the majority of the nobility as a whole. Culturally, it attempted to imbue the kingdom's ruling classes, henceforth united under its aegis, with a new system of values, no longer based on personal honour but on the fatherland and on the State. In short, as the purveyor of the means for social advancement, the monarchical State became a magnet attracting money. As it did so, and even while retaining the legacy of the society of orders, it created a new social structure that paralleled and contradicted the traditional one. It created a new elite or ruling class. (p. 103)

Finally, the third element in Furet's critique concerns the analysis of the revolutionary dynamic. Marxism regards the bourgeoisie as a historical subject without troubling to define the mode of participation of different groups in the Revolution, and without asking why those who led it were not the groups most closely involved in the development of capitalism. It comes up against the fact that there were several revolutions within the Revolution, notably a peasant revolution and a revolution led by the 'little people' of the towns, but, rather than stressing the multiplicity of interests, the contradictions between them, or Jacobinism's function as an ideology of integration and compensation, it preserves its schema by imagining a bourgeoisie which was forced by events and by the need to satisfy its allies to radicalize its methods and objectives in order to defend *its* revolution. The war is therefore seen as an index of economic conflict between the French bourgeoisie and its English rival, and the Terror is seen as a product of the war, as a 'Plebeian way' of carrying through the bourgeois revolution and of eliminating the enemies of the bourgeoisie (p. 127), despite the fact that it was the king and the dispossessed nobility who wanted war, despite the fact that it was only later that the Girondins called for war, and despite the fact that war provided the revolutionary leaders with an opportunity to represent the idea of the nation, to link the unity of the people with the fight against its enemies, and to unite the masses around the new state by mobilizing old military passions in the name of a mission of universal emancipation, despite the fact that, even though the first two episodes of the Terror were indeed associated with a conjuncture of a threat to the nation, it reached its height in the spring of 1794, when the military situation had greatly improved.

That Furet's criticisms do not remove the need for a study of the genesis of the modern bourgeoisie is not in dispute. Nor is the fact that, like all historians, he sees the Revolution as having laid the foundations of bourgeois society. What he does challenge is the view that we can start out with the idea that the bourgeoisie is a class defined by the position it occupies in a system of production; that it is opposed to the nobility simply because of the interests which give it that position; that it forms a totality whose external differences can be explained purely in terms of the diversity of the functions – some practical and others ideological – performed by its members. He further challenges the notion that we can construct a historic individual endowed with needs, modes of knowledge, a will and passions, our only proviso being that its behaviour is determined by its relations with other classes and by the influence of events. No such individual can be identified, either under the Ancien Regime or during the Revolution. Under the Ancien Regime, social division cannot be described solely in terms of class divisions. As we have pointed out, a section of the nobility merges with a section of the common people, both in terms of interests and conditions of existence, and in terms of ways of feeling and thinking; a model of sociability which no longer had anything to do with the norms of the old aristocratic society had imposed itself. This model could indeed be said to contain within it the premisses of a revolution in that it is incompatible with the surviving system of orders, but we would attempt in vain to impute its emergence to the initiative of an actor. As for the Revolution itself, it may well result from a split between the third estate and the nobility, but we cannot conclude that it results from a historical project drawn up by the bourgeoisie, or that it pursues the implications of any such project, as the bourgeois groups which come to the fore are acting within a situation they do not dominate. The power vacuum created by the collapse of the monarchy and the mobilization of the popular masses prevents them from arriving at a formula for a new form of power that is distinct from the people, and removes the markers which allowed them to distinguish between legitimate and illegitimate, real and imaginary, possible and desirable. How, indeed, can we conclude that the Revolution was the work of the bourgeoisie: the principles which the bourgeoisie will later claim as its own were established as early as 1790, when the Revolution was only in its first stages. In any case, the task of understanding the genesis of the bourgeoisie must be subordinate to that of understanding the political form which determined its genesis.

Marxist historiography appears, as we have noted, to be governed by a representation of a break in history and of a split in society; that representation was originally elaborated by the revolutionary actors, and it was first outlined in Sieyè's pamphlet. The criticisms it has inspired therefore require us to remove this first obstacle to interpretation. Furet is convinced of the need to do so, and he urges us to reread Tocqueville because he credits him with having been the first to undertake the task. This, then, is the second articulation of his argument: to demonstrate how Tocqueville divorced the idea of the Revolution from belief in the Revolution (a belief which can, it should be noted, be a source of loathing as well as admiration). But, if we are not to misjudge the line taken by our historian, we must first note that he does not espouse all Tocqueville's theses, and that he uses his work in two ways. He learns both from what it says and from what it does not say, and he can therefore point to its shortcomings. The criticisms addressed to the author of *L'Ancien Régime et la Révolution* are therefore of a different order to those levelled against Marxist historiography. They are not, so to speak, external, but internal. They take shape within the framework of his problematic and are designed to overcome its limitations.

Furet begins by stressing Tocqueville's originality and boldness. Tocqueville casts doubts upon the extent of the innovations of the Revolution; he does not simply register signs of an obvious break, but attempts to detect traces of the continuous process whereby the state was strengthened by administrative centralization, by the democratization of society, and by equality of condition. It would be a mistake to believe that he merely provides a new long-term interpretation. He makes a distinction between revolution as mode of historic action and what our historian describes as revolution-as-process. Nor does he simply substitute previously unnoticed causes for the causes that are normally evoked to explain the revolutionary event; his achievement consists in revealing a dimension of history which was not simply overlooked but actually concealed by the actions and representations of the men who

thought they were making a revolution. We must of course examine
and rectify the direction taken by his analysis. Furet points out the
lacunae in his historical data, and rightly denounces his idealization of
the traditional nobility, his failure to recognize the role played by the
monarchical state in the redistribution of wealth and in the constitution
of a new ruling elite. We do not need to go into his criticisms in detail,
and will simply note in passing that, whilst they are fully justified and
whilst the conclusions he draws as to the nature of the Ancien Régime
are fully convincing, they do not do full justice to Tocqueville's subtlety.
Unlike so many other authors, Tocqueville constantly revises his earlier
statements, and combines the idea of *de facto* changes in administrative
power with the idea of a symbolic change in the status of the state,
the idea of equality and of the increasing similarity of individuals with
the idea of an ever more pronounced inequality and dissimilarity. He
links the idea of the standardization of the social field with the idea
of the heterogeneity of modes of behaviour and beliefs. Finally – and
this ambiguity is decisive because of the way it influences his evaluation
of the Revolution – he combines the idea that the Ancien Regime was
an immense historic transition or a process which broke down
aristocratic society with the idea that the Ancien Regime was a system
which, despite its contradictions, held together and displayed an almost
organic internal unity.

The manner in which Furet exploits Tocqueville's approach is
particularly noteworthy. Being convinced that it is a legitimate
approach, he demands that it must be pursued, and that the fact of
the Revolution itself, the sequence of events that were experienced as
the French Revolution must be constituted as a distinct object of
analysis. In Furet's view there is a 'blank page' that Tocqueville never
filled even though it was essential for him to do so (p. 23). He avoids
the very question his own analysis raises: why did the process of
continuity between the old regime and the new involve a revolution?
And what, in those circumstances, is the significance of the revolutionaries' political commitment?

We see here the third articulation of the argument. The discovery
of a revolution which began before the Revolution and which continued
after the Revolution had ended (the revolution which Tocqueville
initially calls the 'democratic revolution' and which he later associates
with the rise of state power) simply makes the French Revolution still
stranger, and the need to interpret it in all its strangeness is therefore
all the more urgent. In other words, the motor of knowledge is surprise,
if I can put it that way. It is because Tocqueville rejects the Revolution's
appearance of being a process of destruction-advent that he enables
us to explain its appearance. The two ideas have to be taken together:
the Revolution does not coincide with its self-representation, but there
is in its concept something 'that corresponds to its "experienced"
historical reality', something that we cannot dissolve into the Revolution-
as-process, something which does not obey the sequence of cause and

effect; and Furet tells us that it is 'the appearance on the stage of history of a practical and ideological mode of social action totally unrelated to anything that came before' (p. 23).

Two difficulties arise at this point. The author sets himself the task of interpreting the exorbitance of the Revolution but, if he is not to renounce the ideal of historical intelligibility, he must also bear in mind a second task: that of interpreting the relationship (and it is not one of causality) between the old and the new, which is in excess of the old. Thus, the question, 'And what ... is the significance of the revolutionaries' political commitment' must not make us forget the earlier, 'Why did the process of continuity ... involve a revolution?' On the other hand, interpreting the Revolution as such now proves to mean interpreting it both in its practical modality and in its ideological modality; it means interpreting the new both under the sign of socio-historical invention, and under the sign of the birth of a new imaginary representation of history and society.

We will begin by examining the second difficulty because, although they are related, it is only with the next stage in the argument that the first difficulty will become fully apparent. In the passage we are discussing, Furet formulates the need to appreciate the dynamic of the Revolution. He again rejects the explanatory schema which makes the Revolution 'a natural occurrence in the history of the oppressed' and which overlooks the fact that, in most European countries, neither the bourgeoisie nor capitalism required a revolution to assert their presence. He then makes an unequivocal statement: 'But France was the country that, through the Revolution, invented democratic culture, and revealed to the world one of the basic forms of historical consciousness of action' (p. 24). A few lines later, he clarifies this statement by examining the circumstances which led to the outbreak of the Revolution: 'The Revolution tipped the scales against the State and in favour of society. For the Revolution mobilized society and disarmed the State; it was an exceptional situation which provided society with a space for development to which it does not normally have access' (p. 24). He then adds the following comment: 'The Revolution was the historical space that separated two powers, the embodiment of the idea that history is shaped by human action rather than by the combination of existing institutions and forces' (p. 25). Finally, he stresses the universal impact of the French Revolution. Whereas the English Revolution was 'too preoccupied with religious concerns and too intent upon its return to origins', the French Revolution develops 'the one notion that made Robespierre's language the prophecy of a new era: that democratic politics had come to decide the fate of individuals and peoples' (p. 26–7).

This last formula does, it is true, seem ambiguous, as it makes it impossible to distinguish the effects of a dynamic of social innovation from the effects of an ideological dynamic. What is certain is that, throughout the passages we have been discussing, the theme of social and historical invention, of the invention of a new world of human action and human communication, of the invention of the idea that history and society are the space within which the ultimate meaning of human values is inscribed, does remain clearly defined, although it does also become intertwined with the theme of the birth of ideology, of the fantastic belief that human actions and the social-historical world can be free of contradictions. In short, what Furet is suggesting is that 'the moment of the discovery of the political' – by which I mean the moment of the diffusion of questions as to the basis of power and of the social order, and therefore, of every question pertaining to the foundations of truth, legitimacy and reality, the moment, that is, of the formation of the modern sensibility and of the modern democratic spirit, the moment of the institution of a new social experience – is, to use Marx's expression, the moment of the *political illusion*. Furet further suggests that the moment in which the historic dimension becomes fully apparent and in which a question of universal import is invested in the idea of history – in the idea that society is a purely human society – coincides with a 'kind of hypertrophy of historical consciousness', and that 'From the very beginning it was ever ready to place ideas above actual history, as if it were called upon to restructure a fragmented society by means of the imaginary.' (p. 25, translation modified)

In my view, the idea that the meaning of the revolutionary process acquires a double meaning is much more fertile than the idea of our historian previously advanced in his attempt to locate within time the break between the liberal Revolution and the terrorist Revolution, namely the idea that the process 'skidded out of control'. For whilst he is right to detect this break as a turning point in the Revolution, it is even more important to recognize, as he now asks us to recognize, that the Revolution was from its very origins caught up in the political illusion and that ideas were placed above actual history – as Burke saw so clearly in 1793, even though he remained blind to the nature of the democratic foundation. It is equally important to recognize that it was until the very end the source of a proliferation of initiatives, of a mobilization of collective energies which transformed society's relations with its institutions and which opened up a world of possibilities.

It is, however, to be regretted that Furet does not pursue these suggestions, that he concentrates the whole weight of his analysis on the ideological dynamic of the Revolution and merely mentions the invention of a 'democratic culture' or a 'democratic politics' without finding any signs of them within the fabric of events; without specifying what distinguishes these inventions from the fantasmagoria of popular power; and without showing how much modern debates about politics, and the practice, style and content of social conflicts owe to the Revolution. It is, however, understandable that his main concern should be to bring out the logic of the imaginary which subtends not only the actions and discourses of its actors, and the sequence of struggles between factions and groups, but also the tangled web of events which historians normally regard as accidents that interrupt the normal course of the Revolution. The Revolution is irreducible to that logic, ideology comes into being only as a result of a mutation of a symbolic order; the political illusion presupposes an opening on to the political; it presupposes that ideas are placed above actual history, and that past and future have acquired a new meaning. It implies the fantasmagoria of liberty, equality and power, of the people and of the nation, of the emancipation of beliefs from authority, from tradition, from the natural or supernatural foundations of existing hierarchies, and from monarchical power. It is, however, also true to say that the Revolution can be represented, that it can be circumscribed within time, and that its various episodes can be articulated to form a sequence that has both a beginning and an end only by virtue of the eruption of representation, and the fantastic assertion that the postulates of thught, discourse and will coincide with self-being and with the being of society, history and humanity.

Furet best expresses the change in perspective which governs his reading of the Revolution when he writes: 'Every history of the Revolution must therefore deal not only with the impact of "circumstances" on the successive political crises but also, and above all, with the manner in which those "circumstances" were planned for, prepared, arranged and used in the imaginary of the Revolution and in the various power struggles' (p. 63, translation modified). He adds: 'The "circumstances" that propelled the Revolution forward were those that seemed to fit naturally into the pattern of revolutionary expectations: having in this sense been "anticipated" by the revolutionary consciousness, they were quickly given the necessary and appropriate meaning' (p. 63). And his analysis of the war, of the Terror and of the complexion taken on by the dominance of the Jacobins does indeed reveal the function they serve within the system of representations, and does show how the use made of them makes them appear necessary even when there is no longer any justification for them in the 'real'.

Rather than making an empirical demonstration supported by the facts, let us describe briefly the features of the revolutionary imaginary. For the first time, there comes into being a representation of society as being political through and through: all activities and all institutions are assumed to contribute to its general construction and to bear witness to it. This representation presupposes that everything can, in principle, be 'known' and 'transformed', that everything derives from the same values; it contains within it the definition of a new man whose vocation it is to become a universal historic agent, and whose public existence merges with his private existence: the revolutionary militant. But, at the same time, it is allied with its opposite: a representation of a society which falls short of what it should be, which is the victim of the egotism of interests, and which must be forced to be good, as well as with a representation of a multitude of evil beings who are responsible for all the failures of revolutionary politics. The figure of the universal man who embodies the whole of society coexists alongside that of the particular man whose very individuality poses a threat to the integrity of the social body. Yet these preliminary observations take on their full meaning only if we can locate the source of the illusion that a society can, ideally, be in harmony with itself and that an individual can be the bearer of its ends. Revolutionary ideoloy is constituted by the insane assertion of the unity, or indeed the identity, of the people. The legitimacy, the truth and the creativity of history are assumed to come together in the people. Now this primordial image contains a contradiction, for the people appear to conform to their essence only if they are distinguished from the empirical popular masses, only if they institute themselves as – and display themselves as being – legislators, as actors conscious of their ends. In other words the idea of the people implies the idea of a constant operation; the people perform operations which allow them to be their own midwives. It also implies the idea that the people must constantly demonstrate to themselves that they are in possession of their own identity. Only in this way can ultimate values coincide with action. The combination of the two motifs which Furet finds decisive – that of *popular vigilance* and that of *the plot* – are the best expression of this imaginary elaboration. The former corresponds to the requirement that a distance which is internal to the people must be made perceptible; it must constantly be displayed in order to prove that it is destined to disappear; the peoples' certainty as to their identity can increase only if they see themselves, only if they never lose sight of themselves as they look for signs of treason. The latter stems from the need to trace treason to an external source: the people cannot conceive of divisions that emanate from within; they cannot imagine the existence of obstacles that cannot be imputed to the evil will of the enemy without.

To raise the question of the content of the representation of the people, and of what it represses, is to raise the question of revolutionary power. Having drawn our attention to the 'central notion of popular vigilance', Furet rightly observes that: 'it was always raising – especially when the Revolution took a new turn – the insoluble problem of what forms the Revolution should take; and of who was speaking in its name. Which group, which assembly, which meeting, which consensus was the trustee of the people's word? That issue, a matter of life and death, determined the course of events and the distribution of power' (p. 29).

Paradoxically, it becomes impossible to determine where power lies or to determine who holds power at the very moment when the existence of a fully legitimate power is proclaimed, namely the power of a people with a universal existence, which is fully active, which devotes the same energy to all its tasks, and which is fully conscious of its goals. In one sense, the definition of power coincides with that of the people: the people are assumed not only to hold power, but to be power. And yet, as the people are what they are only insofar as they extract themselves, thanks to their vigilance, from the empirical society in which they are embedded, it might also be said that the people assert their identity when a universal agency of knowledge and decisiveness appears in the visible place of power. But that interpretation cannot be valid, for whenever the people are embodied in power, and whenever an organ is created and claims to have been entrusted with the will of the people, or even simply to be exercising it, it becomes obvious that there is a discrepancy which has no *de jure* status between the institution and the institutor. On the one hand, we have the Assembly which claims to represent the people by making laws in their name; on the other we have the men of the Sections and the clubs, or the masses who participate in the revolutionary *journées* and who claim to embody the people in action. Yet when those same men appear for what they are, namely minorities, they expose themselves to being denounced as *de facto* groups who are betraying the people, simulating their identity and acting as usurpers.

Without going into the details of Furet's convincing analysis of the strategy of Robespierre, who cunningly escapes the trap the Revolution sets for all its actors by never staying in any definite place and by combining the positions of the Assembly, the clubs and the streets, let us bring out the essentials of the argument: power becomes excessive when it is invested with the might of the Revolution and of the people, but it proves to be unexpectedly fragile when, by taking on the visible shape of an organ or of men, it reveals itself to be divorced from, and therefore external to, the Revolution and the people. It must be clearly understood that what is at stake here is not simply the image of the individuals who are trying both to identify with power 'and through its mediation, with the people', and to seize power. It is the image of power itself, which is perceived both as a force produced by the people, as the force which makes the people what it must be, and as a force which can be divorced from the people, as a potentially alien force which could turn against the people.

The idea of power and the idea of the plot are therefore bound up together in two ways. Power is recognized as revolutionary and as being internal to the people when it designates the enemy position where aggression is being fomented. It needs the aristocratic plot to mask its own position because it is always threatened with having to reveal that it is particular and not universal. But, by producing evidence of a plot and by pointing its finger at a focus of aggression, it establishes the image of the Other-as-enemy. The danger is now that that image will be transferred on to power, that the site of power will appear to be the site of the plot.

In this respect, the few pages which Furet devotes to the rivalry between Robespierre and Brissot during the debate on the war are quite remarkable. It seems that Brissot was the first to understand the function of the war within the dynamic of the Revolution, as we can see from the famous formula he used in his speech to the Jacobins in December 1791: 'We need great acts of treason: therein lies our salvation ... great acts of treason will be fatal only to those who perpetrate them; they will serve mankind.' Surprisingly enough, Robespierre objects to a machination which he and his supporters will later use to such great advantage. But Brissot has only partially understood the mechanism of the Revolution. He thought that simply by conjuring up the figure of the enemy, he could arouse the people's patriotic faith, make it aware of its unity and thereby fully legitimize the power that was leading it in its struggle. Robespierre displays an intimate understanding of the Revolution. Not only does he suspect his adversary of duplicity, of planning to seize power whilst pretending to defend the people. At a more profound level – for there can be no doubts as to his own political ambitions – he realizes that the Revolution will not be content with any power or any treason which can be circumscribed or which speaks its name. He realizes that it requires a form of treason which is hidden, but which is everywhere, and a form of power which does not show its face. His great achievement is to suggest that, in the policy of the Girondins, the Revolution conceals power, and that power conceals a plot. And so, as Furet puts it so nicely, 'He pushed his rival into the very trap Brissot had baited for Louis XVI and his advisers' (p. 68). As for Robespierre himself, we are given to understand that: 'The war was to carry him to power; not to the ministerial power of which Mirabeau and Brissot may have dreamt, but to the mastery over opinion that was inseparable from the Terror' (p. 68).

Furet's comments on the mastery of opinion bring us to the final stage of our analysis of revolutionary ideology, and we can now make a radical distinction between that ideology and the imaginary formations of the past. It is not enough to identify the key representations around which it is organized: that of a society which is political through and through; that of a society mobilized in order to create the new man; that of the militant entrusted with a universal mission; that of a people who find unity in equality, and their identity in the nation; and that of a power which simply expresses the will of the people. Nor is it enough to appreciate the symbolic mutation which accompanies these representations: the fusion of the principle of law, the principle of knowledge and the principle of power, and the resultant transformation of the *real* into the guarantor of the validity of the system of revolutionary thought. These changes must also be related to changes in the status of speech and in the status of opinion.

The people, the nation, equality, justice and truth in fact exist only by virtue of the speech which is assumed to emanate from within them and which at the same time names them. In that sense, power belongs to the individual or individuals who can speak on their behalf or, to be more accurate, to the individual or individuals who appear to speak on their behalf, who speak in the name of the people and give them their name. The best illustration of the 'displacement of power', to use Furet's expression once more, is not its explicit transfer from one focus of sovereignty to another, but its migration from the fixed, determinate but occult place it occupied under the monarchy to a place which is paradoxically unstable and indeterminate, whose existence is indicated only by the incessant work of its enunciation; it becomes detached from the body of the king, which housed society's leading organs, and moves into the impalpable, universal and essentially public element of speech. This fundamental change marks the birth of ideology. The use of speech was of course always bound up with the exercise of power, and took the mode of the founding word. But whereas it was once the speech of power which ruled, it is now the power of speech.

It must therefore immediately be added that speech can rule only because it conceals the fact that it is power; militant speech or public speech which addresses the people in the name of the people can never speak of the power it contains. Its power can only be unmasked by other militant words which topple it into the trivial register of seditious speech and rob it of its symbolic function in order to claim it as their own. And so, whenever a target is hit, power undergoes a metamorphosis and re-establishes itself by dropping only its support: a particular individual or a group of particular individuals. As Furet explains, the concealment of the power that resides in words is a precondition for its appropriation, and it also creates the preconditions for an incessant political competition based upon the denunciation of the adversary's secret ambitions. It is because 'Power resided in the word' that 'Power was always at stake in the conflict between words, for power could only be appropriated through them, and so they had to compete for the conquest of that evanescent yet primordial entity, the people's will' (p. 49).

Yet the means whereby power is won and the mechanisms of competition remain obscure if we do not also take into consideration a new figure: that of opinion, which is not to be confused with either power or the people, but which provides the intermediary that allows them to be related to one another in the imaginary. On the one hand, opinion is a substitute for the people, for the current reality of the people is never what it should be. This is not to say that it provides a fully determined representation of the people; in order to exercise its function, it must, like the people, escape all given definitions, for if it were to be defined, it would cease to appear to be a source of meaning and value. But it does at least have the ability to manifest itself and, provided that it achieves a certain degree of homogeneity, the capacity to provide signs of the people's presence. On the other hand, the relationship between power and opinion is extremely clear, for, when it manifests itself, opinion either imposes real constraints upon what political actors can say or simply provides them with a reference they cannot elude without revealing their words to be private words. If, that is, some individual or some group proves able to speak in the name of the people, it is only because their words are accepted, disseminated and recognized as the words of the people, or because they are amplified by a voice which appears to belong to no one, which appears to be devoid of any particular social support and which, by its very anonymity, bears witness to the presence of a universal force.

The function of opinion in the Revolution calls for two comments. On the one hand, the power of the word presupposes that a pole of opinion has been constituted; and, because of the collapse of the pole of the monarchy, the legitimacy of the pole of opinion can be asserted to be unlimited. On the other hand, opinion remains shapeless; it cannot be localized in a body and it cannot be reduced to a set of statements as it is constantly being created and re-created, and as the power of the word is conquered through the art of stimulating its expression. In concrete terms, this means that unanimity is manufactured in ad hoc spaces such as clubs or societies through the adoption of motions which bear no mark of individual intentions. In that sense, power succeeds in concealing itself in the word only to the extent that the word has succeeded in insinuating itself into opinion and in passing unnoticed.

At this point in his analysis, Furet begins to follow the trail blazed by Augustin Cochin (to whom the final essay in the book is devoted in its entirety). Their paths have, of course, crossed before because, as Furet reminds us, Cochin set himself the very task he outlines in his own critical extension of Tocqueville's project. Cochin does not explain the Revolution in terms of its balance sheet, and nor does he reinsert it into the continuity of a long-term process; he sets himself the task of interpreting 'the rending of the historical fabric' (p. 171) and the logic of the explosive character of the Revolution. He pursues his analysis at the level at which the explosion itself occurred – the ideological and political level – and he reveals the effects of a new system of legitimacy which implies the identification of power with the people. But, according to Furet, one of Cochin's greatest merits is to have undertaken a sociological analysis of the mechanisms of democratic ideology by demonstrating the role 'philosophical societies' [*sociétés de pensée*] played in the production of opinion. He regards Jacobinism, which he sees as the clearest expression of the meaning of revolutionary practice and ideology, as a combination of a system of action and a system of representation, as a heritage and as 'the fully developed form of a type of political and social organization' (p. 173) that had become widespread in the second half of the eighteenth century. Literary circles and societies, masonic lodges, academies, and cultural or patriotic clubs were all manifestations of the phenomenon.

Just what was a philosophical society, according to Cochin, and just what was its purpose? His interpreter provides the answer:

It was a form of social life based upon the principle that its
members, in order to participate in it, must divest themselves of
all concrete distinctions and of their real social existence. It was
the opposite of what the Ancien Regime called a corporate entity
(*corps*), defined by a community of occupational and social
interests ... The purpose of the philosophical society was not to
act, to delegate or to "represent": it was to deliberate and to cull
from its members and from discussion a common opinion,
a *consensus* to be subsequently expressed, propounded and
championed. A philosophical society had no authority to delegate
nor any representatives to elect on the basis of shared ideas or
as a voting block; it served as a tool designed to produce
unanimous opinion ... (p. 174)

And what light does this shed on Jacobinism? Jacobinism is, we are
given to understand, the fully developed model of the philosophical
society, as transformed by the dissolution of the model of the *corps*
and by the collapse of monarchical power. The notion of the abstract
individual, of the member of the philosophical society thus becomes
the notion of the citizen; the notion of unanimous opinion shores up
the representation of the People-as-One, and all the processes whereby
debates are manipulated, and whereby members and militants are
selected to further the production of homogeneous discourses acquire
both a practical and a symbolic efficacity: the power which conceals
itself in words in order to ally itself with opinion is converted into
political power.

It is, however, also at this point that we find the final articulation
of Furet's argument, and that the difficulty we alluded to earlier arises.
The reader may well be surprised at the reappearance of a question
which had, it seemed, been disposed of: the question of the conditions
which allowed the Revolution to emerge from within the Ancien
Regime, if not that of its causes. Has Furet simply transferred the idea
of the continuity of history, which others thought they could find in
the register of modes of production and class struggle or in the register
of the growth of the state and of administrative centralization, to the
register of 'democratic sociability'? The difficulty is, in my view, worthy
of mention, not because it invalidates his interpretation, but because
it is a further reason to admire his approach. It is in fact quite true
that, in his turn, Furet does look for signs of what will become
revolutionary ideology in the Ancien Regime. But his search for signs,
and it is more sophisticated and more detailed than I may have
suggested, does not lead him to abandon his principles. He argues that
we must abandon the fictional viewpoint which allows us to take an
overview of the Revolution and which confirms that the new springs
from the old just as effects spring from causes. We must conceptualize
the particular political form the Revolution takes as it breaks with the
past. And it is his examination of that political form that leads him to

identify the outline in which it began to take shape. Ultimately, he does not view the Revolution as the product of an earlier history, and he does not claim that, if we simply replace it in, say, the context of the mid-eighteenth century, we will see its birth. It reveals the past, but what it reveals is not the whole of the Ancien Regime – a historian of the Ancien Regime can pursue his studies a long way without having to investigate the Revolution. What it does reveal is the internal decomposition of the representations which governed all social relations, the crack which opened up in the system of legitimacy, and the abyss which is at once revealed and concealed by absolutism. It does not reveal the spread of democracy or of new ideas, which can be seen throughout Europe and especially in England, but it does reveal how much the idea of the equality of individuals, and of the homogeneity and transparence of the social, owes to a contested reference to an omnipotent and omniscient power.

It is not this which inspires me to express reservations about the wisdom of following in Cochin's footsteps. Cochin saw the advent of philosophical societies simply as a prefiguration of Jacobinism, and the formation of opinion simply as a prefiguration of an anonymous power which dissolves within it the diversity of individual points of view. Whilst it is true that he touches here upon an extremely important phenomenon – and the creation of modern revolutionary parties was to reveal its later developments – he fails to see its obverse: the new irrigation of the social fabric by associations which took it upon themselves to analyse the problems of political life; the breaking down of the barriers between the private spaces circumscribed by corporate entities; the spread of critical methods of knowledge and discussion; and the establishment of the exchange or communication of ideas which subtends opinion. Unlike Tocqueville, he does not perceive the ambiguity of individualism, which, for Tocqueville implies both independence of thought, a sense of initiative and the true form of freedom, and at the same time the isolation of everyone, the degradation of the individual that results from the rise of society, and the increasing subjugation of the individual to the power which is assumed to embody society. Whilst Furet obviously does not espouse all Cochin's theses – he explicitly criticizes him for failing to see the embryonic movement towards representative democracy which develops at the beginning of the Revolution and which persists, despite its failures, under the Jacobin dictatorship itself – his interpretation is marred by the lacuna which we mentioned when we noted with surprise that he speaks of 'the invention of democratic culture' without trying to define it. Furet would say that his project was to interpret the *Revolution* within the French Revolution, that it is the pressure of ideology which makes it a revolution, and that his primary concern was therefore to stress the importance of ideology and of all the factors that made it so important, rather than to explore every aspect of a change which did not necessarily require a revolution. We have already said that this answer is perfectly justifiable, and that Furet supports it with a rigorous analysis of the dynamic of the Revolution. But we still have to return to the question of the *excesses* of the Revolution. Do we not have to recognize that its 'excesses' go beyond the limits of ideology? Do we not have to see them as an index of the irreducible gap that suddenly appears between the symbolic and the real, of the indeterminacy of both – and of a gap in the being of the world which we still experience? Our author rightly notes that the Revolution 'provided society with a space for development to which it does not normally have access.' Does this not suggest that representative democracy was powerless to establish itself, not simply because the political illusion estranged men from themselves, but because it is not in itself enough to preserve an opening on to that space, and because, when it claims to be able to do so, it appears to close a space that has only just been cleared? Our author also perspicaciously notes that the revolutionaries fell under the spell of the absolutism they wanted to destroy, and that they secretly adopted the project of gaining complete mastery over the social that was bequeathed them by the Ancien Regime; but, by revealing the political dimension of the Revolution, he also urges us to take stock of the extraordinary event of the end of the monarchy, and of the new experience of a society which could no longer be apprehended in the form of an organic totality. And does not that event institute an open-ended debate as to the foundations of legitimacy, a debate which means that democracy can never be purely a matter of institutions?

Tocqueville and Quinet couched their final verdicts on the Revolution in the same words, or almost the same words. Tocqueville said that it inaugurated 'the cult of the impossible', and in saying that he denounced its flight into the imaginary. Quinet said that it gave birth to 'faith in the impossible', by which he meant that the negation of what is assumed to be the real is constitutive of the history of modern society. We would certainly be wrong to divorce these notions.

6

Edgar Quinet: The Revolution That Failed

It is in the preface which opens the third volume of his *Histoire de la révolution française* ('De la méthode et de l'esprit de ce livre') that Michelet voices his most radical criticisms of the Terror:

> Far from honouring the memory of the Terror, I believe that it cannot even be excused as a measure of public safety. I know that it had to overcome infinite difficulties; but the clumsy violence of the Terror's first attempts to overcome them had the effect of creating millions of new enemies for the Revolution at home, of losing it the sympathies of peoples abroad, of making all propaganda impossible, and of uniting peoples and kings against it in a close alliance. It had incredible obstacles to overcome, but the most terrible of those obstacles were of its own making. And it did not overcome them; they overcame it.[1]

He expresses this view in an attack on a tradition, which we would now describe as left-wing, which promoted the idea that the Terror was salutary and which held up its agents for admiration. In the preface, he attacks Esquiros, Lamartine and Louis Blanc, but his primary targets are the men who inspired them: Buchez and Roux, the authors of the *Histoire parlementaire de la Révolution Française*, to whom he devotes several pages. Their work is not simply one target among others: 'I would not dwell in this way on the *Histoire parlementaire*, were it not that this easily-consulted collection is a constant temptation for the host of readers who have little time.'[2] What are his basic criticisms? He criticizes the authors for describing the Revolution as the culmination of the history of France, for seeing it, that is, as a sequel to the work begun by the monarchy before it became corrupt, and for confusing the spirit of the Revolution and the spirit of Catholicism to a scandalous extent. Their views result in a justification of both the Inquisition and the Terror.

A cursory glance at the commentaries, most of them in the form of prefaces, which Buchez appends to the revolutionary documents published in the *Histoire* is in fact enough to convince one that Michelet's criticisms are quite justified.[3] Buchez, a former disciple of Saint-Simon who saw himself as the great architect of the restoration of the Catholic tradition and, at the same time, as an ardent revolutionary – the defender of 'the most numerous and poorest class' – borrows from his master the idea of an opposition between organic periods and critical periods, and this provides him with a key to the nation's history. He therefore praises the kings who had, until the era of Louis XIV, worked to unify the territory and the social body. Like his master, he believes that no society can maintain its unity unless it is duly hierarchical and unless it is mobilized around an 'activity goal' [*but d'activité*]. Buchez's contribution is to ascribe knowledge of that goal to political power. Being convinced that Catholicism is the national religion *par excellence* and that it could both maintain order and instil respect for authority, he sees the Reformation as the moment which exposed the social body to the greatest of all dangers: the threat of the rise of individualism and the threat of unrestrained egotism. Armed with this principle, the author of the *Histoire parlementaire* finds nothing of fundamental value in the first period of the Revolution; in his view, the Declaration of the Rights of Man merely sanctions the triumph of individualism, and, in more general terms, the work of the Constituent Assembly is simply a continuation of the negative critical work of the *philosophes* of the eighteenth century.

The rise of the real revolutionary movement, in contrast, begins with the realization of the importance of public safety. It is not that Buchez sees the Terror as a cause for celebration; he sees it, rather, as resulting from the state of corruption which French society had reached. In his view the Terror was unavoidable if the community was to be saved from the threat of destruction. The September massacres in particular were unavoidable – as was the Saint-Barthélemy massacre – because of the need to put a stop to the development of anti-social forces. Only one criticism is addressed to the authors of these massacres: they could not publicly justify their actions in the name of a principle, and therefore gave the impression that what was in fact a measure of public safety was a crime. In short, Buchez criticizes them for knowing nothing of the philosophy of history to which he has at last found the key. But at the same time, he attempts to explain their lack of a philosophy by making a distinction between history, which is governed by freedom, and the course of events, which is governed by fatality. The former unfolds beneath the aegis of an awareness of a goal, and presupposes an *active* humanity; the latter unfolds beneath the aegis of blind necessity, of a sequence of cause and effect. The September massacres, like the Saint-Barthélemy massacre, are thus seen as inevitable events, as the product of an era of passivity; they represent a final reaction in the face of an ultimate threat, but those who initiated them cannot fully understand them.

The most astonishing element in this construction is the thesis that history is moving inexorably in the same direction, regardless of whether people are conscious or unconscious of its goal. Only its rhythm varies; people may exercise their freedom and become active subjects; alternatively, they may remain passive, in which case they are forced to undertake tasks whose ultimate rationale they cannot understand. If that is the case, results which action could have achieved in the short term and with an optimal economy of means are achieved only after numerous digressions, by overcoming multiple obstacles and at the cost of great suffering. There can be no doubt as to the function of this hypothesis: it allows Buchez to bridge the gap between two conceptions which appear, respectively, to be purely voluntarist and purely fatalistic. Fatality is dominant in that, no matter how people behave, they are marching towards a final goal, and in that nothing can remove that goal. Freedom dominates in that, not only do people in theory have the power to know and to will that goal and to mobilize in order to achieve it; even when they are caught up in a blind cause and effect sequence, they are still capable of choosing the path that leads to salvation. From this point of view, the history of France can, despite its twists and turns, be seen as a single history which is inevitable, but whose goal is constantly amenable to consciousness. From this point of view, the Revolution allows us to glimpse a split between a pole of activity and knowledge which is associated with the rise of the revolutionary government, and a pole of activity and ignorance which attracts the enemies of the people, the moderates and the *indifférents*. From this point of view, finally, the Terror appears to be one of those moments when, as a result of conditions generated in passivity, it becomes possible to make the transition to activity, when at least the preconditions for a possible return to the path leading to the common goal exist.

Whilst it may seem quite alien to the modern mind, if only because it is constantly bound up with a theology, it would not be difficult to show that Buchez's language derives from categories which for a long time governed the thought of a certain revolutionary left, and which continue to do so: activity and passivity, freedom and necessity, cohesion and dispersal, egotistic interests and public safety, a creative power and masses which depend upon its action. But the reader can be left to make the transpositions which suggest themselves. Let us return to Michelet.

His interpretation of the Revolution contradicts Buchez's point by point, but there is still a parallel between the two, for Michelet too is interested in situating the events that took place between 1789 and 1794 within the history of France and, more specifically, in interpreting the relationship between the revolutionary government and the monarchy. He too associates the Terror with the idea of public safety;

and, finally and perhaps most significantly, he too attempts to explore the religious meaning of the French Revolution.

There is no need to dwell on Michelet's thesis that there was a break between the spirit of the revolution and the spirit of Catholicism, between the principle of justice and the theologico-political principle, between the terror of the Inquisition and the spirit of the rights of man, and between the age of authority and the age of liberty. For our purposes, it is more interesting to note the idea that the break which ushered in the modern world could not be consummated, and that the Revolution was marked by the return of the representations and practices of the past. In the preface we are discussing, Michelet does not simply express his annoyance with a conception which, in order to justify the Terror, invokes the precedent of the Inquisition; he himself speaks of a Jacobin inquisition, and in his view it is the claim that it reveals signs of the revolutionary spirit that is truly scandalous. He takes delight in comparing the two inquisitions and observes that, if we accept Buchez's theory, that of the Middle Ages should have been victorious:

> As a form of terror, it is superior because its repertoire includes the torments of eternity as well as ephemeral tortures. As a form of inquisition, it is superior because it has prior knowledge of the object of its enquiries; the man whose thoughts it is trying to read was once the boy it brought up, and it used all the educational means at its disposal to penetrate his mind; it used the practice of daily confession to penetrate his mind anew, and could exercise two systems of torture, one voluntary and the other involuntary. Having none of these means at its disposal, the revolutionary inquisition could not distinguish the innocent from the guilty, and was reduced to making a general admission of its impotence; it applied the adjective "suspect" to all.[4]

Nor does he challenge the view that the Terror stems from the idea of public safety or salvation [*salut public*], and that that idea had been decisive in previous centuries. But he does see the doctrine of public safety as a denial of justice. In his view, it is the repeated denial of justice that signals a historical continuity:

> Although they were very courageous and devoted, the men of the Revolution lacked the spiritual heroism which could have freed them from the old doctrine of public safety; from the thirteenth century onwards, this doctrine was applied by theologians, and professed and formulated by jurists, notably by Nogaret in 1300, who referred to it by its Roman name of "public safety" , and then by the ministers of the kings, who referred to it as *State interests* or *raison d'Etat*.[5]

The Terror – the last avatar of the theory we find in Rousseau, the philosopher who momentarily succeeded in establishing the unconditional value of right – is on the agenda when it is proclaimed that 'justice will be based upon the general interest'. I am drawing attention to Michelet's views here because they lead him to detect signs of the religious failure of the Revolution in the very phenomena which the author of the *Histoire parlementaire* would see as revealing its loftiest inspiration. He writes: 'Those who forced the Revolution to descend from justice to safety, from a positive idea to a negative idea prevented it from becoming a religion. No negative idea ever founded a new faith. The old faith could then triumph over the revolutionary faith.'[6] And this failure reveals the sterility of both the Jacobins and the Montagnards, and explains why they were swept away by the Terror.

Michelet hints at this interpretation in the preface, but he makes it quite explicit in a chapter entitled 'La Révolution n'était rien sans la révolution religieuse'. Here, he criticizes the Jacobins and the Girondins for being no more than 'political logicians'; he observes that even Saint-Just, the most advanced of all of them, 'did not dare to attack either religion, education or the basis of social doctrines'. He describes the Revolution they led as 'political and superficial': 'No matter whether it speeded up or slowed down, no matter whether it went more rapidly or more slowly along the single line it was following, it was doomed to founder.'[7] It had no foundations: 'It lacked the religious revolution which could have assured its success, the social revolution from which it could have drawn support, strength and depth.' Thus the real reason for its failure: its intellectual sterility. 'It is a law of life; either it increases, or it declines. The Revolution did not increase the patrimony of vital ideas bequeathed it by the philosophy of the century.' And the result of its sterility was the Terror: 'All the fury of the parties could not deceive anyone as to the quantity of life contained within their doctrines. Being both ardent and scholastic, they were all the more ready to proscribe one another in that there was no basic difference between them, in that they could only be certain of the nuances that divided them if they introduced the *distinguo of death*.'[8] But why did the revolutionaries, Girondins and Montagnards alike, 'have neither the time to look for new things nor any thought of doing so'? Because, although they were convinced that they alone could save the people, these men were not sons of the people, had no understanding of its instincts, and never dreamt of probing its aspirations. They were all bourgeois. The Girondins were scribes and lawyers who 'thought they could rule the people through the press'; the Jacobins believed themselves to be infallible, and readily incited the people to violence, but they did not consult the people': 'They boldly pronounced on national issues with only an imperceptible minority, displayed such horrifying scorn for the majority, and believed with such unshakeable faith in their own infallibility that they sacrificed a world of living men to it without any remorse.'[9]

Their haughty claim to be in possession of knowledge and power indicates a return to the past, but far from testifying to a happy historical continuity, it signals the oppression of the monarchical and aristocratic tradition. It is no accident that Michelet should find 'a terrible aristocracy' among the new democrats. He recognizes the mark of old mentalities in new modes of behaviour, and does not hesitate to assert that 'the monarchy was reborn after the death of Danton'. It is not enough for him to say that the old faith triumphed over the revolutionary faith: their political notion of authority seems to him to have re-emerged from the depths of the Ancien Regime. He does, however, suggest that something new can be detected in the moment of repetition. We noticed this earlier when we looked at the ironic comparison he draws between the Jacobin inquisition and the Catholic inquisition. The latter proved superior, not because it was better grounded in truth, but because it derived from a system in which the inquisitor knew his object in advance: the man he had educated. Compared with that era, the terrorist revolution appears to have an external relationship with its object: an abstract object constructed in the name of a false science of the social body. It adopted the principle that, if they were used properly, amputation and purges could preserve the integrity of the nation; but this was the science of 'inept surgeons' who 'in their profound ignorance of the nature of their patient [believed] that they could save the whole body by applying their scalpels at random.'[10] According to our author, then, the doctrine of public safety thus merges with the insane idea that incisions must be made into the social body if it is to be saved – with a rationalist myth.

This is why Michelet's narrative never explains the Terror simply in terms of circumstances, no matter what importance they may be accorded. This is why he sees that it began or 'took its first steps' long before its presence was declared. He sees it as beginning early in 1792, when the Jacobins resolve to purge the press, to persecute the monarchists, and take an oath 'to defend the life and fortune of anyone who denounces conspirators'; and when they prepare their first law on emigration which leaves a host of people who had not until then taken sides, but who were not hostile to the Revolution, with no alternative but to flee or to live under the constant threat of denunciation. And this is also why he contrasts the characters of the old terrorists and the new, and demonstrates that, unlike the knowledge of the inquisitors of old, the new surgical science can, if need be, ally itself with the philanthropy, the tearful rhetoric and the fanaticism of the failed artist.[11]

EDGAR QUINET'S INTERPRETATION

The passages from Michelet which we have been discussing give some idea of the debate that took place within the revolutionary left in the nineteenth century – between, that is, certain writers who sensed a common need to defend the French Revolution as a political, social and religious revolution, and who shared a desire to give it a new future. And yet, let there be no mistake about it, it is not Michelet but Quinet who provides the most rigorous critique of the Terror and of those who defend it. It is his study, published in 1865, which brings out the full implications of the principles he shared with his friend – so much so that they quarrelled briefly – and which goes so far as to describe the French Revolution as *a revolution that failed*. Whatever criticisms Michelet may be inspired to make of the achievements of the Revolution, it is in his view fully positive if it is viewed as a whole; his interpretation is intended primarily as an apologia. Quinet takes the opposite view. The change of tone radically alters the meaning of the picture. The achievements of the Revolution do of course appear immense to Quinet too, but he sees the task as being one of rediscovering something of its original inspiration. But there can be no doubt as to his overall verdict: the Revolution changed into its opposite, and its inability to establish liberty led to the re-emergence of servitude. The primary task is, then, to understand the reasons for its failure.

Quinet's intentions are clear from the very first lines of *La Révolution*: 'The French Revolution has no need of apologias, either true or false, but our century abounds in apologias . . . What remains to be discovered and explained is why the immense efforts and the many sacrifices that were made, and the prodigious numbers of men who perished, produced results that are still so incomplete or so distorted. A whole people cried out in millions of voices: 'We will be free or we will die'. Why were men who were able to die so admirably unable to be free?'[12] Quinet's great project is to evaluate the attraction servitude exerted over a people which did, even so, make an extraordinary effort to free itself, and to understand how the force of repetition destroyed hopes of innovation.

It is therefore not enough to abandon the thesis of an emanation of popular fury, to refuse to explain that fury in terms of a fear of foreign invasion (he shows clearly that the Terror intensified when the danger was over), or to admit that, as Michelet says, the Terror had to overcome obstacles of its own making and was finally overcome by them; we have to conclude that the meaning of the Revolution became inverted, that a process of regression towards despotism was at work within it. We have here more than a simple statement of fact. It is true that we must denounce the 'sophism of the plebeians', according to which evil becomes good if it is done in the name of the Revolution; that we must agree that 'plebeian despotism produces the same results as monarchical despotism: servile souls who beget yet more servile souls'; and that we must realize what effects it has in the context of 'a people made up of docile bourgeois and cowardly citizens', to use a phrase which Quinet quotes from Tocqueville (vol. I, p. 203). But we must also grasp the specific character of the history of France. Its character is cruelly underlined in the first chapter of *La Révolution*; 'If we are to draw any conclusion from the above, it must be this: what we call order, in other words obedience to a master and peace under arbitrary rule, is in France rooted in the bedrock of the nation; and it is almost inevitably reborn, both of itself, and of immemorial traditions. Order, understood in this sense, is protected by the ages; its very antiquity works in its favour and guarantees its safety' (vol. I, p. 9). Throughout his book, Quinet constantly reiterates this view and supports it with factual evidence, much of it relating to the Terror.

It is because the Revolution is in his view essentially political and religious that the Terror is so central to his argument. For one cannot conceptualize the political without understanding the beliefs that govern the relations human beings establish with one another and the general relationship that exists between them and power. In this respect, Quinet is very close to Tocqueville (whom he had read very carefully), and he makes a similar distinction between the transformation of the social state and the political revolution. When, for example, he speaks of the night of 4 August, he observes: 'The great levelling force which had long drive French society and which nothing could halt now faltered. There remained the problem of liberty; in other words the whole problem remained intact.' Now the problem of liberty and the problem of power are one and the same. In his general survey of the beginnings of the Revolution, he notes: 'So long as no attack was made on power, everything was easy, and everything was accomplished automatically. Things, places, memories, interests, privileges, kinship, racial hostilities and even idioms all gave way. But on the day that a desire for political freedom was born, everything changed, and men seemed to be pitting themselves against the impossible' (vol. I, p. 119). In a later passage in which he describes the progress that had been made in dividing up landed estates (a process which began before the Revolution) he again expresses similar views to Tocqueville: 'The division took place despite events simply because it was a movement which had begun outside politics; the Revolution accelerated it; but there was no need for a Revolution to authorise something that had been prepared for without a Revolution ...'. But the conclusion he reaches is very different to Tocqueville's, and is indeed explicitly critical of him. To regret, as did Tocqueville, the fact 'that the Revolution was not accomplished in the name of an absolute power' or to think that 'a despot would have done less to destroy the spirit of freedom than did the very genius of the nation' is, he claims, to border on the satirical (vol. I, p. 121). No doubt we can accept that 'if the great crises of the Revolution had been avoided', men would have achieved 'results which they could not fail to have achieved through the effects of time alone', but if we cling to that view we lose sight of the revolutionary essence of the Revolution, of the very thing that set

France ablaze: 'And so, we always have to come back to the same point: questions of religion and politics, that is, questions of liberty, alone unleashed the storms' (vol. I, p. 123).

The phenomenon of the Terror then becomes intelligible only if it is placed within its political and religious context. Quinet devotes a section of his work to the Terror (Book 17: 'La Théorie de la terreur'), but his interpretation goes far beyond the limits of that section; it also informs his analysis of religion (Books 5 and 16) and his analysis of dictatorship (Book 18).

If we attempt to collate these scattered comments, four arguments emerge; they are inter-related, and all are bound up with the idea of the return of servitude.

A substitute for a religious revolution

According to our author, when the revolutionaries retreated in the face of the task of making a religious revolution, they found themselves faced with a *spiritual void*. In that sense, the Terror appears to be a substitute for the one action which could have united the revolutionary actors in one faith, and which could have revealed to them the respective positions of past and present, the identity of their enemies, the nature of their own cause and the nature of their own identity. In the absence of that creative action and of its guiding idea, the distinction between self and other or between the people and its adversaries no longer had any referent in reality. It was impossible to locate the enemy, who became one with the suspect, and the revolutionary himself lost the criterion of his own morality. He sought it in the imaginary, in the ability to assume the risk of death in the service of the Revolution but, having no understanding of the nature of the Revolution, he could only resort to terror. In other words, and to use Quinet's own terms, 'The revolutionaries were afraid of the Revolution'. And they concealed their fear behind a mask of heroism which meant only this: overcoming death, with the fear of the other and the death of the other as their guarantee.

Quinet thus attacks most interpreters of the Revolution from the rear, for it had become a commonplace to see the Terror as an excess, as a sign of extreme audacity, regardless of whether it was seen as a folly or a necessity. He, on the other hand, sees it as a sign of weakness in the face of difficulty.

The author pinpoints the great event which seems to inaugurate the era of religious freedom (Book 5, chapter 6): 'The Constitution guarantees every man the right to practise the religion of his choice. At this point, certain people thought that the Revolution was complete. Such a great freedom, which was the very soul of the age, must necessarily have seemed to guarantee all future freedoms' (p. 199). But he immediately casts doubts upon the efficacy of such a principle in a society in which one religion – Catholicism – was so deeply rooted that no one could imagine a change. Under such conditions, he notes, 'To grant freedom of belief is to grant nothing' (p. 151). One may as well establish freedom of conscience in Mecca, Tunis or Japan – compare the French Revolution with the religious revolution of the sixteenth century. The latter attacked established religion with the utmost vigour; it forged new institutions, changed the temperament of the people, and it was only later that 'the door was re-opened to the old religion which, having fallen into abeyance, no longer inspired fear' (ibid). No other road was open to it: 'It was in this way, and in no other, that England, the Scandinavian states, Holland, Switzerland and the United States, and all the other peoples who were born of the Reformation were able to acquire a new soul. Without exception, they all saw the old religion as the enemy' (ibid). In France, by contrast, the revolutionaries were concerned with only one thing, despite the murmurings of the Constituant Assembly: they wanted 'to break with tradition without appearing to do so' (p. 161). This road led nowhere. 'As soon as they began to indulge in subtleties, they were lost. If the sixteenth century had adopted that tone, it would not have conquered a single parish. An innovator gives orders, imposes his will, and strikes; he does not prattle. It is impossible to make a religious revolution without admitting that one is doing so. One cannot displace a god without making a noise.' (p. 162).

Quinet goes against the accepted representation by revealing the revolutionaries' 'timidity of mind', a timidity which contrasts with their apparent ferocity. But he also says something more: their ferocity compensates for their timidity: 'How could all the external violence, all the accumulated ferocity, compensate for their timidity of mind?' (p. 163).

He returns to this theme on a number of occasions, notably at the beginning of Book 16, where he leaves us in no doubt as to the relationship between terror and timidity. The author describes the indignation of the Jacobins when Vergniaud dares to question the status of Catholicism during the debate on the constitution in 1793: 'I do not think that we can sanction principles which are absolutely alien to the social order in a declaration of social rights.' 'Having the temperament of *ligueurs*, they were not man enough to displace the Ultimate God of the Middle Ages' (vol. II, p. 137). A few lines later, he adds: 'Could it be true that, with all their colossal boldness, they believed themselves incapable of bending a reed in the moral realm? ... The less they dared to attempt in the moral realm, the more they were forced to dare all in the physical realm. This was a sterile boldness! For all that they made death into an idol, that could not redeem their timidity of mind' (p. 138).

Whence the timidity? Quinet gives the answer in Book 6: 'The truth is, if we are willing to admit it, that not a day went by, so to speak, without these terrible men trembling before the genius of the past.' Their servitude relates less to their submission to the old God than to their fear of making a break between past and present, of an event that meant that they would have to convince the people of a new truth, rather than seducing them by flattering their habits. Quinet then recalls Camille Desmoulins's words when he rebuked Manuel for having obtained a decree against the Corpus Christi procession: 'My dear Manuel, the kings are ripe for the picking; God is not' (p. 181). He then comments: 'The fear the terrorists felt is the underlying reason for the fall of the Revolution because, being secretly afraid of being rejected by the people, they dared not tell the people of anything in advance or prepare them for anything' (p. 182). But, before the Revolution collapsed, the Terror was unleashed as a result of the loss of the markers of morality and truth. 'These men affected a religion in which they did not believe, and they denied the philosophy in which they did believe. They found themselves far from any road, without a compass or a star to guide them. Soon, all that remained was ferocity in the darkness. It is not surprising that they slaughtered one another in the dark' (p. 183).

Camille Desmoulins, Danton, the terrible Marat, Cambon, Bazire, Saint-Just and even Robespierre himself all display the same prudence or the same cunning because they are afraid and have no imagination. But the last, whose revolutionary intransigence caused him to be both admired and detested, does seem to merit the harshest criticisms, for no one did more to protect Catholicism than Robespierre. Whilst he pretends to believe that its authority has been weakened, does he not pay homage to its principles – notably in a speech in which he goes so far as to declare that: 'Little remains in the minds of men but those imposing doctrines which lend their support to the moral ideas and to the sublime and touching doctrines of virtue and equality which the son of Mary once preached to his fellow citizens' (vol. I, p. 185). Robespierre even reiterates this strange view: 'Take consolation from the thought that the religion whose ministers are still paid by the State at least offers us a morality analogous to our own.' The quotations he accumulates lead Quinet to the following conclusion: 'The void which the terrorist system created in the spiritual realm is fully visible here.' And the void is all the more conspicuous in that the immunity of Catholicism is proclaimed at the very moment when preparations are being made to condemn the king. The revolutionaries prove incapable of grasping the profound inter-dependence of the monarchical principle and the theological principle.

Quinet extends his criticisms in Book 16, where he examines the dechristianization movement. Being convinced of the popular nature of the revolt against Christianity, he recalls that it was 'those who devastated churches, broke images and plundered reliquaries' who ensured the success of the Reformation. And he contrasts the sincerity of their protests against the clergy with the parodies of the revolutionary period, which disarm protests and condemn the new faith in Reason to ridicule. The parody organized by Chaumette and Hébert: Reason, 'they believed, could be represented by a beautiful woman who played the role of wisdom on a platform for an hour.' They improvise an act of idolatry, choose an actress who, borne on the shoulders of four men, makes her appearance in the Convention; the Convention is then forced to process to Notre-Dame, which is to become the temple of Reason. 'A rough stone or a worm-eaten piece of wood would have had a much greater hold over people's imagination than an actress who was stripping off her dress an hour after her deification' (p. 144). Quinet then comments: 'This sterility was truly disastrous, as was the inability to see the religious revolution as something more than a feast for the eyes and a *coup de théâtre*.' Then there was the sinister parody organized by Robespierre. 'The first cult at least represented pleasure; the cult Robespierre dedicated to the Supreme Being was based upon fear, and he had to crush the iconoclasts' (p. 146). This time, 'In order to keep the people inside the doors of the former church and to prevent them leaving, the terrorists forced them to stand between scaffolds' (p. 151).

'Here we see the real void at the heart of the French Revolution', repeats Quinet:

> In no other revolution did the leaders act in a manner so directly opposed to their goals; they used all their might to frustrate their own goals. It is this which gives the French Revolution its characteristic ferocity, a ferocity unprecedented in human affairs. It is as though we were watching a blind natural cataclysm rather than an upheaval directed by the will of human beings. (p. 152)

'The Theory of the Terror'

A very different interpretation of the Terror is advanced in Book 17, which is entitled 'La Théorie de la Terreur'. Here, Quinet seeks its premises in the Revolution itself. He accepts that it originates primarily in 'a clash between two irreconcilable elements: the old France and the new France' (vol. II, p. 181), that 'this feeling that there were two absolutely incompatible forces incited men's souls to fury', and that, as reprisals led to further reprisals, anger turned to frenzy. But he then immediately points out the change that occurred when 'Certain minds began to see the reprisals, which had occurred because of force of circumstances, as forming a system' (p. 183). At this point, a policy of Terror replaced the spiral of reprisals. 'Robespierre, Saint-Just and Billaud-Varenne wanted to turn what had been an accident into a permanent state. They turned what had initially been a flash of anger, or of despair, into a principle of government ... They turned ferocity into a cold instrument of government and salvation.' This initial explanation does not, however, go to the bottom of things, as it does not allow us to understand why the most terrible of the Jacobins acquired a following. Quinet finds the explanation in the Convention's realization that it was difficult, if not impossible, for a corrupt nation 'which had grown old in slavery' to accede to liberty. They therefore resolved to 'force the French to be free by using the methods which the politicians of Antiquity had applied in analogous circumstances'. But even that is not in itself an adequate explanation. We still have to look for the origins of revolutionary voluntarism. 'The third cause,' notes Quinet, 'is their scorn for the individual, that sad legacy from the oppression of old. "Be like nature," said Danton. "She looks to the preservation of the species, and is not concerned with individuals." If the so-called terrorism of nature is applied to human affairs, it becomes necessary to behead humanity itself' (p. 184). Here, we see the outline of one of the great themes to which Quinet will return later: the fiction of a revolution which is elevated to superhuman status, which becomes an entity in itself and for itself. 'From the outset, we turned the Revolution into an abstract being like nature, into an idol which we deified and which needed no one, which could, without any danger to itself, swallow up individuals one after another and wax strong on the annihilation of all.' This fiction combines with another, which does more to explain the mechanisms of the Terror: that of the original goodness of man, which is borrowed from Jean-Jacques Rousseau. 'Who would believe that philanthropy itself could also lead to Terror?' exclaims Quinet (p. 185). His answer is remarkable for its acuity. The belief in the goodness of man can be challenged only by imputing the difficulties the Revolution encountered to 'the designs of the wicked'. The revolutionaries 'began by putting "man is good" on the agenda and, when they encountered difficulties in establishing justice, they concluded that they were caught up in a vast conspiracy, *and failed to see that in most cases it was things themselvs that conspired against them*' (emphasis added).

Quinet's exploration of the effects of philanthropy – the ultimate reason for the Terror – is, I believe, unprecedented. Not content with demonstrating 'how suspicion was at work in the minds of Robespierre and the Jacobins', he shows that it also gnawed away at the souls of the terrorists: 'Not only did the half-tamed past roar around them; they bore part of that past within them; without realizing it, they too were implicated in the conspiracy they had uncovered, and which they denounced in all things. Who, then, could they trust, if they bore the enemy within them?'

These, then, are the elements of the 'theory of the Terror'. It is, however, to be noted that, although he expounds them in the first section of Book 16, in Book 17 Quinet relates what seemed to be a product of the revolutionary spirit to the heritage bequeathed by the Ancien Regime. 'In private life,' he observes, 'it is unjust that the sons should expiate the sins of their fathers ... But in the life of peoples, this philosophy does not hold, and present generations must certainly be punished for the sins of previous generations. *This is the only way in which we can find a moral explanation for the reign of the Terror*'

(p. 189, emphasis added). He adds: 'The sword struck at every rank in society because servitude had been the work of all. In these years of horror the history of France came to its frenzied conclusion.' Quinet then reminds us of whose footsteps the revolutionaries were following:

> Each stage was mapped out in advance: Merlin de Douai followed the example of Louvois (the man responsible for the Revocation of the Edict of Nantes), and Fouquier that of Baville ... The drownings in the Loire were based on a model: in the seventeenth century, a certain Planque had suggested drowning the protestants at sea. Carrier took note. Villars threatens to put whole communities to the sword; he is already speaking the language which Collot d'Herbois will use. Montrevel invented the hostage law; the Directory had only to revive it.

No doubt the nature of servitude did change with the Revolution, but its newest features were already imprinted on the past. And, as Quinet was to ask at the end of his work, 'Does servitude cease to be servitude because it is voluntary?' (vol. II, p. 560).

The Terror as farce

There is, then a close affinity between the two arguments we have briefly reconstructed, although one places the emphasis primarily on the religious phenomenon, whilst the other stresses primarily the political phenomenon. It would be a mistake to assume that there is any contradiction between the idea that the revolutionaries were afraid of the Revolution, and the idea that they made an idol of it. The two ideas are complementary. By deifying it, they petrified it, because they were afraid of being carried away by a movement that might have destroyed the basis of their old beliefs. By elevating it above individuals and by making it an abstract being, they avoided the task of setting everyone free, of allowing everyone the ability to base their faith on the dictates of conscience. The Terror is a sign of their inability to break with the past in either the political or the religious realm.

The interpretation becomes more complex when our author describes the revolutionaries as being unable to rediscover the old meaning of the violence which had once been used to found religions or to establish dominance. We are told basically that, when they believe they are innovators, they remain trapped by their identification with a principle of authority, and that, when they think they are imitating the past, they lapse into parody. Without their being aware of it, the modern spirit, the democratic spirit, undermines their plans. It is then not only the Revolution that appears to have been a failure: the Terror itself was a failure. It was cruel, but it was also absurd and derisory.

The same argument is applied to the realm of the religious and the realm of the political. But here, the meandering, ironic and subtle approach of the analyst is no less worthy of interest than the argument itself. In a word, Quinet constructs what will later come to be known as an *ideal type* of terror as foundation, which he sees as essentially religious, and then an ideal type of despotic terror, and uses his models to investigate the revolutionary Terror.

Let us summarize the initial argument, which is made quite explicit in the first section of Book 16 ('Le Terrorisme français et le terrorisme hébraïque'). The question Quinet asks is as follows: 'What in itself is a system of Terror when it is applied to the regeneration of a people?' He then immediately establishes its features:

> The ideal form of this system was conceived and perfected by Moses. His people were dying in slavery in Egypt. He undertook to save them by regenerating them. In order to do so, he first obliged them to foreswear the old Egyptian idols; he then undertook the re-creation of their traditions, and their education. To succeed in doing so, he led them into the desert, and kept them there in fear and trembling for forty years. This was indeed government through fear. (vol. II, p. 132)

The French Terror appears to derive from the same system as the Hebraic Terror: there is the same desire to 'tear the people away from their old loyalties'; and the plan to 'alter even the most inveterate habits, the names of the months, the days and the seasons' reveals a similar plan 'to lead them into the desert where they became lost', as does the dream of a completely new system of education. But at the same time, a comparison of the two reveals differences. The revolutionaries failed to perform the first task required of any lawgiver: they could not institute the people on a religious basis. If Moses had acted like them, if he had consecrated old idols 'stained with the blood of the twelve tribes [he] would now seem execrable to posterity'.

In the second section of the same book, Quinet draws a conclusion from these criticisms: 'Falsity begets absurdity, and absurdity begets horror' (p. 140). His conclusion appears to rest upon the conviction that it was only by being intolerant that the Revolution could become religious. Quinet accepts that the Convention of 1793 formulated a magnanimous principle, but he also states that 'it contained the seeds of counter-revolution'. This argument appears to converge with that outlined above, but it soon becomes apparent that it has a very different function. There is no suggestion to the effect that the Revolution should have taken the Hebraic Terror as a model. Quinet certainly regards a religious revolution and intolerance as incompatible. He notes, for example, in Book 5 that a choice had to be made between a policy of tolerance and a policy of proscription, and that by proclaiming one and practising the other, the revolutionaries were doomed to lose on both counts (vol. I, p. 125); in the same book, he points out that, as the spirit of tolerance is the spirit of modernity itself, temporary recourse to intolerant measures should have been enough to ensure its triumph. He even goes so far as to remark: 'Who knows what offspring the genius of France might have produced in this void, when it was lost in the desert; or what all the free energies of the modern spirit might have produced to fill the gulf opened up by the collapse of the old world?' The question is linked with this comment: 'If they had felt themselves to be united against a common adversary [the terrorists] would not have killed one another' [vol. II, p. 170). There can, however, be no doubts as to what he is thinking, and Quinet himself dispels any possible misunderstanding in Book 16:

> I beg the reader not to pretend to misunderstand me here. I know as well as anyone that freedom of worship is the principle that must prevail, and that it is the basis of the modern consciousness. But I do think that I can say that the revolutionaries were being self-contradictory when they reverted to the old law of terror and, at the same time, safeguarded the rights of their enemies. And that contradiction inevitably destroyed them. (vol. II, p. 178)

It is this contradiction that Quinet is striving to bring out. He is not attempting to make an imaginary reconstruction of the course the Revolution might have taken; he is trying to destroy the theses of those historians who see the Terror as the inevitable outcome of the attempt to regenerate the social body and to ensure public safety. His other purpose is to convince his contemporaries that the Revolution was a failure, and to alert them to the question raised by any change which is at once political, social and religious. (It should not be forgotten that he was writing in exile, at the time when Louis-Napoleon was on the throne in France.)

There is obviously a Machiavellian inspiration behind the decision to construct a model of terror as foundation in order to reveal the derisory elements – the element of falsity, absurdity and horror – in the revolutionary Terror's attempt to imitate that model. This is not surprising: Quinet had read Machiavelli more attentively and with greater understanding than any of his contemporaries. Like Machiavelli, he was enamoured of liberty, and of new ideas and new institutions – *principi nuovi* – and he too mocks would-be realists and sages who preach fatalism but who are in fact always ready to conceal oppression. He too catches them in the trap of the consistency of ends and means. Thus, having posited the hypothesis of terror as foundation, he asks what conclusions we are to deduce from it, provokes a scandalous response, and reveals the terrorists' 'timidity of mind' in the very actions which seemed to show their great boldness. In doing so, he also reveals the 'stupidity' of the historians, to use an expression which he will discuss at length at the end of his book.

Any doubts as to Quinet's debt to Machiavelli should be dispelled by an examination of the second part of the argument under discussion here. The comparison he now draws between Revolutionary terror and despotic terror admirably reveals the irony that lies behind the objective argument. The French terrorists failed, he writes

> To see the true genius of Terror; their popular spirit prevented them from using this instrument of domination with the requisite sang-froid. It requires the greatest impassivity; Louis XIV, Philip II and Richelieu did not proceed with this outward violence ... Only the aristocracies and the monarchies of old had the necessary phlegm to use these weapons without injuring themselves. Democracy is useless for these purposes; being too impetuous and too immoderate, it can insult, but it cannot calumniate; when it thinks it is striking at the enemy, it is striking at itself. (pp. 211–12)

The self-destruction of terrorism is therefore absurd. 'The Inquisition never struck at the Inquisitor.' Discussions as to the limits of the Terror and the attempts some make to moderate it are also absurd: 'The nature of this government requires an element of uncertainty, of the unknown, of extremism in all things. It must be unrestrained; it must know no bounds' (p. 213). The belief in a peaceful future is also absurd: 'The principle of this government must be the destruction of all hope.' The tortures applied in 1793 and 1794 are, finally, wretched; Terror requires

> Hidden and silent tortures; exile in distant lands where the climate is certain to be fateful; silken nooses in the seraglio; prisons which no one leaves alive ... the *in pace* of the Inquisition over the lagoons. One could also mention exile in Siberia, or the mines of the Urals ... These are the punishments fit for a regime of horror; they fill the imagination without exhausting it, and they haunt it constantly. Evils one sees and cannot grasp are fearful. (p. 214)

The French terrorists who have been so admired and so execrated were not up to their task:

> The world shrinks from exemplary deaths, from permanent scaffolds, and from blood that is spilt in broad daylight for all to see. He who dies in the midst of the people feels that he is living to the very end. Death in the darkness, far from the living; an unknown, forgotten death which has no repercussions; that is real Terror. That was not the Terror of 1793. (p. 215)

Ignorance of the People, Scorn for the People

The three arguments we have discussed finally combine with a fourth which was outlined in Book 17 ('La Théorie de la Terreur'), but which finds its clearest expression in the following Book ('La Dictature'). We have already seen this argument in Michelet: the men who took it into their heads to save the people, to force the people to be free, were foreign to it. This criticism is primarily directed against the Robespierristes. We must therefore modify the earlier thesis that they systematized the ferocity of the people; it would be more accurate to say that they wanted both to repress and exploit its ferocity so as to replace it with a solemn and orderly programme for domination. This idea is formulated in the first section of Book 18: 'La République classique et la république prolétaire'. Here, Quinet examines the episode of the elimination of the Hébertistes. He has no sympathy for them, and we quickly learn that he does not regard them as being spokesmen for the people. 'Hébert and his co-accused were' he writes, 'the inevitable product of the regime of the Terror: a sick imagination, unbridled and deranged minds, who saw extreme measures as providing the only hope of salvation' (p. 254). There are no grounds for believing their rage to be sincere, or for forgetting their initial dependence upon the Jacobins: '... who removed the brake, who taught them their ferocity, if not those who killed them?' But it is equally certain that, in destroying them, Robespierre and Saint-Just were displaying their hatred of a terrorism which had damaged the ideals in which, being bourgeois men of letters, they believed:

> In crushing the Hébertistes, Saint-Just was crushing the pleb, the obscure masses ... Men who have studied the classics know little of the temperament of the masses, and it is characteristic of them to see the blind passions of the mob as being inspired by foreign agents. (vol. II, p. 253)

And Quinet adds a valuable comment:

> No tribune in the world ever spoke a less popular, more learned or more studied language than Robespierre and Saint-Just. Anyone who tried to speak the language of the people immediately and naturally seemed hateful to them; *that language seemed to them to debase the Revolution*. They always saw the Revolution in terms of the pomp of Cicero and the majesty of Tacitus. (emphasis added)

His comment recalls his earlier remarks about the reasons for the elimination of the Hébertistes:

> Saint-Just punished them for replacing his Lacedaemonian

formulae with the language of the crossroads. It was the classical, lettered revolution of the Jacobins which crushed the uneducated and plebeian revolution of the Cordeliers. Robespierre was acting out a classical tragedy. Anything that went beyond its orderly conventions – life, spontaneity, popular instinct – appeared to him to be a monstrosity. And he attacked it with sword and fire. (p. 225)

The same theme runs throughout this section, and it is particularly clear in the description of the struggle between Saint-Just and Danton, and between Robespierre and Chaumette.

If Quinet is to be believed, the literary transposition of events, and the erection of an ideal stage upon which actors perform carefully rehearsed gestures and speeches, require the annihilation of everything that challenges the nobility of the revolutionary project. In that sense, the conspiracy which haunts the imagination of the Jacobins can also find an abode in the triviality of the real, in the stubborn prose of the quotidian.

But his criticisms do not stop there. It is to be noted that he does not spare the language of the Hébertistes either: 'Anyone who takes the trouble to follow the saturnalia of *Le Père Duchêne* will see that Hébert himself could not grasp the true language of the people; he adds an oath to every declaration, and pretends that this gives him a popular accent. Theatrical rags stitched together with sans-culottes tatters.' We are, then, being asked to see a double idealization, which at once comes from above and from below – an idealization inspired by a *terrible* will to deny the existence of the men and women who effectively make up the people in order to speak and act in the name of the people.

Is Quinet's last comment anything more than an extension of Michelet's reflections? Perhaps not. But it does help him to reach a conclusion which takes him beyond Michelet, as it does not apply to the Jacobins and the Hébertistes alone, or even to the revolutionary factions as a whole. It applies to the very principle of the idealization of the people, a principle which, although it is used to different ends, still governs the interpretations put forward by historians. The lesson is clear: the people should no more be deified than should history, or France. On the contrary, if we are to learn the truth about history, the nation or the people, we must undertake the revolutionary task of demystifying them. Only then will we finally be in a position to detect the origins of the Terror and the power of the beliefs that are still used to justify it.

They sacrifice everything to I know not what idea of a messianic people which demands blood sacrifices. But at that price, all peoples can claim to be messiahs. They all want their violence, their iniquities and their savagery to be worshipped as though

they were sacred ... Let us have done with this bloody mysticism;
let us at least set history free. Ferocity is ferocity, no matter
which people exercises it. It is no longer permissible to be
idolatrous. No more prejudices. No more systems of blood. No
more fetishization of history. No more Caesars or Robespierres,
and no more God-People. Would that our experiences might
teach us to remain human. (pp. 194–5)

When he cries 'No more God-People' and adds that 'The Terror
was the fatal legacy of the history of France', Quinet lends his critique
a vigour which makes him break with all those who claim to be the
heirs of the Revolution, and which distances him from Michelet himself.
No doubt it also helps us to undertand why his work has been so
deliberately, so obstinately *forgotten*.

7

The Revolution as Principle and as Individual

It was in Italy, during the last period of his life, that Joseph Ferrari acquired a certain reputation as a politician. In France, where he settled in 1838 and where he lived for more than twenty years, the audience he found as a philosopher and writer remained, however, very restricted, even though the publication of his major works and his contributions to *La Revue des deux mondes* and *La Revue indépendente* brought him some renown. Being an exile, he was of course in a difficult position, but his main problem was that he clashed with the new 'intellectual power', which did its best to silence him. He was appointed as a philosophy lecturer at the University of Strasbourg, but was soon dismissed on ministerial orders. He did not succeed in passing the philosophy *agrégation*. At the end of 1848, he was appointed to a teaching post in Bourges, but the repression that followed the *journée* of 13 June 1849 forced him to leave his post precipitately before he could be officially dismissed. His independence of mind, the strength of his republican convictions and his refusal to come to terms with Catholicism won him the hostility of the establishment. The fact is that, for his part, he was scarcely tactful in his dealings with the establishment. He was particularly harsh on Victor Cousin, who had momentarily lent him his support, and on those he called the 'salaried philosophers', to use the title of one of his essays. A short passage he devotes to them in his *Machiavel juge des révolutions*, which is the book we will be discussing here, gives some idea of the force of his criticisms.[1] When he evokes the reign of Louis-Philippe, he observes in passing that: 'Philosophy had its policemen, and their leader; a self-professed advocate of the methodical search for success, forced a calculated mixture of erudition and servility on the teaching profession by setting himself up as the sycophant of legend and as the enemy of every free-thinker' (p. 117). True, some great minds thought highly of him. He established links with Proudhon and Leroux, corresponded with Quinet, won the admiration of Barbey d'Aurevilly, and aroused the interest of Baudelaire. But the general public found little of interest in a foreign philosopher who repelled some readers with his apologia for the Revolution – which he thought was still in progress – and others with his pitiless analysis of the errors of the revolutionaries. His words were not designed to please.

The fate that befell Ferrari in his own lifetime is not surprising. What is more surprising is that his *Machiavel* should have fallen into oblivion, as it has more than one claim on posterity's attention. The work has never been reprinted, and one never sees it mentioned; one would look for it in vain in many great libraries. Yet it has a modern flavour which, whilst it might not have appealed to his contemporaries, would have delighted their descendants: the readers Stendhal expected to find. The name is not a random association. Did Ferrari read Stendhal? We do not know. Or did his training as a jurist, together with his vocation as a writer, mean that he shared Stendhal's love of the *Code civil*? Or did he inherit his freedom of tone, his taste for paradox and his liking for surprises – and it is tempting to describe them as Stendhalian – from the author of *The Prince*? Whatever the truth of the matter, his style is sober, concise and sinewy. He eschews emphasis, and does not linger over descriptions or arguments. His essay stands out from political literature of the period. He does not indulge in fine phrases, lyricism or prophecy. He never uses the rhetorical devices we find even in Constant. Tocqueville's grandiose and architectural use of language does not suit him. He addresses the reader without, it sometimes seems, even troubling to try to convince him. He takes no heed of others' objections, and scorns to take the precautions that might disarm his critics. He unpicks the fabric of Machiavelli's discourse and that of the events of his own age with equal dexterity, extracts from them their 'principle' and, once he has found it, hurries to his goal, and writes with the rhythms of a conquering hero. His extensive erudition is that of a historian, in the sense in which the new school understands that term, but his temperament is that of an essayist. He is not afraid to cram the major events in the adventure Italy lived through from the Middle Ages onwards into twenty-five pages, or, when he is dealing with France, to thread together Robespierre, Bonaparte, Charles X, Louis-Philippe, the republicans of 1848 and Louis-Napoleon as though their names formed a rope of pearls which he can place around the neck of the Revolution. And, despite the brevity and apparent linearity of his arguments, he does capture the attention of the reader, who is carried away by a sort of philosophico-political romance which has a very different appeal to a fictionalized history or an illustrated philosophy.

To promote Machiavelli to the status of the judge of modern revolutions may well seem a foolhardy undertaking. Yet, despite the objections the argument comes up against, the approach proves to be more subtle than the title might suggest: Ferrari weaves a meditation upon the conditions of political action into his reading of the facts. His work deploys a very singular space in which events prove to both reveal and generate the meaning of the Revolution, whilst the thought which provides the key for their interpretation – that of Machiavelli – proves to be embedded in history and to be disclosed by its future. The interplay between narrative and criticism supports the idea that the apparent irrationality of history provides, *a contrario*, a confirmation of its logic.

The brilliant unravelling of the Italian imbroglio which takes up the last long chapter of the work is reminiscent of Marx's *Eighteenth Brumaire*. Both authors have mastered the art of demystifying events by examining the ins and outs of political intrigue, the art of the virtuoso analyst who can swivel the stage around to reveal what is happening behind the scenes. Both use irony to reveal the comedy that lies behind the tragedy of history, to reduce supposed heroes to the dimension of their mediocrity, to dissolve the medley of ideologies into the grey tonality of interest and, at the same time, to reveal signs of the ineluctable gestation of a new world. If Ferrari's analyses did not enjoy the same success as those of Marx, it is not for lack of brio or subtlety. It is probably because he does not urge his readers to identify with a subject who will bring about the emancipation of humanity, because he does not mobilize passions and because, unlike Marx, he combines a conviction that events do form an intelligible sequence with a disturbingly detached view of the agents, methods and circumstances of the Revolution.

The following example will illustrate his style. In the penultimate chapter, Ferrari addresses Louis-Napoleon, who has just ousted Cavaignac from the Presidency of the Republic. Machiavelli prompts the argument, but Ferrari certainly makes it his own. Everything is designed to disconcert the reader, be he liberal or socialist. Listen to Ferrari as he suggests to the apprentice dictator that he should base his fortunes on an alliance with the people: 'Imitate the Medicis; rely upon the dregs of society; be the dictator of the plebeians' (p. 121). Listen to him again: 'They will tell you that you were elected by the forces of reaction, but you were elected unanimously. They will tell you that a unanimous vote is an invitation to found an Empire, that it means the proscription of the Republic; know then that the votes of the people are instinctively revolutionary, but that necessity will make them plebeian.' The hypothesis would be less scandalous if the author shared Proudhon's momentary illusions as to the personality of the victor; one might think him naive. He has no such illusions. A moment later, he adds: 'Unfortunately, we have been dreaming here. Louis-Napoleon was brought to power by the forces of reaction' (p. 123). The vision of history in which events unfold logically, even if they do offend morality, is a dream. The unnatural alliance he briefly imagines does of course serve the cause of democracy, and ultimately, we are told, the principle of democracy will overcome all obstacles. But can democrats listen to a voice which mingles the accents of faith with those of cynicism without finding it repellent? Ferrari tells Louis-

Napoleon to free himself from the past:

> Leave these ruins alone ... it is the people who will save you. You need a religion, and it is the people who will provide it ... What was once the religion of a few men of the Renaissance is now the religion of His Majesty the People; the parvenu wants his success to be worshipped ... Hold fast to the religion of the people; it is in the ascendancy, and the new fortunes of the Republic will help you to rise. (pp. 122–3)

His conclusion is still more surprising: 'If the Prince forgets his role, what becomes of the role of the Republic? Machiavelli has the answer: "You must imitate the folly of Brutus." You must continue a discusison they have been calling a folly for eighteen years.' Ferrari offers no solution, and issues no call to action; in his view, those who understand the principle or the science of history accept that they should not draw conclusions or ask questions. 'Democracy's ideas are still confused; they have not yet won over the masses, and they are aspirations rather than doctrines. Seek and ye shall find; strive and ye shall arrive at an immutable system like the principles of 89 or of 1830 and then the mad will triumph'. This strange language does not imply that we have to distance ourselves from the contemporary world, but nor does it sanction the hopes human beings place in the ability of political action to come to grips with the problems of the day. 'In the meantime, no illegality, no insurrection.' Do nothing, he suggests, which an adversary could seize upon as a provocation. And finally, no speculations about catastrophe. The advantages offered by the regime you are fighting are not, he suggests, to be ignored, but the best one can expect of them is that they will generate the conditions for its overthrow. 'They complain at seeing royalists in control of a republic; their presence is useful if they have the means to re-establish credit; it is essential if they declare bankruptcy. When that happens, the time will have come for a republic without royalists.' Ferrari thus combines a serene realism with a confidence in the inevitability of Revolution; a certain cynicism with the ideals of democracy and socialism; and a search for the meaning that lies behind the contingency of events with the idea that humanity has a destiny. He both condemns established religion and places his hopes in something which he still calls a religion – 'the religion of the people', 'natural religion' – but whose faith and doctrines are purely social or political, in the true sense of the word. He wins over certain categories of readers, and then turns them against himself.

But, rather than examining the effects Ferrari's essay had on its readers, let us look at its more unusual features, in both historical and contemporary terms.

Ferrari finds, then, the principles of contemporary history in the work of Machiavelli, and the cradle of the modern Revolution in the Italian Renaissance. It would seem, at first sight, that there is nothing particularly new in this. Machiavelli had for centuries been exploited by those involved in political or politico-religious struggles, either, as was usually the case, in an attempt to discredit an enemy faction or the established authorities by revealing the perfidy of their supposed source of inspiration, or, as happened more rarely, in an attempt to defend the cause of liberty or the thesis of *raison d'état*. The tactic, which had become something of a ritual, appealed to a number of writers during the Revolution and in subsequent years. Both Robespierre and Bonaparte were 'Machiavellianized' in this way. There were many precedents for the invocation of the spirit of Machiavelli, for the pretence that the author was taking down his words or listening to him as he prompted the actors from the wings; Ferrari uses the device at times, and it was to be used many times by later writers. Interpretations based upon a comparison between the French Revolution and some great event that was assumed to have prefigured it had, by the mid-nineteenth century, become something of a tradition. For some writers,like Ballanche and Leroux, it was the birth of Christianity which prefigured the Revolution, but for most it was the Reformation that constituted the first moment in the break between the Old and the New. Conservatives and liberals who had read De Maistre and Bonald, and even Madame de Staël, Constant and Guizot all shared the same conviction, and used it to support their denunciations or their defence of the principles of 1789. After having been extolled as the discovery of liberty or denounced as an act of collective madness, the Revolution finds itself imprinted in history once more. Ferrari, then, simply alters its date of birth. And yet his work stands out from the majority of political pamphlets, and from earlier attempts to reconstruct history. He is not in fact content with borrowing a few striking formulae from Machiavelli and with putting them into the mouths of the great men he execrates or venerates; he produces what is at times a detailed interpretation of his work, and his intention is to discover a latent meaning beneath the manifest meaning. His recourse to Machiavelli is not merely a pretext for polemic; six of the nine chapters are devoted to him. The critical reading implies a new awareness of the temporality of thought. Machiavelli is no longer seen as a spokesman for certain social forces, or as the originator of a political strategy to be used by specific actors; he is shown to be traversed by the contradiction affecting the Italy of his day. In that sense, it is possible to understand Machiavelli only if we investigate the period of the Renaissance, the moment when the project of liberating Italy from the theologico-political model that had come into being under the double authority of Emperor and Pope begins to take shape in both society and culture. The duplicity that has been ascribed to the author of *The Prince* does not, as it has sometimes wrongly been believed, relate to his personality; it reveals his thought's inability to coincide with itself in a world in which a demand for a new right is beginning to be voiced, but in which a belief in the medieval order still persists. That Machiavelli should devote his book to the art of success, that he should be indifferent to the ends pursued by actors, and that he should at the same time dream of the independence and unity of his native Italy is not a sign of his hypocrisy or of his versatility. It reveals that what he cannot grasp is the connection between principle and action, between the historical creation which implies the destruction of the medieval edifice and the forces capable of accomplishing it. It was impossible for him to grasp that connection because the principle had yet to be embodied in reality. Although traditional values had been destroyed, and although a demand for freedom of action, morals and thought had arisen, the work of creation had yet to be taken in hand by the only actors capable of bringing it to a successful conclusion: the masses, who were to place their faith in change. Machiavelli's understanding of his own period enabled him to make predictions, but that in itself did not allow him to understand the principle behind his own work. Renaissance Italy was a privileged arena for all the conflicts that were later to shake the world – class conflicts, political conflicts, conflicts between values – but it was unable to escape the yoke of the double authority of Pope and Emperor. 'At that point, the Renaissance left Italian soil to become the Reformation in Germany and the Revolution in France. Its men, who were useless under Leo X, are now our true contemporaries' (preface). It was a mistake to view Machiavelli as the man who understood the politics of his own time; he has become the man who understands the politics of Ferrari's time, even though he is not in a position to grasp the meaning of his own predictions. He possessed a knowledge which he could not extract from his thought, but the present can set it free. The theories which posterity insists on ascribing to him – and they are contradictory – are of little importance. Ferrari states bluntly that: 'He professes no principles; he is as alien to the Middle Ages he despises as he is to the modern world of which he knows nothing' (ibid). But his experience of the multiple conflicts which arose out of the radical opposition between the Old and the New enables him to perceive the alternatives facing the historical actors, and to grasp the logic which determines whether they will win or lose – and it is this ability which makes him the judge of contemporary history. Without explicitly saying so, Ferrari suggests that, insofar as it is the moment of a new beginning and represents the first flowering of the modern Revolution, the Renaissance contains the developmental law which will govern subsequent events. He further suggests that the new elaboration of a revolutionary discourse had, for its part, the effect of concealing the pre-conditions for a truly political struggle, whereas Machiavelli could discover them at the level of experience alone. It is, he implies, still possible to discover them by reading Machiavelli. Like many other writers, Ferrari does of course invite his readers to go back to Machiavelli in order to find the key that will unlock the doors of the present. But, as we have seen, that is not his only intention. It is modern revolutions that help him to understand the work of the Florentine writer, and that help him to discover the principle that guided him without his knowing it. And the details of the course taken by those revolutions are elucidated by the principle they help him to conceive. The time-difference does not disappear; the interpretation is supported by a philosophy of history.

Whilst the fertility of this approach must be recognized, it is also important to evaluate the interpretation itself. It rapidly becomes apparent that Ferrari's interpretation is governed by one primary thesis: the Revolution is the modern prince. As we know, Gramsci was later to identify the prince with the revolutionary party. He entrusts the party with the mission of translating the aspirations of the proletariat into the language of political realism – the very mission that Machiavelli's hero carried out on behalf of the bourgeoisie. Ferrari, who, unlike Gramsci, refers frequently to Machiavelli's writings (and not only to *The Prince*, but also to the *Discorsi sopra la prima deca di Tito Livio*) tries to make us recognize the Revolution itself as a cunning, omniscient sovereign who exploits his ministers and then abandons them, who combines boldness with prudence, who both strikes suddenly and plays for time, and who, in a word, uses every means to achieve his ends. Such a representation is not unrelated to the representation of Providence that is to be found in the literature of the period, to that of the 'ruses of reason', or even that of the hidden dialectic of communism. But it has a very special character. Ferrari is, as we shall see, inspired by Machiavelli's account of Cesare Borgia's cruel whims, and he seems to erect a stage on which the actors, the heroes of history, are forced to perform and display their talents or their lack of talent at the request of a cruel author-director. To put it more accurately, he portrays the Revolution both as an author in search of characters and of circumstances he can use for his plot, and as a spectator who watches the performance. This is of course a strange fiction, but it does reveal something of the spirit of the times, namely the fantasy that a visionary force or a vision could create a spectacle and make it last until the time finally came for it to vanish with the dawn of democracy or socialism. In that sense, logicism merges with aestheticism.

We must then accept that it is because the Revolution itself is the supreme judge that Machiavelli can be described as the judge of the revolutions of our times. He merely lends the Revolution his voice and, it must be recalled, he does so without realizing it, because he does not understand its principle.

Let us look at how Ferrari describes the Napoleonic adventure in one of the most brilliant passages in his analysis. 'Who is Napoleon?' he asks, and immediately replies, 'Ask Machiavelli' (p. 108). As he sees it, Machiavelli has already portrayed Napoleon: 'Here, we see the new prince.' Or again, 'The general who marches against the fatherland when he has just won victories on its behalf, is the condottiere who, by acting quickly, outwits the suspicions of the Republic which, according to Machiavelli, should be ungrateful, and which, according to Sieyès, *should have him shot* (ibid). Napoleon knows how to govern, how to make the people love and fear him, how to forge an army that is devoted to him, how to surround himself with good advisers, and how to retain his freedom to make decisions, but his position is such that he comes up against the greatest difficulty that any prince can encounter: he appears in the midst of a people which is accustomed to living in a principality, but which has suddenly become free. His fate is bound up with the Republic, but he can expect nothing from its supporters; the only way he can rid himself of his enemies is to establish an almost royal authority. That authority is conferred on him 'by the interests of the new freedom itself' (p. 110). And so, 'His role is mapped out in advance: Napoleon will march against both the old monarchy and the new republic . . .' 'He uses the laws of the Revolution to fight royalism, and the form of the monarchy to fight the Revolution' (p. 111). He creates new names, promotes new men, creates an aristocracy, and founds an empire. But in the long term he falls victim to a contradiction. He is a prince who cannot rule unless religion supplies him with an image that will retain for him the respect of the people; he is torn between the new religion of the Fatherland and the old religion of the kings; he betrays one by signing the Concordat and by demanding to be crowned, and then betrays the other by attacking the Pope. By relying on force of arms, he can subdue Europe. But, once again, he proves unable to choose between the role of the conqueror and the mission of the liberator. He hesitates to put Machiavelli's teachings into practice. Rather than exterminating the dynasties of his enemies and laying waste their kingdoms, he leaves them intact, and therefore stokes up the fires of rebellion everywhere. And when the fortunes of war turn against him, a universal coalition is formed against him. 'This is a republican and a monarchical war, a democratic and royalist war against a man who is neither a republican nor a tyrant' (pp. 113–114). The whole analysis is punctuated with frequent quotations. Machiavelli seems to be spelling out the alternatives, to be tracing a dividing line between the possible and the impossible. He is therefore Napoleon's judge. But finally the curtain rises on a different scene. Like the Girondins, Danton and Robespierre before him, Napoleon falls from power. 'Who then, is the absolute master, the abstract prince to whom so many great victims were sacrificed?' asks Ferrari. 'The Revolution; whenever an instrument becomes odious to it, it breaks it in accordance with Machiavelli's precept that the people should be appeased and stupefied (*satisfatti e stupidi*)' (p. 114).

The new prince is no longer Napoleon, who was momentarily identified with Machiavelli's creation. And nor is the prince a model which can be represented by an ideal actor within the political field; the prince or the true master stands outside that field, and constructs a theatre in which the performers destroy one another. The final image of the people being appeased and stupefied is quite remarkable. It is of course reminiscent of an episode in Borgia's career which is so famous that Ferrari refrains from mentioning it, unless, perhaps, it is that he is reluctant to make an explicit comparison between the Revolution and that haughty, cynical tyrant. Machiavelli describes how, having entrusted a cruel and efficient man with the mission of restoring order in the Romagna – the province had until then been dominated by minor noblemen and robber barons – Duke Valentino took the opportunity to rid himself of his henchman because he feared that his reputation might damage his own. He then restages the execution scene for the reader: 'Cesare waited for his opportunity; then one morning, Remirro's body was found cut in two pieces on the piazza at Cesena, with a bloody knife beside it. The brutality of this spectacle kept the people of the Romagna for a time appeased and stupified.[2] Machiavelli thus invites the reader to take in at a glance both the spectacle and the stupefied public, but he also invites him to imagine Borgia, to imagine the presence of the master as he contemplates the picture he has created. Well aware of the effect he is creating, Ferrari takes the place of Machiavelli, replaces Borgia with the Revolution, and the cruel but unfortunate Remirro with the cortège of illustrious victims who have fallen since 1789. Finally, he leaves his reader to imagine the gaze of the Revolution as it watches the drama it has staged.

Ferrari's critique of Machiavelli appears to be governed by his desire to project the person of the Prince on to the principle of the Revolution. It is based upon a re-evaluation of conflicts whose meaning the Florentine writer failed to recognize, and it therefore implies an attack on the abstract theory which, as a result of that misrecognition, subordinates action to the individual. And yet, the denials which our author forces himself to make, his omissions, and the arbitrary nature of his reconstruction of both the history of Italy and Machiavelli's thought are also worthy of attention. His proofs are designed to promote an aim which he does not mention by name: to provide a figurative representation of the principle of the Revolution which will make concrete the determinations of the modern individual. At the end of the analysis, the Revolution is shown to be more than a force in which the World Spirit is embodied: it is possessed of knowledge, a will and passions, and it acts in secret, motivated by the ambitions of the *parvenu*.

In his attempt to reconstruct the reality of the conflicts which, he claims, Machiavelli mistakenly explains in terms of individuals' appetites for power, Ferrari foregrounds the antagonism between the Guelphs and the Ghibellines, and makes it the motor-force behind Italian history until the nineteenth century. Although he notes at one point that everyone had become a Guelph by the time of the Renaissance, he needs these imaginary actors in order to trace a line of demarcation between the medieval world and the modern world, and to prove that Machiavelli understood neither. He exploits the struggle between the two factions to explain Italy's prolonged subjection to the Popes and Emperors, and does not hesitate to describe one Pope as a Ghibelline because he forms an alliance with Spain or Austria, as though the old principle survived unchanged in the new monarchies, and as though they were imperial in name only. Although he displays a detailed understanding of the history of Florence, he refuses to see that the men whom the defenders of Guelph orthodoxy accused of being Ghibellines in the fourteenth century were 'progressive' elements; that they made a forceful contribution to the emancipation of state power that certain of them formulated the great theses of civic humanism; or, finally, that most of them were *uomini nuovi* who had only recently become citizens and who came into conflict with the conservative faction of the old bourgeoisie. Indeed, Machiavelli is criticized for comparing the upheaval caused by the Ciompi with the plebeian uprisings of the Roman Republic, whereas he should have seen it as an expression of a Ghibelline plot. This extraordinary judgement is designed to suit the purposes of the argument, and the author explicitly contradicts it when, in evoking June 1848, he asks elsewhere: 'What is this struggle? It is the war between the plebeians and the big bourgeoisie of Florence, between the thin people and the fat people, the *Ciompi* and the *popolani*' (p. 119). It is also to be noted that, despite his obstinate desire to discredit Machiavelli's vision of history, he is at one point quite prepared to contrast it with Dante's vision. If Ferrari is to be believed, Dante understood nothing of the times in which he lived, whereas 'Machiavelli ... identifies with the great rebellion ... He understands only republics and lords ... He addresses himself to the Renaissance; he wants it to complete its great task, and it is with that end in view that he teaches it the great art of rebellion' (p. 53).

These inconsistencies would be of little interest, were it not that if we identify them, we will be in a better position to detect the artifice on which Ferrari relies both for his basic criticisms and for his overall project. As we have already said, his basic criticism is that Machiavelli can conceive of nothing beyond the actions of individuals. He therefore confines himself to defining the alternatives that are available to actors, as though they enjoyed complete freedom of action independently of the issues which determine their respective positions. 'Thousands of duplicitous advisers appeared. ... They gave conspirators advice; they informed princes about how conspiracies were developing; every civil-war situation was exhausted by a sort of casuistry' (p. 21). Ferrari takes this observation much further by denouncing the illusion that a subject can free himself, not only from the constraints of any given situation, but also from the constraints imposed on him by his own nature:

The art of success forces the individual to be by turns a liberator and a tyrant, to caress and to kill, to be benevolent and bloodthirsty, as though we could choose to go against our own nature, our own passions and our own ideas, as though our role in the world were not the logical outcome of a primary given which makes it impossible to play both roles. (p. 29)

In a word, he believes that Machiavelli has surrendered to the vertiginous charms of a knowledge which abolishes all the determinations of human beings and things.

Ferrari borrows from Machiavelli only what he can use for his own purposes: a theory of action which he wants to disprove, but which, paradoxically, he reinstates by transposing it on to a different register. He denounces the view that the individual is the master of his actions as a fiction, but takes up the idea of mastery and associates it with the Revolution. Having discredited the art of success which Machiavelli is supposed to have taught his political actors, he in fact reappropriates it in order to reveal its hidden meaning:

There is one thing he did not think of, one goal that he did not foresee, and it is that goal that he attains. Machiavelli's great art is essentially a secret art. Let us divulge the secret. It is an individual art; if we break this symbol of the individual, and replace individuals with principles, we find that Machiavelli has outlined a theory of principles that have succeeded, by which I mean a theory of all the successful revolutions that have taken place in the world. (ibid)

'Let us divulge the secret' ... the formula has already been used to rehabilitate the author of *The Prince*. 'Break the symbol' – this image, which is probably more recent, occurs in a very different register in the work of writers who see the Gospels as a coded history of the French Revolution, and Jesus Christ as the thinly disguised figure of humanity coming into its own presence. But Ferrari does not believe that Machiavelli knows the secret of his own art; unlike Jean-Jacques Rousseau, he does not say that Machiavelli educated peoples whilst pretending to give lessons to princes. Nor does he invoke an emancipatory message which the moderns cannot read. The Revolution speaks through Machiavelli without his realizing it, and it speaks its own name whilst wearing the mask of an individual. We have to recognize that the Revolution has the power that is naively ascribed to the individual. The Revolution is the absolute master, and it has the power to manipulate both human beings and things. It is able to take on any role, and it can combine the viewpoint of the prince with that of the conspirator, as circumstances demand. Although the fiction of an individual who is free to caress or to kill must be rejected, it is a fact, and it has to be recognized as such, that every Revolution 'inspires love before it massacres its enemies; towards the middle of the eighteenth century, the Revolution was haunting the courts and was caressing people; a few years later it turned to killing' (ibid). It is absurd to credit the Prince with having the ability to 'displace centres, wealth and men'; the Revolution, on the other hand, does indeed have that ability.

Our author obviously understands the question formulated at the beginning of *The Prince* – 'How to win and retain power' – to be no more than an introduction to a discussion of the art of success. He has of course explored the whole of Machiavelli's work, and reads it with subtlety. But he wishes to restrict the discussion to this one question. He has been seduced by the representation of a field of force which is objectified by the gaze of the individual who holds the most power, or who aspires to doing so. He falls under the spell of the sequence of hypotheses and choices which reveals the brilliance of the actor. But he refuses to explore the basis of power, or the institution and exercise of power. In his view, the distinction between the republic and the monarchy has no pertinence within the framework of Machiavelli's theory; it is, he believes, only the individual Florentine who prefers the former to the latter. He is therefore unable to understand that it is because of his meditations upon the nature of society that Machiavelli can take the view that, in certain circumstances, the role of a prince is preferable to that of a republic; that, when a ruling class is at its most corrupt, the effects of inequality can be curbed only by royal or quasi-royal authority; and that, for the very same reason, a republic is still the best regime because only a republic can, when conditions are favourable, allow the energies of the people to be mobilized. We said that Ferrari refuses to understand this, but the comparison drawn between different regimes in the *Discorsi* does not in fact escape his notice. He does, however, fail to recognize its import because he cannot grasp the idea that any political society is organized around a central division between the people and the great, between the desire to command and to oppress, and the desire not to be commanded, not to be oppressed. It is the thought of this division which sometimes leads Machiavelli to express the view that the oppression of a ruling class in a republic may be more onerous than the oppression of a prince, because a prince can curb the insolence of the nobility. In more general terms, it is the idea of this division and the critique of the naive belief that a community of interests and aspirations can be embodied in a good government that leads him to look at the various modes of power's insertion into the social whole. Ferrari says nothing about these meditations, about the need for the prince to have a popular base, or about the possibility of an alliance between the prince's desire to dominate, which can only be realized at the expense of the Great, and the people's desire for liberty, which can never be satisfied, but which represents a response to the oppression of the Great. He views Machiavelli's considerations as to the qualities of the prince simply as a lesson addressed to an individual, without seeing that the wiles of the prince are a response to the wiles which constitute power and the social space, because the prince cannot satisfy the people's desire for liberty and at the same time embody the cause of the public good, and because, being unable to dominate without ceasing to be the people, the people are doomed to be deceived. A similar veil is cast over the foundations of princely power and the foundations of the republic. Ferrari regards the model of the Roman Republic as a retrograde utopia. He therefore cannot appreciate the boldness of an analysis which discredits the notions of concord, stability and good government, and which sees social conflict, plebeian uprisings and the demand for liberty as the source of the grandeur of Rome; which destroys the place that is traditionally assigned to the law-giver – the place of an individual who is believed to possess political knowledge; and which reveals the virtues of a power which is challenged, which is condemned to an endless search for its own legitimacy.

This part of Machiavelli's discourse remains opaque to him because of the goal he has set himself. How could he invest the Revolution with the power of the prince, and how could he promote the Revolution to the status of absolute master, if he had to address the question of social division, if he had to accept the idea that power is always *implicated* in the division it overcomes? The only division Ferrari recognizes is a division between two principles, and he places the stage of history under the sign of their antagonism – an antagonism whose outcome is, moreover, known in advance, as the principle of the Revolution is the principle of modernity itself, the conquering principle in which the truth of the future resides.

What is even more striking is that, from this perspective, the question of the content of the principle tends to vanish. Yet Ferrari is most certainly interested in its content. He hints at the advent of a free society, at the disappearance not only of the old monarchical order but also of the inequalities to which modern capitalism gives rise; at the advent of political and social democracy, at its extension beyond the bourgeoisie, and at the completion of the work begun by the proclamation of the rights of man. But a distinction is then introduced betewen the meaning of the Revolution and the idea of its action, and it is this that makes the reconstruction of post-1789 history so curious. Events are judged in terms of the criterion of the principle's *success*, but its ends and its means are not compared. We thus have, for example, not an apologia for the Terror, but a cold evocation of the Terror as an operation that can be deduced from the Revolution, and no discussion of the contradiction between Jacobin oppression and the ideal of liberty. At a more general level, this gives rise to the idea of an inevitable process in the course of which men are crushed by the principle because they cannot serve it to the very end, or because circumstances restrict the choices available to them. In the course of his reconstruction, Ferrari sometimes goes beyond the limitations of his theory, and it would therefore be wrong to restrict discussion to that level. The pages he devotes to describing how the French Revolution always had to be begun anew, and how the Italian Revolution was always blocked are amongst the finest in his work, and they alone justify its interest. He is one of the very few writers to see the sequence of revolutions and coups d'état which began in 1789 as a single historical adventure and to look into its future. Taking his inspiration from Machiavelli, he admirably reveals both the contradictions in which the actors became entangled and their inability to see the ultimate consequences of the choices they made. By silently adopting the very approach he claims to be discrediting, he ironically unveils the misery of a world in which people can be 'neither totally good nor totally evil'. One senses that, having been struck by the mediocrity of Louis-Philippe, he sees the *juste milieu* as a key notion which can be related to that of the *via media*, which Machiavelli denounces so roundly; and that it is this that inspires both Ferrari and his model to make such a corrosive analysis of regimes which cannot find any base in the people. A critique which pursues the historical actors into their own territory in order to pinpoint the moment when their understanding of necessity fails them can therefore eventually be combined with an image of the present as being unable to provide an answer to the problem of democracy, and with the condemnation of both voluntarism and activism in politics. But it is of course because of his outrageous theory that the Revolution dispels all doubts that Ferrari captures our attention so compellingly.

The paradox of a history which is played out behind the backs of human beings and yet still gives them their liberty, the mythology of an invisible power which causes the visible edifices of power to crumble, the transfiguration of the cruelty, stupidity and fear to which the heroes of the Revolution are ultimately condemned into so many signs of the passage of the Revolution, the proud resolve to enter into a pact with the evils of the day – these are elements in an aesthetics of politics which will haunt the modern imagination for a long time to come. It will be recalled that Baudelaire was one of Ferrari's few admirers. Baudelaire thought momentarily of devoting a chapter in his projected essay on literary dandyism to him. That in itself reveals the modernity of a theorist who saw the Revolution as a great individual.

8

Rereading *The Communist Manifesto*

Is is still possible to read Marx? Is it possible to read him without adopting the historian's approach? Is it still possible to find in his writings a stimulus to thought, to establish a dialogue with him, and do the questions he derived from the experience of his time enrich the questions which the experience of our time forces us to address? In my view, there is no doubt as to the answer. The almost incontrovertible fact that Marxism is now in a state of decay does not, as certain frivolous critics believe, mean that Marx's work no longer has anything to say to us. The truth is that his theses are less important than the road he travelled in his attempt to break with the various currents of tradition and to try to understand the new world that was taking shape in nineteenth-century Europe; less important than his attempt to see beyond economic and political institutions, beyond philosophical, religious and moral representations, to grasp the meaning of the practices on which they are based, the principle of their genesis, and, at the same time, to acquire a general understanding of social relations and historical development. There is certainly good reason to believe that the undertaking became embroiled in certain contradictions, and that it gave birth to illusions which later fuelled a totalitarian ideology. But we cannot therefore conclude that the task was undertaken in vain or that only its failure is instructive. Even if it were true that Marx could do no more than oscillate between rationalism and irrationalism, voluntarism and fatalism, extreme subjectivism and extreme objectivism, we would still be faced with the task of assessing his intentions and of discovering how he attempts to overcome those oppositions – and the task is all the more legitimate in that others who came after him also tried to find a formula that could transcend them, and in that we are still looking for it. Even if it were true that he did not succeed in conceptualizing both the specificity of the human world and its implication in the world of nature, or in elaborating a distinction between the real and the imaginary that does not divorce one from the other, we would still have to admit that his work of interpretation still bears the imprint of this objective. Even if we must ultimately denounce his failure to recognize the nature of politics and conclude that it is illusory to reduce it to the effects of class relations which are themselves determined by a mode of production, and even if we resolve that we must return to the great wellsprings of political philosophy, which had, in Marx's view, dried up, we would be wrong to ignore the fact that even that resolve owes a great deal to our acquaintance with his work, and that no serious investigation into the political can escape the question of the social.

Why do I make this distinction between Marx's theses and the body of work which contains them? Because his work, like any intellectual work, cannot be reduced to the assertions it contains. Because we would look in vain for any signs of a rectilinear path leading from a starting point to a conclusion. His work reveals the mark of the obstacles thought creates for itself through the exercise of thought, if it resists the temptations of formal deduction, if it dedicates itself to interpreting that which exceeds it and responds to the attractions of that which eludes its grasp. Whilst theses, because of their assertive power, oblige the implied reader either to accept them or to reject them, a work asks to be read because it opens up the possibility of an intimate debate with the thought that moves through it. It is in that sense that Marx's work still speaks to the reader. Or, to put it another way, it is because Marx is not a Marxist (and we know that he rejected that description with irritation) that he is still alive. A Marxist knows how to define a mode of production, social classes, relations between base and superstructure, and the sequence of social formations. But for Marx, as he is writing, the significance of these concepts is not established in advance; he discovers it by raising questions and through the work of interpretation. Their significance is displaced from one book to another, or even within the space of a single book – especially in *Capital*, the most important of all. He is not afraid of exposing his argument to contradictions, and the digressions he is forced to make when he examines new phenomena reintroduce ambiguities which seemed to have been dispelled. Thus, the notion of the mode of production is shaken by the analysis of oriental despotism. The image of a single history governed by the development of the productive forces breaks down in the face of that of a break between modern capitalism and all precapitalist forms. The idea that social relations finally become transparent in the bourgeois world is contradicted by the description of the 'enchanted world' of capitalism, by the description of large-scale industry as a 'mechanical monster' which makes individuals its organs, and by the image of bourgeois revolutionaries as being haunted by ghosts which whisper their lines to them.

Marx's work does not coincide with itself. Because it opens itself up to the reader in this way, it gives him the ability to explore it, to express doubts or objections, to return to his own concerns as he comes to know it.

But does not this defence of the work of Marx give rise to a further question? Can we still read the *Manifesto*? By 'reading', I do not mean examining it as a document or treating it as an episode in the history of ideas (a view which its author would certainly have rejected); I mean experiencing the attraction that any great text exerts, surrendering to that attraction and forgetting the distance that separates past from present. It might be objected that the question is futile, that we already know the answer in that, although it was planned in collaboration with Engels and written in the name of the Communists, the *Manifesto* is very much part of Marx's *œuvre*, and is, indeed, perhaps the most important part of it. For countless readers all over the world, it contains the founding father's great message; millions of militants lay claim to the science of *Capital*, but this is in fact the only text with which they are familiar. Not only did Marx never reject it; at the end of his life he described it as the best introduction to his work. Yet this is not an adequate answer. For is it contradictory to accept, on the one hand, that we can read the *Manifesto* and compare it with Marx's other writings, provided that we pay attention to everything we find there that undermines its certainties, and, on the other hand, to say that, if we read only the *Manifesto* and apprehend it in itself, it no longer has the power to take hold of us? Well, that is in fact my view.

It is true that this implies that we must revise our initial argument. It is, I said, because he is not a Marxist that Marx is still alive. I observed that he denied being a Marxist, and thus suggested that Marxism is the work of his epigones. This is no more than a half-truth. Once we admit that his thought is irreducible to what Lenin-Marxism, Stalin-Marxism, Trotsky-Marxism and Mao-Marxism have made of it, we have to accept that there is such a thing as Marx-Marxism, and that it finds its purest expression in the *Manifesto*. The *Manifesto* is self-contained; it speaks the truth about the truth, and it leaves the reader outside. It is of course a monument. But is it not Marx's spiritual mausoleum, the mausoleum he built with his pen, and by whose walls only pilgrims may rest?

A thinker's representation of his own work is indeed a strange phenomenon. Marx liked to say that he had abandoned the manuscript of *The German Ideology* to 'the gnawing criticism of the mice'. The mice never appeared, and the book lives on. On the other hand, he expected the *Manifesto* to defy time itself (or at least to last as long as people still felt the need to read it). Perhaps he did give death its due. Perhaps the *Manifesto* simply owes its success to the work of other mice, who carried what has become the holy grail of Communism to mice the world over.

In voicing this opinion, I am not suggesting that the doctrine has its good side and its bad side. That suggestion would still involve us in a Marxist debate which has, I believe, lost all its legitimacy. I am suggesting something very different, namely that we must recognize the existence of Marx the thinker, without concealing the fact that he himself stifled his own thought in order to attain an invulnerable knowledge and that, in attempting to occupy that position, he colluded in the adventure that befell him as Marxist science became conjoined with a power striving to make itself invulnerable. In that respect, the status of the *Manifesto* seems quite remarkable. At this moment, Marx seems momentarily to have stopped thinking, as it were, or even to have tried not to think in order to describe things as they really are, to describe the course of history as though it were simply waiting to be named. The power of illusion is of course immense. But once it has been dispelled, we see only the artifices of a painting in which we find no more than signs of a style and a period.

In an early comment on the decline of Marxism, Merleau-Ponty attempts to uncover the thought that lies buried beneath the ideology. In the introduction to *Signs*, he writes:

> The history of thought does not summarily pronounce: This is true; this is false. Like all history, it has its veiled decisions. It dismantles or embalms certain doctrines, changing them into "messages" or museum pieces. There are others, on the contrary, which it keeps active ... because, as obligatory steps for those who want to go further, they retain an expressive power which exceeds their statements and propositions. These doctrines are the *classics*. They are recognizable by the fact that no one takes them literally, and yet new facts are never absolutely outside their province but call forth new echoes from them and reveal new lustres in them. We are saying that a re-examination of Marx would be a meditation on a classic, and that it could not possibly terminate in a *nihil obstat* or a listing on the Index.[1]

When I read these lines for the first time, I was immediately convinced. They still seem pertinent today, subject to one proviso: history has changed Marx into a classic, but it has also embalmed the element of Marxism in his work. It has changed the *Manifesto* into a museum piece.

The *Manifesto* opens with a preamble informing us as to its character and function. Let us recall its starting point: 'A spectre is haunting Europe – the spectre of Communism. All the powers of old Europe have entered into a holy alliance to exercise this spectre' (p. 80).[2] This is apparently a statement of fact. Marx draws two conclusions: firstly, that Communism is universally recognized as a power (the hatred and fear it inspires are adequate proof of that – lies and legends cannot conceal an incontrovertible fact); and, secondly, that 'It is high time that the Communists should openly, in the face of the whole world, publish [*offen darlegen*] their views, their aims, their tendencies ...' Marx does not put forward these conclusions in his own name: 'To this end,' he writes, 'the Communists of various nationalities have assembled in London, and sketched the following manifesto ...' The author remains in the background; he is merely a mouthpiece for the Communists. The reader remains ill-defined: the Communists are publishing their views, their aims and their tendencies in the face of the whole world. The *Manifesto* claims to be a pure exposition. And it is an exposition in a more profound sense than the word itself might suggest. It is published in the face of the whole world, and it is an exposition of the world itself; the movement of those who are emerging into the full light of day for the first time causes the world itself to appear in all its visibility. It soon becomes apparent that the Communists are not formulating their views, aims and tendencies from within a particular position; although they are publishing in the face of the world, they are not, paradoxically enough, distanced from the world. By appearing in the face of the world, they can reveal the world as essence, regardless of what it may appear to be in the imagination of human beings who find themselves in the world in a historically and socially determined manner. As the second part of the opuscule states: 'The theoretical conclusions of the Communists are in no way based on ideas or principles that have been invented, or discovered, by this or that would-be universal reformer. They merely express, in general terms, actual relations springing from an existing class struggle, from a historical movement going on under our very eyes' (p. 80). The *Manifesto* claims to be an exposition in the most absolute of senses. Marx is not expounding the theory of the Communists, and they are not expressing their own views; it is the world and history which are expressing themselves through them. The *Manifesto* simply asks us to open our eyes and to look at what is happening, at, that is, what is coming into being and what is appearing.

The first three sections seem to correspond to a division between three moments in the exposition of the Communists' position: views, aims and tendencies. But it requires a further two sections to expound their so-called views, because they are intended to be a pure representation of what is visible in the here and now, and to make visible the entire movement of history. The exposition of the Communists' aims cannot but be an exposition of the aims of the movement of history, and the exposition of their tendencies, which differentiate them from other tendencies within socialism, cannot but be an exposition of the division history makes between those it enables to discover its tendencies, and those who remain trapped by an illusion.

The vision of that which exists, of that which is coming into being, sweeps all before it because it must coincide with the actual reality of the emerging world. It obscures Marx's specific position, but it also obscures that of the proletariat, as its sole destiny is to provide a self-representation of its own appearance in history, to act in accordance with the goal that has been assigned to it. Finally, this vision goes so far as to abolish the position of the class enemy, whose lies do not indicate its supposed ability to understand the reasons behind its interests and its struggle, but the fact that the mode of its insertion into history and its historically determined condition do not allow it to see itself, and condemn it irredeemably to dwell in obscurity.

And so, in the middle of a passage in the second section, in which he attempts to use scorn and irony to demolish the objections of the bourgeois, Marx suddenly breaks off what seemed to be a dialogue:

> But don't wrangle with us as long as you apply, to our intended abolition of bourgeois property, the standard of your bourgeois notions of freedom, culture, law, etc. Your very ideas are but the outgrowth of the conditions of your bourgeois production and bourgeois property, just as your jurisprudence is but the will of your class made into a law for all, a will whose essential character and direction are determined by the economical conditions of the existence of your class. The selfish misconception that induces you to transform into eternal laws of nature and of reason the social forces springing from your present mode of production and form of property – historical relations that rise and disappear in the progress of production – this misconception you share with every ruling class that has preceded you. What you see clearly in the case of ancient property, what you will admit in the case of feudal property, you are of course forbidden to admit in the case of your own bourgeois form of property. (p. 83)

There is, then, no point of view to defend, to put forward against that of the enemy. Marx sees the reality behind the bourgeois; he sees what the bourgeois cannot see, not because he hides it from himself, but because he is, by virtue of his class position, denied self-knowledge. This is also one of the few passages in which Marx allows himself to indulge in argument and polemic. The way in which he then abandons that tactic is therefore all the more remarkable. Polemic and argument imply the presence of an interlocutor, but the *Manifesto*, which appears to expound the Communists' theory and which in fact makes way for an exposition of bourgeois society, of history and of the world, cannot with impunity admit the presence of the word of another; it cannot evoke anyone who is a speaking subject. Hence the paradox we mentioned earlier: although the *Manifesto* is published in the face of the whole world, it is, despite appearances, addressed to no one. Its discourse is deployed in the pure element of generality. It is not intended to convince; it exhibits a truth which resides in things themselves, in their development.

True, this does exempt Marx from having to claim, either on his own behalf or on that of the Communists, to be the leader of the revolutionary forces, or from having to announce the formation of a party which will supplant other parties, and which can claim to have a monopoly on political power. If Marx is to be believed, the

Communists are in fact destined to exercise no more than a sort of spiritual power, if we can use that sacrilegious expression by way of an illusion to Saint-Simon and Comte. As the second section tells us: 'The Communists do not form a separate party opposed to other working-class parties. They have no interests separate and apart from those of the proletariat as a whole' (p. 79). In that sense, it has rightly been noted that the Leninist conception of the party is quite alien to the spirit of Marx. But it is still true to say that an unprecedented adventure is being played out at the level of knowledge, and that it would be foolish to deny that it has effects at the level of action. The *Manifesto* posits a coincidence between the real and the rational, and one would look in vain for even a trace of this notion in the philosophy of Hegel, who does not confuse what he terms the real with the details of historical events, and who does not invest any social actor with the function of embodying the universal or of realizing the concept in the sensible experience of a class. It has of course also been pointed out that Marx maintains a precious distinction between theory and practice. Theory is the concern of the Communists. The proletariat alone is the actor, for the movement of history is imprinted on it. The Communists are not there to teach it lessons. But there cannot, by definition, be anything in practice that escapes theory, for practice encompasses theory as its own expression. What theory cannot designate is the face of the future, of the society in which the old relations of domination and exploitation will be abolished. But its refusal to make predictions by no means implies that it recognizes its own limitations, for that which cannot yet be represented is strictly predetermined in the present. The proletariat cannot give birth to a society which does not conform to its nature, and its nature is such that nothing within it remains opaque. Even supposing that the proletariat does fail in its mission – a hypothesis which is not even mentioned – the only effect of its failure will be regression.

Communism is such an obvious fact that it cannot tolerate any description of what is to come. But the description of the world which is appearing before our very eyes leaves us in no doubt as to its gestation or as to its results. The primary objective of the refutation of bourgeois objections which takes up most of the second section is to show that, whilst they serve to defend specific interests, they are also part of an argument which presupposes the ineluctable development of Communism. Marx's irony echoes the irony of history, which means that the bourgeois's every objection rebounds against him, and that the refutation of Communism can in its turn be refuted. The bourgeois are outraged at the idea of abolishing private property. Marx replies that, if by 'property' they mean the fruit of a man's own lasbour or the ground work of all personal freedom, activity and independence. 'There is no need to abolish it; the development of industry has to a great extent already destroyed it, and is still destroying it daily' (p. 80). If they mean modern bourgeois private property, he replies that it is not purely personal but social. The capitalist has no individual existence; he is the agent of capital, which is a social power, and it is only its social character that the Communists wish to transform. More generally, it is pointless to criticize them for wanting to abolish private property, for private property is already done away with for nine-tenths of the population. Are the theses on abolishing the family, on the community of women or on education scandalous? Quite apart from the fact that the bourgeois family is based upon capital, on private gain, and that this state of things finds its complement in the practical absence of the family amongst the proletarians, and in public prostitution, the bourgeois sees in his wife a mere instrument of production, and bourgeois marriage is in reality a system of wives in common. As for education, the fact that it is already determined by social conditions proves that the Communists have not invented the intervention of society in education; they are concerned solely with rescuing children from the influence of the ruling class. They are further reproached with the crime of desiring to abolish countries and nationality. But capitalism has given birth to the proletariat, to a class which has no country and no ties. How can Communism be criticized for taking away from it what it has not got?

In a word, the Communists have invented nothing. They are simply demonstrating how consequences arise out of premises. Of course they are calling for a revolution! But in doing so, they are simply saying what they have to say because of a necessity which is inherent in language and thought, and which reflects the necessity of social production. Insofar as they are a group, it is not for them to command the proletariat; insofar as they are individuals, it is not for them to rally to it, enrol in its ranks or espouse its cause. Although he is an intellectual, Marx has no inkling of the drama intellectuals will have to face when they are torn between the feeling that they belong to the bourgeoisie, their awareness of being 'bastards' [*salauds*], and the attractions of commitment. It is because he is speaking from within theory that he knows with much certainty that he is caught up in the practice of the proletariat, just as it is through his own practice that the worker discovers himself to be a theorist. Revolutionary speech is as *natural* as revolutionary action; both are involved in a natural history.

A *natural* history? It is indeed a process whose developmental laws can be known, but knowledge is part of the process itself, and its laws account for the fact that it becomes intelligible at this moment in history. As Marx asks:

Does it require deep intuition (*Bedarf es tiefer Einsicht*] to comprehend that man's ideas, views and conceptions, in one word, man's consciousness, change with every change in the conditions of his material existence, in his social relations and in his social life? What else does the history of ideas prove, than that intellectual production changes its character in proportion as material production is changed? The ruling ideas of each age have ever been the ideas of its ruling class. (p. 85)

In other words, there is nothing which is not visible; nothing is more *profound* than that which is manifested materially; men's ideas are a skin which is produced and transformed at the same time as the social tissue it covers. There is no need to probe into the past; nothing in the past is concealed from contemporaries because, in every age, everything formed a whole and was governed by the same movement; and because, as a result of that movement, everything changed at the same time, and was necessarily ordered into a new form. This change in form can be seen on the surface of the present because the material, social and intellectual organization of the present reveals the marks of the dissolution of the previous organization, and because the latter itself resulted from the dissolution of the organization that went before it.

Those who reject the image of a metamorphosis in intellectual production will of course evoke the constants of the human mind. For them it is not enough to admit that the decline of the ancient world and the advent of feudal society explain the rise of the Christian religion, or that the decline of that religion and the expansionof the bourgeoisie explain the rise of the idea of the Enlightenment, or, more specifically, that 'the ideas of religious freedom and freedom of conscience merely gave expression to the sway of free competition within the domain of knowledge' (p. 85). Marx therefore takes their argument into consideration: 'Undoubtedly, it will be said, religious, moral, philosophical and juridical ideas have been modified in the course of historical development. But religion, morality, philosophy, political science and law constantly survived this change. There are, besides, eternal truths, such as freedom, justice, etc. that are common to all states of society. But communism abolishes eternal truths ...' (pp. 85–6) Its answer is that, given that all past societies were organized around class antagonisms, it is 'no wonder ... that the social consciousness of past ages, despite all the multiplicity and variety it displays, moves within certain common forms, or general ideas, which cannot completely vanish except with the total disappearance of class antagonism' (p. 86). The vision of history in which nothing remains in shadow itself proves, then, to be inscribed within the movement which, having displaced the terms of the antagonism, now generates the conditions of its resolution.

So long as Marx was ironically refuting the objections of his adversaries, one could still suppose that his refusal to define a non-bourgeois liberty, morality or law was a precautionary measure. No such doubts are permissible when he explicitly rejects what he calls eternal truths. He does, of course, state that the old bourgeois society will be replaced by 'an association, in which the free development of each is the condition for the free development of all' (p. 87). But at this point, the word 'free' is as meaningless as the earlier assertion that all production will be concentrated 'in the hands of a vast association of the whole nation'. One would attempt in vain to seize upon these declarations in order to promote a democratic or libertarian interpretation. Other texts may well provide a basis for such an interpretation, but not the *Manifesto*. When he refers to the 'free development of each and all', Marx simply means that there will be no restrictions on the development of the productive forces. He does not accept that, in order to be free, one must want to be free, that freedom is something other than a state. And his conception of association – which is in fact quite widespread in so-called utopian literature – leaves no room for individuals who can apprehend themselves as individuals, who can demand the right to be unique and different from everyone else; Communist society appears to be a natural society, just as the whole of history appeared to be a natural history. It is for precisely the same reason that the ideas of freedom and law are said to have arisen in order to guarantee and mask the practice of a ruling class, and that they are said to be destined to vanish in a world which has been freed from class divisions. We are, then, left with a paradox: the history of humanity, which unfolds in its entirety before the eyes of the Communists, leads to a society *without ideas*, to a society which coincides with itself to such an extent as to preclude the possibility of judgements being formulated within it. This is why Marx refuses to imagine what it will look like: its existence is sufficient unto itself. It precludes all self-representation; it cannot be said to be free and just, and it cannot describe itself as such. And this paradox reveals the *Manifesto* to be a fantasmagoria, for how can Marx take the *liberty* of conceiving of humanity as being one, as remaining the same throughout its metamorphoses, and by what *right* can he speak of oppressors and oppressed, of the struggle of the oppressed for their emancipation, unless he recognizes that liberty and right are at work in history?

Why does Marx's naturalism escape notice? Because it is half-concealed behind a dramatic composition. The *Manifesto* does not, as we know, begin with a description of what anyone with eyes to see can see at once, or of what we will subsequently learn, namely that the movement of material production is accompanied by a sequence of social and intellectual transformations. The first section opens with a description of a procession of classes which have come into conflict:

> The history of all hitherto existing society is the history of class struggles. Freeman and slave, patrician and plebeian, lord and serf, guildmaster and journeyman, oppressor and oppressed, stood in constant opposition to one another, carried out an uninterrupted, now hidden, now open fight, a fight that each time ended, either in a revolutionary reconstitution of society at

large, or in the common ruin of the contending classes. (pp. 67–8)

It has often been pointed out that elements in Marx's picture are borrowed from the Saint-Simonians and that it is in many respects inaccurate (the most significant error is the description of the first bourgeois as the descendants of serfs), but we will not dwell on the details here.[3] The remarkable thing about it is that Marx demonstrates the unity of humanity and the continuity of history by describing a war which has been going on since the very earliest times and which is still going on. The protagonists change, but the war always has the same character. Indeed, if the oppressed do not emerge victorious from the battle and do not establish a new order, or if the adversaries succeed only in exhausting one another, the war requires new combatants. The class war is, then, always beginning anew. It is a single war fought out in many episodes, and it is a sort of civil war in that its one theatre is the human 'city'. In modern times, the meaning of the drama becomes clear, and, for the first time, the meaning of its dénouement can be glimpsed. The present proves to be an extension of the past; bourgeois society reveals the conflict between oppressors and oppressed in that: 'It has but established new classes, new conditions of oppression, new forms of struggle in place of the old ones' (p. 68). The reason that we can now say this is that what was once hidden is now fully visible, that everything is now moving in the same direction and is governed by the same antagonism. Whereas societies were once heterogeneous, and whereas the dividing line between the ruling class and the ruled was once blurred by a tangled web of links of dependency, bourgeois society 'has simplified the class antagonisms'. Society is 'splitting into two great hostile camps'. From now on, the duel will be fought out on the forestage. In the past, social transformations took place so slowly that it was impossible to perceive their sequence, but history is now speeding up, and change is taking place before our very eyes. Whereas change once took place within a limited framework, the whole world has now been subordinated to its accelerated rhythms, and it has been set ablaze by the class struggle. And whilst the bourgeoisie is merely a substitute for the ruling classes of old, its behaviour is radically different. Once they had established themselves, the old ruling classes were concerned solely with their own self-preservation; the bourgeoisie is carried away by its enthusiasm for destruction and innovation. It is of course a class which succeeds other classes *in* history, but history is imprinted on it, and it has made change the very principle of its existence. It is indeed the product of a revolution which was the last link in a long chain of revolutions,but it has not left that revolution behind it. The part it plays is, as Marx notes, 'a most revolutionary part': no tradition can withstand it. It has torn asunder the feudal ties which bound man to his natural superiors. It recognizes only naked self-interest. 'It has drowned the most heavenly ecstasies of religious fervour, of chivalrous enthusiasm, of philistine sentimentalism, in the icy water of egotistical calculation' (p. 70). There are no limits to its conquests. As a result, men lose their ties with the land, and with their nation; their relations become universal; both material production and intellectual production are reduced to the same common denominator. Even the most barbarian nations are swept into the vortex. 'In one word, it creates a world after its own image' (p. 71).

Marx paints a veritable portrait of the bourgeoisie. This modern conqueror destroys everything that stands in its way, and it allows no trace of the past to survive; but at the same time it unleashes the formidable creative power which humanity possessed without realizing it. The bourgeoisie 'has been the first to show what man's activity can bring about. It has accomplished wonders far surpassing Egyptian pyramids, Roman aqueducts, and Gothic cathedrals; it has conducted expeditions that put in the shade all former exoduses of nations and crusades' (p. 70). 'The bourgeoisie, during its rule of scarce one hundred years, has created more massive and more colossal productive forces than have all preceding generations together' (p. 72). As Marx asks, 'What earlier century had even a presentiment that such productive forces slumbered in the lap of social labour?' (p. 72).

Under the rule of this conqueror humanity serves its apprenticeship in disenchantment. The social itself is revealed in all its plasticity beneath the apparent rigidity of the institutions which assign everyone a position and a function; the historical itself is revealed by the incessant movement of the consumption of the past. 'All that is solid melts into air, all that is holy is profaned, and man is at last compelled to face with sober senses, his real conditions of life, and his relations with his kind' (pp. 70–1). Disenchantment and the inevitable experience of reality are one and the same. But seeing reality does not mean accepting the established order; it means dispelling the illusion that the bourgeoisie can maintain its rule by pursuing its work of creation–destruction, that it can go on retreating behind class barriers and continue to exclude the exploited masses from the process of socialization at a time when all hierarchies are breaking down.

Marx uses his description of bourgeois society to outline the plot of a *Bildungsroman*. But it is a very strange novel, for if the hero is to understand its moral, his nature must be such that nothing in the past appeals to him and that nothing in the present gives him the illusion that he exists; his temporality and his sociability must be pulverized. Such is the almost unrepresentable figure of the proletariat. It is because it *sinks* deeper and deeper below the conditions of existence of the exploited in earlier societies (and as it sinks, all intermediate classes fall into its ranks), because it has no family, national or religious ties, that the proletariat can find its way to revolution and Communism solely as a result of its struggle against the threat of death. For our purposes the history of its gradual transformation into a fighting, self-conscious and political class is of little import; we will simply note that, unlike *Capital*, the *Manifesto* does not see the development of bourgeois society or its role in large-scale industry as the basis of the proletariat's strength. It is purely because it is crushed by its social existence that it rises, and when it does rise, that will be sufficient to bring about a total revolution: 'The proletariat, the lowest stratum of our present society, cannot stir, cannot raise itself up, without the whole superincumbent strata of official society being sprung into the air' (p. 78).

Marx's naturalism is, we noted, half-concealed behind a dramatic composition. But could we not also say that the drama, the plot and the hero take on a certain consistency only because the description of how relations of production emerge from the natural development of the productive forces speaks to our imagination? Thus, in one single passage, Marx describes bourgeois society as having conjured up gigantic means of production and of exchange – he compares it to a sorcerer who is no longer able to control the powers of the nether world he has called up – and then, without any transition, reverts to the language of strict determinism, describing the clash of modern productive forces against the relations of production as the condition for the existence of the bourgeoisie and its rule. More generally, the two dramas tend to overlap, and it is the artificial parallelism between them that fosters the illusion that history is visible in its entirety. But it takes a great deal of credulity to cling to that illusion, for each drama has its own logic, and each contradicts the truth of the other. In one, the bourgeoisie is transformed into a sorcerer; in the other it appears as a spineless and unresisting agent of the progress of industry.

Finally, we cannot explain why the *Manifesto* has such a lasting appeal for such a wide audience if we do not take into account the eloquence of its author, who so carefully stands back from his discourse or painting. He accomplishes a minor miracle: he seems to take in the whole of history at a glance, and the truth is heard as a single sentence in which the words philosophy, economics, politics and morality mingle. Marx combines a prodigious talent for vulgarizing knowledge with a particular gift for moving his reader. Not that Marx is attempting to make anyone sympathize with the sufferings of the proletarians. He only mentions their sufferings in passing; and in the final section he criticizes utopians for caring chiefly for 'the most suffering class'. He wants to set the heart of the mind beating to the sound of the drums of knowledge. He describes a succession of contending classes, the stages of capitalism from the discovery of America to the advent of large-scale industry, the successive assaults made by the productive forces on property relations (the latter 'became no longer compatible with the already developed productive forces; they became so many fetters. They had to be burst asunder; they were burst asunder', (p. 72), and the successive forms of proletarian organization ('And that union, to attain which the burghers of the Middle Ages, with their miserable highways, required centuries, the modern proletarians, thanks to railways, achieve in a few years' (p. 76). At times the rhythm of the narrative reminds one of a military parade, at times of the flow of a river, and at times of the inexorable movement of a machine. The spellbound reader has no option but to follow, or to beat a cowardly retreat into the ruins of the past. And Marx foresees even that option. The section devoted to 'Socialist and Communist Literature' forbids the reader to feel any nostalgia. The *Manifesto* proceeds to make a rigorous purge of all claimants to a revolutionary theory that is tinged with sentimentality. It categorizes them, ascribing to each his degree of immaturity, illusion or complicity with the decadent classes, and then removes the lader on which they seem to have perched. For the present words and the present gaze can only be born of the very spectacle, the very discourse of history.[4]

Part III

On Freedom

9

Reversibility

Political Freedom and the Freedom of the Individual

Tocqueville's opinion of the role played by men of letters in the eighteenth century and of the responsibility they bear in preparing for the Revolution is well known. As a result of their influence, 'Every public passion was disguised . . . as a philosophy; in literature, political life was violently repressed' (AR, vol. I, p. 193).[1] Less attention has been paid to the reflections he is inspired to make by the appearance of a new category of theorists 'who are commonly termed economists or physiocrats'. Tocqueville accepts that they did not exert the same influence as the *philosophes*, but it is, he believes, in their writings that 'we can best study the true nature' of the Revolution. Indeed, he goes further:

> In their books, we can already recognize the revolutionary and democratic temperament we know so well; not only do they loathe certain privileges; diversity itself is hateful to them; and they would worship equality even if it meant servitude. Anything that stands in the way of their projects is fit only for destruction. Contracts inspire little respect in them; they have no regard for private rights; or rather, and to speak more truthfully, private rights are, in their view, already a thing of the past; all that remains is public utility. (Ibid., p. 210)

They do not, we are told, wish to stir up the people or to destroy the monarchy; on the contrary, they display a love of authority and order. Our author happily describes them as 'men of gentle and tranquil manner, wealthy men, honest magistrates and skilful administrators'. What lies behind their concern for public utility? A complete indifference to political freedoms. The remarkable thing is that this indifference goes hand in hand with a strong attachment to economic freedoms: 'They are, it is true, very much in favour of free trade in goods, and of laissez-faire or laissez-passez policies in trade and industry; but as for political freedoms in the true sense of the word, they never think of them, and whenever they impinge upon their imaginations, they immediately dismiss them' (ibid.).

There is no need to follow Tocqueville's argument or to take up the question of the kinship he detects between the conceptions of these wealthy men and 'the destructive theories which, in our day, are designated by the name of socialism' (p. 213). It is enough to recall that there is an essential difference between political liberalism, as formulated by Tocqueville, and economic liberalism. He does not hesitate to recognize that the latter may ally itself with despotism; the view that free institutions and respect for the rights of individuals are indissociable is part of his critique of omnipotent power. In that respect, Tocqueville's sensibilities are similar to those of Benjamin Constant or Madame de Staël, or to those of a small number of his French contemporaries. What distinguishes him from them is, however, his understanding of the dynamic of the modern state, and of the new characteristics of despotism. Whereas Constant confines himself to a critique of the absolute sovereignty of the people, couches it in speculative terms, and regards the composition of a model in which individual interests disappear before the general interest simply as a mistake, or as a sign of a return to the past, Tocqueville detects within it aspects of 'the revolutionary and democratic temperament we know so well'. His observations are not restricted to the comment that 'Finding nothing close to home that seems to conform to [their] ideal, they [the economists] look for it in distant Asia'. He elaborates the idea of a form of power which is no longer content to demand obedience from all its citizens, which takes it upon itself to transform them or even to produce them:

> According to the economists, the role of the State is not merely to govern the Nation, but to shape it in a certain fashion; it is the task of the State to shape the minds of its citizens in accordance with a model that has been proposed in advance; its duty is to imbue their minds with certain ideas, and to inspire in their hearts such feelings as it judges necessary. In reality, no restrictions are placed upon its rights, and there are no limits as to what it can do; it does not merely reform men, it transforms them; and, if need be, it will simply create other men. (Ibid., p. 212)

These remarks are closely related to those made in the last section of *Democracy in America*, even though the image of a tutelary state and that of a state which attempts to create a society and men in accordance with a preconceived model do not overlap completely. The writer is convinced that the economists' project is gradually being imprinted on the real; a project of absolute power is being combined with a project of knowledge and production which applies both to society as a whole and to individuals. His intuitive understanding of the process that is at work goes further:

The immense social power of which the economists dream is not only greater than any power they see before them; its origins and its character are different. It does not derive directly from God; it is not part of a tradition; it is impersonal; its name is no longer the King, but the State; it is not a family heirloom; it is the product and the representative of all, and it must bend the rights of each to the will of all. (Ibid., p. 216)

In my view, there can be no doubt about it: Tocqueville has pinpointed an event which marks the irruption of an unprecedented domination, one which is so novel that, as he observes in *Democracy in America*, 'the old words *despotism* and *tyranny* are inappropriate' (DA, vol. II, p. 318).[2] The ability to transform the men who attach themselves to power proves, paradoxically, to be bound up with the mode of its generation within society. In that sense, it fully merits the name *social power*. When it is divorced from the person of the prince, freed from the transcendental agency which made the prince the guarantor of order and of the permanence of the body politic, and denied the nourishment of the duration which made it almost natural, this power appears to be the power society exercises over itself. When society no longer recognizes the existence of anything external to it, social power knows no bounds. It is a product of society, but at the same time it has a vocation to produce society; the boundaries of personal existences mean nothing to it because it purports to be the agent of all.

The apparent impersonality masks an unprecedented division between 'all' and 'each'. The 'all' is condensed into the organ of power, whilst 'each' individual is defined as being equal to every other individual, and therefore loses his own individuality. We therefore have a picture of: 'A people composed of individuals who are almost alike and entirely equal, an undifferentiated mass which is recognized as the sole legitimate sovereign, but which is carefully denied all the faculties that might allow it to direct and supervise its government. Above it there stands a single representative who is mandated to do everything in its name without consulting it' (AR, vol. I, p. 213).

To whom is Tocqueville addressing himself when he spells out the danger of modern despotism, when he remarks in *Democracy in America* that: 'I have always thought that servitude of the regular, quiet and gentle kind which I have just described might be combined more easily than is commonly believed with some of the outward forms of freedom, and that it might even establish itself under the wing of the sovereignty of the people' (vol. II, p. 319)? Presumably a writer is always speaking to an indeterminate reader who exists in both the present and the future. It should also be noted that we now have a wealth of experience that allows us to understand Tocqueville better than his contemporaries could understand him, and that the picture he paints must have seemed all the more outrageous in his day in that the signs of the extension of social power and equality were minimal, in comparison with the spectacle offered by the society in which we live. But it is still true to say that, either consciously or unconsciously, any writer privileges certain interlocutors or adversaries. Tocqueville is addressing himself primarily to men who thought they were liberals and who, like him, belonged to an enlightened elite, who regarded the upheaval in property ownership that had been brought about by the French Revolution and by the Rights of Man as a *fait accompli*; but who were haunted by the threat of the extension of political freedoms and individual freedoms, by the fear that the social body would break up, by a fear of anarchy; who believed that a strong government would protect tranquillity, but who failed to foresee the rise of despotism. It is with them in mind that he asks: 'Amid the ruins which surround me shall I dare to say that revolutions are, not what I most fear for coming generations?' (DA, vol. II, p. 329), and that he states: 'I am convinced ... that anarchy is not the principal evil that democratic ages have to fear, but the least' (ibid., p. 288). He adds: 'The love of public tranquillity becomes at such times [after a revolution] an indiscriminate passion, and the members of the community are apt to conceive a most inordinate devotion to order' (ibid., p. 301). With the same people in mind, he states: 'In our days, men ... attend only to the amazing revolution that is taking place before their eyes, and they imagine that mankind is about to fall into perpetual anarchy. If they looked to the final consequences of this revolution, their fears would perhaps assume a different shape' (ibid., pp. 314–15). And again: 'A great many persons at the present day are quite contented with this sort of compromise between administrative despotism and the sovereignty of the people; and they think they have done enough for the protection of individual freedom when they have surrendered it to the power of the nation at large' (ibid., p. 319). It need scarcely be stressed that Tocqueville had no sympathy for revolutions. As a race, revolutionaries seemed to him to be hateful. In 1848, he shared the emotions of his class, and he saw in the origins of the proletarian insurrection no more than 'a mixture of greedy ideas and false theories.'[3] His encomia of the freedom of the press, of the civil and political associations and of the universal suffrage he sees in America are always tempered by cautious reservations. His ability to break out of the circle of his prejudices is therefore all the more remarkable. In his view, democracy's prime virtue is its characteristic agitation, and not its potential ability to facilitate the selection of the best and to improve the government's ability to conduct public affairs. Whilst he agrees that the people often conduct their affairs very badly, he does not see that as something to be condemned, since it seems to him that the agitation which reigns in the political sphere spreads to the rest of society: it encourages initiative in every domain by promoting the circulation of ideas and by expanding everyone's field of curiosity. 'This ceaseless agitation which democratic government has introduced into the political world influences all social intercourse. I am not sure that, on the whole, this is not the greatest advantage of democracy; and I am less inclined to applaud it for what it does than for what it causes to be done' (DA, vol. I, p. 251). A later comment is even more lucid: 'Democracy does not give the people the most skilful government, but it produces what the ablest governments are frequently unable to create: namely, an all-pervading and restless activity, a superabundant force, and an energy which is inseparable from it and which may, however unfavourable circumstances may be, produce wonders' (ibid., p. 252). He does, of course, consistently contrast the democracy that is to be found in Europe, where it has been 'abandoned to its lawless passion' (ibid., p. 11) with that to be found in America, where 'it has been able to spread in perfect freedom' (ibid., p. 13). And yet, even assuming that the function of the initial comparison is simply to win over his readers – 'timid minds' who are afraid that reforms might lead to anarchy – he is so carried away by the logic of his principles that he puts forward a formula which, in my view, expresses his thought admirably: 'Thus it is by the enjoyment of a dangerous freedom that the Americans learn the art of rendering the dangers of freedom less formidable.' (ibid., p. 119). One could not hope for a better description of the unique character of the democratic adventure. Tocqueville rejects the hypothesis that this adventure can be mastered thanks to the emergence of a power which, because it represents the will of all, can subordinate the rights of each individual to its idea of the public good and of the direction that should be imprinted on society. Nor, despite his concessions to the then-fashionable theory of enlightened self-interest (and, once again, we have to ask whether they might not be purely tactical), does he base his judgement on the principle of the natural self-regulation of interests. The fiction that harmony can arise out of a combination of individual passions is quite alien to him. His analysis suggests that, in the course of history, individuals *discover* that they are all independent and shaped in each other's likeness as a result of their increasing equality of condition; and it further suggests that citizens *discover* that, as citizens living among other citizens, they are all equally destined to exercise public authority or to supervise its exercise. This discovery cannot be interpreted within the limitations of a historicist conception; it is not a contingent event bound up with one of several equally legitimate modes of social organization. Tocqueville makes his views on this point perfectly clear in *L'Etat social et politique de la France*: 'According to the modern democratic and, I venture to say, the *correct* notion of freedom, every man, being presumed to have received from nature the necessary intelligence to conduct his own affairs, acquires at birth an equal and imprescriptible right to live independently of his fellows in all respects that concern him alone, and to govern his destiny as he sees fit' (AR, vol. I, p. 62, emphasis added). The notion of individual freedom is, we are given to believe, both a product of history and correct. One would object in vain that men with a sense of their independence existed prior to the advent of democracy; no one is more aware of the strength of that feeling in aristocratic society or of the extraordinary effects it could have; he is even convinced that this strength of feeling diminishes when independence is not something that is won by the few, and is socially recognized. It is, however, true to say that, when it is translated into right, individual independence ceases to be the privilege of the few and to be exercised at the expense of the subjugation of others; it becomes unconditional; it is a human attribute, and it reveals the vocation of humanity. There is nothing in this recognition of right to sanction the illusion that the existence of individuals precedes that of society; in a democracy, individuals emerge from within society, and they do not simply appear to be similar: they are defined as such and can declare themselves to be similar. In the same passage, Tocqueville also makes it clear that: 'Once it becomes apparent that absolute power was no more than a material fact, an ephemeral accident . . . obedience is no longer a matter of morality.' In other words, although political freedom itself is a product of history, it is not reducible to a system of institutions designed to protect individual freedom; both freedoms stem from the same cause, namely emancipation from any personal authority which can arrogate the power to take decisions affecting the destiny of all in accordance with its own ends. Political freedom in its turn becomes unconditional: it reveals the essence of the political. In saying that, in democracy, men discover themselves to be individuals and citizens, we are also implying that nothing can materialize their freedom, regardless of the weight of the institutions that support it. And this is why a new form of servitude might be compatible with the outward forms of freedom (DA., vol. II, p. 319). The new science of politics which Tocqueville appeals for so strongly in the opening pages of *Democracy in America* is, then, highly unusual. It is not confined to an understanding of how institutions function; and still less does it have anything to do with the pseudo-science preached by those who argue the case for a social body whose movements are carefully regulated, and in which everyone is assigned their rightful place in order to fulfil the function that is most beneficial to all. It is a philosophy rather than a science. It avoids the illusions of organizational theory, and it is designed to educate the reader about the dangers of freedom, not in order to make freedom seem unattractive, but in order to make its dangers acceptable, to show that risks have to be taken to ward off other threats. The entire analysis of the freedom of the press, of civil and political associations, and of universal suffrage is governed by this over-riding concern.

It is not simply because individual freedom and political freedom form a happy combination and support one another that, in Tocqueville's view, they are inseparable; it is because freedom cannot be localized, because it is not an attribute of human existence or coexistence, because it is constitutive of them, and because it is indivisible. It is revealed in what Bergson calls a retrograde movement of the truth. A comparison with Benjamin Constant's concepts will reveal the originality and boldness of Tocqueville's conception. Tocqueville does of course share Constant's hatred of arbitrary power; and his idea of freedom, like Constant's, has nothing in common with the theory of economic liberalism. It is, moreover, to Constant's credit that he not only denounces the fiction of an absolute sovereignty of the people which finds its expression in the right to constrain every individual in the name of all, but that he also discerns the difference between the spirit of the Moderns and that of the Ancients. It is to his credit that he shows that in the cities of Antiquity, which the revolutionaries of the eighteenth century admired so much, the price of participation in public affairs was the renunciation of individual rights, whereas the enjoyment of those rights has now become an irrepressible need which makes the exercise of direct democracy both impossible and undesirable. But in his *Principes politiques*, Constant is not content with asserting that 'there is one part of human existence which, of necessity, remains individual and independent, and which, by right, lies beyond any social competency';[4] with contrasting the rule of arbitrary power with the fixity of contracts; or with recommending the observance of forms – the 'tutelary divinities which watch over human associations' – because in their absence, everything is 'obscure' and subject to 'the lonely dictates of conscience and the vacillation of opinion' (p. 411). His argument constantly tends to make individuals both the condition and the end of the political order. Having enumerated the modern civil institutions that make up 'the boulevard which now surrounds individual freedom', he states: 'This individual freedom is in effect the goal of all human associations' (p. 408). He confuses contracts with political associations themselves (p. 410). He defines forms as 'the only relations between men' (p. 411). He regards the violation of individual freedom as destroying all those guarantees which are 'the first condition and the only goal which allow men to unite under the rule of law' (p. 412). Similarly, it is not enough to demonstrate that individual freedom is the 'greatest of all modern needs' and that 'we must therefore never ask for it to be sacrificed in order to establish political freedom' (p. 506). In his view, political freedom is no more than a guarantee (p. 509). The necessity of preserving political freedom must not make us forget that 'the more time the exercise of political rights leaves us for private interests, the more precious freedom becomes' (p. 152). The real reason why we should not completely reject the 'division of political power' relates, then, to the danger that those who have been entrusted with authority might take advantage of the indifference of those who gave them their mandate and might dispose of those guarantees as they see fit; it relates, that is, to the danger that individuals might lose their 'enjoyment of private rights' [*jouissances privées*]' (p. 513). We must not be deceived by the fact that, at the end of his famous discourse on 'La liberté comparée des anciens et des modernes', Constant suddenly adopts a different tone and, in a few emphatic phrases, rejects the view that happiness is the ultimate goal of the human race, and describes political freedom as 'the most powerful and the most forceful means of achieving perfection that Heaven has granted us'. His vision of modern democracy is very different from Tocqueville's. It is not that the latter rejects the statement that 'Among the moderns ... the individual is independent in his private life, but, even in the freest states, he is sovereign only in appearance' (p. 496), or the view that 'his personal influence is an imperceptible element in the social will which imprints its direction on the government' (p. 448). But that observation – and we know how he will develop it – concerns only one aspect of the dynamic of democracy; and it does not lead him to ignore the vitality of a society which promotes initiatives in every domain. And, whereas for Constant, this observation simply supports the idea of an irreversible movement towards the enjoyment of private rights [*jouissance privées*], for Tocqueville it reveals the void which appears when everyone retreats into their own sphere – the void in which social power is engulfed.

The representation of the individual therefore becomes inconsistent if it is extracted from the representation of the political. Perhaps it would be more accurate to say that the problematic of the individual is completely transformed by the new notion of the political. Constant uses that notion to designate a sphere of actions and relations governed by the imperative of the common interest. Political power is circumscribed within society because of the specific function it performs; maintaining public tranquillity by ensuring the protection of the security of all, raising the forces and funds required for the smooth transaction of all the various types of business in which citizens take part, and providing for defence against possible foreign aggression. Constant follows tradition in that the three departments of the state – justice, finance and defence – are enough to define its field of intervention. The public realm is separate from the private realm; common goals are different to private goals. At the same time, power is beyond the reach of individuals, regardless of the influence they may exert on governmental action via suffrage or through the expression of opinions. It could not, of course, be said that Tocqueville provides a new definition of the political. The fact is that in his analysis of American democracy he reserves a particular significance for that term by making a distinction between the social state and its political consequences, between civil associations and political associations, between administrative power and political power, between ideas and feelings, and morals, and between despotism and political freedom. But, despite these distinctions – and the criteria on which they are based are, in the event, often unstable – the reader cannot fail to perceive in democracy a *form of society* whose singularity becomes apparent if it is compared with a different *form*, such as aristocratic society. Despite his efforts to see equality of condition as the fundamental fact from which all others seem to be derived, he leaves us in no doubt that the meaning it acquires in democratic society is very different from the meaning it had under the Ancien Regime. By identifying administrative centralization as a specific phenomenon and as something distinct from governmental action, he gives it a symbolic import and reveals that, quite apart from the technical modifications it implies, its effects permeate the whole of society, and influence both mentalities and morals. He is not inviting us to recognize a mode of activity which has its specificity at a certain remove from the political; on the contrary, he invests with a political meaning something that escaped the notice of earlier meditations that were confined to the sphere of government and parties. Similarly, he does not and cannot confuse civil associations with political associations, and still less does he confuse the temporary groupings that are formed to defend an interest or a particular right with national parties; but his analysis does reveal an indivisible truth about associations as such. One would attempt in vain, he says in substance, to limit freedom of association to particular activities; if men lose the freedom to act together in great things, they will lose their taste for association in little things which concern them more closely. Conversely, if their interventions are restricted to the minor details of social life, they will be unable to think or feel for themselves. 'For my own part, I should be inclined to think freedom less necessary in great things than in little ones, if it were possible to secure the one without possessing the other' (DA, vol. II, p. 320). He immediately adds:

> Subjection in minor affairs breaks out every day and is felt by the whole community indiscriminately. It does not drive men to resistance, but it crosses them at every turn, till they are led to surrender the exercise of their own will ... It is vain to summon a people who have been rendered so dependent on the central power to choose from time to time the representatives of that power; this rare and brief exercise of their free choice, however important it may be, will not prevent them from gradually losing the faculties of thinking, feeling and acting for themselves, and thus gradually falling below the level of humanity. (Ibid., pp. 320–1)

Tocqueville is certainly not suggesting that everything is the same, but he is suggesting that everything in the dense fabric of society is interdependent, and that a lesion at any one point in the tissue of democracy will tear it apart.

To convince ourselves that this is so, we have only to examine the repetitive and methodical use he makes of the concept of social power. The author of *Democracy in America* replaces the notion of a power that can be localized, of a visible power whose action depends upon those who are entrusted with it, with that of a diffuse, invisible power, which is both internal and external to individuals; which is produced by individuals and which subjugates individuals; which is as imaginary as it is real; and which is imprinted on government, administration and opinion alike. And so, although he follows Constant's example in attacking arbitrary power, he does not leave matters there. He perceives the more serious danger that is inherent in the representation of society's absolute right. His tone may seem similar to that of Constant when, for example he states that: 'No citizen is so obscure that it is not very dangerous to allow him to be oppressed' (DA vol. II, p. 327). But his point of view is not the same. The problem is not simply that, by violating the rights of one individual, power undermines the convention which binds him to others, and that everyone therefore fears for his own safety. The evil comes from both above and below. It is a sign that men have been dazzled by the image of a society which merges with power. The fact that the individual no longer feels that an attack on his neighbour is an attack on him means that the relationship beween self and other has disappeared, that individual existence has become accidental, as compared with the substantive power of society. Tocqueville makes this point on at least two occasions: the idea of social power dominates the imagination of both those who govern the state and those who obey it: 'The notion they all have of government is that of a sole, simple, providential, and creative power. All secondary opinions in politics are unsettled; this one remains fixed, invariable and consistent ... those who govern and those who are governed agree to pursue it with equal ardour' (ibid., p-p. 291–2). He repeats this conviction when he analyses the new taste for uniformity: 'Thus the government likes what the citizens like and naturally hates what they hate. These common sentiments, which in democratic nations constantly unite the sovereign and every member of the community, establish a secret and lasting sympathy between them' (ibid., p. 295). No matter whether he is talking about the new freedom or the new servitude of the individual, he sees it as being exercised within a form of political society – but, in his view, the institution of the form of that society can never be disassociated from the institution of the individual.

The acuity of his vision of democracy is, moreover, such that it allows him to grasp not only the complicity between those who govern and those who are governed, but also the complicity between the resolute supporters of order, who are prepared to increase the government's power because of their fear of anarchy, and its adversaries, who, in order to further the cause of the people, either call for a new revolution or construct models of a society in which all antagonisms disappear:

Even those which are most at variance are nevertheless agreed on this head. The unity, the ubiquity, the omnipotence of the supreme power, and the uniformity of its rules constitute the principal characteristics of all the political systems that have been put forward in our age. They recur even in the wildest visions of political regeneration; the human mind pursues them in its dreams. (Ibid., vol. II, p. 291)

Tocqueville again opens up a different perspective to that adopted by Constant. The socialist utopia is in fact sustained by a truth which no theory of liberalism narrowly based on the theory of the interdependence of individuals can perceive. Arguing against Constant, Saint-Simon therefore denounces the idea of a society whose sole justification is the protection of individuals. His preface to *Le Système industriel* is in every sense the antithesis of the doctrine of the *Principes politiques*, as outlined in the chapter on 'De la liberté individuelle'. Basically, Saint-Simon derides the idea that freedom is the goal of all human associations: a human association is governed by an activity goal [*but d'activité*]. In any given period, freedom can be defined only in terms of that goal; the goal is primary, and freedom is merely the ability to pursue it. The idealization of the notion of contract therefore conceals a mystification: human beings do not unite in a society in order to make laws for one another; one may as well imagine individuals coming together to draw up new conventions for the game of chess, and believing that this makes them chess-players. The jurists who served the monarchy talked a lot about forms, but forms mask content; and those who control the destiny of modern society must consider the content of all things. As for political freedom, if it means the exercise of everyone's right to govern or to control the government, it is tantamount to leaving authority to chance, or to denying that there is such a thing as competence in the management of public affairs, even though the existence of competence is recognized in all other matters. Although they are obviously different, the arguments do at least have a common basis: a critique of the abstractions that characterize the liberal theory of the individual. Tocqueville's writings are not simply beyond the reach of this critique; he will in fact take it into account and will reveal the hidden connection between it and the principles of the defenders of political realism. These criticisms do not affect him because, as we have said, he does not posit the view that individuals are the first terms in an association whose sole justification is that it procures for them guarantees of their independence. The only rationale for contracts and forms is that they explain and stabilize those guarantees. They have the virtue of maintaining and making visible the markers of the differentiation and articulation of social relations, which tend to be destroyed by the belief in the absolute right of society. A government elected by universal suffrage does not enjoy the advantages of competence: it is to be applauded less *for what it does than for what it causes to be done*. In short, Tocqueville attacks Saint-Simon on his home ground. He is no less interested than Saint-

Simon in the rise of modern society. His purpose is to demonstrate, using America as an example, that it is at its most vigorous when the illusion that its organization can be mastered is dispelled, when the activities and opinions of human beings escape state control. Rather than replacing the notion of the sovereignty of the individual with that of the sovereignty of society, he unmasks the fiction concealed by the latter notion: the fiction of a collective individual, of a great being who can be defined and whose contours can be outlined, the fiction that its *content* can be seen and that its *goal* can be established. And he demonstrates that this fiction is indissociable from the image of omnipotent power. It is irrelevant that in a utopia this power is assumed to do away with coercion, that it is placed under the aegis of science, that it can be termed spiritual, or that it can be based upon the consent of its subjects: it is still essentially despotic. We can thus understand why, for Saint-Simon, the position of the individual is, if not obliterated, at least rigorously subordinated to the imperative of social cohesion. This is not simply a result of the primacy that is accorded to organic periods – in critical periods, individualism can come into play only because old principles have been dissolved, and their dissolution is a precondition for the gestation of a new form. The double image of a society which has achieved self-knowledge and of an organ which actualizes society implies that the individual is imprinted on it, that the individual is *known*. It might be added that, given that only a small number of people are competent, citizens would be left to dwell in obscurity, if the goodness and rationality of the social organization, and the functions which devolve upon them, were not made visible; if citizens themselves did not participate in the great spectacle of the careful construction of the social machine. The individual is, then, plucked from obscurity – the danger of his becoming lost in the crowd is warded off – when his gaze is concentrated on the common goal thanks to the numerous ceremonies and festivals which give society a face, which celebrate the various roles of its members, both in industry and in the family, and which ensure that everyone is both visible to everyone else and able to see everyone else.

Nothing tells us more about the principles of Tocqueville's liberalism than this model, which is its explicit negation. If we look beyond the formulae that bear the hallmark of classical theories, we find in Tocqueville a new concept of the individual combined with a critique of the new conjunction of power and science, and of the ideal of the total visibility of society. His acceptance of the freedom of individuals, of the irreducible element in every individual goes hand in hand with a valorization of a political society that is instituted through a new awareness of what cannot be known or mastered. At the same time, the underlying tendency of this society – if, that is, it is not overthrown by the dangers it creates – is to deny the possibility of a full vision of the being of the social in which everyone is included. It is not that Tocqueville is unaware of the threat posed by the isolation of individuals

or of the new phenomenon of *the man lost in the crowd*. We know
that he sees this as one of the twin effects of equality of condition –
the other being a love of independence – but he does regard the
reversal of the phenomenon into its opposite as an event that can give
rise to despotism. He is so firmly convinced that equality of condition
is irreversible that he cannot conceive of the establishment of a
community in which everyone lives beneath the gaze of all and in
which everyone can see everyone else. Aristocratic society conformed
to that model. It was organized in terms of multiple networks of
personal dependency. Tocqueville does of course note that a single
chain bound the last link to the first, the peasant to the king, but he
also notes that: 'The outline of society itself was not easily discernible
and was constantly confounded with the different powers by which the
community was ruled' (DA, vol.II, p. 328). It was in the castle, the
seigniory, the commune and the corporation that men related to one
another; everyone could see someone above him or below him. The
disappearance of the figure of the other-as-fellow and the collapse of
an authority which guaranteed the nature of the social bond in the
here and now has, however, a twofold effect: the individual acquires
the notion of a society in which he is defined as being shaped in the
likeness of others, but he cannot see it – he can see neither himself
nor its other members. And in that society he inevitably loses the
markers of his identity because he surrenders his individual perspective
and allows himself to be absorbed into an anonymous vision. 'As the
conditions of men become equal among a people,' notes Tocqueville,
'individuals seem of less and society of greater importance; or rather,
every citizen, being assimilated to all the rest, is lost amongst the
crowd and nothing stands conspicuous [*l'on n'aperçoit plus que*] but
the great and imposing image of the people at large' (ibid., vol. II,
p. 290). His understanding of the alienation that accompanies the
vision of the people (and the vision of society and power, whose
images replace the image of the people in subsequent lines) is
remarkable. When individuals, who are constituted as such by the
operation which isolates them from one another, become lost in the
crowd, the vision that conjures up this great being suppresses them
and swallows them up in the anonymity of *on*. It need scarcely be
pointed out that the writer's target here is not Saint-Simon (though it
is not irrelevant that the reference to 'dreams' should appear in the
same chapter); he is analysing a process which is intimately bound up
with the democratic experience in order to reveal its dangers. Not only
does utopianism fail to see the origins of those dangers; it tries to
actualize 'the great and imposing image of the people', and it even
wants that image to accompany the lives of individuals, because it is
motivated by a desire to pluck individuals from their anonymity and
to relocate them in the bright light of a communal space in which
everyone and everything can see and be seen.

Tocqueville does not contrast the dream of a society which can accede to full self-visibility with the advantages of a mechanism which allows everyone to conduct his own affairs without being seen by others, and which ensures the cohesion of society withou anyone being able to form an idea of society. When he notes that in aristocratic ages the image of society was not easily discernible, he is not singing their praises. His remarks to the effect that the correct notion of freedom coincides with men's recognition that they are shaped in each other's likeness and with their feeling of belonging not only to one society but to one humanity leave no doubts as to his intentions. He is suggesting that the new meaning of 'fellow', 'society' and 'humanity' can only be reconciled with freedom if the representation of their realization in the real is held in check. The desire to realize it would result in a flight into the imaginary, and that in turn would have the effect of introducing a scission between, on the one hand, the realms of opinion, power and science and, on the other, the people who are subject to them. His entire work is designed to convince the reader that the idea of equality, of society, or of humanity must remain latent if it is not to become a terrifying fiction, and that it emerges from the coming together of multiple individual perspectives. The truth of the independence of the individual is not, therefore, that it is an indivisible unity but that it provides the ultimate symbol of singularity.

One possible question remains to be asked: in emphasizing so forcefully the harmful effects of democracy, does Tocqueville preclude the possibility of the further pursuit of the adventure of individual and political freedom? At the end of the penultimate chapter of *Democracy in America*, he does, it is true, alter the implications of an argument that seemed to imply the inevitability of despotism. Having noted that 'The men who live in the democratic ages upon which we are entering have naturally a taste for independence', he revises his earlier views and adds that: 'They are naturally impatient of regulation, and they are wearied by the permanence even of the condition they themselves prefer. They are fond of power, but are prone to despise and hate those who wield it, and they easily elude its grasp by their own mobility and insignificance' (vol. II, p. 33). The optimism which finds expression in the conviction that 'these propensities . . . will furnish new weapons to each succeeding generation that struggles in favour of the liberty of mankind' is not based upon observation of the facts alone, since, although it seems to Tocqueville that the individual has acquired a taste for independence, it must not be forgotten that that taste itself is bound up with a political event with a metaphysical significance: the collapse of an unconditional authority which, in one or another social context, *someone* could claim to embody. It must, however, be admitted that Tocqueville has little to say about the nature of this taste for independence; it appears to result from equality, but it implies no more than 'a taste for following in their [men's] private actions no other guide than their own will' – a taste which soon inspires 'the notion and love of political freedom' (ibid., p. 287). The link he establishes between the figure of *someone* and the idea of an unconditional authority is no less disappointing. Tocqueville describes the phenomenon of personal dependence which characterizes the aristocratic world well, but he merely mentions, without really examining it, the function the monarch performed when he manifested legitimacy in his person, when he was believed to be the embodiment of the nation, when his power was believed to derive from God or from the new secular divinities known as Reason and Justice. He therefore does not appreciate the import of the extraordinary event signalled by the rise of modern democracy: the formation of a power which has lost its ability to be embodied and the ultimate basis of its legitimacy, and the simultaneous establishment of relations with law and knowledge which no longer depend upon relations with power, and which imply that it is henceforth impossible to refer to a sovereign principle transcending the order of human thought and human action. Although Tocqueville examines the new representation of social power, which testifies to the fact that society is confined within its own frontiers – and rightly interprets it as a perversion – and although he simultaneously rejects the hypothesis of a return ot the Ancien Regime and a theologico-political order, he goes no further than that. He is reluctant to conclude that the experience of political and individual freedom, and the advent of a new idea of power and right, coincide with a new experience of knowledge, with the advent of a new idea of truth. It must be stated that this mutation implies that what was once no more than the seed of an idea in the minds of a small number has germinated, spread and imprinted itself on social life. Although he is bold enough to say that 'He who does not seek freedom for its own sake is doomed to serve' (AR, vol. I, p. 114), Tocqueville does not go so far as to say that he who does not seek truth for its own sake is doomed to believe – and to serve. Following an inspiration similar to that of La Boétie, he invites us to recognize that freedom cannot be taught to anyone who does not desire it, that it is not a specific commodity that can be named, and that to desire it is to possess it. Yet for some reason he holds back from the idea that the quest for truth and the truth itself are one and the same, that modern society and the modern individual are constituted by the experience of the dissolution of the ultimate markers of certainty; that their dissolution inaugurates an adventure – and it is constantly threatened by the resistance it provokes – in which the foundations of power, the foundations of right and the foundations of knowledge are all called into question – a truly historical adventure in the sense that it can never end, in that the boundaries of the possible and the thinkable constantly recede.

I have attempted elsewhere to examine the consequences of the new phenomenon of the disincorporation of power, the most important being the experience of a society which can no longer be represented by the model of the body, and which accepts division and the effects of division in every domain. Here, I will therefore simply point out that the changes that can be identified in the mode of the institution of the social can also be seen in the mode of the institution of the individual. It cannot simply be argued that, once the individual escapes the authority the *other* embodied for him because of his social pre-eminence, the only standard by which he can judge his conduct is conformity to justice and reason, as determined by the free examination of his own conscience, and that his only rule of conduct in all things is his will. This idea, which has so often been formulated by liberal discourse, in all its variants, allows us to overlook the fact that, whilst reason and justice become solemn references which are available to all, they are subject to interpretation by all, and are linked to a discovery which no individual can disassociate from the mobilization of his capacity for knowledge and speech. When he is defined as independent, the individual does not, as Tocqueville seems to assume, acquire a new certainty in place of the old – the new certainty being one he derives from his autonomy or one which binds him to the power of opinion or of science. He is doomed to be tormented by a secret uncertainty. Once truth cannot be divorced from the exercise of thought, and once the law by which the existence of the individual is posited proves to be linked to his ability to enunciate it, knowledge and non-knowledge converge, and it is impossible to separate them. Even the distinction between thought and right cannot account for the novelty of this event, for the exercise of thought changes when the right to think is asserted; it is certainly a right that cannot be defined, but it is one which is constantly being extended into areas that were formerly forbidden. Such a right cannot be circumscribed within the limits of the political; it affects all the relations the individual establishes with the world and with others; it affects his every thought, and *founds* them in the sense that it brings them into being.

Everything that, in Tocqueville's day, was portrayed by the novel and by literature as a whole, is an index of the individual's new mode of existence within the horizons of democracy: giving one's thoughts their due, agreeing to live with them, accepting conflict and internal contradictions, granting one's thoughts a kind of *equality* (no matter whether they are noble or base, no matter whether they take shape under the aegis of knowledge or passion, as a result of contacts with people or with things), and accepting that the inner–outer distinction has become blurred. The emergence of the individual does not merely mean that he is destined to control his own destiny; he has also been dispossessed of his assurance as to his identity – of the assurance which he once appeared to derive from his station, from his social condition, or from the possibility of attaching himself to a legitimate authority. To paraphrase Tocqueville's description of America, we can readily agree that the individual is prey to a 'ceaseless agitation', that his uncertainty as to his identity produces 'a restless intellectual activity' and a 'superabundant energy' which he was 'unable to create' when he governed his passions in accordance with a legitimate model. Or, to paraphrase our critique of Saint-Simon's utopia, we can readily agree that the individual discovers that he is undefined, and has no contours, no content and no goal.

Now if we agree that the individual is in part constituted beneath the pole of a new indeterminacy which opens him up to himself, which turns truth into a question to which there is no answer, but which also traverses him whether he realizes it or not, we have to reject the alternative formulated by Tocqueville, or at least refrain from posing it in absolute terms. If Tocqueville is to be believed, the individual either appears in the fullness of his self-affirmation, or disappears completely as a result of his weakness and isolation, and is swallowed up by opinion or by social power. This implies both an underestimation and an overestimation of the individual; it implies a failure to recognize that his strength does not reside in his full positivity as a subject, and that any attempt, no matter how refined, to enslave him will fail because there is within him something that escapes objectification.

Tocqueville's idea that democratic freedom can be transformed into servitude still survives in our day. And not without good reason. It is not worth describing yet again all the signs of this trend, the most noticeable being the repeated efforts that have been made to 'normalize' the individual. It is, however, true to say that those who accept Tocqueville's view and who denounce this threat most vocally even go so far as to believe that the project can reach completion; they readily conclude that the individual will soon be annihilated, but they reserve themselves the right to conceive of that eventuality, and they do so as though they were fully independent. Now, it is one thing to perceive the ambiguities of the democratic adventure; it is quite another to conclude that the question of the individual, bound up as it is with the question of truth, can be suppressed. Despite all its vices, democracy is, for those who are suffering totalitarian oppression, still the only desirable form of society, because it preserves the double idea of political freedom and the freedom of the individual.

The most remarkable feature of critiques of democracy is the durability of the representation of *the man lost in the crowd*. It fuels both a horror of anonymity and a longing for an imaginary community whose members experience the joys of being together. Tocqueville was immune to such longings. It is therefore all the more striking that his aversion towards any form of popular mobilization, which he shared with the men of his class, should not have prevented him from seeing the crowd as a sign of the degeneration of the individual. And in that respect, is it not worth noting an ambiguity? Is anonymity an absolute evil? Those who wish to make the individual or the community – or both – an active subject assert that it is. But if we accept that the individual escapes his own perception in the very act of relating to himself, that he has to come to terms with the unknown element within himself, why deny that there is a link between solitude and anonymity, why deny that recognition of the other as being shaped in our likeness implies that we must also accept that we cannot know the other, and why, finally divorce the truth of association from the truth of isolation, when we should be taking them together? The answer is obvious: it is as though, for almost two hundred years, we had been forced to oscillate between making an apologia for individualism and making an apologia for mass democracy, between disavowing one and disavowing the other.

10

From Equality to Freedom

Fragments of an Interpretation of Democracy in America

Few authors have experienced the feeling of having discovered and named the object on which their meditations are concentrated to the same degree as Tocqueville. His examination of American society reveals to him that equality of condition is 'the fundamental fact from which all others seem to be derived' (vol. I, p. 3).[1] Observing that equality of condition has attained its extreme limit in America, he becomes convinced that Europe is constantly approaching it. Equality of condition therefore seems to him to have the character of a 'providential fact': 'It is universal, it is lasting, it constantly eludes all human interference' (p. 6). The men of his time must, he asserts, 'be convinced ... that the gradual and progressive development of social equality is at once the past and the future of their history' (p. 7). And what does equality of condition mean? A 'social state'. What does its gradual and progressive development mean? A 'social movement' or a 'social revolution'. And what is this social state; what is this social movement? Democracy, 'the democratic revolution'. In the introduction to the first volume of *Democracy in America*, there is a constant interplay between the concept of equality of condition and that of democracy.

Equality of condition is, however, no more than a 'fundamental fact'. In the very first lines of his introduction, Tocqueville describes it as such: 'it exercises a prodigious influence on the whole course of society', on public spirit and laws, and has no less effects on civil society than on the government (p. 3). We can therefore conclude that the democratic revolution is not reducible to this fundamental fact, that it encompasses both that fact and its effects. If, however, it affects society at every level, it is still true to say that the nature of the change depends upon the milieu on which it is imprinted, and that the milieu has been shaped by history. How, then, can we distinguish between the accidental and the necessary in history?

The answer appears to be as follows. American society fully reveals the connection between the fundamental fact and its effects insofar as the origins of the nation coincide with the origins of democracy. In America, then, the course of history has not been disrupted. America reveals the democratic phenomenon in its pure state whereas in Europe it is difficult to distinguish between factors pertaining to the essence of democracy and factors attributable to the disorders resulting from the destruction of the Ancien Regime; from, that is, the effects of the great Revolution. In France, in particular, democracy

> has overthrown whatever crossed its path and has shaken all that it has not destroyed. Its empire has not been gradually introduced or peaceably established, but it has constantly advanced in the midst of the disorders and the agitations of a conflict. In the heat of the struggle each partisan is hurried beyond the natural limits of his opinions by the doctrines and the excesses of his opponents, until he loses sight of the end of his exertions, and holds forth in a way which does not correspond to his real sentiments or secret instincts. (p. 11)

In America, by contrast, 'the great social revolution ... seems to have nearly reached its natural limits. It has been effected with ease and simplicity; say rather that this country is reaping the fruits of the democratic revolution which we are undergoing, without having had the revolution itself' (p. 13). The beginning of the second chapter appears to confirm our initial answer: America is the only country in which 'it has been possible to witness the natural and tranquil growth of society, and where the influence exercised on the future condition of states by their origin is clearly distinguishable' (p. 27) Tocqueville also states here that: 'America, consequently, exhibits in the broad light of day the phenomena which the ignorance or rudeness of earlier ages conceals from our researches' (p. 27).

Let us also consider Tocqueville's initial approach. Chapter 1, which is entitled 'Exterior form of North America', obviously functions as a preamble; the author gives a brief account of the natural environment and of the Indian communities who occupied certain parts of the territory before the arrival of the colonists. The second chapter is entitled 'Origin of the Anglo-Americans and importance of this origin in relation to their future condition'. It introduces us to a history which is transparent because the birth of the nation is visible. 'The entire man is, so to speak, to be seen in the cradle of the child' and, just as we condemn ourselves to ignorance if we begin to study the man in his maturity, so the meaning of history in general escapes us because the origins of peoples remain invisible to us (p. 26). An understanding of the American starting point is so productive that Tocqueville even ventures so far as to say: 'The readers of this book will find in the present chapter the germ of all that is to follow and the key to almost the whole work' (p. 28). The third chapter is devoted to 'The social condition of the Anglo-Americans'. In a brief introductory section, the author notes that social condition 'is commonly the result of circumstances, sometimes of laws, oftener still of these two causes united; but when once established, it may justly be considered as itself the source of almost all the laws, the usages and the ideas which regulate the conduct of nations: whatever it does not produce, it modifies' (p. 46). The section which ends this chapter (pp. 53–4) describes the 'political consequences of the social condition of the Anglo-Americans': it is general in scope, and it contains a thesis which both stands as a preliminary conclusion and anticipates later developments. After this, the analysis deals with political laws (the principle of popular sovereignty), democratic government (at the level of townships, states, and of the Federal State), institutions (associations and the press), morals, ideas ... The first three chapters, and more specifically chapters 2 and 3, therefore definitely form a whole, and provide us with the means to understand the following chapters. A correct understanding of the historical starting point and of the fundamental sociological cause, which coincide so happily, is assumed to facilitate an understanding of the articulations of the democratic model.

If, however, we look at Tocqueville's argument in detail, it becomes a source of astonishment. How does he begin? By describing the English emigrants. Although they 'differed from each other in many respects', they had 'certain features in common', and 'were all placed in an analogous situation' (p. 28). Not only did they all speak the same language, and not only were they children of the same people; they shared the same political heritage: 'They were more conversant with the notions of right and the principles of true freedom than the greater part of their European contemporaries' (p. 28). More specifically, they had already had experience of collective forms of government: 'that fruitful germ of free institutions which was deeply rooted in the habits of the English; and with it the doctrine of the sovereignty of the people had been introduced into the very bosom of the monarchy of the house of Tudor' (ibid.). It is only after he has made this initial observation that Tocqueville explains why colonization could not give birth to an aristocracy (the origins of the emigrants and the exploitation of the land precluded that possibility). He immediately continues: 'All the British colonies had striking similarities at the time of their origin. All of them, from their beginning, seemed destined to witness the growth, not of the aristocratic liberty of their mother country, but of that freedom of the middle and lower orders of which the history of the world had as yet furnished no complete example' (p. 29). The comment is reminiscent of a remark made in the author's introduction: 'The emigrants ... somehow separated the democratic principle from all the principles it had to contend with in the old communities of Europe, and transported it alone to the New World' (p. 13). We therefore have to recognize that in the New World, where the principle of society coincides with the principle of democracy, democracy implies freedom.

Tocqueville then takes into consideration the North–South opposition and establishes that the real starting point is to be found in the North, in the New England states. It was there that 'the two or three main ideas that now constitute the basis of the social theory of the United States were first combined' (pp. 30–1). We are now given to understand that the starting point is not simply a social fact, but a moral and political fact. There can be no mistake about it: the author then describes the social condition of the emigrants of the North, and the singular phenomenon of a society containing 'neither lords nor common people, and we may almost say neither rich nor poor (p. 31), but he does so in order to make it clear that it was their intelligence, their morality and above all their convictions that distinguished them from other colonists. They had not been obliged to flee England out of necessity: their 'object was the triumph of an idea' (p. 32).

We are of course told that they had religious motives; the remainder of the chapter brings out the role of religion by examining the emigrants' stories and quotations from the pioneering puritans. Tocqueville is awed by the admirable combination of a spirit of religion and a spirit of freedom (p. 43) which is so cruelly lacking in Europe. But these considerations never make him forget that freedom is the starting point and that democracy is originally *political*. 'Puritanism was not', he asserts, 'merely a religious doctrine, but corresponded in many points with the most absolute democratic and republican theories' (p. 32).

It is also to be noted that, whilst he is amazed at the role played by religion, he does not hesitate to make a distinction between those elements of legislation which reveal the marks of 'a narrow, sectarian spirit', and 'a body of political laws which, though written two hundred years ago, is still in advance of the liberties of our age' (p. 39). Within the body of laws shaped by New England (the intervention of the people in public affairs; the free voting of taxes; the responsibility of the agents of power; personal liberty; trial by jury) he identifies 'fruitful principles' which were destined to be 'applied and developed to an extent such as no nation in Europe has yet ventured to attempt' (p. 39).

Why is this so surprising? Because nothing that has been said here allows us to deduce these fruitful principles, these political principles and these principles of liberty from any first fact, from any social fact, or even from the supposedly fundamental fact of equality of condition. Equality of condition does indeed appear to exist, but it is bound up with the *idea* of equality of condition, and that idea cannot, at the starting point, be divorced from the idea of freedom.

The contradiction we have just glimpsed becomes more pronounced as we read the final section of the third chapter. Ignoring his earlier analysis, Tocqueville attempts to determine a first cause, as though it could be distinguished from the starting point, as though the first cause were sociological and could be divorced from the historical starting point. But it is self-evident that if the second chapter were intended to supply no more than a description of the beginnings of American democracy, the author would not have pointed out that it contained 'the germ of all that is to follow and the key to almost the whole work' (p. 28). And it is equally obvious that the analysis of the effects of the law of inheritance, which takes up the greater part of the third chapter, has as much to do with a historical as with a sociological perspective. Indeed, the two are always associated in Tocqueville's argument, and it is that which gives it its force. Yet he does not hesitate to 'deduce' political consequences from a social state (equality of condition); in other words, he deduces a political state, defined as an effect, from a social state which is given the status of a cause.

The deduction itself is so disconcerting as to merit careful examination.

Tocqueville begins by asserting that equality must necessarily 'find its way into the political world, as it does everywhere else' (p. 53). It is, he adds, impossible 'to conceive of men forever remaining unequal upon a single point, yet equal on all others ... they must in the end come to be equal upon all' (p. 53). He concludes that equality will find its expression in the political world either through popular sovereignty or through despotism (rights given to every citizen, or none at all to anyone). This certainty is based, he implies, on the description he has just given of the social state, which 'is just as liable to one of these consequences as to the other'. Two objections can, however, be levelled against these initial propositions. The equality of condition Tocqueville has described coexists alongside multiple inequalities. He has in fact only demonstrated that, in the United States, 'The last trace of hereditary ranks and distinctions is destroyed'. This, it would appear, is the limit that has been reached by equality of condition; this is the complete form of what in Europe is still a gradual and progressive development. Tocqueville himself observes that there is 'no lack of *wealthy individuals*' in America: 'I know of no country, indeed, where the love of money had taken stronger hold on the affections of men and where a profounder contempt is expressed for the theory of the permanent equality of property' (p. 51). He therefore has no grounds for deducing 'equality upon all points' from 'equality upon a single point'. And yet he clings firmly to that argument, as is evident from the passage in the introduction in which equality of condition is described as a 'providential fact'. That passage is reproduced word for word in the preface to the twelfth edition, which was written in 1848, that is, almost fifteen years after the publication of the first volume:

> Would it be wise to imagine that a social movement the causes of which lie so far back can be checked by the efforts of one generation? Can it be believed that the democracy which has overthrown the feudal system and vanquished kings will retreat

before tradesmen and capitalists? Will it stop now that it is grown
so strong and its adversaries so weak? (p. cv.)

The argument put forward in the introduction was no more convincing,
for we have already learned that equality was to a large extent the
result of the actions of kings, who proved to be 'the most active and
most constant of levellers' (pp. 4–5). Shortly afterwards, the author
points out that democracy 'suddenly ... acquired supreme power'
(p. 8). No cause and effect relationship has been established between
equality of condition and the defeat of the kings or, more generally,
between a social state and a political regime. It can no doubt be
accepted that equality of condition implies the destruction of aristocratic
society. But the two phenomena appear to be aspects of a single
process. It is therefore impossible to argue the case in terms of cause
and effect. Indeed, given that the king is at the origin of this double-
edged process, we have to choose between two hypotheses. The first
is that he himself destroyed aristocratic society by seizing absolute
power – in which case it is difficult to see why he should necessarily
have been vanquished by a social process which he instigated and of
which he was the beneficiary: that can only be explained in terms
of contingent events (democracy's sudden acquisition of power).
Alternatively the democratic revolution has a logic of its own, even
though it was provoked and encouraged by the actions of kings; in
which case the phenomenon cannot be restricted to an increasing
equality of condition. If it tends to destroy first royalty and then the
power of the bourgeois and the wealthy, it must have a political
vocation; the stakes are not limited to the abolition of hereditary ranks
and distinctions, and the democratic revolution must be directed against
all visible forms of domination, against all the modes of its incarnation
in individuals or classes. And if that is the case, how can one say that
it is 'as liable to one of these consequences as to the other', as likely
to lead to the establishment of absolute power as to freedom? We find
an eloquent expression of the ambiguities of Tocqueville's thought in
the 1848 preface. Having reproduced the 'prophetic' lines from the
introduction, the author seems momentarily to regard the advent of
the Republic as irreversible:

> Though it is no longer a question whether we shall have a
> monarchy or a republic in France, we are yet to learn whether
> we shall have a convulsed or a tranquil republic, whether it shall
> be regular or irregular, pacific or warlike, liberal or oppressive,
> a republic that menaces the sacred rights of property and family,
> or one that honors and protects them both. (p. cvi)

But, no sooner has he formulated this 'fearful problem', than he
modifies the terms of the alternative: 'According as democratic liberty
or democratic tyranny is established here, the destiny of the world will

be different; and it may be said that this day it depends upon us whether the republic shall be everywhere finally established or everywhere finally overthrown' (p. cvi). In my view, this strange displacement betrays an uncertainty as to the nature of democracy.[2] On the one hand, democracy appears to imply a republican regime, the only question being whether it will be regular or irregular; on the other, it is assumed to be compatible with both tyranny and freedom; although it has effects on the political world, its development occurs outside it.

The manner in which these alternative views are linked cannot be ignored. It is as though, having surrendered to an initial impulse which led him to recognize the political vocation of democracy, Tocqueville suddenly corrected himself, and relegated democracy to the register of equality of condition. The deduction made at the end of chapter 3 gives the same impression: although freedom was said earlier to be inscribed within the American 'starting point', it is suddenly denied its primal status and is reintroduced merely as a possible effect.

Even this change of perspective does not seem to be enough. The author is not satisfied with the conclusion that the social condition of the Anglo-Americans is as liable to one consequence as the other (the sovereignty of all and the absolute power of one man respectively). The discovery that the passion for equality is ambivalent – that it both tends to eievate the humble to the status of the great and reduces everyone to the status of the lowest common denominator – leads him to a further conclusion which destroys the earlier balance of political possibilities. Two very different arguments pave the way for this conclusion. To summarize the first: democratic peoples do indeed have an instinctive taste for freedom, but they make only 'rapid and sudden efforts' to obtain it; equality, on the other hand, is their idol, and they would rather perish than lose it. But, curiously enough, the 'manly and lawful passion for equality' and the 'depraved taste for equality', which were previously regarded as being distinct, are not an index of conflict; they have the same effects and they merge into a single obsession which distracts men from the need to guard against the threat of servitude. According to the second argument, 'in a state where the citizens are all practically equal, it becomes difficult for them to preserve their independence against the aggressions of power' because no one individual is strong enough to resist it and because only a general combination can 'protect their liberty'. Tocqueville's final reflections are based upon both arguments: 'The Anglo-Americans are the first nation who, having been exposed to this formidable alternative, have been happy enough to escape the dominion of absolute power. They have been allowed by their circumstances, their origin, their intelligence, and especially by their morals to establish and maintain the sovereignty of the people' (p. 54).

The terms of the alternative have of course been preserved in a formal sense. But democracy seems destined to lead to absolute power, while freedom is bound up with a contingent situation. It is in effect an accident that the Americans were able to escape the fate that awaited them. That accident is comprehensible only if we take into consideration the advantages they enjoyed thanks to the size and relative isolation of their territory, and the exceptional conditions of their undertaking: they founded a society without a revolution; the founding fathers were virtuous, came from the most enlightened strata in old England, and were inspired by their love of God.

We therefore find once more a divorce between a sociological first cause and a historical starting point, a divorce which we have already described as illegitimate. But Tocqueville's interpretation of American democracy now becomes paradoxical in the extreme. The introduction has led us to believe that American democracy represents democracy in a pure state, in that the distortions resulting from the people's struggle against the aristocracy and from the aristocracy's resistance are not found in it, and in that everything in it is perfectly visible. The American case now proves to be impure; in America, the democratic revolution appears to have been driven off course (in a positive sense) by specific causes – circumstances, origins, intelligence and morals. When we examine it, the visible and the invisible change places. What Tocqueville claims to find in it is that which cannot be seen: the link between equality and absolute power. What can be seen is the link between equality and freedom, which is assumed to be an effect of the Americans' prehistory (the past of the emigrants) or of the conditions under which they settled the territory, and which is therefore not visible within the limits of the social state and the political world.

Can we escape this paradox? The introduction does, it is true, indicate one path which we have failed to explore. Europe, and France in particular, are described as a scene of disorder. In Europe, democracy has advanced without guidance, and those who were in a position to *guide* it have failed to do so. Tocqueville contrasts this with the model of America, where democracy has gradually reached its natural limits, and where it has been effected with ease and simplicity. He claims to be able to draw lessons from this model (but points out, as he does throughout his work, that what applies to one people may not necessarily apply to another). We can assume that these lessons shed light both upon the internal logic of democracy and upon the safeguards which allow the Americans to avoid the dangers it creates. We can also accept that in the United States these safeguards are an effect of the national character (which has been shaped by the past of the emigrants) or even of circumstances, and that they provide indications which will help the enlightened men of the Old World to guide democracy correctly. In short, Tocqueville appears to believe that what was in the United States the work of chance can be converted by Europeans into the work of science. The fact is that, having described the democratic revolution as inevitable, he states that:

The first of the duties that are at this time imposed upon those who direct our affairs is to educate democracy, to reawaken, if possible, its religious beliefs; to purify its morals; to mould its actions; to substitute a knowledge of statecraft for its inexperience, and an awareness of its true interest for its blind instincts, to adapt its government to time and place, and to modify it according to men and conditions. A new science of politics is needed for a new world. (p. 7)

Democracy in Europe might be compared with a child whose nature cannot be changed but who must be disciplined by receiving a good education: 'Democracy has ... been abandoned to its wild instincts, and it has grown up like those children who have no parental guidance, who receive their education in the public streets, and who are acquainted only with the vices and wretchedness of society' (pp. 7–8). And as the teachers understand nothing of the nature of children, the best they can do is to observe how a child develops when it enjoys peaceful conditions, and use their observations to invent artifices that can replace the education provided by a good environment. Tocqueville's comments on religion appear to confirm this hypothesis. 'By a strange coincidence of events, religion in France has been for a long time entangled with those institutions which democracy destroys' (p. 12), with the result that the religionists attack equality and freedom because they fail to see that Christianity is not hostile to democracy on principle, and that those who defend new ideas attack religion because they fail to understand that all institutions are based upon morals and beliefs. Both parties should therefore appreciate the good fortune of the Americans and should try to combine religion with democracy, regardless of their own convictions.

A division is, it appears, being introduced between a realm of necessity, which is limited to the extension of equality of condition, and a realm of contingence, between the curious history of the peoples of Europe and that of the people of America. And it is being suggested that our task consists of learning the lessons of happy accidents in order to correct the effects of unhappy accidents.

Without wishing to deny that Tocqueville's discourse has pedagogic and pragmatic intentions, it cannot be said to be satisfactory. If we simply note the existence of democracy in Europe and in the United States and ascribe the features of these two political worlds to particular causes, the very idea of a 'fundamental fact' disappears. It is then impossible to verify the hypothesis that the democratic revolution has a logic. The essence of democracy remains concealed from us as our perception of its development is always distorted by accidents.

We would attempt in vain to avoid the difficulties we have noted; if we do so, we simply compound them. But if we explore them, we begin to perceive a question which both governs Tocqueville's thought and mobilizes the objections we have met with: the question of Europe and America, of convulsed democracy and tranquil democracy, of the logic of the democratic revolution and of accidents, of the social state and the political world, of the people and their leaders. It concerns freedom and the relationship between freedom and equality.

Indeed, if we content ourselves with the idea that Tocqueville never departed from an aristocratic conception of freedom, further research will be pointless and the conclusion, being given in advance, will be neither new nor productive. It is much more important to detect signs of the indeterminacy of a thought which is trying to come to grips with the enigma of democracy – an enigma which, to a certain extent, it helps to formulate.

The opening chapter of the second book of Volume II is worthy of attention because it draws a lengthy and explicit contrast between the love of equality and the love of freedom and because, as the title indicates, it attempts to show why the former is more ardent and enduring than the latter. Its premisses are in fact no less important than its conclusions: Tocqueville speaks of equality and freedom *as such* before turning to the passions they inspire. First moment:

> It is possible to imagine an extreme point at which freedom and equality would meet and blend. Let us suppose that all the people take a part in government, and that each one of them has an equal right to take a part in it. As no one is different from his fellows, none can exercise a tyrannical power; men will be perfectly free because they are all entirely equal; and they will all be perfectly equal because they are entirely free. To this ideal state democratic nations tend. This is the only complete form that equality can assume upon earth. (vol. II, p. 94)

The argument is designed to disconcert the reader, even though Tocqueville describes only the ideal pole of democracy. He is in effect implying that equality of condition is no more than an inferior form of equality because, in its complete form, equality is political and blends with freedom. Nothing in the earlier chapters of his work allowed the reader to imagine this state of completion and perfection, not only because real forces frustrate its emergence, but also for two other reasons. First, equality of condition appeared to acquire its full meaning as a social fact and to manifest itself on a level other than that of political, economic and juridical equality. And second, equality seemed to be an effect of a historico-natural determinism, whereas freedom was a matter of art. But although they blend insofar as their essences are taken into consideration, they are immediately differentiated once more, apparently as a result of a return to empirical observation.

Second moment: 'This is the only complete form that equality can assume upon earth; but there are a thousand others ...' (p. 94). Tocqueville argues, in substance, that equality may prevail in civil society without prevailing in the political world; it may even prevail in civil society in the absence of freedom, the only requirement being that all are alike, live under one master and are equally willing to serve his power. Third moment: this argument is complemented by an examination of freedom. Freedom, we are told, can be found where equality does not exist. The two arguments are not, however, symmetrical. Having deduced from his first argument that there is good reason to distinguish between equality and freedom, Tocqueville notes that the taste for equality and the taste for freedom are 'two unequal things' (p. 95). In order to convince his reader of this, he introduces a historical dimension which has previously been absent from his reflections by asserting that there is in every age 'some peculiar and preponderant fact' which gives birth to 'some pregnant fact or some ruling passion'. This device clearly reveals the element of uncertainty in his argument. The singular and predominant fact is in fact confined to democratic ages, and it is, as we know, equality of condition. Tocqueville's only comment on freedom, on the other hand, is the observation that 'Freedom has appeared in the world at different times and under various forms; it has not been exclusively bound to any social condition, and it is not confined to democracies' (p. 95). The choice of words is eloquent. Tocqueville does not say that freedom is the peculiar and predominant fact that characterizes aristocratic societies. Two reasons prevent him from doing so. On the one hand, it is possible to take the view that free institutions existed in aristocratic societies and that the nobility or the urban elite had a taste for freedom, but freedom was not 'the distinguishing characteristic of the age' (that phrase is reserved for democracies, and refers to equality). On the other hand, and for our purposes this is more important, freedom, according to our author, does not belong to the realm of *fact*, in the sense in which the word is being used here. The 'fact' is the social state. And in the aristocratic world, the social state is inequality of condition.

The divorce between freedom and equality thus goes further than one might have at first thought. The historical perspective which is introduced in order to clarify it in fact obscures it. To put it more accurately, it does not reveal the phenomenon Tocqueville is attempting to conceptualize: the first appearance within history of 'a fundamental fact from which all others seem to be derived' (vol. I, p. 1). The event remains concealed beneath a representation of different ages which surreptitiously borrows from Montesquieu's notion of the distinctive features of different regimes. The historical perspective is in fact introduced solely to convince the reader that freedom can prevail in the absence of equality, and that equality can prevail in the absence of freedom. But, no sooner has it been introduced than it vanishes in the face of the assertion that freedom is not 'caught up' in history. It is not bound up with any one social condition (and the image of binding in itself suggests that it is not imprinted on society), and nor is it inscribed within time.

We still have to ask why Tocqueville's thought follows this tortuous line. There can be no doubt as to his conception of equality. He articulates it at the beginning of his general introduction: equality of condition is not a social fact like any other; it is the product of an irreversible revolution, and it shows men 'at once the past and the future of their history' (vol. I, p. 7). Yet he refrains from reformulating that conception here. To do so would destroy the opposition he has established between freedom and equality. If it is true that, as he established in the first moment of his argument, equality attains its complete form when it blends with freedom, how can it be maintained that it follows an irreversible course throughout history, that it tends to attain its extreme limit without accepting that it tends to result in political freedom? By ignoring the historical character of equality (its inevitable development), Tocqueville avoids the problem of the history of freedom. By showing that, unlike equality, which is rooted in a social state, freedom is not bound up with any particular social state, he severs its historical roots, but he does so, so to speak, indirectly, without confronting the difficulty he raises. And in doing so, he exposes himself to a further objection based upon his own principles. For once equality is no longer defined as a universal historical fact, there appears to be no reason why it cannot be found in different social states, or why it cannot be said to be 'bound up' with them, just as freedom is bound up with them. It is not enough to note that it can prevail in civil society without prevailing in the political world (which is another way of locating it in a social state), or even that it can penetrate the political world in the absence of freedom (which does not challenge its status as a first cause). It must be recognized that aristocratic society in particular provides an example of a nobility whose condition is, of course, different from that of other social classes but which displays an internal equality. Tocqueville brings out this phenomenon elsewhere, he does not take it into consideration here. Why not? Because, I believe, to do so would force him to conceptualize equality in terms of a history which transcends the limits of democracy, and because that would also oblige him to re-examine its relationship with freedom, from which he wants to divorce it both in theory and in practice.

This last objection re-introduces a question we have already raised: is equality of condition an aspect or a degree of equality, or is it a fact *sui generis*?

To recapitulate, let us clarify the three propositions we are attributing to Tocqueville. The first establishes that, in its complete form, equality blends with freedom. The second, that equality is circumscribed within a specific social state which is historically determined, namely modern democracy, and that it is its distinctive feature. The third establishes that freedom transcends the realm of the political and the historical. When stated baldly, these propositions are contradictory. The problem posed by the status of freedom is no less difficult than that posed by the status of equality. It is tempting to think that the former problem determines the latter, because it challenges the meaning of past and future history, and not only the objective evaluation of social change.

Let us now consider the remainder of the chapter. It is devoted to demonstrating that, in a democracy, men prefer equality to freedom. The argument is based upon the opposition we have just noted. In the first place, a people's taste appears to be shaped by its social state, and equality is so deeply imprinted on its life that considerable energy would have to be mobilized in order to extirpate it. An unnatural feeling would, so to speak, have to manifest itself: 'Their social condition must be modified, their laws abolished, their opinions superseded, their habits changed, their manners corrupted' (vol. II, p. 96). Freedom, on the other hand, is not a natural attribute of the people, even though they enjoy it; in other words, it is not part of their social being. It is a commodity: 'political liberty is more easily lost; to neglect to hold it fast is to allow it to escape' (p. 96). Although Tocqueville himself does not put it in these terms, we might say that in a democracy men *are* equal, and that they love equality because they tend to persist in their being. But they possess – or do not possess – freedom in the sense that one possesses – or does not possess – an attribute or a dignity. In the second place, freedom itself proves to be almost invisible; only its excesses are visible. In other words, freedom is an ideal commodity, and it only becomes a material commodity if it is debased to the level of conduct, of rules which go against the preservation of a social order: the dangers of anarchy are obvious to all. Equality, on the other hand, is visible to the majority; its charms are felt and are within the reach of all, and only its excesses are invisible, for its evils 'creep gradually into the social frame' (p. 96). In other words, the inertia or torpor of the social body, the dislocation of its members and the disaffection of individuals from the *res publica* are signs which usually escape our consciousness. The evils of equality are visible from afar, and they are such that 'they are seen only at intervals; and at the moment at which they become most violent, habit already causes them no longer to be felt' (p. 96). In the third place, and this argument is implicit in the second, political freedom does not inflame the passions of the masses: it 'bestows exalted passions from time to time upon a certain number of citizens'. In order to enjoy it, men must purchase it by 'some sacrifices' and 'they never obtain it without great exertions'. The charms of equality, on the other hand, are 'self-proffered; each of the petty incidents of life seems to occasion them, and in order to taste them, nothing is required but to live' (p. 96). Freedom, that is, refers us to the pole of the subject, of will and of action, whilst equality refers us to the pole of nature.

We now have to re-examine this picture. When Tocqueville speaks of equality, he implicitly gives it the restricted meaning of equality of

condition, which he sees as an established social state. He contrasts it
with freedom, which has to be won. But do we not find traces of a
conquest inscribed within the social state? Tocqueville avoids this
question. Yet in the first section of this chapter, where he asserts that
equality may prevail in civil society without prevailing in the political
world, he describes it in these terms: 'There may be equal *rights* of
indulging in the same pleasures, of entering the same professions, of
frequenting the same places; in a word, of living in the same manner
and seeking wealth by the same means, although all men do not take
an equal share in the government' (vol. II, pp. 94–5, emphasis added).
It is no accident that he should use the word *rights*. It indicates that
he views the social state as a state in which rights have become
sedimented. It must, however, be admitted that this sedimentation has
the effect of establishing a situation which can now be regarded as
being almost natural to society. The hypothesis implies, then, that this
situation marks the end of the march towards equality, and that changes
of a political, economic, juridical and moral order originate therein.
For Tocqueville himself this, however, is no more than a half-truth.
Towards the end of the passage we are discussing, he evokes the
intense passion that is aroused in democratic peoples at certain times.
This extreme passion arises:

> At the moment when the old social system, long menaced, is
> overthrown after a severe internal struggle, and the barriers of
> rank are at length thrown down. At such times men pounce upon
> equality as their booty, and they cling to it as to some precious
> treasure which they fear to lose. The passion for equality
> penetrates on every side into men's hearts, expands there, and
> fills them entirely. (pp. 96–7)

Equality now appears in a very different light, and we would have
great difficulty in distinguishing it from freedom. Its progress depends
upon a series of struggles. It cannot be regarded as a fact of nature.
It triumphs when the barriers that once separated citizens are cast
down. We cannot ignore the fact that those barriers separated inferiors
from superiors. The process of equalization is not simply one of the
removal of differentiation; it is the process of the destruction of the
positions occupied by citizens who dominate society, who possess
power, honours and wealth. In that sense, it cannot be said that
equality is imprinted on social life. Like freedom, it is won, and it can
be defined as a commodity. And, far from being circumscribed within
certain limits and becoming the cause of certain changes, its internal
momentum makes it overcome all limitations, because it penetrates on
every side in men's hearts and expands there.

It must, however, be admitted that we are giving the text a meaning
that does not correspond to Tocqueville's intentions. It might be
objected that it is not certain that, when he speaks of men having the

right to live in the same way in a democracy, he believes that they won that right through their struggles; or that, when he speaks of barriers being thrown down, he imputes that event to the actions of the people; or even that the phrase 'men pounce upon equality as their booty' implies that they labour under the illusion of having won it. Indeed, a reading of the final part of the text strongly suggests that this is not what he means. This section, which is devoted specifically to modern European nations, tells us that 'Absolute kings were the most efficient levelers of ranks among their subjects' (p. 97). The comment is intended to convince us that 'equality was therefore a fact of some standing when freedom was still a novelty' (p. 97), that the former had already crept into the habits of men, that it was part of their lives and that they loved it before the latter became an affair of opinion and taste. This argument, however, raises new and yet more serious difficulties. The gap between equality and freedom is now so great that the initial statement that they tend to blend with one another becomes incomprehensible. Equality proves to be the result of an action which levels the social field. We can quite understand that it implies inertia on the part of citizens, or even that it leads to a situation in which they become complacent. But the terms of the problematic of equality have changed. To say that men are equal now means simply that their ranks have been levelled. To say that they love equality now means that they love servitude or a power disguised as a single master. And, once again, the social problematic of democracy disappears behind a political problematic. The thesis that the social state (equality of condition) has the status of a first cause thus loses its content; the first cause is now the power which breaks up the social body.

At the end of the chapter, Tocqueville himself finally provides us with proof that he has not forgotten his starting point. At the end of the passage we have been discussing, he asserts without any transition that: 'I think that democratic communities have a natural taste for freedom; left to themselves, they will seek it, cherish it, and view any privation of it with regret. But for equality, their passion is ardent, insatiable, incessant, invincible . . .' And he concludes that: 'They will endure poverty, servitude, barbarism, but they will not endure aristocracy' (p. 97). Freedom and equality are of course still divorced. But freedom has been reinscribed within the nature of democracy, and the failure of freedom now appears to result from the perversion of equality.

Although the discrepancies in Tocqueville's thought are very obvious in the chapter we have been examining, if we wish to take full account of them, we must glance at the next six chapters which, taken together with chapter I, appear to form a distinct section. As we must then compare Book II with Book IV, to which it is closely related.

In chapters 2 to 7, the author exploits the disjunction he has introduced between equality and freedom. Indeed, he accentuates it by taking into account only one extreme form of equality – the separation of social agents – and therefore describes freedom as an artifice designed to remedy it. His initial remarks are concerned with individualism. They are not simply a continuation of the preceding argument, and they refer back to the opening chapters of Book I. 'I have shown how it is that in ages of equality every man seeks for his opinions within himself; I am now to show how it is that in the same ages all his feelings are turned towards himself alone' (vol. II, p. 98). It will, however, be recalled that in his opening discussion Tocqueville revealed the ambiguous relationship between two tendencies; one favourable to intellectual freedom, and one which, by removing the old guarantees of individual belief, gave similarity of opinions a new force (the tyranny of the majority). Here, the analysis of individualism concentrates solely upon the process which separates, isolates and *privatizes* individuals, a process which is wholly prejudicial to society. To that extent, it is a new extension of the critique of democratic egalitarianism. The image of a fragmented society is superimposed upon that of a society which has been levelled. The process of both fragmentation and levelling is revealed by the contrast between the aristocratic model and the democratic model. In the aristocratic model, all individuals are closely related to one another in both space and time. On the one hand, change is imperceptible, and time is almost immobile: 'As families remain for centuries in the same condition, often on the same spot, all generations become, as it were, contempo-raneous.' On the other, institutions 'have the effect of closely binding every man to several of his fellow citizens' (p. 98). Democratic society, in contrast, is a theatre of constant change, and breaks down duration: 'The woof of time is every instant broken and the track of generations effaced' (p. 99). As each class gradually approaches others, 'its members become undifferentiated and lose their class identity for one another' (p. 99). The comparison finds its clearest expression in the proposition that: 'Aristocracy had made a chain of all the members of the community, from the peasant to the king; democracy breaks that chain and severs every link of it' (p. 99). It is, then, the fact of decomposition of the social, or of what we would now call the process of the atomization of the individual, that Tocqueville sees as the essential factor. But it is worth pointing out that he still has reservations about aristocratic ages, as they will be voiced again at the end of his work. Thus, 'It is true that in these ages the notion of human fellowship is faint and that men seldom think of sacrificing themselves for other men' (p. 99). Why are these reservations important? Because they indicate that, in a sense, Tocqueville can see the other side of the picture he is painting; looking beyond the decomposition of the social, he glimpses the advent of humanity – or of the society which makes itself the representative of humanity. It is, however, still true to say that the major opposition between the phenomenon of association (typical of aristocracy) and the phenomenon of disassociation (typical of democracy) is so central to his argument as to suggest that the function of freedom is to remedy the evils generated by equality.

It is not necessary to retrace Tocqueville's analysis of American institutions in any detail. When he speaks of local life, of civil associations, of the press and of political associations, he always makes the same points: freedom pertains to the art of restoring life to the social body, of repairing the woof of a fabric that has been torn, and of countering the centrifugal movement of elements whose sole beneficiary is despotism. He writes, for example, that: 'The Americans have combated by free institutions the tendency of equality to keep men asunder' (vol. II, p. 103), and that: 'Free institutions ... remind every citizen ... that he lives in society' (p. 105). He also remarks that 'When men are no longer united among themselves by firm and lasting ties, it is impossible to obtain the cooperation of any great number of them unless you can persuade every man that his private interest obliges him voluntarily to unite his exertions to the exertions of all the others' (p. 111), and that 'A political association draws a number of individuals at the same time out of their own circle' (p. 116). The science of association – the 'mother of science' (p. 110) – thus tends to become one with the science of freedom.

The argument appears to be consonant with one of the themes of the first chapter of Book II, and the same theme is developed in the introduction. But we find once more that the author cannot sustain it to the very end. He contradicts it, at least tacitly, in the seventh chapter, where he compares the virtues of the associations that are formed in civil society with those of the great associations which mobilize men around political objectives. For a moment, he does of course continue to speak of freedom as a defence against the threat of the decomposition of society. But his picture of democracy changes. Great political associations or parties are no longer seen as artifices which elites can use to remedy the disadvantages of individualism; they correspond to the aspirations of the majority, to its desire to participate in the management of public affairs. We find, then, that it is no longer a question of stimulating men's initiative, but of not obstructing its free development. Having noted that 'when some kinds of associations are prohibited and others allowed, it is difficult to distinguish the former from the latter' and that 'in this state of doubt men abstain from them altogether', Tocqueville makes this remarkable observation:

> It is therefore chimerical to suppose that the spirit of association, when it is repressed on some one point, will nevertheless display the same vigor on all others ... When the members of a community are allowed and accustomed to combine for all purposes, they will combine as readily for the lesser as for the more important ones; but if they are allowed to combine only for small affairs, they will be neither inclined nor able to effect it. (vol. II, p. 117)

We spoke of a reversal of perspective; this last argument is in fact based upon the conviction that men have a natural penchant for freedom, that the threat it poses to public tranquillity cannot be avoided and that, on the contrary, great risks have to be taken to avoid the dangers implicit in a 'restricted' freedom which is liable to explode into anarchy or to be extinguished by despotism. 'Thus it is by the enjoyment of a dangerous freedom that Americans learn the art of rendering the dangers of freedom less formidable' (p. 119).

It is true that Tocqueville never loses sight of the evils of individualism, but his views as to the blessings of freedom are no longer based upon his initial premisses. He suggests that democracy gives birth to two tendencies, one leading to the isolation of individuals, and the other to the promotion of trade and of joint initiatives. 'In their political associations the Americans, of all conditions, minds and ages, daily acquire a general taste for association and grow accustomed to the use of it' (p. 119).

The reservations the author expresses at the end of this chapter, where he evokes the case of the nations of Europe, are an eloquent testimony to the ambiguity of his interpretation. Recalling the criticisms of unrestrained freedom of association that were put forward in Book I on the grounds that, in political matters, 'if it does not throw them [the people] into anarchy . . . it perpetually brings them, as it were, to the verge of it' (vol. II, p. 119), he now makes the point that civil peace, respect for the laws and stability of government are precious blessings but that, if political freedom is to be sacrificed to them, the cost to the nation must be weighed: 'I can understand that it may be advisable to cut off a man's arm in order to save his life, but it would be ridiculous to assert that he will be as dextrous as he was before he lost it' (p. 120). The vitalist metaphor finally does away with the artificialist metaphor which has constantly been used in previous chapters. Political freedom returns to the pole of nature. The art of politics still has its place, but it consists of compromising with political freedom in one way or another, and not of introducing it into an amorphous democratic mass.[3]

Book IV (and we will only be dealing with those aspects of it which are relevant to our purposes) represents Tocqueville's final attempt to reformulate, rectify and, to some extent, reorient his analysis of equality and of its relationship with freedom. We have already pointed out that it is closely related to Book II. He states explicitly that his aim is to show the influence of democratic ideas and feelings on political society or, as he puts it in a brief preamble, on 'the government of human societies' (p. 287). He has, however, broached this subject on a number of occasions, notably when he claimed to be describing the influence of ideas and feelings – here, the order of the argument is reversed – on democracy. We must therefore recognize that, as well as revealing signs of a division whose pertinence is very relative, Book IV also contains an attempt to embrace the logic of democracy or to determine the course of the democratic revolution. 'To succeed in this object,' he notes, 'I shall frequently have to retrace my steps, but I trust the reader will not refuse to follow me through paths already known to him, which may lead to some new truth' (p. 287). The most novel truth would appear to be found in chapter 6 with its description of the 'immense and tutelary power' which arises in modern democracy:

> I think ... that the species of oppression by which democratic nations are menaced is unlike anything that ever before existed in the world; our contemporaries will find no prototype of it in their memories. I seek in vain for an expression that will accurately convey the whole of the idea I have formed of it; the old words despotism and tyranny are inappropriate; the thing itself is new, and since I cannot name, I must attempt to define it. (p. 318)

As everyone knows, this analysis has done more to ensure Tocqueville's posthumous fame than the rest of his work taken together, and I would not dream of denying either its originality or its fecundity. But, given that we are trying to locate discrepancies or even contradictions in his thought, it must not blind us to the author's starting point, which, if we compare the first chapter to the opening chapter of Book II, is in itself new. In the latter, we observed, the initial assertion that, in its highest state, equality blends with political freedom prepared the ground for a divorce between equality and freedom. Here, the author begins with a eulogy of democracy for which nothing in his earlier criticisms has prepared us. The title of the chapter announces that 'Equality naturally gives men a taste for free institutions', and the first lines of the text explain why this is so:

> The principle of equality, which makes men independent of each other, gives them a habit and a taste for following in their private actions no other guide than their own will. This complete independence, which they constantly enjoy in regard to their equals and in the intercourse of private life, tends to make them look upon all authority with a jealous eye and speedily suggests to them the notion and love of political freedom. Men living at such times have a natural bias towards free institutions. Take any one of them at a venture, and you will find that, of all governments, he will soonest conceive and most highly value that government whose head he has himself elected and whose administration he may control. (p. 287)

Equality is, it is true, once more presented as a fundamental fact, but it is so immediately linked with its effect – freedom – that the latter is again related to the pole of nature (social nature) and grounded in instinct. This masks a logical hiatus: how can it still be claimed that freedom is introduced into an egalitarian society from the outside? And it masks a historical hiatus: how can it still be claimed that

Europe's misfortunes result from the fact that equality is long-standing and that freedom is recent? It is impossible, finally, to sustain the idea that they meet and blend only at their extremes: they have been shown to be consubstantial. The tendency towards freedom is inseparable from the tendency towards equality: men have a natural bias towards free institutions. The body of the chapter does not refute this eulogy of democracy; in fact the conclusion reinforces it as the author makes what is in effect a profession of faith:

> Personally, far from finding fault with equality because it inspires a spirit of independence, I praise it primarily for that very reason. I admire it because it lodges in the very depths of each man's mind and heart that indefinable feeling, the instinctive inclination for political independence, and thus prepares the remedy for the ill which it engenders. It is precisely for this reason that I cling to it. (p. 288)

It might be said, then, that equality is not an unmixed blessing; it engenders an ill. True. Tocqueville has not forgotten what he wrote about the separation of individuals that accompanies the destruction of hierarchies or, more generally, of networks of personal dependency. But, aside from the fact that the accent is now placed on the good aspect of equality, the word itself, which was once an index of exteriority, has now become an index of freedom's interiority: equality bears within it the remedy for the ills it engenders.

The mention of the dangers implicit in equality is also a clear indication of the extent to which Tocqueville has distanced himself from his earlier theses. He ascribes to 'timid minds' the fear that love of independence inspires. Whereas the break-up of the social was formerly seen as a threat, it now becomes the object of a hypothesis which has no consistency and which is, in a sense, secondary:

> As the citizens have no direct influence on each other, as soon as the supreme power of the nation fails, which kept them all in their several stations, it would seem that disorder must instantly reach its utmost pitch and that, every man drawing aside in a different direction, the fabric of society must at once crumble away. I am convinced, however, that anarchy is not the principal evil that democratic ages have to fear, but the least. (p. 288)

It is as though Tocqueville were his own interlocutor, for it was Tocqueville himself who described the breaking of the links which once made up the chain.

But we still have to ask ourselves why the author discards a representation which seemed to mean so much to him – or, to be more accurate, whether he discards it in absolute terms, or whether he does so on a provisional basis and in favour of some other representation.

In one sense there can be no doubt as to the answer: the representation does indeed change. The idea that the greatest threat is the crumbling away of the social body is, in one way or another, rejected several times in Book IV. It gives way to an idea which has, of course, already been advanced, but which now becomes central to his critique of democracy, namely the idea that fear of anarchy or love of order will pave the way for absolute power. Thus, at the beginning of chapter 3, we read:

> The love of public tranquillity is frequently the only passion which these nations retain, and it becomes more active and powerful among them in proportion as all other passions droop and die. This naturally disposes the members of the community constantly to give or surrender additional rights to the central power, which alone seems to be interested in defending them by the same means that it uses to defend itself. (pp. 293–4)

The same point is made in Chapter IV, where Tocqueville again evokes the case of France, of a people who have emerged from a long and bloody revolution and who are therefore more than ever disposed to increase the functions of central government: 'The love of public tranquillity becomes at such times an indiscriminate passion, and the members of the community are apt to conceive a most inordinate devotion to order' (p. 301).

These last observations, and even more so the broader argument within which they are inscribed, enlighten us as to the motives behind the change that has taken place. It is because the *social void* appears to him to be a fiction that Tocqueville is no longer concerned with drawing attention to the process of the fragmentation or dislocation of society. He sees anarchy as the 'least of the evils' democratic societies have to fear because he is convinced that, even if we accept the worst of all possible hypotheses, it will be no more than episodic. His main conviction appears to be that, on the contrary, democracy tends to give society such plenitude and such solidity that the variety of ideas, feelings and modes of behaviour, the free play of initiative and even the desire for novelty will disappear.

Once again, it is important to refer back to Book II. It will be recalled that the analysis of individualism made in the second chapter affords Tocqueville the opportunity to contrast the democratic model with the aristocratic model so as to bring out their distinctive features: on the one hand, a principle of association; on the other a principle of disassociation. The comparison between the two models is taken up once more in the corresponding chapter of Book IV, but this time it is used to show that one is characterized by social differentiation, which gives rise to the idea of a multiplicity of secondary powers and which makes it inconceivable that uniform rules could be imposed upon all members of the social body, and that the other is characterized by equality of condition, which gives rise to the idea of 'a single and central power' and of 'uniformity of legislation' (p. 289). One could of course take the view that the two ideas are not incompatible, and that they apply to different phenomena. But if the former is taken to its logical conclusion, it is impossible to recognize the emergence of the individual, of a citizen who relates to himself at a distance from other citizens, as a positive sign of independence. It further implies a classic conception of despotism which obscures the novelty of the democratic fact in modern society. This is already apparent from the beginning of chapter 4 of Book II, which is designed to show how Americans combat the effects of individualism by free institutions: 'Equality places men side by side, unconnected by any common tie; despotism raises barriers to keep them asunder; the former predisposes them not to consider their fellow creatures, the latter makes general indifference a sort of public virtue' (p. 102). It is of little import that the author should add that 'Despotism ... which is at all times dangerous is more particularly to be feared in democratic ages' (p. 102); he is superimposing an institution which exists 'at all times' upon the present. The argument does, however, become much more subtle in the final Book, where the author attempts to articulate the fact of a new freedom with that of a new power.

All the more remarkable, therefore, is the reworking of the problematic which occurs when Tocqueville makes central to his argument the themes of a single central power and of uniformity of legislation. These themes mobilize a representation of equality which we have of course seen him outline before, but it now acquires a new status.

To remain, however, with the second chapter of Book IV. Having compared the aristocratic and democratic models, Tocqueville declares that 'As the conditions of men become equal among a people, individuals seem of less and society of greater importance; or rather every citizen, being assimilated to all the rest, is lost in the crowd, and nothing stands conspicuous but [*l'on n'aperçoit plus que*] the great and imposing image of the people at large' (p. 290). This sentence is worthy of detailed examination. As we can see, the initial proposition is qualified. It in fact evokes the familiar image of levelling, but it does not allow us to understand why the debasement of individuals should go hand in hand with the elevation, not of power, but of society. To do that, it would have to be immediately asserted that the individual is necessarily caught up in a social representation, and that his image therefore cannot contract at one pole without the image of society becoming dilated at the other. But the author does not say that. The slippage introduced by the 'or rather' suggests that the identity of each individual becomes lost within a collective identity as a result of assimilation. The break in the sentence and the irruption of the *on* are in themselves eloquent. The image of the people becomes detached from that of individuals, and it is perceived by all from an impersonal viewpoint. But, having introduced the term 'the people', Tocqueville immediately continues:

This naturally gives the men of democratic periods a lofty opinion of the privileges of society and a very humble notion of the rights of individuals; they are ready to admit that the interests of the former are everything and those of the latter nothing. They are willing to acknowledge that the power which represents the community has far more information and wisdom than any of the members of that community; and that it is the duty, as well as the right, of that power to guide as well as govern each private citizen. (p. 290)

The substitution of *society* for *the people* is worthy of note. It is a sign that the process which began with equality is being reduplicated. We have, on the one hand, an identification with all the rest which gives rise to the image of the People-as-One, and, on the other, a schism which gives rise both to a pure multiplicity of individuals reduced to a minimal degree of power [*puissance*], and to society as such. The omnipotence of the real is imprinted on the latter. And this sheds light on power [*pouvoir*] in two ways. Power can embody the people; as has already been suggested, the people are a condensation of opinion; the people exercise the tyranny of the majority, to use a formula from Book I. Power can also *represent* society, which is indefinable but which is also the only thing to have substance and strength and, because it represents society, it seems to all to be an 'imposing power which alone rises above the level of universal depression' (p. 294).

The comment to the effect that the same representation triumphs even where the doctrine of popular sovereignty is most violently rejected immediately proves that we are not on the wrong track. 'The idea of intermediate powers is weakened and obliterated; the idea of rights inherent in certain individuals is rapidly disappearing from the minds of men; the idea of the omnipotence and sole authority of society at large rises to fill its place' (p. 291).

It is in this context that the notion of 'social power' begins to be deployed in systematic fashion. The notion is, it seems to me, an index of a new conception which means that the sphere of the political can no longer be circumscribed at a remove from the sphere of the social. Power does, of course, still appear to be the site of an effective action of levelling. It follows its 'natural tendencies' by encouraging equality and uniformity: 'The government likes what the citizens like and naturally hates what they hate' (p. 295). And where does this entente come from, if not from a sort of chiasmus between a society which elevates itself to the status of power, and a power which is diffused throughout society?

What, then, becomes of equality in Tocqueville's analysis? It is no longer revealed by the spectacle of the dispersal of individuals who were formerly members of a corporate entity (or of more than one such entity), or of individuals who are equal because they are independent units and because, by definition, no one individual is inferior or superior to another. On the one hand, 'equality' designates similarity, and it has the effect of producing the illusion, which is inscribed in the real, of a collective identity known as the People. On the other hand, it appears within the formation of a uniform surface, and has the effect of producing the illusion (which is also inscribed in the real) of an agency which is distanced from it but which understands the law of its construction: the power which *represents* society and which the author describes as 'sole, simple, providential and *creative*' (p. 291, emphasis added).

It is, then, as though Tocqueville recognized the virtues of equality as the moment of the emergence of freedom solely in order to neutralize this representation. He does not discard it, but first downgrades it, and then goes so far as to exploit it anew in order to convince the reader that democracy naturally evolves towards a new kind of despotism. This line of thought is already visible in chapter 3, where the author continues his examination of the phenomenon of the concentration of power. Having noted that love of public tranquillity outweighs all other passions (we have already cited this passage), he seems to want to recall his earlier comments on the taste for independence that is generated by equality. We are then faced with an ambiguity: independence and powerlessness. These are, we are told, 'two conditions which must never be either separately considered or confounded together' (p. 294), but it soon becomes apparent that both lend themselves to the development of power. The debility of the individual makes him feel 'the want of some outward assistance' (p. 294) which he cannot hope to receive from any of his equals, and so he turns his eyes to the imposing power which alone arises above the level of universal depression. The demand for independence, for its part, proves essentially to be voiced at others' expense, but every man's refusal to obey another can coexist alongside 'common dependence' on an absolute third party. 'The man of a democratic age is', notes Tocqueville, 'extremely reluctant to obey his neighbour, who is his equal', but 'he loves continually to remind him of the common dependence in which both of them stand to the same master' (p. 295). This last formula does not, however, appear to be entirely convincing, as it still leaves room for the notion of dependence on someone – the master – and Tocqueville quickly qualifies it by adding: 'Democratic nations often hate those in whose hands the central power is vested, but they always love that power itself' (p. 296). The argument thus seems to be complete; nothing remains of the declaration we noted in chapter 1: 'Men living at such times have a natural bias towards free institutions' (p. 287). Their natural bias now seems to lead them to acceptance of the yoke of power, and at the same time it leads them to avoid all personal dependence. Tocqueville returns then, by an unexpected route, to one of the major themes of Book II: 'Individual independence and local liberties will ever be the products of art' (p. 296).

But this is only a stage. It is in chapter 6 that freedom is finally transformed into its opposite. In chapter 3, the 'love of the power' which resists the hatred shown towards those in whose hands power is vested is directed towards a power which has the function of *representing* society, but we are told nothing about the origins of that power or about the figures in whom it is vested. When Tocqueville then denounces 'the sort of despotism which democratic nations have to fear' and refers to an oppression which is new and which he cannot name, he is not satisfied with defining its characteristics: 'an immense and tutelary power ... absolute, minute, regular, provident, and mild ...' which takes control of every aspect of men's lives and which 'every day renders the exercise of the free agency of man less useful and less frequent' (p. 318). At the end of his analysis, he adds that servitude 'might be combined more easily than is commonly believed with some of the outward forms of freedom' (p. 319). And then, with greater resolution, he reveals to the reader that the regime which is most likely to inscribe this model in reality is the regime which displays the features of political democracy:

> Our contemporaries are constantly excited by two conflicting passions: they want to be led, and they wish to remain free. As they cannot destroy either the one or the other of these contrary propensities, they strive to satisfy them both at once. They devise a sole, tutelary, and all-powerful government, but elected by the people. They combine the principle of centralization and that of popular sovereignty; this gives them a respite; they console themselves for being in tutelage by the reflection that they have chosen their own guardians. Every man allows himself to be put in leading-strings, because he sees that it is not a person or class of persons, but the people at large who hold the end of his chain. By this system the people shake off their state of dependence just long enough to select their master and then relapse into it again. (p. 319)

Even this last proposition is immediately qualified. The momentary respite from dependence itself appears to be illusory:

> It is vain to summon a people who have been rendered so dependent on the central power to choose from time to time the representatives of that power; this rare and brief exercise of their free choice, however important it may be, will not prevent them from gradually losing the faculties of thinking, feeling and acting for themselves, and thus gradually falling below the level of humanity. (pp. 320–1)

The model is condemned in such strong terms that we can forget the reservations that were expressed earlier, namely that the rule of one man or of an irresponsible body would be worse still; that oppression is less degrading when it is exercised beneath the sign of popular sovereignty; that individuals do make some gains when they sacrifice their independence to the public. The ultimate truth appears to be that the new despotism takes on its most definite form when the image of power as representing society combines with that of the people as being concerned solely with their own affairs.

Such, then, is the strange argument that seems to be put forward in Book IV. It is certainly very different to the argument we traced earlier, but it contains just as many surprises. No – we have interrupted it too soon because we are still trapped by the interpretation that has come down to posterity. Let us not forget the final lines of chapter 6. Suddenly the picture changes once more. Tocqueville corrects himself:

> A constitution republican in its head and ultra-monarchical in all its other parts has already appeared to me to be a shortlived monster. The vices of rulers and the ineptitude of the people would speedily bring about its ruin; and the nation, weary of its representatives and of itself, would create freer institutions or soon return to stretch itself at the feet of a single master. (p. 321)

We would therefore be wrong to conclude that tutelary democracy is viable and that the bias towards independence will, if left to itself, lead to a state of servitude. Despite all the arguments that have been put forward to convince us that this is the case, we must finally accept that freedom cannot in the long term conceal servitude, that freedom will be won once more or that, if it is lost, it will disappear completely in the face of despotism. It would also be wrong to think that this last development in Tocqueville's discourse is a sign that a brief and inconsistent concession is being made to hope, that he is moving beyond the framework of his theory. Tocqueville takes his rehabilitation much further at the end of chapter 7. He does of course again describe freedom as a remedy for equality, but he concludes that:

> The men who live in the democratic ages upon which we are entering have naturally a taste for independence; they are naturally impatient of regulation, and they are wearied by the permanence even of the condition they themselves prefer. They are fond of power, but they are prone to despise and hate those who wield it, and they easily elude its grasp by their own mobility and insignificance. These propensities will always manifest themselves, because they originate in the groundwork of society, which will undergo no change; for a long time they will prevent the establishment of any despotism, and they will furnish new weapons to each succeeding generation that struggles in favor of the liberty of mankind. (p. 330)

Every word is directed against the theses that were advanced earlier. It is particularly noteworthy that individuals are no longer prisoners of power because they have been debased; their very insignificance saves them. It is also to be noted that the people no longer love power, even though they hate those in whose hands it is vested (p. 296); despite their love of power, they never lose sight of the hateful and despicable figure of the master.

Finally, it seems significant that this conclusion should stem from a new reflection upon the nature of the aristocratic model and the democratic model: 'I shall conclude with one general idea, which comprises not only all the particular ideas that have been expressed in the present chapter, but also most of those of which it is the object of this book to treat' (p. 328). It is important not to distort his intentions: he intends to show that there was a time when men's efforts tended to increase and strengthen the might of social power, and, now that it has reached its height, it is their task to impose limits upon it, to assert and protect the rights of private citizens, and to preserve the independence of the individual. But his first observation does not concern power alone. Taking up a theme which we have already seen in chapter 2, he remarks that in aristocratic ages, '*the outline of society itself was not easily discernible* and was constantly confounded with the different powers by which the community was ruled' (p. 328, emphasis added). In my view, this judgement determines the chapter's final considerations as to the virtues of democracy. It is therefore all the more surprising that Tocqueville should not make the connection explicit. What one might have expected him to add is that the outline of society is born together with modern democracy (and this would provide the other term of the opposition); or, to be more accurate, and as the term 'outline of society' is ambiguous, that, along with the formation of an image of the people or of society – and these are still determinate images in which a belief in a collective identity or an objective power crystallizes – there is born a desire to see the social as something visible. Yet he holds back from this conclusion; neither the idea of a unique power nor that of uniform legislation can explain the new meaning that has been invested in politics and right.

Need it be stated that this examination of part of Tocqueville's discourse (which some may find too detailed, though it is, to my mind, not detailed enough) was not intended to catch him out in his own contradictions? The results of such a project would be both slight and sterile. As with any great thinker, we can learn from Tocqueville's contradictions. Indeed, I will go further than that: it is perhaps because he is blind to the questions raised by the historical development of freedom that he is capable of finding in modern society features that his contemporaries – bourgeois democratic and socialist thinkers alike – could not discern. Almost one and a half centuries later, we are still faced with the enigma of democracy, and his work helps us to decipher it.

PART IV

ON THE IRREDUCIBLE ELEMENT

11

The Permanence of the Theologico-Political?

There was, in the nineteenth century, a widespread and lasting conviction that one cannot discern the transformations that occur in political society – that one cannot really take stock of what is appearing, disappearing or reappearing – without examining the religious significance of the Old and the New. In both France and Germany, philosophy, history, the novel and poetry all testify adequately to that. This conviction is not of course entirely new, and it can be traced far back into history. I am not thinking of the work of the theologians and jurists, or of their disputations over the links between the authority of Kings and Emperors, and that of Popes; no matter how they exercised it, their thought was still confined within the limits of a theologico-political experience of the world. It is, it seems to me, in the sixteenth century that we detect the first signs of a modern reflection upon politics and religion; it is then that a new sensitivity to the question of the foundations of the civil order is born as a result of the combined effects of the collapse of the authority of the Church and of the struggles that accompanied the Reformation; as a result both of the assertion of the absolute right of the Prince and of challenges to that right. It is, however, still true to say that at the beginning of the nineteenth century a much wider debate is inaugurated as a result of the French Revolution. It is while that event is still a living memory that there arises a feeling that a break has occurred, but that it did not occur within time, that it establishes a relationship between human beings and time itself, that it makes history a mystery; that it cannot be circumscribed within the field of what are termed political, social or economic institutions; that it establishes a relationship between human beings and the institution itself; that it makes society a mystery. The religious meaning of this break haunts the minds of the men of the period, no matter what verdicts they may reach – no matter whether they look for signs of a restoration of Catholicism, for signs of a renewal of Christianity within Catholicism or Protestantism, for signs of the fulfilment of Christianity in political and social life, outside the old framework of the Churches, or even for signs of its complete destruction and of the birth of a new faith. To mention only the case of France, we might say that at one extreme we have legitimists like De Maistre, that at the other we have socialists like Leroux, and that, between the two extremes, we have such individual thinkers as Ballanche, Chateaubriand, Michelet and Quinet; they all speak the same language, and it is simultaneously political, philosophical and religious.

It is true – and let us not forget it – that the same period sees the assertion of a new state of mind, of a tendency (traces of which can be found in the sixteenth century, and which became clearly outlined during the French Revolution) to conceive of the state as an independent entity, to make politics a reality *sui generis*, and to relegate religion to the domain of private belief. As early as 1817, Hegel was already denouncing this tendency in terms which foreshadow its future developments. Arguing in the *Encyclopedia* that 'the state rests on the ethical sentiment, and that on the religious', he adds this valuable commentary:

> It has been the monstrous blunder of our times to try to look upon these inseparables as separable from one another, and even as mutually indifferent. The view taken of the relationship of religion and the state has been that, whereas the state had an independent existence of its own, springing from some source and power, religion was a later addition, something desirable perhaps for strengthening the political bulwarks, but purely subjective in individuals: – or it may be, religion is treated as something without effect on the moral life of the state, i.e., its reasonable law and constitution which are based on a ground of their own.[1]

Before long, similar criticisms became widespread in France, but they were based upon different premises, were inspired by humanism or by a socialism tinged with a new religiosity, and were addressed to adversaries who came to the fore when the reign of Louis-Philippe ensured the triumph of a pragmatic or even cynical politics which Victor Cousin painted in more favourable colours as eclecticism. This 'bastard philosophy', to use Leroux's expression, certainly celebrates the indestructible virtues of religion, but it does so in order to subordinate them to the preservation of a political order which, to cite Hegel once more, is based on a ground of its own.

We therefore have to recognize that what is now the dominant conception of politics goes back a long way. Its origins seem to merge with those of the bourgeois spirit – with the spirit of a bourgeoisie which has become politically dominant. Without wishing to dwell on the vicissitudes of ideology that drove it from the intellectual scene, we ought, then, to say that it is not in the work of the thinkers we first mentioned that we find the first signs of our modernity, but in eclecticism. The 'monstrous blunder' which Hegel denounces would therefore appear to designate the truth of modern times, the truth of our own times. The judgement of history which he evokes so often appears to have gone against him, to have denounced his blunder. In more general terms, we would then have to conclude that, if those thinkers who sought the religious truth of the political revolution they had witnessed (and I am referring to the democratic revolution) seem so alien to the sensibilities of our time, it is because they had no understanding of the new. But can we leave matters at that, and wax ironic about their wild imaginings? For these thinkers, the Ancien Regime was something that had existed in living memory. They still lived in the gap between a world that was disappearing and a world that was appearing, and their thought was still haunted by questions which knew no limits – by which I mean that it was not yet restricted by any presuppositions as to how to define objects of knowledge or as to how to define politics, religion, law, economics or culture. Might we not ask ourselves whether these thinkers may, even if they were mistaken, have had a singular ability to grasp a symbolic dimension of the political, of something which was later to disappear, of something which bourgeois discourse was already burying beneath its supposed knowledge of the real order of society?

Before we attempt to answer that question, we must first define our terms.

It is certainly a fact that political institutions have long been separated from religious institutions; it is also a fact that religious beliefs have retreated into the realm of private opinion. The phenomenon is observable even in countries where Catholicism remains the dominant religion. True, this statement has to be qualified if we also take into consideration those European countries that have come under totalitarian domination. But, whilst that phenomenon is thought-provoking, let us ignore it for the moment in order to concentrate on our general observation. Does it have any meaning in itself? Can we say that religion has simply disappeared in the face of politics (and survives only on the periphery of politics) without asking ourselves what its investment in the political realm once meant? And do we not have to assume that it was so profoundly invested therein as to have become unrecognizable to those who believe its effects to have been exhausted? Can we not admit that, despite all the changes that have occurred, the religious survives in the guise of new beliefs and new representations, and that it can therefore return to the surface, in either traditional or novel forms, when conflicts become so acute as to produce cracks in the edifice of the state?

According to the former view, the 'modern' notion of politics is not in doubt, and derives from our actual experience. According to the latter, it is an index of our ignorance or disavowal of a hidden part of social life, namely the processes which make people consent to a given regime – or, to put it more forcefully, which determine *their manner of being in society* – and which guarantee that this regime or mode of society has a permanence in time, regardless of the various events that may affect it. Following that line of argument would not necessarily take us back to those interpretations (and they are, moreover, contradictory) which regarded the link between the religious and the political as indissoluble, but we would at least have to recapture something of their inspiration.

If, however, we specify the terms of our question in this way, we cannot fail to notice that they are closely related to the meaning we give to the words 'the religious' and, more important still, 'the political'. We must, then, examine their meaning.

We can define 'the religious' in broader or narrower terms, and the threshold beyond which the word loses all pertinence is a matter for debate; it would, however, seem that we can readily agree that certain beliefs, attitudes and representations reveal a religious sensibility, even though the agents concerned do not relate them to any dogma; even though they do not imply any fidelity on their part to a church; and even though they may, in certain cases, go hand in hand with militant atheism. The expression 'religious sensibility ' retains a fairly precise content if we relate it to historically and culturally determined phenomena: in other words not to religion in general but to the Christian religion, whose various manifestations we can identify without any risk of error. The word 'political', on the other hand, brings us face to face with an ambiguity that must be resolved if we are to know what we are talking about. The fact that we can choose to say either *the political* [*le politique*] or *politics [la politique*] is, as we all know, an index of this ambiguity. What is certain is that the delimitation of the domain known as 'the political' does not result from methodological criteria alone. The very notion of 'limits' in fact derives from a desire for an 'objective' definition – a desire that lies at the origin of the political theory, political science and political sociology that have developed in the course of our century. No matter whether we attempt, for example, to circumscribe an order of social relations which are intelligible in themselves, such as power relations; to conceive of a body of social functions whose necessary articulation signals the coherence of a system; to distinguish a superstructural level, based upon relations of production at which class domination is at once expressed and disguised by institutions, practices and representations which supposedly serve the general interest; or, finally, to identify from empirical observation which of the mass of social facts relate directly or indirectly to the exercise of power, the underlying assumption is always the same: we assume that the object can have substance only if it is particular. In other words, the epistemological operation through which we relate to the object – be it posited as 'real' or as 'ideal' – makes it appear by separating it from other defined or definable objects. The criterion of what is *political* is supplied by the criterion of what is *non-political*, by the criterion of what is economic, social, juridical, aesthetic, or religous. This operation is not innocent; it hides behind a truism borrowed from the domain constituted as that of exact knowledge: science deals only with particulars. It need scarcely be pointed out that this disposition has never prevented anyone from looking for articulations between that which pertains to politics and that which pertains to different realities or different systems; on the contrary, it usually acts as an encouragement to do so. How, for example, do power relations combine with juridical relations? How is the political system integrated into a general system as a sub-system? How are the political institutions, practices and representations which are essential to the preservation of a mode of production determined, and what is their specific efficacy in different socio-historical formations? How do they in their turn exploit a given state of culture, law or religion? Theorists and observers are only too willing to formulate such problems. Indeed, those who take a relational, a Marxist, a functionalist or a descriptive stance urge us to use our historical experience as a means to identify the various modes of the articulation of social relations, sub-systems and superstructural levels. But it is still true to say that any attempt to conceptualize the ways in which the combinations vary derives from the preliminary operation of breaking down social data in order to find something intelligible. And it is also true to say that that operation is inspired by a principle which erects the subject into being a pure subject of knowledge, gives it a scientific neutrality, and guarantees it its self-assurance by virtue of the coherence of its constructs or observations.

We arrive at a very different idea of *the political* if we remain true to philosophy's oldest and most constant inspiration, if we use the term to refer to the principles that generate society or, more accurately, different forms of society. It would be absurd to claim that we then apprehend the political in its wider acceptation. We are elaborating a different idea and we are guided by a different requirement of knowledge. We do not need to evoke the centuries-old debate that makes up the history of political philosophy in order to specify the meaning of this idea or of this requirement. For it is not relevant to our purposes to ask how the philosopher's search was, in the past, guided by his investigations into the essence of man, into the transition from a state of nature or into reason's self-realization in history. The idea that what distinguishes one society from another is its *regime* – or, to be more accurate and to avoid an over-worked term – its *shaping* [*mise en forme*] of human coexistence has, in one form or another, always been present, and it lies, so to speak behind the theoretical constructs and behind advances in philosophical thought which are tested against the transformation of the world. In other words, it is simply because the very notion of society already contains within it a reference to its political definition that it proves impossible, in the eyes of the philosopher, to localize the political *in* society. The space called society cannot in itself be conceived as a system of relations, no matter how complex we imagine that system to be. On the contrary, it is its overall schema, the particular mode of its institution that makes it possible to conceptualize (either in the past or the present) the articulation of its dimensions, and the relations established within it between classes, groups and individuals, between practices, beliefs and representations. If we fail to grasp this primordial reference to the mode of the institution of the social, to generative principles or to an overall schema governing both the temporal and the spatial configuration of society, we lapse into a positivist fiction; we inevitably adopt the notion of a pre-social society, and posit as elements aspects that can only be grasped on the basis of an experience that is already social. If, for example, we grant to relations of production or the class struggle the status of reality, we forget that *social division* can only be defined – unless of course we posit the absurd view that it is a division between alien societies – insofar as it represents an internal division, insofar as it represents a division within a single milieu, within one 'flesh' (to use Merleau-Ponty's expression); insofar as its terms are determined by relations, but also insofar as those relations are themselves determined by their common inscription within the same space and testify to a common awareness of their inscription therein. Similarly, if we make a rigid distinction between what belongs to the realm of economics or politics (defined in modern science's sense of the term), or between what belongs to the juridical or the religious in an attempt to find within them signs of specific systems, we forget that we can arrive at that analytic distinction only because we already have a subjective idea of the primal dimensionality of the social, and that this implies an idea of its primal *form*, of its political *form*.

The difference between the idea of the political – in all its variants and all its moments – and political science – in all its variants and all its moments – is not that the latter is concerned with society as a totality and that the former rejects 'totality' as an illusory object. Marxist science, for example (and I am not referring here to Marx himself; his thought is at once more ambiguous and more subtle than this) does indeed claim to be able to reconstruct a real or ideal totality; Parsonian science also claims to be able to rearticulate systems of functions within what it terms a general system. The opposition manifests itself at a different level. The philosopher is not necessarily in search of an elusive object such as a totality; he looks at different regimes or forms of society in order to identify a principle of internalization which can account for a specific mode of differentiation and articulation between classes, groups and social ranks, and, at the same time, for a specific mode of discrimination between markers – economic, juridical, aesthetic, religious markers – which order the experience of coexistence.

We can further specify the notion of shaping [*mise en forme*] which we have introduced by pointing out that it implies both the notion of giving meaning [*mise en sens*] to social relations (the expression *mise en sens* is taken from Piera Aulagnier), and that of staging them [*mise en scène*]. Alternatively, we can say that the advent of a society capable of organizing social relations can come about only if it can institute the conditions of their intelligibility, and only if it can use a multiplicity of signs to arrive at a quasi-representation of itself. But we must again stress that the shaping or institution of the political cannot be reduced to the limits of the social as such. As soon as we posit as *real* the distinction between what is social and what is not social, we enter the realm of fiction. We have just said that the principle of internalization which enables us to conceptualize the political presupposes a mode of discriminating between the various markers that organize the experience of coexistence; and that experience is inseparable from the experience of the world, from the experience of the visible and the invisible in every register. It need scarcely be stressed that discrimination between real and imaginary, true and false, just and unjust, natural and supernatural, and normal and abnormal is not restricted to the relations people establish in social life. The elaboration attested to by any political society – and not simply the society in which the subject who is trying to decipher it lives – therefore involves an investigation into the world, into Being as such. Understanding how the experience of an *objective* world, of a world which is what it is independently of particular collective experiences, arose – at least partially – in the course of history – and it is tempting to describe it in Husserlian terms as a transition from the socio-political *Umwelt* to the *Welt* – would of course be a formidable task, and a further task for political thought.

For the moment, however, we will restrict ourselves to an examination of the difference between political philosophy and political science. We can agree that the latter encounters problems which bear the hallmark of philosophical research but, for political science, they are of course no more than *problems* to be circumvented, along with other problems, during the process of reconstructing or describing the workings of society. In fact the theorist who analyses politics in terms of power relations cannot but ask himself how and why they stabilize in any given configuration in such a way that the dominant power does not have to exercise its authority openly, irrespective of whether he grants them their own logic or sees them as a reflection or a transposition of class relations which are themselves determined by a mode of production. He cannot but ask how and why they succeed in eluding the understanding of the actors, how and why they appear to be legitimate or in accordance with the nature of things. Apparently, then, his problem is how to account for the process of the internalization of domination. But he resolves that problem by looking beyond the frontiers of politics for the nature and origins of the process, by appealing to the mechanisms of representation he finds in the spheres of law, religion or technical-scientific knowledge. Similarly, the theorist who defines the specificity of political action by subordinating it to functional imperatives (ensuring the unification or cohesion of the social whole, making it possible to formulate and achieve general objectives) is not unaware of the fact that his definition is purely formal. He therefore accepts that such functions can be performed only if social agents internalize the political imperative. And in order to account for that, he invokes the values and norms which determine behavioural models within a given system of culture. But he then assigns specific functions to those norms and values; he seeks to find the preconditions for their efficacy within the coherence of the system whence they derive. In short, whatever the schema of the reconstruction or description may be, his approach always consists of isolating relations and combining them in order to deduce *society* from these operations. The fact that certain of these relations are assumed to provide a key to the modes of the internalization of the social should deceive no one. The theorist is moving to an external element. When he speaks of law, religion, science, values, norms and categories of knowledge, he is simply filling in the blanks in a pre-given schema of actions, practices and relations (defined in either materialist or formalist terms). The second operation depends upon the first. Precisely how the object is repositioned to allow the transition from the level of the real or the functional to the so-called level of the symbolic is of little import. Precisely how the element of the imaginary or of language is introduced is of little import. The conclusion that, in the last analysis, power relations, relations of production or functional relations are always 'represented' or 'spoken' by religious, juridical or scientific signs is also of little import. This notion of the symbolic does not help us to escape an artificialist conception; it is deployed in a play of articulation whose terms have already been separated out, and it is grafted on to something that is assumed to contain within it its own determination.

The opposition between philosophy and science is one between two intellectual requirements. For science, knowledge finds its self-assurance by defining functional models; it operates in accordance with an ideal of objectivity which introduces a sovereign distance between the subject and the social. The externality of the knowing subject is of necessity combined with the idea that the social can stand outside itself. Conversely, any system of thought, which takes up the question of the institution of the social is simultaneously confronted with the question of its own institution. It cannot restrict itself to comparing structures and systems once it realizes that the elaboration of coexistence creates meaning, produces markers for distinguishing between true and false, just and unjust, and imaginary and real; and that it establishes the horizons of human beings' relations with one another and with the world. It attempts to explain itself and, at the same time, to explain its object. In that respect, it seems to me that there is no radical difference between our present requirement and those of the philosophy of history or of ancient philosophy. We have lost the criteria of classical reason, refuse to distinguish between healthy and corrupt regimes,

between legitimate and illegitimate authorities – a distinction based
upon the idea of a human essence – and find it impossible to invoke
the idea of the development of Mind – which would allow us to see
the constitution of the modern state as both the completion of an
itinerary and the meaning of the stages (progression, regression and
digression) that go to make it up. Nevertheless, we are still traversed
by our investigation into the meaning of the human adventure that
unfolds in different forms of political society, and that investigation is
still a response to our experience of the political in the here and now.
We look for signs of truth and signs of legitimacy, for traces of the
concealment of truth and right, and we do so because of the tension
inherent in any thought that is trying to define what it has the *right*
to think.

To return to the question with which we began: that of the historical
disentanglement of the religious and the political. In the context of
sociology or political science, their disentanglement is an obvious fact
which leaves intact the categories of knowledge of the social. The
political and the religious are regarded as two separate orders of
practice and relations; the problem is one of understanding how they
are articulated, or how they cease to be articulated, by examining
empirical history. The fact that for hundreds or, rather, thousands of
years, human beings made no such distinction, and that they gave a
religious expression to the functions exercised by authority or to the
power relations whence it arose, does not detract from the need to
recognize the pertinence of a distinction whose value is self-evident in
terms of objective analysis. Now this approach brings us up against a
double difficulty: on the one hand, history, like society before it, loses
all depth; the phenomenon of separation becomes an index of one
general system among others, and science assumes a resolutely relativist
stance. When this happens, science conceals the conditions of its own
formation and, along with them, the basis for the claim that its
operations have a universal validity, as it is the fact of separation which
allows it to identify the specificity of politics. Alternatively, we have
a combination of a dialectical or evolutionary theory and the idea that
the elimination of religion from the political field marks the formation
of a rational, or potentially rational, type of society in which institutions
and practices appear, or begin to appear, for what they really are. But
in that case, the fact of the separation of the religious and the political
tells us nothing in itself; its meaning is established by reference to a
law of historical development or to the laws of the dynamic of social
structures.

The philosopher finds himself in a different position. When he thinks
of the principles that generate society and names them the political,
he automatically includes religious phenomena within his field of
reference. This does not mean that in his view the religious and the
political can coincide. It does, however, mean that one cannot separate
the elaboration of a political form – by virtue of which the nature and

representation of power and social division (divisions between classes
and groups) can stabilize, and by virtue of which the various dimensions
of the human experience of the world can simultaneously become
organized – from the elaboration of a religious form – by virtue of
which the realm of the visible can acquire death, and by virtue of
which the living can name themselves with reference to the dead,
whilst the human word can be guaranteed by a primal pact, and whilst
rights and duties can be formulated with reference to a primal law. In
short, both the political and the religious bring philosophical thought
face to face with the symbolic, not in the sense in which the social
sciences understand that term, but in the sense that, through their
internal articulations, both the political and the religious govern access
to the world. This does not make it inconceivable that there is, in any
society, a potential conflict between the two principles, or even that
it is universally, if tacitly, recognized to exist. Nor does the fact that
there is in the modern world an imperative to make a clear distinction
between the realms they regulate create difficulties for political thought;
this state of affairs in fact meets its requirements, as it has never been
able to submit to the authority of religion without demeaning itself, and
as it demands the right to seek its foundations within its own activities. In a sense, this revolutionary event is the accomplishment of
philosophy's destiny; philosophy is bound up with that event in that it
finds the conditions for its own emancipation at the very moment when
human beings acquire a potential grasp on their own history, a means
to escape the fatalism imposed on their lives by the subjugation of the
social order to religious law, and a means to detect the possibility of
a better regime in their practices and the novelties they create. But it
would be quite illegitimate to leap to the conclusion that religion as
such must disappear or, to be more accurate, that it must be confined
to the realm of personal opinion. How, in fact, could we argue that,
without losing all sense of its symbolic dimension, of the dimension
that constitutes the relations human beings establish with the world?
The fact that differences of opinion are now recognized to be legitimate
does of course have a symbolic meaning, but only, it would seem,
within the limitations of a political system which guarantees every
individual the right to enjoy the respect he must show others. What
philosophical thought strives to preserve is the experience of a difference
which goes beyond differences of opinion (and the recognition of the
relativity of points of view which this implies); the experience of a
difference which is not at the disposal of human beings, whose advent
does not take place *within* human history, and which cannot be
abolished therein; the experience of a difference which relates human
beings to their humanity, and which means that their humanity cannot
be self-contained, that it cannot set its own limits, and that it cannot
absorb its origins and ends into those limits. Every religion *states* in
its own way that human society can only open on to itself by being
held in an opening it did not create. Philosophy says the same thing,

but religion said it first, albeit in terms which philosophy cannot accept.

Philosophy's critique of religion is therefore ambivalent. Whilst, for example, it rejects the truth that the Christian churches find in Revelation and whilst, in theory, it escapes the authority of the Text and refuses to accept the image of a God who comes down to earth and is incarnated in the person of his Son, it does not assume that untruth is a lie or a lure. Nor, when it remains true to its inspiration, does it want to preserve untruth for the simple reason that it may contain beliefs which help to preserve the established political order. What philosophy discovers in religion is a mode of portraying or dramatizing the relations that human beings establish with something that goes beyond empirical time and the space within which they establish relations with one another. This work of the imagination stages [*met en scène*] a different time, a different space. Any attempt to reduce it to being simply a product of human activity is doomed. Of course it bears the mark of human operations in that the script for the performance bears witness to a human presence and borrows from human sense experience. Human beings populate the invisible with the things they see, naively invent a time that exists before time, organize a space that exists behind their space; they base the plot on the most general conditions of their lives. Yet anything that bears the mark of their experience also bears the mark of an *ordeal*. Once we recognize that humanity opens on to itself by being held in an opening it does not create, we have to accept that the change in religion is not to be read simply as a sign that the divine is a human invention, but as a sign of the deciphering of the divine or, beneath the appearance of the divine, of the excess of *being* over *appearance*. In that sense, modern religion or Christianity proves to be teaching the philosopher what he has to think. He rejects religion insofar as it is the enunciator of Revelation but, insofar as it is a mode of the enunciation of the divine, he at the same time accords it a power of revelation which philosophy cannot do without if, that is, it ceases to divorce the question of human nature from the question of human history.

To simplify the argument to extremes: what philosophical thought cannot adopt as its own, on pain of betraying its ideal of intelligibility, is the assertion that the man Jesus is the Son of God; what it must accept is the meaning of the advent of a representation of the *God-Man*, because it sees it as a change which recreates humanity's opening on to itself, in both the senses in which we have defined it. Modern philosophy cannot ignore its debt to modern religion; it can no longer distance itself from the work of the imagination or appropriate it as a pure object of knowledge, once it finds itself grappling with the question of its own advent, once it no longer conceals from itself that there is also such a thing as the philosophical *work of thought* and that the focus of its investigations can be displaced, even though it may indulge in the fantasy of being able to put a halt to its displacements. The philosopher's pretentions to Absolute Knowledge notwithstanding, the substitution of the concept for the image leaves intact the experience of alterity in language, and of a division between creation and unveiling, between activity and passivity, and between the expression and impression of meaning.

These last remarks may, perhaps, bring us closer to the most secret reasons for the philosopher's continued attachment to the religious. Justified as his demand for the right to think may be, and even though it frees him from every established authority, he not only realizes that any society which forgets its religious basis is labouring under the illusion of pure self-immanence and thus obliterates the locus of philosophy; he also senses that philosophy is bound up with religion because they are both caught up in an adventure to which philosophy does not possess the main key. And so, when he proclaims that Christianity's end has come, he still invokes the birth of a new faith, because he is unable to divorce his knowledge from a primordial knowledge which is at once latent and widely shared. Despite appearances, he therefore refuses to accept the historical fact of the separation of the religious and the political. As we have said, he argues that those who accept it as an established fact have a mistaken notion of the political. But in doing so, he runs the risk of denying that appearances have sufficient consistency to represent a new practice, to inscribe themselves in some way in the reality of power and the state. But, given that he accords representation a symbolic status and that he still thinks it impossible to divorce the position of power from its representation, a problem should now arise as to how to evaluate the change implied by the representation of a form of power which has no religious basis. Unless this problem arises, a philosophical critique will have no import, or will consist simply of the denunciation of erroneous opinions. But as we have already seen, that was not its objective; its object was the possibility of so shaping society that the religious world would be merely misrecognized or disavowed.

The future that the thinkers of the nineteenth century were attempting to decipher is to some extent our past and our present. The meaning of our present itself is of course dependent upon an indeterminate future; but we enjoy the advantage of an experience that was denied them and which brings a new relief to their debates. In their day, the political form we know as modern democracy was only just coming into being. All its premises had been established, but it still kept its secret, even though its dynamic and its ambiguities were partly visible, as we can see, in particular, from certain of Tocqueville's extraordinary insights into the future. The project of totalitarianism, however, still lay beyond the horizons of their political thought, and there can be no doubt but that it both helps to shed light on the secret of democracy and urges us to investigate anew the religious and the political.

Modern democracy testifies to a highly specific shaping [*mise en forme*] of society, and we would try in vain to find models for it in the past, even though it is not without its heritage. The new determination–representation of the *place of power* bears witness to its shaping. And it is certainly this distinctive feature that designates the political. I deliberately refrained from stressing this earlier because I was concerned with bringing out the difference between political science and political philosophy by showing that the former attempts to circumscribe an order of particular facts *within* the social, and that the task of the latter is to conceptualize the principle of the institution of the social. But now that the danger of ambiguity has been removed, we no longer need to be afraid to advance the view that any political philosophy and any political science is governed by a reflection upon power. Precisely because of this, they do not deal with specifics, but with a primal division which is constitutive of the space we call society. And the fact that this space is organized as *one* despite (or because of) its multiple divisions and that it is organized as *the same* in all its multiple dimensions implies a reference to a place from which it can be seen, read and named. Even before we examine it in its empirical determinations, this symbolic pole proves to be power; it manifests society's self-externality, and ensures that society can achieve a quasi-representation of itself. We must of course be careful not to project this externality on to the real; if we did so it would no longer have any meaning for society. It would be more accurate to say that power makes a gesture towards something *outside*, and that it defines itself in terms of that outside. Whatever its form, it always refers to the same enigma: that of an internal–external articulation, of a division which institutes a common space, of a break which establishes relations, of a movement of the externalization of the social which goes hand in hand with its internalization. I have for a long time concentrated upon this peculiarity of modern democracy: of all the regimes of which we know, it is the only one to have represented power in such a way as to show that power is an *empty place* and to have thereby maintained a gap between the symbolic and the real. It does so by virtue of a discourse which reveals that power belongs to no one; that those who exercise power do not possess it; that they do not, indeed, embody it; that the exercise of power requires a periodic and repeated contest; that the authority of those vested with power is created and re-created as a result of the manifestation of the will of the people. It could of course rightly be pointed out that the principle of a power which men are forbidden to appropriate had already been asserted in classical democracy, but it need scarcely be pointed out that power still had a positive determination in that the representation of the City and the definition of citizenship rested upon a discrimination based upon natural criteria or – and this in the event comes to the same thing – supernatural criteria.

The idea that power belongs to no one is not, therefore, to be confused with the idea that it designates an empty place. The former idea may be formulated by political actors, but not the latter. The first formulation in fact implies the actors' self-representation, as they deny one another the right to take power. The old Greek formula to the effect that power is *in the middle* (and historians tell us that it was elaborated within the framework of an aristocratic society before being bequeathed to democracy) still indicates the presence of a group which has an image of itself, of its space and of its bounds. The reference to an empty place, by contrast, eludes speech insofar as it does not presuppose the existence of a community whose members discover themselves to be subjects by the very fact of their being members. The formula 'power belongs to no one' can also be translated into the formula 'power belongs to none of us' (and in historical terms, this appears to be the earlier of the two). The reference to an empty place, on the other hand, implies a reference to a society without any positive determination, which cannot be represented by the figure of a community. It is because the division of power does not, in a modern democracy, refer to an *outside* that can be assigned to the Gods, the city or holy ground; because it does not refer to an *inside* that can be assigned to the substance of the community. Or, to put it another way, it is because there is no materialization of the *Other* – which would allow power to function as a mediator, no matter how it were defined – that there is no materialization of the *One* – which would allow power to function as an incarnation. Nor can power be divorced from the work of division by which society is instituted; a society can therefore relate to itself only through the experience of an internal division which proves to be not a *de facto* division, but a division which generates its constitution.

It should also be added that, once it has lost its double reference to the *Other* and to the *One*, power can no longer condense the principle of Law and the principle of Knowledge within itself. It therefore appears to be limited. And it therefore opens up the possibility of relations and actions which, in various realms and in particular in those of production and exchange, can be ordered in terms of norms and in accordance with specific goals.

If we wished to pursue this argument, we would have to examine in detail the processes which regulate the establishment of democratic power, in other words the controlled challenge to the authority vested with its exercise. It is enough to recall that this requires an institutionalization of conflict and a quasi-dissolution of social relations at the very moment of the manifestation of the will of the people. These two phenomena are both indicative of the above-mentioned articulation between the idea that power is a purely symbolic agency and the idea that society has no substantial unity. The institutionalization of conflict is not within the remit of power; it is rather that power depends upon the institutionalization of conflict. Its institutionalization is the result of a juridical elaboration, and, in this first sense, it allows us to identify a field specific to politics – the field of competition between protagonists whose modes of action and programmes explicitly designate them as laying claim to the exercise of public authority. This immediately reveals the link between the legitimacy of power and the legitimacy of a conflict which seems to constitute politics, but it must also be noted that this phenomenon presupposes the coming together of a number of conditions relating to social life as a whole: freedom of association and of expression, and the freedom of ideas and of people to circulate. In this respect, the idea of a division between the sphere of the state and the sphere of civil society that is so often invoked seems to blur rather than to elucidate the features of the democratic phenomenon. It prevents us from identifying a general configuration of social relations in which diversity and opposition are made visible. It is, I believe, also noteworthy that the delineation of a specifically political activity has the effect of erecting a *stage* on which conflict is acted out for all to see (once citizenship is no longer reserved for a small number) and is represented as being necessary, irreducible and legitimate. That each party claims to have a vocation to defend the *general* interest and to bring about *union* is of little importance; the antagonism between them sanctions another vocation: society's vocation for division. It is also of little importance that what is at stake in the political conflict does not coincide with what is at stake in the class struggle or the struggle between interests; whatever the degree of distortion introduced by the shift from the political level to the social level, the important point is that all *de facto* divisions are transfigured and transposed on to a stage on which division appears to exist *de jure*. This phenomenon is, as we have noted, combined with the singular procedure of universal suffrage, which is based upon the principle of popular sovereignty but which, at the very moment when the people are supposed to express their will, transforms them into a pure diversity of individuals, each one of whom is abstracted from the network of social ties within which his existence is determined – into a plurality of atoms or, to be more precise, into statistics. In short, the ultimate reference to the identity of the People, to the instituting Subject, proves to mask the enigmatic arbitration of Number.

Let us stop and retrace our steps after this first stage in our analysis. The representation of politics which lies at the origins of social science is, it must be agreed, generated by the very constitution of democracy. For it is indeed true, as social science asserts, that power no longer makes any gesture towards an *outside*, that it is no longer articulated with any *other* force which can be represented, and that, in that sense, it is disentangled from the religious. It is indeed true that power no longer refers to any point of origin which coincides with the origins of Law and Knowledge and that, in that sense, the type of actions and relations which cluster around its pole can be distinguished from other types of actions and relations which might be termed juridical, economic and cultural; and it is therefore true that something can be circumscribed as being *politics* [*la politique*]. The one thing that remains hidden from the gaze of the scientific observer is the symbolic form which, as a result of the mutation in power, makes this new distinction possible: the essence of *the political* [*du politique*]. The illusion that the political can be localized within society is therefore not without a certain consistency, and to dismiss it as a mistaken opinion would mean surrendering to one more illusion.

Modern democracy is, we said, the only regime to indicate the gap between the symbolic and the real by using the notion of a power which no one – no prince and no minority – can seize. It has the virtue of relating society to the experience of its institution. When an empty place emerges, there can be no possible conjunction between power, law and knowledge, and their foundations cannot possibly be enunciated. The being of the social vanishes or, more accurately, presents itself in the shape of an endless series of questions (witness the incessant, shifting debates between ideologies). The ultimate markers of certainty are destroyed, and at the same time there is born a new awareness of the unknown element in history, of the gestation of humanity in all the variety of its figures. It must, however, also be made clear that the gap is merely indicated, that it is operative, but that it is not visible, that it does not have the status of an object of knowledge. It is the attributes of power that are exposed to our gaze, the distinctive features of the contest in which power appears to be the prize. The things that capture our attention and that are designated as objects to be known are the mechanisms which control the formation of a public authority, the selection of leaders and, more generally, the nature of the institutions vested with the exercise and control of that authority. And so the symbolic dimension of the social passes unnoticed, precisely because it is no longer masked beneath a representation of the difference between the visible world and the invisible world.

This, then, is the paradox: regimes in which the figure of power stands out against an *other* force do not completely obscure the political principle behind the social order. As the religious basis of power is fully affirmed, it appears to be both the guarantor and the guardian of the certainty which supports the experience of the world; at the same time, it appears to be the keeper of the law which finds its expression in social relations and which maintains their unity. In contrast, democracy, in which the figure of the *other* is abolished, in which power is not divorced from the division which generates it – I will not say that power is stripped bare, as that would imply surrendering to yet another realist fiction – and in which power therefore eludes our grasp (escapes appropriation and representation), is a regime which cannot be apprehended in its political form. Whilst the contours of society become blurred, and whilst the markers of certainty become unstable, there arises the illusion of a reality which can explain its own determination in terms of a combination of multiple *de facto* relations.

Now, does not an analysis of this type also lead us to ask whether political philosophy, which does, for its part, continue to search for the principles that generate modern society, might not be caught in the trap of appearances in that it takes the view that society's religious basis is indestructible? That conviction is no doubt based upon the idea that no human society, whatever it may be, can be organized in terms of pure self-immanence. But is this the only reason for its attachment to the religious? Is not political philosophy guided by a quest for an ultimate knowledge which, although it is won in response to the requirements of reflection, is still formulated in terms of knowledge of the *One*? Is not this the inspiration it wishes to preserve, and does it not sense that the advent of democracy threatens to do away with it? I am not forgetting that, in its effective movement, it contradicts this inspiration, places thought in the realm of the interrogative, and deprives it of the religious element of certainty and that, in that sense, it is, as we have noted, bound up with a political constitution which no longer permits human activities to be placed beneath the sign of a primal law. But taking its effective movement into account does not mean that we have to ignore its representation of its aims. And does not the fact that it is drawn towards the religious indicate that it is retreating in the face of a political form which, by subjecting human beings to the experience of division, fragmentation and heterogeneity in every register, and to the experience of the indeterminacy of the social and of history, undermines the ground on which philosophical knowledge was built, and obscures the task it sets itself? The assertion that a society can never lose its religious basis can, in other words, be understood in one of two ways. The philosopher may mean to say that it would be illusory for society to claim to be able to confine the principle of its institution within its own limits. But in that case he fails to see that whilst modern democracy does foster that illusion, it does so by breaking down old certainties, by inaugurating an experience in which society is constantly in search of its own foundations. He fails to see that it is not the dimension but the figure of the *other* that it abolishes, and that, whilst there is a risk involved in the loss of the religious, there is also something to be gained by calling the law into question, that freedom is a conquest. Alternatively, he may mean to say that religion elaborates a primordial representation of the One, and that this representation proves to be a precondition for human *unity*, but we then have to ask ourselves about the reasons for the attractions of unity. We have to ask how much its attractions owe to its opposite, namely the repugnance inspired by division and conflict. We have to ask how the philosophical idea of the One colludes with the image of a united society. We have to ask why unity must be conceived beneath the sign of the spiritual, and why division must be projected on to the material plane of interest.

In order to evaluate fully this reluctance to admit that there is a separation between the political and the religious, we must go beyond the level of analysis at which we have been working. It is in fact impossible to ignore the fact that the image of union is generated or re-generated at the very heart of modern democracy. The new position of power is accompanied by a new symbolic elaboration and, as a result, the notions of state, people, nation, fatherland and humanity acquire equally new meanings. If we take no interest in these notions or restrict our discussion to the function they may play in the process of legitimating power, we adopt the artificial point of view which we described as characteristic of science. They derive, of course, from what we have called the shaping [*mise en forme*] and staging [*mise en scène*] of society, and from the process of giving it meaning [*mise en sens*]. The only problem is to determine whether or not they are essentially religious.

It is also true that, even if we do take the view that these notions are essentially religious, we will not necessarily agree as to how they are to be interpreted. It is one thing to say – in a society based upon individual freedoms – that Christianity delivers human beings from the domination of needs and from the image of their temporal finiteness, that it inspires in them a feeling of community, fraternity and obedience to an unconditional moral principle, and that, in the absence of Christian belief, there would be no place for an ethic of service to the state or for patriotism. It is quite another thing to say that the very principle of Christianity implies a depreciation of worldly values, that religious feeling has broken with Christianity, is being re-created and is now invested in love of the nation or of humanity. According to the former argument, social morality and the state still rest upon religion, to cite Hegel once more; according to the latter, social morality is self-sufficient because it has become religious. But, important as that distinction may be, it does not alter the terms of the question we are asking. For both interpretations appear to accept that anything which expresses the idea of having social roots, of sharing a feeling of belonging, of identifying with a principle that shapes human coexistence must derive from a religious feeling.

Is this beyond all doubt? Do we not have to ask whether the religious might not be grafted on to a more profound experience as a result of some *determinate* representation of origins, community and identity?

Our brief comments on the notion of the people in democracy suggest that it is bound up with an ambiguity which cannot adequately be translated into religious terms. The people do indeed constitute a pole of identity which is sufficiently defined to indicate that it has the status of a subject. The people possesses sovereignty; they are assumed to express its will; power is exercised in their name; politicians constantly evoke them. But the identity of the people remains latent. Quite apart from the fact that the notion of the people is dependent upon a discourse which names the people, which is itself multiple and which lends the people multiple dimensions, and that the status of a Subject can only be defined in terms of a juridical constitution, the people are, as we have noted, dissolved into a numerical element at the very moment of the manifestation of their will.

A similar ambiguity arises if we examine representations which have been accorded a religious significance. When we speak of the state as a transcendent power, we mean that it has its own *raison d'être*, that, in its absence, society would have neither coherence nor permanence and that, in that sense, it demands unconditional obedience and the subordination of private interests to the imperative need for its preservation. But we then fail to see that democracy disassociates political power from the existence of the state. It is no doubt as a result of that disassociation that the state acquires its great might, that the characteristic impersonality of its operations allows it to subdue all social activities and relations to its interests, and even to foster the illusion that it is a great individual, that everyone has to recognize its will as its own, to paraphrase Hegel. But it is equally certain that this tendency is held in check because the political competition and social conflict mobilized by the democratic process of contesting the exercise of power led to an indefinite transformation of right and to a modification of the public space. Reason of state threatens to become an absolute, but it is powerless to assert itself because it remains subject to the effects of the aspirations of individuals and groups in civil society and, therefore, to the effects of such demands as can be inscribed within the public space. When we evoke the nation, we look to it as the source of a religious faith. But do we not have to ask how it is defined, and to evaluate its debt to the discourse which enunciates it? Do we not have to ask how the notion and the feelings it inspires were, in Europe, transformed as a result of the discourse of the French Revolution and, in the nineteenth century, as a result of the new constructs of the historians who contributed so much to the formation of a new political consciousness? In the case of France, we have only to think of the role Thierry, Guizot, Mignet or, somewhat later, Michelet played in portraying the nation's destiny, in introducing a new perspective, in reshaping values, in giving events a new depth and in breaking history down into significant sequences. We have only to observe how effective this 'composition', which was modified as a result of both the progress of knowledge and ideological imperatives, was in moulding our collective memory, how it is imprinted on monuments, commemorations, place names, school textbooks, popular literature, and both major and minor political discourses. We would be wrong to conclude that a new religion is inscribed within this phenomenon simply because it implies the depiction of the origins and permanence of a community. For all signs and symbols which mobilize belief lend themselves to interpretation, to re-interpretation, and are bound up with modes of anticipating the future, with the idea of the goals which social actors imagine to be real and legitimate. The idea of the nation does not refer to a text which exists prior to the commentary; it is of course supported by an accretion of materials and representations, but it can never be separated from a discourse on the nation – a discourse which, whilst it enjoys a privileged relationship with the discourse of power, is still not amenable to appropriation. Paradoxically, it is because it is a historical entity that the nation eludes the religious imagination, which always tries to establish a narrative, to master a time that exists outside time. Whilst the nation bestows a collective identity, it is at the same time implicated in that identity. It remains a floating representation, and the origins of the nation, the stages of its foundation and the vectors of its destiny are therefore constantly being displaced and are always subject to the decisions of social actors – or those who speak for them – who want to establish themselves within a duration and a time which allows them to name themselves.

And why should this demand for a *name* be wholly ascribed to either the register of religion of that of ideology? Perhaps more than any other, the idea of the nation urges us to make a distinction between the symbolic, the ideological and the religious.

The difficulty of analysing modern democracy arises because it reveals a movement which tends to actualize the image of the people, the state and the nation, and because that movement is necessarily thwarted by the reference to power as an empty place and by the experience of social division. The movement of which we are speaking must be described with greater precision: when society can no longer be represented as a body and is no longer embodied in the figure of the prince, it is true that people, state and nation acquire a new force and become the major poles by which social identity and social communality can be signified. But to assert, in order to extol it, that a new religious belief takes shape is to forget that this identity and this community remain indefinable. Conversely, to find in this belief a sign of pure illusion, as liberal thought encourages us to do, is to deny the very notion of society, to erase both the question of sovereignty and that of the meaning of the institution, which are always bound up with the ultimate question of the legitimacy of that which exists. It means, for example, reducing power – or the state, which is wrongly confused with power – to an instrumental function, and the people to a fiction which simply masks the efficacy of a contract thanks to which a minority submits to a government formed by a majority; and, finally, it means regarding only individuals and coalitions of interests and opinions as real. If we adopt this view, we replace the fiction of unity-in-itself with that of diversity-in-itself. We thereby deny ourselves the means to understand that, far from signalling a regression into the imaginary, the aspirations that have been manifested in the course of the history of democratic societies under the slogans of establishing a just state or emancipating the people have had the effect of preventing society from becoming petrified within its order, and have re-established the instituting dimension of right in the place of the law which served to establish both the respective positions of rulers and ruled, and the conditions for the appropriation of wealth, power and knowledge.

If we reject both these modes of interpretation (not forgetting that they were outlined as a result of the constitution of a new type of society), might we not finally be able to detect the paths by which a return to the religious might be effected?

A return? It will be objected that the term presupposes that the religious never disappeared. Indeed. But it is one thing to say that beliefs have survived in their traditional form, and quite another to accept that a fire which has gone out can be relit. It is, moreover, worth asking, as Merleau-Ponty used to ask, whether anything in history has ever been superseded in an absolute sense. In the present case, the analysis we were outlining reveals the possibility of situations in which the symbolic efficacy of the democratic system is destroyed. If, in effect, the mode of the establishment of power and the nature of its exercise or, more generally, political competition, prove incapable of giving form and meaning to social division, a *de facto* conflict will appear throughout society. The distinction between power as symbolic agency and power as real organ disappears. The reference to an empty place gives way to the unbearable image of a real vacuum. The authority of those who make public decisions or who are trying to do so vanishes, leaving only the spectacle of individuals or clans whose one concern is to satisfy their appetite for power. Society is put to the test of a collapse of legitimacy by the opposition between the interests of classes and various categories, by the opposition between opinions, values and norms – and these are no less important – and by all the signs of the fragmentation of the social space, of heterogeneity. In these extreme situations, representations which can supply an index of social unity and identity become invested with a fantastic power, and the totalitarian adventure is under way.

For our purposes, it is not important to distinguish between the various modes of the formation of totalitarianism. We cannot of course ignore the fact that in one case the image of the people is actualized through the sanctification of the proletariat, and that in the other it is actualized through the sanctification of the nation; that the former process is shored up by a redefinition of humanity and that the latter is shored up by a redefinition of a race: communism and fascism are not to be confused. But, in terms of the question we are posing, the similarity between the two is striking. Both attempt, in one way or another, to give power a substantial reality, to bring the principles of Law and Knowledge within its orbit, to deny social division in all its forms, and to give society a *body* once more. And, it should be noted in passing, we find here an explanation as to why so many contemporary philosophers – and by no means only minor figures – have become compromised in the adventure of Nazism, fascism or communism; the attachment to the religious which we noted earlier traps them in the illusion that unity and identity can be restored as such, and they see signs of its advent in the *union* of the social body. It is not because they submit to a charismatic authority that they lend their support to totalitarian regimes, particularly not if they rally to communism; they surrender to the attractions of a renewed certainty and, paradoxically, they use it as a pretext to assert their right to contemplate freely the basis of any experience of the world.

We should of course be careful not to reduce the totalitarian phenomenon to its religious aspects, as certain imprudent commentators have done. It is, rather, by exploring the genesis of ideology, by identifying the metamorphoses of a discourse which, by placing itself under the aegis of knowledge of the real, claims to escape the indeterminacy of the social, to master the principle of its institution, to rise above division so as to enunciate its terms and conditions and to inscribe it within rationality, either by preserving it in its present state or by subjecting it to the movement of its own abolition; it is by detecting the new relationship that is established between the viewpoint of science and the viewpoint of the social order, that we can best arrive at an understanding of totalitarianism. This regime represents the culmination of an artificialist project which begins to take shape in the nineteenth century: the project of creating a self-organizing society which allows the discourse of technical rationality to be imprinted on the very form of social relations, and which, ultimately, reveals 'social raw material' or 'human raw material' to be fully amenable to organization. It would, however, be futile to make a sharp distinction between the ideological and the religious, for whilst the latter is disavowed insofar as it indicates an *other* place, we can also see that it is reactivated in the quest for a *mystical* union and in the representation of a body, part of which – the proletariat, the political party, the leading organ, the egocrat (to use Solzhenitsyn's phrase) – represents both the head of the people and the people in its entirety. The reproduction of this model in one sector of society after another then converts individuals into members of multiple micro-bodies.

Within the framework of ideological discourse, it is even conceivable that the representation of the organization (or, more accurately, of the machine) can combine with that of the body. Not only does extreme artificialism tend to be interchangeable with extreme organicism because of the demand for the full affirmation of the social entity; this discourse can only hold up if it becomes a body and only if – no pun intended – it can embody the subjects who speak it: it tends to abolish the distance between enunciation and utterance, and to be imprinted on every subject, regardless of the signification of words.

The increasingly perceptible effects of the failure of totalitarian ideology are no less instructive. The reappearance of a divide – deeper here than in any other regime – between the discourse of power and people's experience of their situation indicates the impossibility of precipitating the symbolic into the real, of reducing power to a purely social definition, of materializing power in the persons of those vested with it, of representing society as a body without supplying it with an external guarantor of its organization and limits, and of abolishing social division. The nature of this discourse is in fact such that the subject either loses all notion of its own position or perceives it as being totally alien, as a mere product of a group which manipulates words in order to conceal facts. Once belief in communism is shaken, it gives way to the image of a party or a power which rules through force; to the image of an external force which subjugates the society it claims to embody; to the image of a law that is its property, of a law that is designed to conceal the rule of the arbitrary; to the image of a truth of history that is designed to conceal lies. And when signs are inverted, when the plenitude of communism reveals a void, when the people break up and morals break down, or when, to use Hegel's language once more, social morality and the state collapse, we see the return of democratic aspirations and, along with them, the old faith, which means primarily the Christian faith. In response to the fantastic attempt to compress space and time into the limits of the social body, there reappears a reference to an absent body which symbolizes a time-span that can be neither appropriated, mastered nor reduced. Certainty is reborn, together with a singular ability to attack the image of the 'new man' and of the 'radiant future' by deriding it.

Might it not, however, be a further mistake to believe that the new links that are being forged between the democratic opposition and the religious opposition bear witness to the democratic essence of Christianity or to the Christian essence of democracy? If we accept that, do we not lose sight of the meaning of the adventure that began when they became disentangled in the nineteenth century? To put it more simply, do we not have to admit that they come together in a restoration of the dimension of the *other*, which totalitarianism tries to suppress with its representation of the People-as-One?

We have until now been asking how we can conceive the links between the religious and the political, and the possibility of their being broken. But is this the appropriate language to use? Is there any sense in trying to apprehend the religious *as such* by extracting it from the political and then specifying its efficacy in one or another form of society? Or, to be more specific, and since the scope of our investigation has from the beginning been restricted, are we entitled to refer to an essence of Christianity and to relate certain features of modern political societies (that is, societies instituted since the beginning of the Christian era) to that essence? The question may be disconcerting insofar as Christianity is based upon a narrative, or a body of narratives, to which we are free to refer, whatever degree of veracity we may accord it, in order to identify it as a specific religion which appeared at a given epoch in the history of humanity. Even at this stage, however, we cannot ignore the fact that the birth of this religion has a political meaning. That fact was of course stressed and discussed by theologians for centuries, long before Dante based his apologia for a universal monarchy on the argument that the Son of God resolved to come to earth and to take the form of a man at a time when humanity was united under the authority of the Roman Emperor who was, metaphorically, the Emperor of all humanity – and that, more specifically still, He resolved to do so at a time when the first census of all the Emperor's subjects was being carried out. It is, however, more pertinent to note that one cannot derive the principles of a political order from the sacred texts; attempts to do so were made over and over agian, but the point is that they involved making digressions through multiple and often contradictory interpretations. The new religion reformulates the notion of a duality between this world and the next, and between man's mortal destiny and his immortal destiny; it depicts a mediator who is a God-made-man. It is believed to bring together not only one people but the whole of humanity; the body of Christ symbolizes the unity between men and God, and the union of all men in the eucharist. Christ lives on in a Church of which he is simultaneously the head. The very fact that the event of his birth took place at a specific time and in a specific place indicates that he was born to be the new Adam; and a link is established between the idea of the fall and the idea of redemption, and thus makes tangible the historical dimension of the divine. All these themes lend themselves to political elaborations, but their meaning is in itself uncertain. It is when a definite relationship is established between a certain type of political institution and a certain type of religious institution that the religious basis of the political order becomes legible, as does the political basis of the Church, for the Church ceases to merge with Christian humanity, and is circumscribed within a space, organized under the aegis of a power, and imprinted on a territory.

Let us now, then, qualify a formula which appeared to take us to the heart of the problem. We asked ourselves whether religious belief might not have been transferred on to philosophical thought at the very moment when the latter claimed to be able to discern the persistence of the religious in the political; whether, in short, it might not have misrecognized itself by misrecognizing the meaning of the new society which began to take shape in the last century. It might be more accurate to ask: does not this thought bear the imprint of a theologico-political schema? Is it not because it is secretly governed by a curious identification with *the royalty of the spirit* that it is drawn to the One?

The work of Michelet appears to me to provide the perfect justification for asking this question. He is not, of course, a philosopher in the sense in which scholars understand that term, but the reader has already been warned that we are not using it in its restrictive sense. The fact is that he does not belong to the species 'scientific historian', which had yet to come into being; his history is interpretative and is bound up with an investigation into the meaning of Humanity's development and, more specifically, into the political and religious revolution which he thought was going on before his very eyes, despite the forces which were trying to hinder it or to reverse its course. I find his thought exemplary because it testifies to a debate which we rarely see taking place within the mind of one man. His initial stance is to espouse and combine two conceptions which see the Revolution as being the heir to the work already accomplished by Christianity and by the monarchy respectively. Breaking with this inspiration, he then makes a radical critique of the Ancien Regime as a theologico-political formation whose destruction was inaugurated by the Revolution. But his critique is such that it re-exploits seemingly discredited theologico-political categories to make an apologia for modernity. Yet this very operation, and we may well wonder to what extent it is conscious or unconscious, brings him up against the idea of a right or a freedom which can found themselves; the idea of a humanity which displays signs of its self-transcendance, of a heroism of the spirit (the expression is an early borrowing from Vico), of an infinite questioning of any given configuration of knowledge.

The movement that takes us from the *Introduction à une histoire universelle* or the *Origines du droit français* to the *Bible de l'humanité* or the 1869 Preface to the *Histoire de France* via *La Révolution française* describes a trajectory in which we find a constant tension between the idea that religion is the ultimate horizon of human life and the idea that right is the ultimate source of human self-creation or, to be more accurate, that right is an internal principle that allows human beings to transcend themselves. These two ideas determine, respectively, the notion of having roots in a place and a time, the notion of tradition and of an identity between self and being (people, nation, humanity), and the notion of the rootlessness, the wandering and the turmoil of being, the notion of a wild assertion of the self as being free from all authority, as being supported only by the work that is being accomplished.

It is obviously my intention not to summarize Michelet's itinerary but, by making a digression, to shed light on the question which concerns us here. Let us go back, then, to the starting point provided by the *Introduction à une histoire universelle*. What is its relevance? It is not that it reveals the author's originality. To put it briefly, it is a condensation of the interpretations of Guizot and Ballanche. The monarchy is seen as a levelling and centralizing agent which has the virtue of creating conditions of equality and of making society increasingly homogeneous. Michelet sees in Christianity the advent of a religion of equality and fraternity, of a religion based upon a love of humanity. The idea that the old monarchy became useless once the construction of society had been completed is borrowed from Guizot; the idea that the spirit of Christianity has been invested in social institutions is borrowed from Ballanche. It is important at least to note that Michelet rapidly arrives at a double reading of the history of France, that he reads it in both religious and political terms; in his view, the distinctive feature of France is that the 'feeling of social generality' was born in that nation. Despite inequality of condition and of morals, and despite the regional differences which survived until the Revolution, a people comes into being thanks to the double effect of a principle of material unification and a principle of spiritual unification. We will not dwell upon the formulae which signal France's pre-eminent role in 'bringing heaven to earth'; a few examples will suffice: 'the moral world found its Word in Christ, the son of Judaea and of Greece, and France will explain the Word to the social world'; France's role is to 'break the news of this new revelation'; France speaks 'the Word of Europe', and holds 'the pontificate of the new civilization'. We will, however, pick out at least this judgement, which he will later invert: 'The name of the priest and the king, of the representatives of what is most general, that is, most divine in the thought of a nation lent, as it were, the obscure right of the people a *mystical envelope* in which it grew and became stronger' (emphasis added).

In *La Révolution française*, Michelet transforms this 'mystical envelope' into an illusion: he completely divorces right and justice from the name of the king and the priest, who are now seen as concealing them in order to stifle them. And yet, he still finds the basis of Ancien Regime society in the 'priestly monarchy'. Indeed, if we are to believe his own account, his conversion to the struggle against Christianity and his decision to write his *Révolution* originated in something similar to a religious revelation. The authenticity of the scene he reconstructs in 1869 is irrelevant; it is an admirable illustration of how symbols change place in the construction he himself built and of how that construction survives despite inversions of meaning.

His *Histoire de France* had, he tells us in the Preface, brought him to the threshold of the 'monarchical ages' when an 'accident' upset his plans.

One day when I was passing through Reims, I saw the magnificent cathedral, the splended Coronation Church, in great detail. When one walks around the internal gallery eighty feet above the ground, one sees the ravishing wealth of its flowery beauty as a permanent alleluia. In this empty immensity, one always seems to be able to hear the great official clamour which was once called the voice of the people ... I reached the last little tower. There, I found a spectacle that astonished me greatly. The round tower was garlanded with sacrificial victims. One has a rope around his neck; another has lost an ear. The mutilated are sadder than the dead. How right they are! What a terrifying contrast! The church of festivals, the bride, has adopted that lugubrious ornament for her wedding necklace! The pillory of the people has been placed above the altar. But might not those tears have fallen down through the vaults and on to the heads of the kings? The fearful unction of the Revolution, of the wrath of God. "I will not understand the monarchical ages" I said to myself, "unless I first establish within me the soul and the faith of the people, and, after *Louis XI*, I wrote my *Révolution* (1845–1853).

This astonishing description is more eloquent than many historically or theoretically based arguments, and it does more than they ever could to help us understand the position Michelet adopts to mount his attack on the theologico-political. Where is his position? Inside the cathedral of the coronation, the very place where Christian France was shaped and then reshaped. It is there that he takes up his position; indeed he explores it thoroughly. He ascends its heights, just as the souls of the kings were believed to ascend to take their place at the side of God, to the acclamation of the people; and, in this new liturgy, his thought takes its place at the side of the people. Michelet moves through the church like an actor; he makes it undergo a true metamorphosis, but he is still there. He watches the king being crowned, but he secretly transforms the coronation into a deposition so as to reveal the second coronation which, so to speak, reduplicates it. He uses all the old symbols: the coronation, the acclamation which welcomes the elect into the communion of saints, the marriage between the Church and Christ, between the kingdom and the king, the sacrificial victim, the cross that stands above the altar, the unction which raises the king head and shoulders above his assembled subjects. But for Michelet the coronation is that of the people. It is the true voice of the people that he hears in the nave; he imagines the celebration of a different marriage; the garland of sacrificial victims replaces the martyred Christ; the pillory stands above the altar; tears replace the sacred liquor; the Lord's anointed becomes the anointed of the Revolution, which becomes God's epic poem. And, it must be added, he becomes sensitivized to a time which, whilst it does not exist outside time, does not exist within time either: the time of a people, of the people who await their incarnation, who are in a sense always invisible, but who reveal themselves for one moment in history – and who demand faith.

It must not be believed that the scene in Reims Cathedral is simply a fantasmagoria; it is a condensation of many of the themes that determine the intellectual work which went into *La Révolution française*. It is not necessary to identify all the references, even though they are explicitly religious. The image of the Church appears in both the 1847 and 1869 Prefaces. Michelet's reply to those who mourn the fact that the Revolution could not use the spirit of the Reformation to combat Catholicism is that it adopted no Church for the very good reason that 'it was itself a Church' (a criticism addressed specifically to Quinet, although he is not mentioned by name). Michelet's reply to those who criticize his book and claim to be the heirs of the Girondins or the Jacobins is that he is reluctant to argue with them because he 'did not want to destroy the unity of the great Church'. But the mystical conception of the Revolution is at least as important as the words themselves, if not more so. The Revolution was of course an event which occurred in a specific place but, as he writes at one point and as he constantly suggests, 'it knew nothing of time or space'. The event was modelled on Christ's appearance on earth. It bears witness to the fulness of time, to use St Paul's expression, but it also abolishes time. It inaugurates an era, but it escapes all temporal determination, and represents a spiritual unity which allows humanity to accede to its own presence; in that sense, it proves to be indestructible, to exist outside the field of continuing political battles, and to condemn all attempts to restore the old order as being in vain. With the Revolution, humanity rises above itself and, henceforth, it is only from these new heights that it can relate to itself and survey the vicissitudes of its history. When he analyses the Fête de la Fédération, Michelet adopts the language of the theologian, and speaks of it as though it were France's marriage with France, as though it were modelled on the marriage between Christ and the Church or that between the king and the kingdom. And when he returns to the theme of humanity's search for its own body, he evokes the moment when the world said to itself: 'Oh, if only I were one ... If only I could at last unite my scattered members, and assemble my nations.' And when, in the 1869 Preface, he returns to 1790, he adds: 'No other *agape*, no other communion was comparable with this.' In the same passage, he turns the war of 1792 into a 'holy war'. We saw then 'the absolute, infinite nature of sacrifice'. This is enough for him to refute once more Quinet's thesis that the Revolution could not find new symbols: 'Faith is all; form counts for little. What does it matter how the altar is draped? It is still the altar of Right, of Truth and of Eternal Reason. Not a stone from it has been lost, and it waits peacefully.'

It is the establishment of certainty and the new relationship that has been forged between certainty and revelation which bear witness to the reinscription of Michelet's thought within the matrix of the Christian religion. But we must never lose sight of the fact that the monarchical reference is combined with a Christological reference. Michelet does not simply adopt the notion of a duality between the temporal and the non-temporal, transpose it on to a new register and link it with an event which allows the non-temporal to be read within the temporal; he reappropriates the image of the king and the idea of the sovereignty of the One in order to celebrate the People, Spirit or Reason, and Justice or Right. Like the Revolution, the People are divided in their existence. Insofar as the People exist within time and space, they can appear fallible, divided or even despicable, as when they take on the features of 'mob rule' or 'popular caprice', as when they adopt the gross gesticulations of the parvenus of the Paris Commune, and as when they grotesquely allow themselves to be ruled by 'buffoons'; they can become 'the most dangerous of judges' when they are 'in ferment' (the references are to the chapter on the trial of Louis XVI). In their atemporal existence, they win their true identity, and reveal themselves to be infallible and at one with themselves, to be in legitimate possession of an absolute right. And when they take on this status, they occupy the position of the king. Michelet is not indulging in rhetoric when he says that, as a historian, he has taken the 'royal road' and comments that: 'to me, that word means popular' (Livre III: 'De la méthode et de l'esprit de ce livre'); in raising the question of the legitimacy of the condemnation of Louis XVI, he is asserting that 'the people are all' and designating 'the true King: the people'. One cannot fail to see in certain of these formulae a resurgence of the theologico-political myth of the double nature of the king.

The repeated eulogies of right as being the Sovereign of the world (a formula borrowed from Rousseau) are equally significant, as is the moment when, in the course of his pitiless description of the wrong-doings of the priestly monarchy, Michelet elevates Buffon, Montesquieu, Voltaire and Rousseau to the status of the founding fathers of the new humanity (he even calls them 'the great doctors of the new Church'), and when, reappropriating an expression whose illusory effects he never ceases to denounce, he elevates 'royalty of spirit' above the world. We see here the workings of the transference to which we referred earlier. 'Until then, unity had been based upon the idea of a religious or political incarnation. A human God, a God made flesh was required to unite Church and State. Humanity was still weak, and placed its union under the sign, the visible sign, of a man, an individual. From now on, unity will be purer, and will be freed from this material condition; it will lie in the union of hearts, in the community of the spirit, in the profound marriage of feelings which joins each to all.' A more detailed analysis of Michelet's language would further reveal a symbolic architecture which is very similar to that elaborated at the end of the Middle Ages, an architecture which placed the king in a position to be a sovereign mediator between justice and people, and justice in a position to be a sovereign mediator between reason and equity.

As we have already said, the fact that we find in Michelet's thought the imprint of the theologico-political he is so determined to destroy does not, however, discredit his interpretation of the mutation that occurred in the transition from Ancien Regime to Revolution. He is one of the few thinkers of his day to recognize the symbolic function of power in shaping social relations. Anyone who doubts that this is so has only to read or reread the introduction to *La Révolution française*, a veritable essay in political philosophy whose major insight seems to me to have lost none of its acuity, despite the fragility of the historical reconstruction. Compared with that made by Tocqueville, the analysis of the Ancien Regime may, of course, seem summary and sociologically poor. But we do not have to choose between them, and the difference between them is not that between an ideological history and a conceptual history. In fact Michelet sees and tries to conceptualize something that escapes Tocqueville's thought. The latter notes every sign of the gradual centralization of the State and of the increasing equality of condition, and interprets them as proof that society is indeed being transformed, despite the seeming permanence of its order. It could not be said that he is insensitive to the symbolic dimension of the social. In one sense, it does not escape him for, rather than the *de facto* growth of equality and centralization, it is, I believe, the establishment of a principle of similarity governing both conduct and morals and the establishment of the *point of view of the state* that attracts his attention. But it is precisely because he erects this into a model – an ideal model whose coordinates in time and space are never defined – that he loses interest in the figure of power, and tends to reduce the history of the Ancien Regime to the break-up of aristocratic society to such an extent that the new society appears to be no more than the final product of that process, and that the Revolution becomes unintelligible except insofar as it designates the moment of a flight into the imaginary. Michelet, on the other hand, decodes the symbolic by transposing it on to another register; within this register, the mainspring behind domination and behind the organization of institutions is, as he puts it, the most *obscure* and the most *intimate* element in the position and representation of power (and let me repeat that one cannot exist without the other). He expresses his views most clearly when, having drawn up a balance sheet of the state of France on the eve of 1789, having noted that, 'I see the Revolution everywhere, even at Versailles', having judged inevitable and visible to all 'the defeat of the nobility and the clergy, and having described the boldness and blindness of Calonne, he concludes: 'The only obscure question was that of royalty. This is not, as it has so often been said, a question of pure form, but a fundamental question, a question more intimate and more perennial than any other question in France, a question not only of politics, but of love and of religion. No other people so loved their kings.'

This interest in the obscure, the profound and the primal, which inspires all Michelet's works from *Les Origines du droit français* to *La Sorcière*, helps him to discover something which Tocqueville fails to see: the mystery of the monarchical incarnation – beyond the conscious representation of a divine-right king whose power restores something of the presence of Christ and thereby makes justice appear in his person, there lies an unconscious representation of a society embodied in a king, of a society whose political institutions are not simply ordered in accordance with a 'carnal principle', but whose members are so captivated by the image of a body that they project on to it their own union, that their affects are precipitated in an amorous identification with that body. If we read him carefully, we find that Michelet in fact combines two arguments which, whilst they are connected, do not overlap.

The first relates the political law of the Ancien Regime to religious law – indeed, it would not be going too far to say that the one is derived from the other. Christianity proves to be both the system that shaped the monarchy and the body of institutions that supports it. This is in fact obvious from the very plan of the Introduction: the first part is entitled 'De la religion au Moyen Age', and the second 'De l'ancienne monarchie'. Michelet therefore immediately formulates the question: 'Is the Revolution Christian or anti-Christian? Logically and historically, this question comes before all others'. And the answer is not long in coming: 'On the stage, I still see only two great facts, two principles, two actors and two persons: Christianity and the Revolution.' He even goes so far as to assert: 'All the civic institutions that the Revolution invented either emanated from Christianity, or were modelled on its forms and authorized by it.' From this point of view, the schema is simple: Christianity is 'the religion of grace, of free, arbitrary salvation, and of the good pleasure of God.' The human monarchy is constructed in the image of the divine monarchy: both govern on behalf of an elect. Arbitrary power, masked as justice, has taken up its abode in society: it is found 'with depressing regularity in political institutions'. It is a 'carnal principle' that supports the social organization, the division between the orders and the hierarchy of conditions; this is a principle which 'puts justice and injustice in the blood, which makes them circulate along with the flux of life from one generation to the next'. The theologico-political system is, he suggests, such that it glorifies love, the personal relationship that exists between man and God, between man and king; the spiritual notion of justice is materialized; love is put 'in the place of law'. To paraphrase freely, using the same terms that we used earlier: when the law is fully asserted and when divine might and human might are condensed within a single person, Law is imprinted upon power; Law *as such* is abolished; the motive behind obedience is no longer fear, but a loving submission to the monarch. At the same time, the obverse of the love demanded by Christianity is revealed to be its hatred of all who perturb order: 'The incredible furies of the Church during the Middle Ages', the Inquisition, the books that were burned, the people who were burned, the history of the Vaudois and the Albigenses. Compared with that terror, the revolutionary Terror makes one smile. The love inspired by the king also has its obverse: torture, the Bastille, *lettres de cachet* and the *Livre rouge*.

But Michelet's second argument, which first emerges in the articulation between the first and second parts of the Introduction, takes a different direction. The might of the king does not simply descend from the heights of Christian arbitrariness; it is also constructed by his subjects. It is they who built 'this sanctuary, this refuge: the altar of the kingdom'. It is they who invented 'a series of legends and myths embroidered and amplified by all the efforts of genius: the holy king who was more of a priest than the priest himself in the thirteenth century, the knight-king in the sixteenth century, the good king with Henri IV, the God-king with Louis XIV.' In one sense, they are obeying the same inspiration as the great thinkers of the period, observes Michelet: Dante was similarly inspired to seek the salvation of humanity in unity and to imagine a monarch who, because he embodied the One, would possess unlimited authority and would be set free from mortal passions. But, 'we must dig deeper than Dante, we must dig into the earth, and uncover and contemplate *the profoundly popular basis on which the colossus was built*' (emphasis added). Men did not simply believe that they could 'save justice in a political religion', and they did not simply create 'a God of Justice out of a man'; they made kings the object of their love. Theirs was a singular love: 'an obstinate, blind love which saw all its God's imperfections as virtues. Far from being shocked at seeing the human element in him, they were grateful for it. They believed that it would bring him closer to them, that it would make him less proud and less harsh. They were glad that Henri IV loved Gabrielle.' The remarkable thing about the description of this love, about the evocation of Louis XV, the 'well-beloved', a God-made-flesh, and about the pages devoted to Louis XVI as he returns from Varenne to his execution is that they suggest that we have to re-examine the representation of the king's two bodies. This, as formulated in the Middle Ages, was based upon the notion of the two bodies of Christ and, in sixteenth-century England, generated the juridical fiction that the king was two persons in one, one being the natural king, a mortal man who was subject to time and to common laws, who was vulnerable to ignorance, error and illness, and the other being the supernatural king, who was immortal, infallible and omnipotent within the time and space of the kingdom. This representation gave rise to numerous commentaries on the part of the English historians, and Ernst Kantorowicz analyses them with unrivalled erudition and subtlety.[2] Michelet does not of course bring this out, but he does deal with the issue indirectly, and in such a way as to reveal the limited extent to which this representation can be formulated in juridical or theologico-political terms, even though it was primarily such a formulation that caught the attention of contemporaries. As we read Michelet, it becomes apparent that, over and beyond this representation, it is the natural body which, because it is combined with the supernatural body, exercises the charm that delights the people. It is insofar as it is a sexed body, a body capable of procreation and of physical love, and a fallible body, that it effects an unconscious mediation between the human and the divine; the body of Christ, although mortal, visible and fallible as well as divine, cannot ensure that mediation because, whilst it indicates the presence of God in man, it cannot fully indicate the converse: the presence of man and of the flesh in God. By breaking with the argument which derives the human monarchy from the divine monarchy, Michelet uncovers an erotico-political register. In his view, that register is, no doubt, established simply because religion has put love in the place of Law, but he does outline a logic of love in the political, and it is surprising that he does not see that it is older than Christianity. The modern king who is portrayed as God's representative on earth, as a substitute for Christ, does not derive all his power from that image. It is through the operation of sacrifice alone, in the element of suffering alone that man becomes as God, identifies with Christ and shuffles off his mortal coil. At this point, love values the king above life itself. And it is through the double operation of sacrifice and pleasure [*jouissance*] that the king's subjects experience rapture. Love both nourishes their life and justifies their death. It is the image of the natural body, the image of a God made flesh, the image of his marriage, his paternity, his liaisons, his festivals, his amusements and his feasts, but also the image of his weaknesses or even his cruelties, in short all the images of his humanity, that people their imaginary, that assure them that the king and the people are conjoined. A carnal union is established between the great individual and his mass of servants, from the lowliest to the most important, and it is indissociable from the mystical union between king and kingdom. According to theology and the jurists, the immortal king possesses the gift of clairvoyance as well as that of ubiquity; but, at the same time and even as he escapes the gaze of his subjects, he has the gift of attracting the gaze of all, of concentrating upon himself the absolute visibility of man-as-being: since he is a unique focal point, he abolishes differences between points of view and ensures that all merge in the One.

Michelet's extreme sensitivity to the enigma of the monarchical incarnation and of the role it gives to the natural body within the supernatural body is particularly evident in his analysis of the condemnation of Louis XVI. We will examine only those elements of it that are relevant to our purposes. The question of whether or not the trial should have taken place is not an issue for Michelet. It is obvious that it should have taken place. It had a double utility. On the one hand, it restored royalty to its rightful place – 'within the people' – by making the people a judge; on the other, 'it brought out into the light that ridiculous mystery which a barbarian humanity had for so long turned into a religion: the mystery of the monarchical incarnation, the bizarre fiction that the wisdom of the people is concentrated in an imbecile.' Given that royalty was embodied in a man, the problem was to establish how the evil could be excised so as to destroy the incarnation and so as to prevent any man from ever becoming a king. The historian gives his answer immediately, and then supports it with numerous arguments. 'Royalty had to be dragged into the broad light of day and exposed on all sides, and it had to be opened up to reveal what was inside the worm-eaten idol, to reveal the insects and worms inside the beautiful golden head. Royalty and the king had to be condemned usefully, judged, and placed under the blade. Did the blade have to fall? That is another question. When he merged with the dead institution, the king was no more than a head made of wood, empty, hollow, no more than a thing. If, when that head was struck, even a single drop of blood flowed, that was proof of life; people began to believe once more that it was a living head; royalty had come back to life.' (Livre IX, p. 7).

This penetrating analysis can be reformulated as follows: men regard royalty as a condensation of immortal life, and that life takes the form of a living man: the king. It has to be demonstrated that the symbol of life is the product of an illusion; belief has to be rooted out, and the idol has to be shown to be an idol; in short, the inner shadows of this pseudo-visible entity have to be destroyed; he must be laid low and torn to pieces. That action alone will ensure that the living individual loses his life. The empty head of Louis XVI appears in the empty crown. If, on the other hand, Louis XVI is struck, and if his blood is shed in the belief that this will annihilate his body, it will be found that we have here a living man, and, given that this living man represents eternal life, royalty will be resurrected. In general terms, Michelet is trying to explain that, as royalty is embodied in a man, the royal fantasmogoria is revived when the man is turned into a spectacle. Hence his bitter commentary on the detention of Louis XVI in the Temple. It was believed, he suggests, that the deposition of the individual would have the effect of desanctifying him. On the contrary: 'The most serious and the cruellest blow that could have been struck against the Revolution was the ineptitude of those who constantly kept Louis XVI before the eyes of the population, and who allowed him to relate to the population both as a man and as a prisoner.' Why? Because the more he was revealed in his human singularity, and the more visible the living individual became, the more he remained a king. His sufferings inspired love even before he was executed, but beyond that love there lay, so to speak, *the attraction of the unique object of every gaze.* Michelet succeeds admirably in showing that Louis XVI appears to be unique precisely because he is so commonplace, because he is seen in the bosom of his family, a mere man amongst mere people, caught up in the insignificance of everyday life. All the signs which designate him to be a man restore his kingship.

I cannot refrain from pointing out the remarkable manner in which the writer portrays Louis XVI. He shows him to his readers, but he does so in order to prevent him from delighting the eye. He describes him as 'ruddy-faced and replete', as eating too much over-rich food, as walking along with 'the myopic gaze, the abstracted expression, the heavy gait and the typical swaying walk of the Bourbons', and as giving the impression that he is 'a fat farmer from the Beauce'. By doing so, he does not make him any less commonplace, but his neutral observations do tend, as it were, to dissolve his individuality into a genre painting.

The crucial moment in the interpretation, however, concerns the execution. Michelet is not insensitive to the arguments of the Montagne, as it believes that it did have the merit of recognizing the imperative need to destroy the incarnation. The Montagne believed, 'not without reason', he adds, that 'a man is as much a body as a spirit, and that one could never be certain of the death of the monarchy until one had touched, felt and handled it in the shape of the dead body of Louis XVI and his severed head.' He suggests, in a sense, that if the people were to be elevated to the rank of royalty, they needed, perhaps, more than the image of the Law; that they needed, perhaps, an image of punishment. But he also suggests that, whilst the imagination is not extinguished by the light of justice, nothing stimulates it more than the sight of a corpse. The blood of the dead man does not destroy the incarnation; it revives it. Royalty and religion are reborn at the very moment when the revolutionaries lapse into the illusion that sustained them; namely the illusion that they were imprinted upon a real body. Such then are 'the terrible effects of the legend of the Temple', of the legends that were unleashed by the execution:

> The kings of the scriptures are called Christs; Christ is called a king. There was not a single incident in the king's captivity that was not seized upon and translated into an episode in the Passion. The Passion of Louis XVI became a sort of traditional poem which peasants and women passed on by word of mouth: the poem of Barbarian France.

How can the thinker who is so devoted to rooting out beliefs which give rise to, sustain or restore the mystery of the monarchical incarnation consent to their being transferred on to the sacred image of the People, the Nation, Humanity and the Spirit? The problem would become more complex if we were to follow a further strand in his interpretation of the Revolution, but to do so would be beyond the scope of the present essay. These all too brief remarks must suffice: although he posits an antithesis between the Ancien Regime and the Revolution, Michelet is still blind to the internal contradictions of the Revolution. He sees Robespierre's acquisition of power as a resurrection of the Monarchy (a process which began with the death of Danton, he notes in the 1868 preface); he attacks the Jacobin doctrine of public safety by comparing it with the absolutist idea of reason of state and the Christian doctrine of salvation. He denounces both the Montagnards and the Girondins as arrogant intellectual elites ('There is a terrible aristocracy among these democrats'); he even goes so far as to say of Robespierre that 'On the day that the director was revealed to be the future king of the priests [after the trial of the Mother of God], a reawakened France set him at the side of Louis XVI' (Livre III: 'De la méthode et de l'esprit de ce livre'). He wishes, we said, to ensure that the Revolution will not be confused with any one of its episodes, and to prevent it from being appropriated by any one clan; but, whilst he detemporalizes it in one sense, in another he restores to it a temporality that cannot be mastered, and describes its progress in such a way that the creation and destruction of men and ideas become indissociable; although he asserts the unity of the spirit of the Revolution, he sees it as being deployed in different places and as stirring up so many currents that he makes a distinction between a truly peasant revolution and an embryonic socialist revolution.

Perhaps the contrast between two of his formulae reveals just how ambiguous his conception of the Revolution is. Both, as it happens, have become famous: 'history is resurrection' and 'history is time'.

The reader of the rapid sketch we have outlined cannot have failed to sense the weakness in Michelet's argument. When he derives the human monarchy from the divine monarchy and political institutions from religious institutions, he is relying upon an outrageous simplification of Christianity. This does not invalidate his thesis that both types of institution are inscribed within a single schema, but it is by no means proven that the latter are modelled on the former. As we have indicated, any such proposition presupposes that one can conceive of an essence of Christianity without taking into account the political fact. Michelet in fact half glimpses the arbitrary element in this hypothesis when he states that the Gospel contains no specific teachings: 'Its vague morality', he concedes to his adversaries, 'contains almost none of the doctrines which made Christianity such a positive, absorbing and compelling religion and which gave it such a hold on men.' (Introduction) He therefore makes it clear that he is taking as his object religion as it is fully instituted by Catholicism. As, however, he discovers that the theme of grace is the principle behind its doctrine, one might have expected him to take the phenomenon of Protestantism into consideration, and to look at the mode of its insertion into modern political societies, rather than simply remarking in passing that it merely 'formulates in harsher terms' the doctrine of the Catholic world. He remains silent about this point. When he outlines his major opposition between Christianity and revolution, he deliberately ignores events in America. It escapes his notice that it was the puritans who founded free institutions in New England, and that they constantly referred to the Bible in their political proclamations, whereas his contemporary Quinet finds in the combination of Protestantism and freedom a lesson which has considerable implications for any understanding of modern democracy. Yet this lacuna in Michelet's argument, or rather, this occultation of a puritan revolution, is relevant to our argument, not so much because it is a sign of his failure to understand or recognize the true nature of Christianity, as because we can see in it an index of his determination to circumscribe the efficacy of the religious. Michelet's purpose is of course to show how Christianity shaped the European monarchies and, more specifically, the French monarchy. It should, however, also be noted that, whilst Quinet is careful to distinguish between Christianity and Catholicism, and even to stress the liberating virtues of Protestantism, he has no more insight than Michelet into the specific efficacy of the religious. Also, for his part, he is looking for a formula for a new faith which can be invested in the People, in the Nation, in Humanity and, at the same time, in Right or Justice and Reason. It is also pertinent to ask whether the ideal of political freedom that is affirmed by the break with the values of the monarchical regimes might not, thanks to puritan discourse, be able to coexist alongside a definite increase in conformism at the level of opinions and morals, and whether, in that sense, it might not coexist with a new disavowal of the effects of the social division which sets democracy free. It is in fact as though, although they are working on different premisses, the thinkers who are most alert to the advent of modernity and to the irreversibility of the course of history (and, in the case of France, I am not thinking only of Michelet and Quinet, but also of liberals like Guizot and Tocqueville and of socialists like Leroux) all looked to the religious for the means to reconstitute a pole of unity which could ward off the threat of the break up of the social that arose out of the defeat of the Ancien Regime.

This, then, is the question to which we return after our digression through Michelet's problematic and which we now have to reformulate. Rather than attempting to redefine relations between the political and the religious in order to assess the degree to which one is subordinated to the other and to examine the question of the permanence or non-permanence of a sensitivity to religious thought in modern society, might it not be more appropriate to posit the view that a theologico-political *formation* is, logically and historically, a primary datum? We might then be able to see in the oppositions it implies the principle of an evolution or, if we prefer to put it this way, the principle of a symbolic operation which takes place in the face of events; and to detect how certan schemata of organization and representation survive thanks to the displacement and transference on to new entities of the image of the body and of its double nature, of the idea of the One, and of a mediation between visible and invisible, between the eternal and the temporal. We would then be in a better position to ask whether democracy is the theatre of a new mode of transference, or whether the only thing that survives in it is the phantom of the theologico-political.

If this is so, what we will discover is a network of determinations, of which the 'priestly monarchy' supplies only one element, albeit a constituent element, and in which the development of City-States, urban corporations, trade-guilds and the exploitation of the heritage of classical humanism all become caught up in their turn. We will also discover a dynamic schema imprinted upon the complex play of chiasmata which Ernst Kantorowicz analyses with such subtlety; these are not, I repeat, chiasmata between the theological and the political, as his formulations sometimes suggest, but, if I may be forgiven the barbarism, between the already politicized theological and the already theologized political.

It need scarcely be stressed that this schema is legible only if we bear in mind the horizons of the real history in which there take place changes in the economic, technological, demographic and military realms, changes in the balance of power between the dominant actors, and changes in the categories of knowledge – and in that realm, the renaissance of Roman law and of ancient philosophy marks a decisive moment. If, moreover, we accept Kantorowicz's argument, that schema cannot be projected in its entirety on to empirical history, even though its articulations can be grasped within a temporal dimension. The four formations identified by the author – Christo-centric, juridico-centric, politico-centric and humano-centric kingdoms – testify to a displacement of the representation of the king's two bodies, but what is displaced on each occasion is not eradicated, and proves to contain the kernel of a future symbolic configuration. Thus, the fact that royalty is originally supported by the image of Christ does not mean that it must abandon that image when the Christological reference loses its efficacy as a result, in part, of the strategy of the Pope and his exclusive claim to be the Vicar of Christ. Long after the disintegration of the tenth-century Othonian myth, the *Traité du sacre* written for Charles V explicitly makes him a substitute for Christ, and indeed, as Michelet rightly notes, Louis XVI could still benefit from that identification. Similarly, the fact that in the age of Frederick II and Bracton the representation of the king is firmly supported by that of Justice and Right should not make us forget that a veritable religion of Right was reformulated in the sixteenth century and that it contains within it elements of a future system in which the body politic or the kingdom will appear to be the sacred body of the king. And nor should we forget that when, in his *De Monarchia*, Dante paints a portrait of an Emperor who, insofar as he possesses a univeral authority, can represent the One and can therefore represent the coming together of humanity as a body, despite the multiplicity of its members and the sequence of generations, his theologico-political vision of humanism cannot be explained away in terms of contemporary conditions (and still less can it be reduced to a nostalgic longing for the Empire). Dante's vision was prefigured by the lengthy labours of the Italian jurists, and it will be reactivated in the period of Charles IV, Elizabeth, François I and Henri III. When imperial ambition is combined with a universal language, the ideas of the *De Monarchia*, and the double figure of Augustus and Astra, of might and justice, will be exploited anew and will be used to promote the edification of a new monarchy and the conquest of the world. The essentials remain unchanged: the theologico-political is revealed in the deployment of a system of representations whose terms may be transformed, but whose oppositional principle remains constant.

When royalty is made sacred by the institution of unction and coronation, it is possible for the king to argue the case for a sovereignty which removes him from the rest of humanity, which allows him to be a Vicar or minister of Christ, to seem to have been made in his image, and to have both a natural, mortal body and a supernatural, immortal body. At the same time, it is possible for the Pope, who controls the rite of coronation, to seize the emblems of the monarchy and to imprint his power on the temporal realm (and this possibility was later realized through the Gregorian reforms and with the dispute over investitures). When, in an attempt to undo the imbrication of secular and priestly functions that came about as a result of the sanctification of royalty, the Church acquires the strength to circumscribe its domain and to become a functional body modelled on the emergent States, it tries to differentiate itself radically from all other political entities and to preserve its spiritual mission by claiming to be a mystical body (*corpus Ecclesiae mysticum*) – the very body of Christ, who also represents its head. At the same time, a religious vocation is re-imprinted on the kingdom, which defines itself as a mystical body (*corpus Republicae mysticum*) – the body of the king, who also represents its head. When the re-exploitation of Roman law and of Aristoteleanism provides theology and political theory with a new conceptual framework, the ancient concepts of *imperium, populus, communitas, patria, perpetuitas* and *aevum* (a notion intermediate between that of time and that of eternity) are reworked to represent, in their respective registers, a new relationship between the *particular*, which is still inscribed within the limits of a body, of an entity which is organized spatially and temporally, and the *universal*, which is still related to the operation of transcendance. The ideas of reason, justice and right, which inspire both a return to the principles of classical thought and a movement towards a secularized ethic, are themselves caught up in a theologico-political elaboration. The prince (and we have already alluded to this event) comes to occupy the position of the mediator between Justice and his subjects; the old Roman definition of the Emperor as being at once above the laws and subject to Law is modified to put him in that position; he appears to be both his own superior and his own inferior; grace makes him divine, but his nature makes him human. He both institutes and reveals justice, and is both its vicar and its image within the State – and, symmetrically, Justice, like Christ, becomes an object of worship, and insinuates itself into a position in which it can mediate between Sovereign Reason and Equity, between a substitute for divine law and a substitute for human law.

Particular attention should be paid to the series of divisions which accompanies and sustains the representation of bodies, a representation which was originally inspired by the model of Christ; not only can they

be substituted for one another; they support one another. The principle
of the schema is, let me repeat, established when a new kind of royalty
is instituted by the rite of coronation. As Marc Bloch demonstrates,
we are now in the presence of a complex phenomenon which calls into
question both the status of temporal power and the status of spiritual
power . . .[3] When the king is blessed and crowned as the Lord's
anointed, his power is spiritualized but, although he is the earthly
replica of Christ, he differs from his model in that, whilst grace makes
him divine, his nature makes him human. It is not simply that he
cannot truly take the place of the sacred one (and no doubt no one
has ever been able to do so); it is also that his person makes visible
both the union of natural and supernatural, and the division between
them. Despite the attempts made by the Othonian Emperors, the path
to a complete identification with a God-made-man remains blocked.
At the same time, the king comes up against another earthly force:
the priest from whose hands he receives grace, and who is in a position
to claim to be his superior. The division of the body of the king
therefore goes hand in hand with the division between royal (or
imperial) and papal authority. What happens at the latter pole is
equally significant, for the claim that the Pope is superior to any
temporal power is bound up with his ambition to imprint his own
spiritual power on a territory. In that respect it should be recalled that
the circumstances surrounding the pact signed between Pépin le Bref
and Etienne II – the first pact between a pope and a king – are not
anecdotal; they have a symbolic significance. Pépin converts his father's
bid for power into an act of usurpation: he asks the Church to establish
the basis of his legitimacy. Etienne, for his part, tries to enlist the
king's help in seizing the Exarchate of Ravenna by exploiting a forged
document – the so-called Donation of Constantine, which surrenders
Rome's possessions into his hands. A double fraud is thus covered up
by a new combination of religious law and human law. The new
formation is indeed theologico-political through and through, by which
I mean that it is determined by a double struggle for power. It is,
however, yet more important to note that we can from the outset
discern two simultaneous movements towards a universal authority
that is both scriptural and temporal. But neither can be carried through
to completion: unrestricted political domination is impossible, and so
is the creation of a theocratic monarchy.

   The fragmentation of authority which is characteristic of feudal
organization, on the other hand, has the result of outlining the position
of a king who, within the framework of a limited territory, appears to
have no superiors – that is, no temporal superiors – and who is defined
as being an Emperor within his own kingdom (*imperator in suo regno*).
And it is at the very moment when this claim is being so clearly
asserted, in, that is, the mid-thirteenth century in both France and
England, that the monarchical configuration begins to be deployed in
its Western singularity.

The work of inscribing power and laws within a territory, the delineation of a political society with definite frontiers and the winning, within that space, of the allegiance of all to the authority of the king, are accompanied by the process of the sanctification and spiritualization of the kingdom. The process of secularization and laicization which tends to deprive the Church of its temporal power within the framework of the state and which tends to include the national clergy within the community of the kingdom is paralleled by the process of the incorporation of those religious representations which are capable of investing a 'natural' space and social institutions with a mystical signification. Throughout the fabric of society, a division is effected between the realm of the functional and the realm of the mystical; though, given that it is revealed in terms of that representation, it would be more accurate to speak of it being effected throughout the fabric of the *body politic*. The division of the body politic occurs together with the division of the king's body; at the same time, the body politic is part of his body; his immortal and supernatural body remains that of a person whom grace makes divine, and in whom God dwells, but at the same time it migrates into the body of the kingdom; whilst a single body is defined both as the body of a person and as the body of a community, its head remains the symbol of a transcendance that can never be effaced. Thus, in the famous essays he devotes to the reign of Philippe le Bel, Joseph Strayer shows how the conquest of the unity of political society under the slogan of 'defence of the kingdom' succeds in mobilizing religious affects – the defence of the kingdom is a continuation of the defence of the kingdom of Christ; a feeling for the earthly fatherland replaces a feeling for the heavenly fatherland; the warriors who sacrifice their lives become brothers to the crusaders who fell in order to deliver Jerusalem and who were promised to the glory of God.[4] The historian reveals how the figure of the warrior king becomes that of the Most Christian King, just as the territory is transformed into a *holy land*, and the mass of subjects into a chosen people (see his essay, 'The most Christian country, The Chosen people and the Holy Land'). It is pointless to dwell upon precisely how the Roman notions of *patria*, *communitas* and *populus* are reactivated and reshaped within a religious symbolic; I would simply like to draw attention to what is now a well-known phenomenon: the installation of representations of the People, the Nation, the Fatherland, of Holy War and of the salvation or safety [*salut*] of the state within the theological configuration of the medieval monarchy. With reference to Kantorowicz's analyses, it would be no less instructive to examine the process inaugurated in the twelfth century whereby a public domain becomes detached from the person of the king and is defined as a domain of inalienable property; and whereby a further division is introduced between a reference to an objective order and a reference to a sacred order: the *res publica* becomes a *res sacra* modelled on the possessions of the Church, which are themselves the property of Christ. The Crown and the Treasury are placed beneath a pole of impersonality which will later become the pole of the state and, thanks to the same inversion of signs, are defined as persons, as mystical bodies. (Bracton even ventures to define the king as the Vicar of the Treasury, in accordance with the model of the Vicar of Christ.)

Finally, it would also be appropriate to re-examine the relationship that was established between the notion of a power that is confined to a limited territory and a restricted community (a notion which was unknown in the period of the Empire), and the notion of a power which has a vocation for universal domination. And it would be appropriate to re-examine the symmetrical relationship that was established between the notion of a kingdom, a nation and a people which are accorded a definite identity, and the notion of a land and a community in which humanity is imprinted and embodied in a privileged manner. The formula which makes the king an Emperor in his own kingdom contains a contradiction: it makes a gesture towards both an unlimited authority and a limited authority; it indicates that modern monarchs' tacit acceptance that their might is restricted by the might of others has not done away with the fantasy of imperial might – a fantasy which has been revived again and again throughout the ages. And this contradiction drifts into the framework of the kingdom; it is as though empirical frontiers are conceivable only if the kingdom finds itself to be entrusted with universal values. In order to appreciate its full import, we would perhaps have to elucidate it further by re-examining the role played by the idea – which receives its initial impetus from Dante – that humanity will become *one* and will live in peace under the sole authority of the *One*, an idea which combines the power of the spirit or Sovereign Reason with political power. This idea was strongly challenged by those who saw humanism as providing the basis for a critique of the temporal monarchy – a critique which began to be formulated by the end of the fourteenth century in Florence and which spread throughout Europe in the sixteenth – but it may also be worth asking whether it might not have retained its theologico-political efficacy in the realm of philosophy, and whether it might not resurface whenever philosophy attempts to reformulate the principle of what, following Michelet, we have termed the Royalty of Spirit.

What conclusions are we to draw from this brief incursion into the theologico-political labyrinth? That we must recognize that, according to its schema, any move towards immanence is also a move towards transcendence; that any attempt to explain the contours of social relations implies an internalization of unity; that any attempt to define objective, impersonal entities implies a personification of those entities. The workings of the mechanisms of incarnation ensure the imbrication of religion and politics even in areas where we thought we were dealing simply with purely religious or purely profane practices or representations.

If, however, we look back at the democratic society which began to take shape in the nineteenth century and which the philosophers and historians of the period were exploring, do we not have to agree that the mechanisms of incarnation were breaking down? The disincorporation of power is accompanied by the disincorporation of thought and by the disincorporation of the social. The paradox is that any adventure that begins with the formulation of a new idea of the state, the people, the nation or humanity has its roots in the past. In that sense, Tocqueville has more reason than he might suspect to denounce the illusion that the French Revolution was a radical beginning, and to want to reconstruct the prehistory of democracy. Although we have been able to do no more than allude to the fact, there was at the time of the Renaissance such a thing as a humanism tinged with a political religiosity, and Michelet could still find traces of it, almost without realizing it. Far from leading us to conclude that the fabric of history is continuous, does not a reconstruciton of the genealogy of democratic representations reveal the extent of the break within it? And so, rather than seeing democracy as a new episode in the transfer of the religious into the political, should we not conclude that the old transfers from one register to the other were intended to ensure the preservation of a *form* which has since been abolished, that the theological and the political became divorced, that a new experience of the institution of the social began to take shape, that the religious is reactivated at the weak points of the social, that its efficacy is no longer symbolic but imaginary and that, ultimately, it is an expression of the unavoidable – and no doubt ontological – difficulty democracy has in reading its own story – and of the difficulty political or philosophical thought has in assuming, without making it a travesty, the tragedy of the modern condition?

12

The Death of Immortality?

Not all those who were exiled to Jersey after the Bonapartist coup d'état in the middle of the last century shared the same political sensibilities, but, perhaps more than anything else, it was the question of immortality that divided them. Indeed, that question itself had a political import. Astonishing as it may seem to us, in order to be a true republican, a true democrat or a true socialist, one either had to deny or affirm a belief in immortality. Victor Hugo and Pierre Leroux both had definite ideas on the subject, and saw those ideas as a precondition for the understanding and edification of the society of the future. Their discussions were acrimonious. The former expresses his irritation with the 'religion of humanity' which dissolves the identity of the individual, absorbs him into a collectivity during his lifetime and discards him after his death. The latter amuses himself with rigged conversations with 'spirits'. The 'Philosophie' preface to *Les Misérables* and *La Grève de Samarez*, which were both written a few years after the event, testify to their debates. Hugo appears to have abandoned the doctrine of metempsychosis in 1860, but he still clings to the belief in the migration of spirits: 'Space is an Ocean, and the worlds are islands. But there must be communications between the islands. These communications take the form of spirits being sent from one world to another.'[1] He allies his faith in 'The Being ... that miracle that cannot be enumerated' with the belief that the self is indestructible because 'it partakes of the indivisible'. He suggests that the humanity which the new prophets venerate has been reduced to its own devices, that it has been cut off from the world and from God, that it is 'an empty humanity. A spectre'. A long argument which lends itself to the fiction of a history from which freedom and responsibility have been banished leads him to conclude: 'Immortality; there we have the residue of the argument; something which survives and which is answerable; there we have the basis of the syllogism.'[2] This is as much a political conclusion as a philosophical or theological conclusion, since it implies that the extension of freedom increases the degree to which man is responsible for what he was on earth;

> The more you give life to do, the more you leave the tomb to do. The slave has no responsiblities; ultimately, he could die completely, and death would have nothing to say to him. The citizen, in contrast, is of necessity immortal, and he must be responsible. He was free. He has accounts to render. This is the divine origin of freedom.[3]

Hugo does not mention by name his adversaries, the upholders of the religion of humanity. But presumably Leroux is not his only target. He also finds repellant the wild imaginings of Comte or Enfantin. Not even Ballanche's *Palingénésie* finds favour in his eyes, even though it is inspired by a faith in a divine Creator; Ballanche is concerned solely with how humanity is reborn after its successive deaths.

As for *La Grève de Samarez*, it expresses the conviction that theologians understand nothing of the doctrine of immortality, and that Leroux's 'illustrious neighbour' Hugo is too preoccupied with himself, his image and his art to understand the implications of the theory that all beings are interdependent.[4] When he acts out his torments and raptures on the beach at Samarez, Leroux quite happily summons up ghosts, questions them and makes them speak, but he shows no interest in converting his ecstasies into the farce of real communication with spirits from another world. In a passage cited by Pierre Albouy, our author puts these words into the mouth of his interlocutor:

> I converse with spirits. Your whole religion is false. . . . Humanity, which you regard both as an ideal being and a real being, does not exist. It has never come to my tables. The future life is not what you say it is . . . I am not certain that we go to the stars; but I am greatly inclined to believe it.[5]

We will not describe Leroux's conception of immortality. He is careful not to define it, for, contrary to Hugo's suggestions, it is not an attribute of either a real or an ideal humanity. But we will at least point out that there is in his view no divide between the visible and the invisible; nothing invisible can be circumscribed within space – in the stars, as his friend Reynaud, with whom he quarrelled over this point, would say – or within time, in a future life divorced from our present life; no representation of immortality can be divorced from the experience of a human presence throughout history, from an initiation into speech through the use of reading and writing.

Our contemporaries may read Hugo the philosopher, Saint-Simon or Ballanche with interest – and not simply out of historical interest – but we can all agree that they will see their comments on immortality as mere curiosities.

They feel much more at home with Tocqueville, whose thought breaks with these wild imaginings and is already sociological. The fact is that in a chapter on individualism in the second volume of *Democracy in America* – which was, it will be recalled, published in 1840 – Tocqueville compares aristocratic society and democratic society, and describes the transformation which occurs in their respective conceptions of time and of collective space. Aristocratic society was, he tells us, such that everyone had a rank and a station, and was caught up in a vast network of dependence: 'Aristocracy had made a chain of all members of the community, from the peasant to the king.'[6] And the dominant notion was that time was immutable, that it existed outside any sequence of events or of individuals: 'As families remain for centuries in the same condition, often on the same spot, all generations become, as it were, contemporaneous.'[7] This is enough to make us grasp the almost natural sense in which humanity understood immortality. As the author remarks in another chapter: 'Amongst the aristocratic nations of the Middle Ages generation succeeded generation in vain; each family was like a never dying, ever stationary man, and the state of opinions was hardly more changeable than that of conditions.'[8] The contrast with this model brings out the singularity of democracy: 'New families are constantly springing up, others are constantly falling away, and all that remain change their condition; the woof of time is every instant broken and the track of generations effaced. Those who went before are soon forgotten; of those who will come after, no one has any idea.'[9] Tocqueville concludes his argument with this comment: 'Thus not only does democracy make every man forget his ancestors, but it hides his descendants and separates his contemporaries from him; it throws him back forever upon himself alone and threatens in the end to confine him entirely within the solitude of his own heart.'[10] The author in fact goes beyond this picture, which might suggest that the reactivation of the belief in immortality at the beginning of the nineteenth century is no more than a survival from the past. He investigates its nature and its function in democracy in two chapters entitled, rsepectively, 'Why some Americans manifest a Sort of fanatical spiritualism' and 'How religious belief sometimes turns the thoughts of Americans to immaterial pleasures'. He is struck first of all by the appearance of sects which endeavour to strike out extraordinary paths to eternal happiness, and by the popularity of 'religious insanity', and then by the true religiosity of the American people. His interpretation of the first phenomenon stems, in part, from what might be termed a sociological reflection. He argues, in substance, that the desire to escape the world is born of a search for well-being and that, in a democracy, that desire is heightened because men are not satisfied with the enjoyment of material goods, and 'feel imprisoned within bounds, which they will apparently never be allowed to pass.'[11] As the majority allow themselves to be imprisoned within these bounds, the religious insanity of the minority intensifies: 'If ever the faculties of the great majority of mankind were exclusively bent upon the pursuit of material objects, it might be anticipated that an amazing reaction would take place in the souls of some men. They would drift at large in the world of spirits, for fear of remaining shackled by the close bondage of the body.'[12] Tocqueville adds: 'It is not, then, wonderful if in the midst of a community whose thoughts tend earthward a small number of individuals are to be found who turn their looks to heaven. I should be surprised if mysticism did not soon make some advance among a people solely engaged in promoting their own worldly welfare.'[13] The reader might rightly wonder at the subtlety of the interpretation. The picture meets his intellectual expectations: mysticism appears on the fringes of a common ideal of worldly happiness; people react against the feeling that they are being swallowed up by the real by seeking the impossible in the here and now. But if we wish to discover Tocqueville's ideas rather than a projection of our own, we have to admit that his argument takes him beyond the framework of a sociological analysis. Between noting the religious insanity that accompanies the proliferation of bizarre sects and advancing the hypothesis of the rise of mysticism, he ventures a comment on human nature:

> It was not man who implanted in himself the taste for what is infinite and the love of what is immortal; these lofty instincts are not the offspring of his capricious will; their steadfast foundation is fixed in human nature, and they exist in spite of his efforts. He may cross and distort them; destroy them he cannot.[14]

It might be said that we can explain away these lines by saying that Tocqueville's Christian convictions have overcome his scientific ambitions. But, even supposing that to be true, we have to ask ourselves whether it is permissible to draw a dividing line between his knowledge of democracy and the principles which allow him to discover within it the seeds of both the best and the worst, to uncover both the dynamic of democratic despotism and the dynamic of democratic freedom. That hypothesis does, however, appear to be debatable. The second chapter I mentioned contains an observation which in fact reappears several times in the work: 'The Americans show by their practice that they feel the high necessity of imparting morality to democratic communities by means of religion.'[15] Here, we have to accept that a distinction is made between *religion* and *religious insanity*: the word 'religion' designates Christianity. And yet the comment brings out a truth with a universal import: 'What they think of themselves in this respect is a truth of which every democratic nation ought to be thoroughly persuaded.'[16] This truth relates, not to the essence of Christianity, but to the nature of the human mind, which has to defend itself against the threat of its debasement. Tocqueville gives that threat another name: materialism. This 'among all nations, is a dangerous disease of the human mind', but it is more especially to be dreaded in a democracy than in any other society. Tocqueville does of course take the view that Christianity is a higher religion. But it is because it is so deeply rooted in modern humanity that he clings to it; and, his own preferences notwithstanding, he is certainly not greatly interested in the nature of religious feelings. 'When, therefore, any religion has struck its roots deep into a democracy, beware that you do not disturb it': that is his view.[17] He perceives, then, how dangerous it would be in his day to create a vacuum of belief by replacing one faith with another. Tocqueville is interested primarily in belief, rather than in the diversity of Christian religions or in the diversity of religions in general. In his view belief, whatever it may become, derives its truth from the same source in all regimes in a democracy; and, at bottom, that source is a belief in immortality. He is therefore not afraid to assert that: 'Most religions are only general, simple and practical means of teaching men the doctrine of the immortality of the soul. That is the greatest benefit which a democratic people derives from its belief, and hence belief is more necessary to such a people than to all others.'[18] This is followed by an even more daring proposition, which finally blurs the distinction between 'religious insanity' and the Christian religion:

> The doctrine of metempsychosis is assuredly not more rational than that of materialism; nevertheless if it were absolutely necessary that a democracy should choose one of the two, I should not hesitate to decide that the community would run less risk of being brutalized by believing that the soul of men is the carcass of a hog than by believing that the soul of man is nothing at all.[19]

Our contemporaries like Tocqueville; they believe that he has to be recognized as a very modern writer; *Democracy in America* attracts a wide readership, and is praised for its sobriety. On the other hand, the very few people who know *La Grève de Samarez* or the preface to *Les Misérables* have the impression that they are fanciful texts. And yet, should we not ask why it is that the sober Tocqueville can sympathize with equally fanciful ideas? It would in fact be an instructive exercise to ask the political scientists who know *Democracy in America* so well to read the following sentence, which is taken from the last chapter we discussed:

> The belief in a supersensual and immortal principle, united for a time to matter is so indispensable to man's greatness that its effects are striking even when it is not united to the doctrine of future reward and punishment, or even when it teaches no more

than that after death the divine principle contained in man is absorbed in the Deity or *transferred to animate the frame of some other creature.* (emphasis added)[20]

Would they be able to identify the author?

The Death of Immortality is the title of a fragment from *Minima Moralia.*[21] At first sight, the formula is convincing. Note that Adorno does not place a question mark after it. He simply records the event. Without dwelling on his argument, which is less assured than the formula might suggest, let us at least provisionally accept a statement which appears to concur with the common sense of our time. The death of immortality, then – but is not the corollary of this that there is nothing but death? Or, rather, since we cannot speak of death without bringing into play the thought of death, nothing but the thought of death? It is rather difficult to accept this. Sociologists and historians have for a number of years been looking at changing attitudes towards death and, more specifically, at the change which appears to them to have characterized recent decades. The conclusion to be drawn from Philippe Ariès's pioneering, and rightly famous, study would appear to be this: the death of the idea of death.[22] If he is to be believed, a mutation has occurred, and it is of a different order to all those mutations that punctuate the history of Western societies. He sums it up most adequately with the provocative formula: 'death inverted'.

The rituals which once accompanied the final event are no more. Death is no longer the drama which people once saw as setting the seal of destiny on a life. No more grandiose *mise en scène*; no more division of roles between the dying man, as he awaits his end and spends his time preparing for it, and his relatives and family. The spectacle of death seems, to say the least, to have been displaced, as have the ceremonial aspects of funerals and mourning. Following Gorer, who takes the view that death has been declared taboo and that the only other thing to have ever been subject to such a strict taboo is sexuality, Ariès notes our contemporary repugnance at anything that makes an exhibition of death, and even goes so far as to speak of a feeling of obscenity. A remarkable inversion of signs indeed. The poetic death that allowed the dying to look down on the world of the living appears to have given way to a prosaic death; the ostentation of death has given way to invisibility. Whereas death was once erected into a crucial moment in the family adventure or, more generally, the collective adventure, it is now private and solitary; whereas it was once personal and almost heroic, it is now anonymous. There are indeed many indications that our era has seen an attempt to dissolve the phenomenon into the banality of the quotidian. Whilst the dying are urged to pretend not to be dying, their relatives try to conceal their pain and mourning. It is as though everyone had to slip away discreetly without disturbing the living, to collude with the living in masking the void. Let me add that the new willingness of doctors – and this is commonplace in the United States – to inform their patients of the inevitability of their fate does not, despite appearances, alter the picture: telling someone who does not know he is condemned 'the truth' still indicates a desire to play down the drama; and in most cases, it indicates, not an obedience to a religious or moral imperative, but conformity to the rules of hygiene and bureaucracy. It places the patient under an obligation to accept his doctor's final orders, to make a clean death, to put his affairs in order, and to carry out the last duties society expects of him.

Does not this removal of drama imply a disavowal of death? Ariès frequently suggests that this is the case. And, at least at one point, he dares to express his own opinion: 'Technically, we accept that we might die, and we take out life insurance to protect our families from poverty. But deep inside, we feel that we are not mortal.'[23]

Is it not, then, worth asking whether the disavowal of death and the disavowal of immortality might not in our day simply be two aspects of a single phenemenon? Far from replacing an illusion with a sense of reality, does not the loss of belief in immortality help to cover up a question which, until a very recent date, constantly haunted the human mind? But how can we say that? Anyone who reads Ariès can accept that death has become the object of a disavowal, even though he himself conforms to the new customs. No matter how little room we give the event, it cannot be abolished. We all see others die, and never doubt that we too will die. We know enough to retain some idea of what we refuse to accept. And, it has to be said: the books we are discussing have not caused a scandal. Indeed, they have sold well. But how can we hear the words *disavowal of immortality* without feeling an unreasonable urge to *assert* our immortality? If, as Ariès and Gorer state, the representation of death now seems obscene, the representation of immortality is even more obscene. The taboo on immortality seems to be total and unavoidable. Historical analysis does of course allow us to identify it as a taboo. But there is still a reluctance to conceive its object: the fact of immortality or of something non-mortal that goes by that name. We would certainly find no symmetry between a history of attitudes to death and a hypothetical history of attitudes to immortality. The historian of the former retains his freedom of judgement. Whilst he agrees that signs of a disavowal can be found in the practices of our time, he can also find a disavowal in the practices of the past: was not the pomp of death a way of concealing something that escapes representation and discourse? The historian of attitudes to immortality does not have the same freedom. The difficulty is that immortality appears to be essentially pompous; anyone who tried to reconceptualize it on the basis of his own experience would expose himself to ridicule. To cite Ariès once more: 'Deep inside, we feel that we are not mortal.' He does not say 'that we are immortal'.

Is he not trying to allay our suspicions? Is he not trying to avoid the taboo? It is true that the negation of mortality is not equivalent to an assertion of immortality. But it is a gesture towards an unknown which ought to take a substantive form: towards a non-death.

To return to Adorno's formula: *the death of immortality*. The play on words is disturbing. It not only tells us that belief in immortality is no more; it also implies the absurd suggestion that immortality once existed. On reflection, however, it is not lacking in pertinence. For the fact is that the word has not been banished from our language; and the thought that it harboured has not been suppressed. True, we no longer believe in immortality, but we do not simply accept that it was once an object of human belief; we readily describe certain men, such as Homer, Dante and Shakespeare (and the three names were associated in significant fashion at the beginning of the nineteenth century), as immortal. It might be objected that we are using one word in place of another, and that we mean that they are unforgettable. In our eyes, the artists, writers, philosophers, statesmen and great soldiers whose names are engraved on humanity's memory are still immortal. We do not, of course, imagine that they dwell in the stars. But do we simply mean that their memory will never perish? We do not describe execrable heroes such as Nero or Attila as immortal, even though their names are familiar. Immortality is an attribute of figures whose words or deeds outlive their ephemeral effects, who seem, in one way or another, to have helped to shape the destiny of humanity. We also apply the word, defined in the same sense, to extraordinary events which we credit with having decided the meaning of history. It is also to be noted that certain of these immortal beings have a special privilege, whilst others had to win their immortality: these are the artists or writers whose language touches us, with whom we can commune across time, as though some element in time had not passed by, who are, as Pierre Leroux puts it, still present in their work. Is it the work, rather than the man, which remains immortal? For our purposes, that is irrelevant. If we replaced the word immortal by 'unforgettable' or 'imperishable', we would impoverish our language considerably. To do so would not remove the feeling that the book we are reading, the canvas we are looking at, or the sonata we are listening to is not dead. Then, then, is the paradox: at some point, immortality died, and yet it lives on, provided that it seems to be a property of beings or things from the past. How can we put it to death if it had its *place*? Its place is essentially invulnerable to the ravages of death, even though we claim that death now has total dominion over our world.

We want to get rid of absurdity. But absurdity is stubborn. If a belief in immortality is absurd, it was as absurd yesterday as it is today, and we have to admit that we cannot make allowance for it by accepting that things that come down to us from the past last indefinitely, and

then denying that the same is true when we apprehend the present
and the future.

The astonishing thing is that we can accept the unthinkable provided
that science dresses it up as a fact. Thus, we learn without being
unduly disturbed that, wherever a trace of a human settlement, no
matter how old, has been found, traces of some funeral ceremony
have also been found. We readily agree that the notion of death is
indissociable from human existence, even that it appears to be a
constitutive element thereof, without drawing the obvious conclusion
that this necessarily implies the notion of non-death. There is no need
to have a profound knowledge of philosophy to understand that
marking a grave means primarily naming death and making a sign or
a gesture which, minimal as it may be, evokes permanence and
establishes a link that can never be broken between the visible and
the invisible. 'Something in the place of nothing' ... we know how
contemporary philosophy has dismissed the formula, but it cannot, of
course, be divorced from an earlier representation: *someone in the
place of nothing* It can be read on the most fragile monuments erected
by human beings to other human beings. And we must further admit
that the gesture which creates the void also erects the monument, that
by saying yes and no to death in the same breath, we create a Word.
The living can no more recognize themselves as the authors of that
Word than they can recognize themselves as the authors of their own
deaths; yet the Word is as indestructible as death is inevitable. The
deceased is a witness to the conjunction of the two. It does not matter
how we establish the stages of his migration; it does not matter whether
the final resting place we give him is in a specific place in the world,
whence he will communicate with the living; whether it is in another
world which will become his eternal home; whether we simply hang
his portrait on the wall in the family home; or whether we merely
think of him – we always exhibit a wish to make something of the
dead. The deceased begets duration. He creates substance. If we fail
to embody him, humanity is dissolved into a time that has been
pulverized.

It is not simply through communication between the living or through
the interpenetration of their perceptions that the world is revealed to
be a *common world*, an external world. And nor is it enough to say
that it is because everyone can see, can be seen by others and is quasi-
visible to himself, that he is imprinted on the being on to which it
opens. The world is at once immutable and inexhaustible, absolutely
present and beyond our present grasp, visible and invisible, unthinkable
and thinkable, only because it arises from the fracture of death, only
because, deep within it, it bears the mark of the division of death. Its
institution cannot be disassociated from the institution in which the
other who has been both lost and named reassures human beings of
the certainty that what *is* will endure.

It is true that recognition of a primal relationship between the idea of death and the idea of something that endures for ever serves only to familiarize us with the inconceivable, and that it leaves us powerless to deal with the specific question of immortality and of its eventual death or semi-death. The notion allows us to formulate, in a singular way, the experience of *that which lasts for ever.* In *The Human Condition*, Hannah Arendt draws our attention to the distinction, or rather the opposition, between immortality and eternity. In her view, immortality is to be recognized when men cannot conceive of a world other than the world they inhabit – a world which displays obvious signs of its permanence. Greek thought bears witness to this experience:

> Immortality means endurance in time, deathless life on this earth and in this world as it was given, according to Greek understanding, to nature and the Olympian gods. Against this background of nature's ever-recurring life and the gods' deathless and ageless lives stood mortal men, the only mortals in an immortal but not eternal world, confronted with the immortal lives of their gods but not under the rule of an immortal God.[24]

Men alone are mortal because, unlike animals, they are not members of a species whose immortal life is guaranteed through procreation. It is therefore as individuals that they aspire to partake of the divine nature by producing works, deeds and words which will leave behind them an imperishable trace. The certainty that the world and the higher beings that populate it will endure for ever is, however, destroyed by the Christian religion and by the new notion of a transcendant God, of a place outside the world where man will find an eternal resting place, compared with which the time of earthly life will count as nothing. But, as Arendt also observes, its destruction is prefigured in Antiquity by the birth of philosophy, when the excellence of the contemplative life is proclaimed at the expense of the active life, the *vita activa*. This event appears to her to be decisive in that it reveals the link between the idea of immorality and political life, as well as that between immortality and life in the world. When man ceases to be defined by his participation in the City and by his relations with his equals – each appearing before all and producing a self-image to be shown to all – his hope of imprinting something of himself on the duration of time disappears. Immortality requires the institution or the deployment of the public space. But it should not be supposed that it is therefore a contingent manifestation which is dependent upon a certain form of society. Political life, in Arendt's sense of the term and in the sense in which it was recognized in the Greek City, is the highest form of the human condition. For her, the loss of a sense of immortality therefore coincides with the loss of a sense of the human condition.

Arendt returns to this theme and develops it further in a chapter in which she evokes the decline of modern humanity. That men have a sensible experience of *a common world*, of a world which pre-exists and outlives every generation, is not, in her view, enough to ensure its consistency and its transcendance.

> Such a common world can survive the coming and going of the generations only to the extent that it appears in public. It is the publicity of the public realm which can absorb and make shine through the centuries whatever men want to save from the natural ruin of time. Through many ages before us – but not any more – men entered the public realm because they wanted something of their own or something they had in common with others to be more permanent than their earthly lives ...

Arendt adds: 'There is perhaps no clearer testimony to the loss of the public realm in the modern age than the almost complete loss of authentic concern with immortality, a loss somewhat overshadowed by the simultaneous loss of the metaphysical concern with eternity.'[25] Hence the conclusion that: 'Under modern conditions, it is indeed so unlikely that anybody should [in our day] earnestly aspire to an earthly immortality that we probably are justified in thinking that it is nothing but vanity.'[26]

Whence the withering away of the public realm in our age? In one sense, its decline appears to be an indirect result of Christianity's devaluing of the earthly world.

> The Christian abstention from worldly things is by no means the only conclusion one can draw from the conviction that the human artifice, a product of mortal hands, is as mortal as its makers. This, on the contrary, may also intensify the enjoyment and consumption of the things of the world, all manners of intercourse in which the world is not primarily understood to be the *koinon*, that which is common to all.[27]

In another sense, the spectacle of modern society further elucidates the phenomenon: it is a mass society in which individuals find themselves trapped in the narrow circle of their private lives, and are at the same time swallowed up in and carried away by an undifferentiated collective vision of the real when they come together. We will not pursue this latter explanation. Let us, rather, retain the hypothesis that the notion of an indefinite time being allotted to men and their works is, for Arendt, intrinsically bound up with the emergence of a space which is, by right, open to all, which stands out against the background of the social, and which gives everyone a universal visibility. The division of time – a time for beings and mortal things, a time for beings and immortal things – coincides with the first division between the private realm and the public realm. This is also the division between a truly social life in which men are still stratified because of the requirements of labour and the satisfaction of needs, and because of political life, which delivers them from their obscurity and inspires in them a passion for their image and for their mode of appearance, a passionate desire to be seen and recognized by their equals. If we follow Arendt, it is, then, futile to look for the basis of the belief in immortality in a religious or metaphysical quietism, or simply in the fear of death, and it is also futile to stress the distinction between personal survival and the survival of the institution. She suggests that, once he appears on the public stage, man comes to dwell in his own image, that he no longer belongs to himself as an individual, that he becomes immortal in his own lifetime, or even by challenging death, regardless of what his representation of his own destiny may be.

We will not, perhaps, understand Arendt's thought if we confine ourselves to a reading of *The Human Condition*, and if we restrict our discussion to the contrast between the ancient City and modern mass society. For her, the *polis* is merely a reference which is intended to shed light upon the political institution of the common world or upon the opposition between immortality and eternity. It is therefore self-evident that, when she speaks of the withering away of the public domain in our era, she is alluding to a recent past in which it was fully deployed. If we refer to her essay *On Revolution*, this becomes obvious: the world that we have lost is the world that was built, momentarily, by the French and American Revolutions. Men then had the strength to break with the Christian ethic – sometimes without realizing it; they were able to rehabilitate life on earth; they passionately set themselves the task of building an eternal city, and identified their own immortality with that of their political achievement:

> Nothing perhaps indicates more clearly that the revolutions brought to light the new, secular and worldly yearnings of the modern age than this all-pervasive preoccupation with permanence, with a 'perpetual state' which, as the colonists never tired of repeating, should be secure for their 'posterity'. It would be quite erroneous to mistake these claims for the later bourgeois desire to provide for one's children and grandchildren. What lay behind them was the deeply felt desire for an Eternal City on earth, plus the conviction that 'a Commonwealth rightly ordered may, for any internal causes, be as immortal or as long-lived as the World.'[28]

At the time of the two great revolutions, modern peoples turned, according to Arendt, 'once more to antiquity to find a precedent for [their] new preoccupation with the future of the man-made world on earth'. At the same time, the individual actor on the political stage was transfigured, and escaped his own mortal existence. Modern politics found its 'briefest and most grandiose expression' in Robespierre's phrase, 'Death is the beginning of immortality'.[29] This is something that our contemporaries would now find inconceivable. If the prophecy is turned into a statement of fact, Arendt could easily, it would seem, endorse Michelet's verdict: 'In times of weakness, it will no longer be possible to understand how, in the midst of these bloody revolutions, and with one foot in the grave, these extraordinary men could dream only of immortality'.[30]

Whilst this interpretation is attractive, we have to go beyond its limitations, as the arguments it mobilizes make it difficult to interpret the representation of immortality which arose out of the Greek political universe. How can one reveal the link between the sense of immortality and the sense of posterity, which is so obvious in revolutionary language, without noticing that it is new? How can one forget that, for the Greeks, there was no question of building 'an eternal city on earth', that their City was essentially divine; that immortal life surrounded them, that works and deeds performed in the present were an invitation to future generations to look upon something imperishable, but that their makers could not remove them from the cycle of history, and could not, so to speak, make them participate in the immortal work of creation? How, on the other hand, can a writer be so alert to the double division of space and time – the obscure space of the social, and the public, luminous space of the political; the time of transience and the time of immortality – without seeing that, in the modern world, it implies a tension of which the ancient world, or at least the epoch which Arendt evokes, knew nothing? A citizen of Athens may well have immortalized himself on the political stage but, insofar as he was a member of society, he owned a fragment of the divine land which gave him the right to be a citizen. Nothing in distant Antiquity suggests the idea that the City, humanity or history could be transcended within the world or within time. And is it not because religion makes it impossible that we find no sign of that idea? Suggestive though it may be, Arendt's formula *'Eternity versus Immortality'* is misleading if it leads us to ignore how the idea of immortality both persisted and was transformed as a result of the belief in *another world*. The only aspect of the Christian religion to which Arendt refers is its devaluing of earthly life; there is of course no lack of solid evidence to support her thesis and she could produce more than one argument in favour of it. But the work of Christianity has to be read in two ways: the notion of the fall of man, who expiates his original sin in his human condition, is combined with the notion of a human incarnation of the divine.

We see the first signs of 'modern' immortality in the body of Christ, a body which, in the Middle Ages, finds substitutes in the bodies of the Pope, the Emperor and the King, and which is actualized in the community, circumscribed as it is within its indestructible space: the Church, and then the kingdom and humanity itself. Dante is merely following an established tradition when he creates the figure of a universal monarchy and gives it the mission of revealing humanity unto itself in all its unity – a unity which transcends the diversity of the 'nations' from the far north to the far south – and in its continuous duration – which transcends the never-ending sequence of the generations, each of which appears as a limb of a single body moving through space. But it is not enough to examine the ambiguity of these religious representations in terms of their explicit content. The remarkable thing about them is the way they become invested in political representations, in the laicized, secularized and worldly representations which crystallize at the end of the eighteenth century, even though they had begun to take shape earlier. The image of the immortal body of the kingdom is grafted on to that of the territorial state. The theme of defending the king allies itself with that of defending the fatherland, and thus ensures that the warrior who dies for its sake will enjoy immortality upon earth, just as the warrior who died in the defence of Jerusalem was certain to enter into Paradise at the time of the Crusades. A whole segment of the history of beliefs remains hidden from us if we ignore how transcendance was transferred into the frontiers of worldly space; and whilst its transference into that space was in part unconscious, it was also the result of deliberate efforts on the part of the politicians and jurists who were striving to elevate monarchical power above all *de facto* powers, to give it a different kind of life to that enjoyed by mortal institutions and mortal men, and to give the state something it lacked and which it had once possessed when it was rooted in a divine land: *permanence in time*. That their efforts were based upon an acquaintance with Roman law and with the philosophy of Aristotle, that they would have been inconceivable without the reactivation of the knowledge of the *universitas*, of the *communitas* which establishes the status of *perpetuitas* as opposed to change – which establishes, that is, an immutable law as opposed to particular customs – should not make us forget that, thanks to Christianity, a new link was forged between the One who exists outside time and the individual or collective body, between a transcendental sovereignty and worldly life.[31]

For centuries, the king was the ultimate symbol of this being in the world, which is at once its own inferior and its own superior, which is at once mortal and immortal. But if we look even briefly at a free city at the moment when it is beginning to evolve towards the state form, at, for example, Florence in the latter part of the fourteenth century, we cannot fail to be struck by the fact that its efforts to constitute itself as a republic in order to leave no place for a tyrant are paralleled by a desire to seize the attributes of monarchy, to produce an image of a sovereignty which is distanced from all its members and which is immortal.

This is especially remarkable in that it is in Florence, in modern Europe, that an ethics of the *vita activa*, as opposed to the contemplative life, begins to be elaborated under the sign of a return to Antiquity, of the restoration of the power of man in the world, and of the renewal of the civic spirit. We therefore cannot deny the originality of humanism by replacing it in the context of a Christian society. Many of the features Arendt regards as being characteristic of what might be called revolutionary humanism, which appeared in the eighteenth century, can already be seen in Florentine humanism, including the belief that works performed by the City contain a universal truth. Particular significance should be given to the double attempt to elevate to immortality both the Florentine fatherland and those citizens who contributed to its greatness – those who distinguished themselves in the conduct of public affairs or in war, or as writers, artists or merchants – an attempt which was at the time, we can legitimately assume, facilitated by the formation of a public space, of a public stage.

We will, however, perhaps be in a better position to grasp the modernity of the sense of immortality and all the features that differentiate it from the Greek conception of the world if we compare it with the former event.

It has rightly been noted that humanism in fact introduces a sense of history, a sense of a time-difference.[32] The ancient world was not discovered, as though it were something that had been lost and then found again. Traces of it survived throughout the Middle Ages, not only in the writings of the great authors – most of whom were of course the object of *studia humanitatis* – and in monuments, but above all in the use of the Latin language. Indeed, historians tell us that it was not perceived as a different world, despite the break between Christianity and paganism. That perception is characteristic of humanism. What we have termed a return to Antiquity therefore implies its institution, the institution of a past which is removed from the present. The experience of *temporal separation* is a precondition for communication, or in its extreme form, identification with the ancients; it is also the precondition for an opening on to the future, an opening created by deeds, knowledge, art and pedagogy, by a work of creation which is legitimized by the creation of the past. The humanists saw themselves as heirs but, at the same time, they acquired a posterity. The dignity of the *vita activa* is combined with the dignity of the life of the citizen, but, in more general terms, it is instituted by a new relationship with the work of art. Hannah Arendt appears to be curiously insensitive to this event. When she speaks of works of art in *The Human Condition*, she accords them a permanence which seems to have the properties of an essence. The world of art appears to her to be *par excellence* a 'non-mortal home for mortal beings'.[33] It is, then, important to investigate both the birth of this feeling of permanence and the significance it acquires when it becomes conjoined with a representation of the work of art as having a singular identity, as being localized in space and time. The idea of permanence alone cannot account for another idea which seems to emerge together with humanism: the idea that works of art are contemporaneous *within* a time-difference; the idea of a conjunction between something that no longer exists and something that does not yet exist. If, however, we concentrate exclusively on the revolution in the experience of time that is introduced by humanism, we will fail to see that it is shaped by a rejection of the 'dark ages', which, in the eyes of those who wanted to escape them, were not yet over. For the humanists, the awareness that Antiquity is a different world whose authenticity has to be restored implies a break with the language, the knowledge and the morals of a degraded humanity, a will to extract themselves from the darkness of a period in which custom replaces truth. The effects of this break are ambiguous in that, on the one hand, it implies emancipation from established authorities in every domain of life, a demand for creativity, and an apprehension of the present – and one of the most remarkable signs of this is the full recognition of the virtues of the vernacular – and in that, on the other hand, it leads to real life being confined within a circle of men of letters who understand the works of the ancients, who can read them and who can use language correctly – and so, paradoxically, Latin is restored to its purity as a canonical language. We might even venture to say that humanism thus paves the way for the emergence of two conceptions of immortality. To a large extent, it stakes its destiny on an attempt to master the experience of contemporaneity within a time-difference, to erect a theatre in which things that seem, in terms of the agreed signs, to deserve not to perish are authorized to appear, and to install the new in a future commensurate with the demands of the present by inviting posterity to participate in the great spectacle of culture. It is therefore not surprising that the project of humanism should have become imbricated with that of Christianity, or that they should have collaborated in 'manufacturing' a transcendance that could take place within the world. Ancient maxims extolling immortal entities such as Reason, Justice, Wisdom and Fatherland are combined with religious references in order to glorify and immortalize the monarchy. Greek and Roman mythology is mobilized through poetry, statuary and painting to represent the presence of the Prince as being beyond time. But this phenomenon also has much wider implications: the notion of the sovereignty of the author or of his work takes on a political and religious meaning, just as the notion of the sovereignty of the Prince or the nation finds support in a scholarly culture and in theology. And it is not illegitimate to ask whether the Revolution might not have put an end to this trade in immortality. Arendt refuses to see the Revolution as anything other than the moment of the foundation or refoundation of the political, of the deployment of a public space, and of the establishment of an *eternal city* built by men for men. It is astonishing that she should see the use of new artifices to resurrect Antiquity and to put it to new ends solely in this light, that she should express her delight with Robespierre's 'Death is the beginning of immortality' without concerning herself with his heroic posture, or with the way politics, culture and history are staged to dazzle the common people.

Edgar Quinet appears to me to display more perspicacity than Arendt
or even Michelet when he observes that:

> No tribune in the world ever spoke a less popular, more learned .
> or more studied language than Robespierre and Saint-Just.
> Anyone who tried to speak the language of the people immediately
> and naturally seemed hateful to them. They always saw the
> Revolution in terms of the pomp of Cicero and the majesty of
> Tacitus.

In an evocation of one of the final episodes of the Terror, he adds:
'It was the classical, lettered revolution of the Jacobins which crushed
the uneducated and plebeian revolution of the Cordeliers. Robespierre
was acting out a classical tragedy. Anything that went beyond its
orderly conventions – life, spontaneity, popular instinct – appeared to
him to be a monstrosity. And he attacked it with sword and fire.'[34]

And yet, we said, we can detect in humanism a different notion of
immortality, which is not subordinate to a representation of sovereignty,
and which can be placed under the sign of *conversation* or, to use a
term which was dated even at the time and which is understood in a
different sense by the moderns, *friendship*. When it is understood in
this sense, there is no mastering of a time-difference, but merely the
feeling that the invisible *other* is closer than the living, that his words
can be heard despite his fate at the hands of time, or that words can
be entrusted to him in some indefinite future. The dialogue with the
dead had, of course, become a genre in itself, and it conferred a
flattering nobility on its author. But, to evoke the Florence of the so-
called Renaissance age once more, listen to the sobriety we find in,
for example, Machiavelli's dialogues with the ancients. In a letter
which was to become famous, he tells his friend Vettori how, when
he had been banished from Florence, he spent his time in rural exile.
Having described the morning he spent in the woods, he mentions
stopping at the inn opposite his house. He plays backgammon, quarrels
with the inn-keeper, the butcher, the miller and two workmen from a
lime-kiln; their oaths can be heard in the next village. He confides
that he has to venture into his 'flea-pit' to prevent his brain from
stagnating completely. Then, as evening falls, it is time for work:

> I returned to my lodgings. I went into my study, and at the door
> I took off my everyday clothes, which were covered in mud and
> dirt, and put on pontifical court dress. Now that I was fittingly
> dressed, I entered the court of the men of Antiquity. They
> greeted me honourably, and I dined on that food that is above
> all mine and which I was born to eat. I felt no embarrassment
> at talking to them or at asking them to explain their actions, and,
> out of human kindness, they were good enough to answer my
> questions. And for four hours I felt no boredom; I forgot all my

troubles, and I even ceased to fear poverty. *I was not even afraid of death*. (emphasis added)[35]

Finally, we are told that these conversations were not fruitless; a little book is coming into being: *De Principatibus* (later to be known as *The Prince*). By describing how he went from the tavern to his study and how he changed his clothes, Machiavelli makes it clear that he is stepping into a time that exists outside time. The change is further stressed by the quality of the clothes he put on. They are not simply any ceremonial garments, and they are not those he wore when he carried out his duties in Florence. He had use for pontifical or royal court dress only when he was sent abroad on mission, when he was dispatched by the Republic as its ambassador. But such dress is indispensable if he is to appear in the presence of Livy, Tacitus, Aristotle or Xenophon, and if he is to converse with them, if they are to recognize that he has been sent on a historical mission, that he is modern humanity's delegate to Antiquity. Without any reference being made to God or to the division between heaven and earth, we have here a representation of a division between this world and the next, between the trivial place we inhabit alongside the living and the place of immortality. Notice, however, that Machiavelli never pronounces the word 'immortality'. He is content to say: 'I was not even afraid of death'. Why is he so serene? Because, in order to speak to the dead, one must speak as though one were dead? No doubt. But it is primarily that he has the feeling of having another life, not in the vague sense that he will endure for ever, but in the very precise sense that he is undeniably present for others, for the world and for himself in a realm beyond time. The invisible interlocutors Machiavelli joins are as alive as his companions in the tavern; he himself is more alive than the backgammon player he dismisses at the door. The inexhaustible conversation becomes a source of constant mutual recognition, the source of his future work.

Machiavelli thus describes an experience which many other writers have described and which, although it finds its clearest expression in the Renaissance, is not confined to that period: the experience of a dialogue which breaks down the barriers of time and which, through the duality of question and answer, speaking and listening, institutes a singularity – the singularity or someone or something – that cannot be broken down into a 'once' and a 'now'. In such an experience, immortality does not look down from on high; it is, rather, a transition through time which reveals its density; beneath its constantly changing surface, the movement of time is reversible. The idea of that which does not die is indissociable from that of the sovereignty of the immortal being – an idea which was, we said, bound up with that of a superhuman power, with that of an invulnerable body which supplied everyone with an image of survival.

Perhaps, however, we can best grasp the sign of this sovereignty at the moment when a glorious immortality meets with a radical challenge; when the proclamation of *perpetuitas* is countered with the proclamation of *vanitas*. The negation reveals the basis of the assertion by turning it inside out. Either *vanitas* becomes a sign that all power belongs to the Eternal, before whom all human creations are as nothing, or, and for our purposes this is more relevant, it promotes an emphatic election of death, and installs death in the place of sovereignty. No one has done more to unveil the complicity between the representation of immortality and death, or their relationship with sovereignty, than Shakespeare. When, having heard of Bolingbroke's rebellion and having proclaimed the invulnerability of his pompous body, Richard II suddenly glimpses the impossible – the fact that he will be parted from it – the image of death's elect replaces that of God's elect: the crown, which was an indestructible substance becomes 'the hollow crown wherein death keeps his court'. ('For within the hollow crown/That rounds the mortal temples of a king/Keeps death his court'.) It should not be forgotten that Shakespeare puts these words into the mouth of a prince; there is no suggestion that he himself believes them. He has too fine a perception of the contradictory nature of the sovereign to want to take his place. He urges us, his readers, to accept the idea of a double time without succumbing to the illusion of a double body, and spares us the alternative of having to give all to immortality or having to give all to death.

To return to our initial question. The thought of the men of the nineteenth century was still haunted by a sense of immortality. That sense of immortality seems to have disappeared or, paradoxically to have survived only by becoming compromised with a respect for the past, only by becoming bound up with a sense of posterity. These, it appears to me, are the most characteristic features of modern times. Perhaps matters become less certain than Adorno and Arendt suggest, if we agree to separate out the various representations implied by the current sense of the word – a task we have just outlined. Perhaps matters become even less certain if we pay attention to the alterations they underwent even in the nineteenth century, in a world which was turned upside down by what Tocqueville called the 'democratic revolution'. I say 'alterations' because in this respect there is no radical discontinuity between the Ancien Regime and post-revolutionary society. Numerous signs testify to the persistence of the theologico-political vision of the immortal body. To extend the discussion beyond the frontiers of Catholicism, the Saint-Simonians, to take only one example, espoused a belief in an organic society which was to be built on the ruins of the revolutionary ages, and which would be able to conceive of and celebrate its own immortality. The invention of the 'religion of humanity'; Enfantin's substitution of the indestructible body of society, or even that of humanity, for that of the king; the substitution of Science for the holy book; of Saint-Simon for the

Messiah – none of these events can conceal the heritage of the past, even though they relate to a completely new vision of industry and of organization, and, more generally, to an artificialist, constructivist philosophy of the social which breaks with Christian tradition. The humanist conception of a glorious immortality, on the other hand, begins to blossom with the rise of the bourgeoisie, and this is a phenomenon with much wider implications. The elaboration of a national history and of a history of humanity, and the legitimation of the individual, which existed only in outline in the fifteenth and sixteenth centuries, supply it with new resources. But we can still see traces of earlier attempts to imprint the nation, the institution and the individual on a monumental time, to sanctify Reason and Right – the Right whose 'immortal principles' were finally established in 1789 – to engrave imperishable names on the collective memory, and to hand on to future generations the torch borne by the living, as thinkers of the period were so fond of saying.

If, however, we compare 'religious insanity' with bourgeois humanism, we see that something new does appear: the function of discourse, which is constantly pressed into service to produce immortality. Not that immortality ever lacked a symbolic, or even propaganda, when it served the monarchy and the republic. But there is no comparison between that and the rhetorical and pedagogical means that are employed to make belief in immortality a guarantee of the durability, not only of a specific regime, constitution or institution – beginning with the institution of the family – but of *civilization itself*. The explanation for this urgent need to express belief in immortality in formulae and eloquent images is that men are haunted by the idea of the break-up of the social, and that democracy threatens, sometimes implicitly and often explicitly, to bring that about. Civic humanism took shape in the fifteenth century, we noted, as a result of a desire to emerge from an age of darkness into the light that the Ancients had known; it flourished in a climate of confidence in a new foundation. The bourgeois humanism of the nineteenth century experiences an ambiguity which undermines its certainties. It does not see barbarism simply as a thing of the past – not to mention the fact that it usually regards barbarism as having two aspects: that of feudal times and that of the Terror, which means that even the light of 1789 cannot make it forget the darkness that surrounds it. Ranged in front of it, it sees the barbarian masses, the 'little people' who have no property and no culture, who are ready to rise, and whose irruption on to the public stage would destroy the eternal foundations of the social order. At the same time, no one can sound the depths of this fear or plumb the void that lies within the proud construction, at the heart of the supposedly imperishable edifice of bourgeois civilization without seeing that it also produces a new feeling that both the principle and the heart of civilization are contingent. The great task, which is best expressed by Guizot, is to make it clear that *the Revolution is over*. But what no one seems able to eradicate is the idea of *the event*, not merely of that specific event, but of the event as such, which no longer exists with time, but which can fracture and undo time, which can give birth to the unknown: it has all the might of disorder, and no established order can be guaranteed to prevent it from being unleashed.

If we accept that the notion of sovereign immortality was bound up with the ultimate legitimacy of the body politic and that it was for centuries bound up with the legitimacy of the monarchy, how could it fail to become fragile after the collapse of the monarchy, and particularly after the tragic failure of a terrorist power which claimed to be the incarnation of Eternal Reason and Justice? The bourgeoisie, of course, tries feverishly to acquire new emblems entitling it to legitimacy and to promote a recognition of its vocation for immortality, but it cannot raise itself up without sensing the void beneath its feet. The power to which it gives its allegiance – representative power – is no longer organically linked to society, and the age on which it wants to inscribe the symbols of its durability is no longer organically linked to earlier ages. In the aftermath of 1830, Chateaubriand finds the words to jeer at the bourgeoisie: 'The only thing that we now lack is the present within the past. That is no great loss! As though the ages did not provide a foundation for one another, and as though the latest age could stand on thin air!'[36] Or again, 'The dynasty of Saint Louis was so powerful thanks to its extensive past that when it fell, it tore away part of society's foundations' – and it is not that he has any desire to see its restoration.[37] And if we also agree that attachment to imperishable things and beings is based upon the experience of a continuity between generations, customs and traditions, how can we fail to be struck by the contrast between the memory of that permanence, and the attempt to establish its signs, and the new vision of change, the acceleration of production, of the circulation of commodities, of the break-up of inherited property, and of mobility of condition, of the whirlwind that sweeps away established positions, morals and ideas? One usually thinks of Marx in connection with this whirlwind: 'All fixed, fast-frozen relations, with their train of ancient and venerable prejudices and opinions, are swept away, all new-formed ones become antiquated before they can ossify. All that is solid melts into air, all that is holy is profaned ...'[38] If we simply retain this passage from the *Manifesto* without mentioning its author's conclusions, we find that it is an expression of of a widespread view. Balzac – a privileged reference for Marx – exhibits a similar awareness of the whirlwind, especially in the astonishing picture of Paris that opens *La Fille aux yeux d'or*, but so too do Tocqueville, Chateaubriand, Michelet and Quinet. When one reads them, and when one reads Chateaubriand in particular, one hesitates to say that the advent of a mass society, the loss of a sense of duration and the ruin of the works or ideas on which it could once imprint itself are recent phenomena. Does the conclusion of the *Mémoires d'outre-tombe* refer to the last century, or to the end of our own century?

> The old European order is expiring. In the eyes of posterity, our current debates will look like puerile struggles. Nothing exists: the authority of experience and age, birth or genius, talent or virtue are all denied; a few individuals climb to the summit of the ruins, proclaim themselves giants, and then fall to the bottom like pygmies.

He goes on:

> In the life of the City, everything is transient; religion and morality are no longer accepted, or else everyone interprets them in their own fashion. In things of a lower nature, we find the same inability to convince, or even to exist; a reputation lasts for barely an hour, a book grows old in a day; writers kill themselves to attract attention; that too is vanity; no one even hears their last sighs.

Let us also look at one last passage, which is not simply a rhetorical flourish. On more than one occasion, Chateaubriand suggests that an era which brings people face to face with the banality of life also brings them face to face with the banality of death. Historians who claim that the death of Death occurred only a few decades ago would be astonished by the picture of cholera which the writer both dreams and describes. First, he dreams it: 'Imagine a shroud floating like a banner from the towers of Notre-Dame, and the canon firing single shots to warn the imprudent traveller. ...' He dreams of it reducing a prostrate people to terror and silence as they tremble at their prayers. And then he describes cholera in Paris in 1817: 'A scourge with no imagination ... walking abroad with a mocking smile in the bright light of day in a completely new world, and carrying a bulletin. ...' Cholera is certainly an agent of terror, but it is an agent of an unknown terror: 'Brilliant sunshine, an indifferent crowd, the ordinary round of life. ...'

The image of a glorious immortality does undergo a renaissance in the nineteenth century, but it conceals a wound to which the turgidity of bourgeois discourse bears witness, and a small number of witnesses know just how deep that wound is. The witnesses themselves have not, however, lost their sense of immortality. And that concerns us closely.

Could it be that they are still heirs to the discreet humanism we described earlier, to a humanism which does not give way to rapture, and which, through the experience of conversation, leads, despite time, to a recognition of men and their works? To a certain extent this is no doubt true. But the notion of time-difference is not the same, once the notion of time itself has changed, once the fracture between *before* and *after* has become immediately tangible, once, as a result of that fracture, humanity's whole past – the Orient as well as Greece, the Middle Ages and the Renaissance – emerges, is summoned into the present, and simultaneously becomes a sign of a world that is vanishing. The past re-emerges, charged with meaning, but also marked with the sign of loss. And nor does the notion that man has two lives – a trivial, prosaic life spent in day-to-day dealings with others, and a poetic life in which he participates in the universe of culture and politics – remain unchanged, once political life and literary production are no longer confined to minority groups, once they permeate the entire space of society, once, to put it another way, the representation of the audience which nourishes the work becomes combined – I will not say confused – with that of opinion.

We would try in vain to dissociate the idea of immortality which haunts the writer and his awareness of posterity from his new experience of temporality and his new relationship with the public. Chateaubriand, whom we evoked earlier, is worthy of mention because, all too often, it is said that he displays an immoderate desire to immortalize himself and to provide a spectacle for posterity – and he does at times display unmistakable signs of that desire. Yet few writers shared his awareness of the void that was opened up by the fall of the monarchy, and of the impossible coincidence between what once was – and it seems to him that it has gone for ever – and what is yet to be – a future which he sometimes imagines to be a constant process of decadence, and which he sometimes recognizes as the era of another society which men are not yet mature enough to accept. The monarchy had legitimacy and immortality on its side, and he says so, but he knows that it is dead. And, however much he may regret the fact that its life-span was cut short by its adversaries, it is impossible to believe that he sees it as being the victim of an accident. His picture of the Legitimist world leaves us in no doubt as to that: 'He enjoys the decrepitude that comes with time; he is blind and deaf; he is frail, ugly and surly; but he looks quite natural, and crutches suit him at his age.' The concession to the *natural* is made only in order to bring out just how ridiculous the survivors of the Empire are. They are not antiques like the Legitimists, and they have not grown old as a dated fashion grows old; they are like the deities that descend from their chariots of gold cardboard on the stage of the opera. The image of the opera itself helps him to reveal the monarchical masquerade. As he describes the theatre in which the Duc de Berry was assassinated, he evokes 'the empty auditorium after the end of a tragedy' and concludes: 'The monarchy of Saint Louis lay dying behind a mask amongst the debauchery of a carnival, in a place which the Church had pronounced anathema.' His respect for the period of the immortal monarchy and the devotion he showed to Charles X after his abdication go hand in hand with the public statement that he never believed in the divine right of kings. He sees legitimacy and the old immortality as no more than simulacra which were useful to the social order. As for his own sense of immortality, not only does he fail to invest it in a sovereignty which could have guaranteed the immortality of his work; it finds expression in his very ability to say both that it has gone and that it was never anything more than a mask. More generally, it finds expression in his ability to occupy a position that cannot be localized in time and space because it is not the position in which he distinguished himself in public life or in literature. It is a position which revealed how far he was from having his roots in reality, because it did not inscribe him in the glorious course of History; but it did open his eyes to what was appearing and what was disappearing in time – or, to be more accurate, for it is not simply a matter of seeing what was falling into the past and what was in gestation, it did give him *time regained in time lost.*

The choice of words is no accident, for no work does more to anticipate Proust than the *Mémoires*. No other work blurs in this way the conventional boundaries between subjective and objective, between the individual and the social, between personal and historical temporality, between being and appearance; no other work tries in this way, as Chateaubriand puts it, to make 'both ends of life meet' by undoing the representation of beginning, middle and end, and that of an outline which allows an imaginary world to be kept at a distance from a real world.

The sense of immortality proves to be bound up with the conquest of a place *which cannot be taken,* which is invulnerable, because it is the place of someone – who is neither an individual in the contemporary sense of the word nor a subject in the philosophical sense of the word – who, by accepting all that is most singular in his life, refuses to submit to the coordinates of space and time and who is so disproportionate that he sets free breaks and relations which no one before him has experienced and which we now experience through him.

We would attempt in vain to reduce this frame of mind to the status of a psychological or psychosociological trait. We are not dealing with a desire for glory that has been reshaped by the new cult of originality. If we believe that, we forget one thing: for us, Chateaubriand is not dead. And why does he live on, unless it is because his thought and his language make him peerless and because (and this amounts to the same thing) they cause to emerge from within thought and language themselves something which is unprecedented but still specific, something which partakes of their essence, something singular which, once it has come into being, bears the strange hallmark of being something that must be.

Can we say that this *place that cannot be taken* has always been the place of the writer, no matter how far back in history we go? Even if that were true, we would have to admit that the writer never knew it. The certainty of being must vanish into the experience of nature, society, time, and language if writing is to become the theatre in which there comes into play the dizzying freedom to create something unique without the guarantee of a model. It must vanish if someone is to assume the *right* to speak without the protection of the law which supposedly founds the organization of speech, or to cease to divorce discovery from the invention of what has to be said. The dissolution of the markers of certainty coincides with the rise of democracy as a result of the collapse of the ultimate sovereignty or legitimacy which the Monarchy had for centuries claimed to embody. But, as we have already suggested, there is another aspect to that event: everything that once bore a meaning that was in search of eternity is now diffused amongst an ever-expanding audience and its fate now depends upon the public reception it is given; the obverse of that event is the expansion of a language which, because it breaks with popular speech or with what Stendhal calls the *natural*, proves to have the quality of a scholarly language, to be organized in accordance with norms, and to have, ultimately, the function of ensuring that the search for eternity is identified with it because they both mean breaking with the masses. And so the writer can only reach the impregnable place he seeks by making a constant effort to escape the apparently voluble but profoundly petrified language of Opinion. He does not simply assume the right to speak without the protection of the law that founds language; he defends himself against the *tyrant* described by Tocqueville: the anonymous power of Opinion, which absorbs all that is thought or spoken – the singular as such – and converts it into a *commonplace*. We took Chateaubriand as an example, but he is presumably not the only true writer of the nineteenth century to have been haunted by the twin images of a stereotyped, standardized language which enslaves all speech, and from which speech must be reclaimed, and a language-abyss into which speech may fall, no matter how novel, nimble or intimate it may be.

But what is this *common place* where the imperishable motto cited in Latin becomes a platitude, where the latest fashionable turn of phrase and concepts that were invented yesterday triumph? Has it nothing to do with the *common world* which Arendt describes as being the basis for any thought of eternity? How can we give immortality a name, when the very word that names it is caught up in the contagion of stupidity? At the end of his *Révolution*, Quinet writes: 'Do you think that, now that it has been relentlessly exploited for four thousand years, stupidity or, to give it its historic name, foolishness, is still a virgin mine? No one who puts his hand into it is likely to exhaust it.' He goes on:

> We become annoyed when we see foolishness; it is infatuated, self-assured, imperturbable and always new. We would be so much more equitable if we knew how sincere and how old this foolishness is, if we knew its noble lineage; if we knew how many stultified generations it has taken to bring it to this perfection of form and content; if we knew how long nature had to work to

spread it around, to choose it rather than any other element, to corroborate its descent from father to son, drawing it from every possible source, causing it to increase, and embellishing and decorating it down the ages; if we knew how nature has passed it down from serf to bourgeois, from robe to sword, from cleric to seigneur in order to produce this prodigy of stultification which confounds us, outrages us and saddens us, and which we should, on the contrary, admire, were it not that we ourselves are part of it.

It is no doubt true that, like many men of his generation, Quinet still has a sense of immortality. But, ultimately, few men display their beliefs outside the framework of the dominant ideology. Hugo and Leroux were two such men, but they rebelled against what Quinet calls 'foolishness ... infatuated, self-assured, imperturbable and always new' and, as it happens, the foolishness against which they rebelled is the assertion that *immorality does not exist*. Their arguments are extravagant, not in the sense that they are not serious, but in the sense that they leave the beaten track, take their adversaries by surprise, use the whirlwind of writing to rescue their readers from the whirlwind of Opinion and, by mingling history, religion, science, politics and writing, make them lose all sense of time and place.

Canetti writes of Stendhal that: 'This rare and free man had, none the less, one article of faith, which he spoke of as simply and as naturally as of a mistress. Without pitying himself, he was content to write for a few, but he was certain that in a hundred years he would be read by many.'[39] The image of a mistress is well chosen in that it captures the idea that immortality is no longer a question for the law, that it has become the most private aspect of human life, and that it has nothing to do with making a glorious appearance in the public space.

Dare we venture to say that the new attitude towards immortality that we find in a small number of nineteenth-century writers helps us to understand the oblivion into which it has fallen in our century? Something that could once be said, provided that it was said unemphatically, can no longer be normally said. But what cannot be said is not necessarily dead, and it is not necessarily a sign of degradation. Arendt is certainly right to denounce the tragedy of mass society, and Adorno is certainly right to denounce one of its effects: the culture industry. But they are only half right. They fail to see that, although it has forgotten immortality, modernity has deified certain tyrants, and has even embalmed the bodies of some of them after their deaths. They also fail to see that, ultimately, there is an element of prudence and virtue in rejecting the representation of an indestructible body. Significantly, Canetti places his eulogy of Stendhal at the end of a chapter entitled 'The survivor'. The lowest form of the passion for survival is, he believes, to be found in the tyrant – the lowest and,

I would add, the most obscene, because he does not simply kill in order to survive; he forces everyone to fix his gaze on him, and violates everyone's consciousness. That in itself should inspire our era to take a more sober view of the idea of immortality and to reject every sign of ostentation. 'Whoever opens Stendhal,' Canetti goes on, 'will find him and also everything which surrounded him; and he finds it *here*, in this life.'[40] We find the same contrast, in even more curious form, between the image of a tyrant who swallows up the living, and the image of a link between human beings that can survive time in a short story by Nabakov. *Tyrants Destroyed* is the story of a man who is literally possessed by the image of the body of a tyrant. He never leaves his double, and once even approaches him. Now, he is familiar with every detail of his life. They rise at the same time, eat the same frugal breakfast, and read through the same newspapers. From morning to night, he imitates the tyrant's every gesture, his every thought. But he thinks constantly of killing him. On the tyrant's birthday, he is carried away by a poem written in his honour. His hatred vanishes; he even wants to die, to be punished. And suddenly, laughter saves him. His laughter reveals that even his own story is ridiculous. But it transforms his desire for death into a desire for immortality. And so he dedicates his story to posterity:

> This is an incantation, an exorcism, so that henceforth any man can exorcise bondage. I believe in miracles, I believe that in some way, unknown to me, this chronicle will reach other men ... And, who knows, – I may be right not to rule out the thought that my chance labour may prove immortal, and may accompany the ages, now persecuted, now exalted, often dangerous and always useful.[41]

Here, the desire for immortality treads a very narrow path. A slender desire, borne along by a puff of laughter. But it is possible that Nabakov has captured an element in the spirit of our time that could not be revealed by the theorist of the *death of immortality*.

Notes

1 THE QUESTION OF DEMOCRACY

1. Leo Strauss, *Natural Right and History* (Chicago University Press, Chicago, 1953).
2. See ch. 10.

2 HUMAN RIGHTS AND THE WELFARE STATE

1. This article provided the basis for a paper read to the Law Faculty of the Facultés Saint-Louis in Brussels on the occasion of a day conference organized by the Dean, François Ost, on *'Actualité des droits de l'homme dans l'Etat-providence'*. In it, I refer to a document drawn up by François Ost and his associates. The reader will forgive me if I occasionally use formulations from an earlier paper entitled *'Droits de l'homme et politique'*, which was first published in 1980 (*Libre,* 7 (1980), reprinted in *L'Invention démocratique* (Paris: Fayard, 1981). Translated as 'Politics and Human Rights', tr. Alan Sheridan, in Lefort, *The Political Forms of Modern Society,* ed. John B. Thompson (Polity Press, Cambridge, 1986). I have found it impossible to eliminate these minor repetitions without destroying the coherence of an argument which was elaborated with different purposes in mind.
2. Alexis de Tocqueville, *Democracy in America,* the Henry Reeve translation as revised by Francis Bowen (Alfred A. Knopf, New York, 1945), vol. II, p. 318.
3. Ibid.
4. Ibid., p. 319.
5. Ibid.
6. Ibid., p. 321.
7. Lefort, 'Politics and Human Rights.'
8. Pierre Manent, 'Démocratie et totalitarisme', *Commentaire,* IV, 16 (1981–2).
9. Pierre Pachet, 'La Justice et le conflit des opinions', *Passé-Présent,* 2 (1983).

3 Hannah Arendt and the Question of the Political

1. Hannah Arendt, Interview with Günther Gauss, 'Was bleibt? Was bleibt die Muttersprache', in Gauss, *Zur Person* (Feder, Munich 1964).
2. Hannah Arendt, *Between Past and Future* (Faber and Faber, London, 1961), p. 14.
3. Maurice Merleau-Ponty, *Adventures of the Dialectic*, tr. Joseph Bien (Heinemann, London, 1974), p. 3.
4. Gauss interview.
5. Hannah Arendt, *The Human Condition* (University of Chicago Press, Chicago, 1958).
6. Hannah Arendt, *The Origins of Totalitarianism* (George Allen and Unwin, London, 1963), p. 338.
7. Ibid., p. 336.
8. Moses I. Finlay, *Politics in the Ancient World* (Cambridge University Press, Cambridge, 1983).
9. Arendt, *Between Past and Future*, pp. 4–5.
10. See also Claude Lefort, 'Hannah Arendt et le totalitarisme', in Colloque des Hautes Etudes en Sciences Sociales, *L'Allemagne nazie et le génocide juif* (Hautes Etudes/Gallimard, Le Seuil, Paris, 1985), pp. 517–35.

4 The Revolutionary Terror

1. Robespierre, speech of 11 Germinal, year II, *Histoire parlementaire de la Révolution*, vol. XXXII (Buchez and Roux).
2. Taine, *Les Origines de la France contemporaine*, vol. III, p. 77.
3. Mortimer-Ternaux, *Histoire de la Terreur, 1792–1794* (Paris, 1863–81).
4. Georges Lefebvre, *Le Gouvernement révolutionnaire, 2 juin 9 thermidor II* (Centre de Documentation universitaire, Paris, 1947).
5. Saint-Just, speech of 8 Ventôse, year II, *Histoire parlementaire*, vol. XXXI.
6. Mortimer-Ternaux, *Histoire*, vol. III, p. 33. [The *chambres ardentes* were courts empowered to condemn criminals to be burned; translator].
7. Ibid., p. 36.
8. Ibid., vol. VIII, p. 376.
9. Ibid., p. 403.
10. Lefebvre, *Gouvernement révolutionnaire*, pp. 119–20.
11. Camille Desmoulins, *Le Vieux Cordelier; Histoire parlementaire*, vol. XXX.
12. Mortimer-Ternaux, *Histoire*, vol. VIII, p. 389; Thiers, *Histoire de la Révolution Française*, vol. IV, p. 365.
13. Billaud-Varenne, speech on the theory of democratic government, *Histoire parlementaire*, vol. XXXII.
14. Robespierre, speech of 8 Thermidor, Year II, *Histoire parlementaire*, vol. XXXIII.
15. Thiers, *Histoire*, vol. V, p. 286.
16. For the documentary evidence, see Mortimer-Ternaux, *Histoire*, vol. III.
17. Ibid., vol. III, p. 133.
18. Buchez and Roux, *Histoire parlementaire*, vol. XXIV, p. 204.
19. Lefebvre, *Gouvernement révolutionnaire*, p. 264 f.

5 INTERPRETING REVOLUTION WITHIN THE FRENCH REVOLUTION

1. François Furet, *Interpreting the French Revolution,* tr. Elborg Foster (Cambridge University Press and Editions de la Maison des Sciences de l'Homme, Cambridge and Paris, 1981).
2. François Furet and Denis Richet, *La Révolution Française,* Hachette, Paris two vols., 1965–1966). A one volume edition was published by Fayard, Paris in 1973.
3. Furet, *Interpreting the French Revolution,* p. 12.
4. Michelet, *Le Tyran,* p. 1009.
5. Michelet, *Histoire de la Révolution Française* (Gallimard, Bibliothèque de la Pléiade, Paris 1979), vol. I, p. 300.

6 EDGAR QUINET: THE REVOLUTION THAT FAILED

1. Michelet, *Histoire de la Révolution,* vol. I, p. 297.
2. Ibid., p. 296.
3. The quintessence of Buchez's interpretation of the Terror will be found in the preface to vol. XXVII: 'Les Journées de septembre.'
4. Michelet, *Histoire,* vol. I, p. 295.
5. Ibid., p. 298.
6. Ibid., p. 299.
7. Ibid., vol. II, p. 622.
8. Ibid., p. 623.
9. Ibid., vol. I, p. 301.
10. Ibid., p. 241.
11. Ibid., pp. 1003, 1086.
12. Edgar Quinet, *La Révolution.* References are to the third edition, 2 vols, Paris 1865, and are given in parentheses in the body of the text.

7 THE REVOLUTION AS PRINCIPLE AND AS INDIVIDUAL

1. Joseph Ferrari, *Machiavel juge des révolutions de notre temps,* Paris, 1849; page references are given in the body of the text; *Les Philosophes salariés,* Paris 1849; reprinted, Payot, 'Critique de la politique', Paris 1983.
2. Machiavelli, *The Prince,* tr. George Ball (Penguin, Harmondsworth, 1961), p. 58.

8 REREADING *The Communist Manifesto*

1. Maurice Merleau-Ponty, *Signs,* tr. Richard C. McCleary (Northwestern University Press, Evanston, 1964), pp. 10–11.
2. Karl Marx, 'The Manifesto of the Communist Party', in Marx, *The Revolutions of 1848,* ed. David Fernbach (Pelican, Harmondsworth, 1973). Page references are given in parentheses in the body of the text.
3. The introduction and notes to Charles Andler's edition of the *Manifesto*

(Petite Bibliothèque socialiste, Paris) can still be read with profit.
4. As we noted earlier, Charles Andler in exemplary detail explores Marx's debt to his predecessors.

9 REVERSIBILITY

1. Alexis de Tocqueville, *L'Ancien Régime et la Révolution Française* (AR), vol. I, p. 193. References are to A.-P. Mayer's edition of the *Oeuvres Complètes*.
2. Alexis de Tocqueville, *Democracy in America* (DA). References are to the revised Reeve translation.
3. Alexis de Tocqueville, *Recollections*, tr. George Lawrence (Doubleday, Garden City, New York, 1971), p. 170.
4. Benjamin Constant, *De la Liberté des modernes*, ed. Marcel Gauchet (Le Livre de poche, Paris 1980). Page references are given in parentheses in the body of the text.

10 FROM EQUALITY TO FREEDOM

1. The page references given in parentheses are to the revised Reeve translation.
2. François Furet brings out the ambiguities of Tocqueville's thought in his essay 'De Tocqueville and the Problem of the French Revolution', in Furet, *Interpreting the French Revolution*.
3. Despite its interest, the remainder of Book II will not be examined here. Tocqueville's views on the development of industry, on the condition of the proletariat, and as to whether or not the industrial class forms an aristocracy in the United States do relate to the problematic of equality and freedom, but their analysis would require a separate study.

11 THE PERMANENCE OF THE THEOLOGICO-POLITICAL?

1. G.W.F. Hegel, *Philosophy of Mind*, tr. William Wallace (The Clarendon Press, Oxford, 1894), pp. 156–7.
2. Ernst Kantorowicz, *The King's Two Bodies: A Study in Medieval Political Theology* (Princeton University Press, Princeton, New Jersey, 1957).
3. Marc Bloch, *The Royal Touch: Sacred Monarchy and Scrofula in England and France*, tr. J.E. Anderson (Routledge and Kegan Paul, London, 1973).
4. Joseph Strayer, *Medieval Statecraft and the Perspectives of History* (Princeton University Press, Princeton, New Jersey, 1971).

12 THE DEATH OF IMMORTALITY?

1. Victor Hugo, *Oeuvres Complètes* (Club français du livre, Paris) vol. XII, p. 49.
2. Ibid., p. 54.
3. Ibid., p. 55.

4. Pierre Leroux, *La Grève de Samarez* (Klincksieck, Paris, 1979).

5. Cited in Pierre Albouy, *Mythographies* (Corti, Paris, 1976). Albouy gives an accurate account of the conflict between Hugo and Leroux and, more generally, of the intellectual climate on Jersey and Guernsey at this time.

6. Tocqueville, *Democracy in America*, vol. II, p. 99.

7. Ibid., p. 98.

8. Ibid., p. 328.

9. Ibid., p. 99.

10. Ibid.

11. Ibid., p. 135.

12. Ibid., p. 134.

13. Ibid., p. 135.

14. Ibid., p. 134.

15. Ibid., p. 143.

16. Ibid., pp. 143–4.

17. Ibid., p. 145.

18. Ibid.

19. Ibid., p. 146.

20. Ibid. For an analysis of Tocqueville's philosophy and of the basis of his interpretation of democracy, see Pierre Manent, *Tocqueville et la nature de la démocratie* (Julliard, Paris, 1982).

21. Theodor Adorno, *Minima Moralia*, tr. E.F.N. Jephcott (Verso, London, 1978), pp. 100–1.

22. Philippe Ariès, *Essais sur l'histoire de la mort en Occident, du Moyen Age à nos jours* (Editions du Seuil, Paris, 1975).

23. Ibid.

24. Hannah Arendt, *The Human Condition*, p. 18.

25. Ibid., p. 55.

26. Ibid., p. 56.

27. Ibid., pp. 54–5.

28. Hannah Arendt, *On Revolution* (Faber and Faber, London, 1963), p. 232. (The quotation is from Harrington.)

29. Ibid., p. 235.

30. Michelet, 1868 preface to *La Révolution Française*.

31. On the advent of the modern state and on its theologico-political foundations, see Kantorowicz, *The King's Two Bodies*, and Strayer, *Medieval Statecraft*.

32. E. Garin, *L'Education de l'homme moderne* (Fayard, Paris, 1962).

33. Arendt, *The Human Condition*, p. 168.

34. Edgar Quinet, *La Révolution*, vol. II, p. 263.

35. Niccolò Machiavelli, letter to Francesco Vettori, in Machiavelli, *Il Principe, e Pagine dei Discorsi e delle Istorie*, ed. Luigi Russo (Sansoni, Florence, 1967), pp. 29–30.

36. Chateaubriand, *Mémoires d'outre-tombe* (Gallimard, Bibliothèque de la Pléiade, 1950), p. 492.

37. Ibid., p. 60.

38. Marx, 'Manifesto', p. 70.

39. Elias Canetti, *Crowds and Power*, tr. Carol Stewart (Victor Gollancz, London, 1963), p. 277.
40. Ibid., p. 278.
41. Vladimir Nabakov, *Tyrants Destroyed* (Weidenfeld and Nicolson, London, 1975), pp. 36–7.

Index